393

P9-ASH-290

Religious Values in Counseling and Psychotherapy

Religious Values in Counseling and Psychotherapy

by Charles A. Curran

SHEED AND WARD : NEW YORK

158.01

Nihil Obstat, Leo J. Steady, Ph.D., S.T.D., Censor Librorum; Imprimatur, ✠Robert F. Joyce, Bishop of Burlington; November 27, 1968. The Nihil Obstat and Imprimatur are official declarations that a book or pamphlet is considered to be free of doctrinal or moral error. No implication is contained therein that those who have granted the Nihil Obstat and the Imprimatur agree with the contents, opinions or statements expressed.

© *Sheed and Ward, Inc., 1969*

Library of Congress Catalog Card Number: 69–16992

Manufactured in the United States of America

Acknowledgments

To the Clergy in America, Europe, the Orient and Africa, and to Sisters, Brothers and religious teachers of all religions who have been students, members of institutes, and associates of mine, I owe a very special debt of gratitude. Most of the ideas here were developed with and through them and the marks of their contribution are everywhere evident.

I must also recognize a particular debt to Msgr. John J. Egan and Fathers Eugene Kennedy, Daniel Tranel and Roland Janisse and, through many years of encouraging friendship, Michael Tabit.

To these must be added Dr. Seward Hiltner, Dr. Granger Westberg and Dr. Carroll Wise as well as Dr. Gardner Murphy and Dr. Paul Pruyser.

For constant aid in the myriad details in the production process of this manuscript, full credit again goes to Rosina Mena Gallagher and Jennybelle P. Rardin.

For grants and research support, I am especially indebted to The Society for Human Relations Research and to Dr. Mary F. Young, Dr. Norma B. Gutierrez and Robert A. Sprecher for special kindness.

Included here also should be Wayne Rogers, William Gallagher, Antonio and Kathleen Aguilar, A. J. Mann and Alain and Alfreda Decombe for much kindness and assistance.

I have gained much from my associations with The Academy of Religion and Mental Health and Charles Bergman and his staff. In a very special way, I, together with all the members of the *Academy*, owe much to Dr. George C. Anderson for his deep and considerate kindness that is always personal and thoughtful.

Here too, I am especially grateful to the *Academy Journal* and, for particular help and encouragement, to its inspiring editor, **Dr.** Harry Meserve, and his assistant, Mrs. Jean Conti.

Lastly, may I express appreciation to Philip Scharper.

Parts of articles appearing in Journals were later completely revised and made a part of this book. General appreciation is here expressed for the use of this material. In *Chicago Studies,* "Counseling and Sacramental Confession," Summer, 1968, pp. 163–174; in *The Journal of Pastoral Counseling,* "On the Nature of Pastoral Counseling," Spring 1968, III (1), pp. 7–24; in *The Journal of Religion and Health,* "Toward a Theology of Human Belonging," April 1965, IV (3), and "Vatican II: A New Christian Self Concept," April 1966, V (2), pp. 91–103; in *The Journal for Scientific Study of Religion,* "Some Psychological Aspects of Vatican Council II," Spring 1963, pp. 190–194; in *Marian Studies,* "Psychological Factors in Marian Devotion," March 1964, XV, pp. 111–126; in *The Catholic Psychological Record,* "The Personality Dynamics of Scrupulosity," Fall 1963, I (2); in *The Journal of Counseling Psychology,* "The Counseling Relationship and Some Religious Factors," VI (4), 1959, pp. 266–270 and "The Role of Sin and Guilt in Psychotherapy," VII (3), 1960, pp. 192–197.

Appreciation is expressed for permission to use these as well as a revision of a chapter in the book, *Constructive Aspects of Anxiety,* edited by Seward Hiltner and Karl Menninger, Abingdon Press, New York, 1963.

Contents

viii *Contents*

DEDICATION
To the clergy and religious teachers;
to all in the scientific, healing and helping professions;
with admiration and respect.

Religious Values in Counseling and Psychotherapy

Introduction: Relevance and Involvement

COUNSELING, psychotherapy and religion are each broad words with a wide variety of meanings and implications. It is therefore immediately necessary to clarify our meaning here by saying that we are concerned with the personal pursuit of religious values. Our focus on counseling and psychotherapy, then, should be narrowed to mean the way these can aid a person to arrive at the integration of religious values and so make religion personally effective in his life. Consequently, we are not treating here all the theories and methods that might be included under counseling and psychotherapy, much less attempting to justify them. We are rather discussing particular sensitivities and skills which facilitate authentic relationships between persons and which can lead to the uncovering and better fulfillment of personal values and—for our purpose here—religious values.

We are also distinguishing, here, counseling from guidance and education. In this relationship, counseling is the process through which a person arrives at adequate integration of his whole self, so that he can absorb and put to use the knowledge and information received from education, guidance and other sources. Counseling then is, in this very special sense, person-centered, and aimed not simply at knowledge but at assimilation, conation and investment.

RELIGIOUS MATURITY

Implicit in religious process and development is a kind of growth paralleling physical and psychological growth. This is emphasized

1

repeatedly in the analogy of milk for infants and meat for the full-grown, and similar comparisons. Such growth involves not simply external dependence on others for guidance and decision but the gradual acquiring of an inner capacity to make such judgments oneself. It demands, therefore, the internalization of religious values.

The aim of this book, then, is to concentrate on those aspects of individual, group and community relationships that lead to such internalization of values, especially religious values. In this way a person arrives at a greater degree of religious maturity. It is here particularly that counseling and psychotherapy can relate to religion.

Since our topic is primarily religious values, we do not, as a rule, treat of particular beliefs and practices except where, as in the consideration of Vatican Council II, this is clearly indicated. We are assuming that religion demands a basic faith commitment and creed and a belief in a personal and sustaining God who is concerned for each man and the universe. We do not suggest, therefore, any psychological surrogate. Nothing in the development of and research in counseling and psychotherapy would warrant such suggestions.[1] What we propose here, then, are rather to be seen as extensions and clarifications and not as substitutions for essential religious concerns.

Moreover, in our focus on the Church as community as well as an organization, we are obviously not initiating something completely new. We are calling attention, rather, to a tradition of community and communication that has always existed. But, in addition, we are suggesting methods adapted from recent psychological developments that would seem to explicate this kind of authentic and creative communication.

RELEVANCE

A central focus of modern religion is summed up in the word "relevance." Additional words like "commitment," "encounter," "engagement" are similarly used to highlight and bring together religion and modern man as he is. In this striving for greater human belonging and identity, group and individual counseling, psychotherapy, and various skilled relationships adapted from these fields, can be of particular importance to religion.

A crucial issue facing many in our time comes from an anxiety about their own personal adequacy and lack of fulfillment and their alienation from others. To alleviate this we are especially turning to various forms of individual and group counseling and psychotherapy. A crucial issue in religion, at the same time, is this pressing question of its own relevance. These two issues can be brought together by the increased interrelationship of counseling, psychotherapy and religion.

Around these issues each has something significant to offer the other. Without confusing or distorting their own contributions, they can, at the same time, counterbalance and complement one another. Greater awareness of, and skill in, methods of personal engagement and relationship adopted from counseling and psychotherapy can give religion an important means of becoming relevant to modern industrial and civilized man. Correspondingly, the effectiveness of counseling and psychotherapy can be reinforced, extended and sustained by genuine religious understanding and experience.

AUTHENTIC CONCERN

Moreover, part of the concern about "relevance" is also a concern for "authenticity." Aspects of modern culture arouse in many a deep resistance based on the feeling of dishonesty, manipulation, and what is often called "being phony." Religious relationships seem to have come increasingly under this same suspicion. In providing, then, some aids and clues to establishing greater integrity within the person and more genuineness in relating to others, counseling and psychotherapy can also benefit religion. For if the salt of religious commitment is not to lose its capacity to bring savor to the human condition, then any religious encounter must, most of all, be characterized by a special authenticity. There must be a genuine gift of self and a profound respect for the freedom, uniqueness and mystery of the other person. Only in this way can it convey a sense of worth and so be personally redemptive.

PERSONAL AND SOCIAL

But "relevance" and "involvement" and similar words commonly have a social as well as a personal meaning. Applied to religion, they are often intended to stress the social significance and responsibilities of religious values. Seen this way they emphasize, too, the fact that purely personal reform is not enough; it must also be social.

This is unquestionably so. We are not implying, therefore, that personal renewal is all that matters or even that it can be, by itself, really effective. The expression "the man is not enough without the moment and the moment is not enough without the man" could be applied to changing social structures and attitudes. One man or a small group of men cannot do this alone. They may, however, be the catalytic agents that initiate such changes, as, say, the early Christians were.

Simply to work for social change, however—basic and necessary as this is in itself—without considering the necessity of a corresponding change in the persons who make up the social fabric where these changes are to occur, is either to fail or to produce artificial change. One has then *plus ça change, plus la même chose,* because only appearances and forms have changed. Real reform, even social reform, must finally come about in and through individual persons. That is, it must invoke and engage each one at the deepest level of himself. Only when this happens to many who represent basic strands in the social fabric does the design and quality of the fabric itself really change.

Nonetheless, the individual cannot be seen in isolation from the community. Consequently, a basic religious concern is the nature of the community which best represents it in our time. Structures drawn from the past may now be less than adequate to meet the demands of present personal and social needs. The nature of community itself, then, and the kind of communion and communication it produces inevitably enters into this discussion. This concern of religion about the nature of community corresponds to a like concern stemming especially, among other influences, from group and individual counseling and psychotherapy. This is coming to be known as "community psychology and psychiatry." These areas are becoming increasingly extended beyond the person himself to his involvement with others and the larger community.

PERSONALIZED KNOWLEDGE AND ACTION

By religion we mean not only the theological meaning of religious concepts but, even more, their personalized value or self-investment implications. Theology, in its original "logos" sense, can be thought of as being concerned primarily with the knowing process, with the significance of concepts relating God and man. Religion would go beyond this to the highly personal kind of knowing indicated by "gnosis."

We might go further and propose that the special kind of knowledge involved here might even be termed *conative knowledge* —to indicate not only its choice or action orientation but its total self-involvement as well. This would include the more personalized knowledge indicated by *gnosis,* but it would suggest the unified levels of emotional, instinctive and somatic involvement also—as the term *conative* would imply.

We have characterized this with the concept "value" to indicate not only the personalized knowing necessary for such relationship to God but also the degree of self-investment that the person himself must make. This self-investment involves the whole person and not simply his adequate knowing. In other words, he must *do* as well as *know,* so that his cognitive process integrates his whole psychosomatic being and results in religious commitment and action.

We might then add the term *theognosis* to theology to reach and imply these new aspects. In other words, we are here concerned with a theology of the unique human condition or, as we will consider in detail later, *a theology of human belonging.*

RELIGIOUS VALUES

This book follows from, and is closely related to, the volume published earlier, *Counseling and Psychotherapy: The Pursuit of Values.*[2] The focus of this book, however, is directly on religious values. We have therefore tried to avoid repetition except when necessary. Reference is then made to the more extensive treatment in the previous work. Consequently, concepts like "meaning," "values," "convalidation," "authentic relationship," "creative affiliation," and the like, while important in our treatment, will be only briefly explained, since one can find these same questions discussed in greater detail in the previous volume and elsewhere.

By "religious values" we mean, then, the particular area of personal application and not the whole field of theology. We are especially concerned here with the way relationships—patterned from counseling and psychotherapy but redesigned for their special religious purpose—might prove helpful. Their helpfulness might be precisely in the manner by which a degree of real self-investment is facilitated. This is clear from the delineation we have given to our use of the word "value" as signifying *meaning plus self-investment*.

COUNSELING THERAPY

While our concentration here is, in fact, on counseling, we have included "psychotherapy" in the title itself because, in the theoretical contributions and practical research data and skills, psychotherapy cannot be clearly distinguished from counseling. They have both noticeably affected concepts of personality dynamics and development.

We see *counseling as a normal process*. It is in this sense especially that counseling, and skilled individual and group relationships patterned from it, could offer an important and practical aid to the implementation of religious values in a person's life. But there is also a wide area of both theory and practice which clearly relates religious values to psychotherapy. The whole question of sin and guilt, for example, would be an evident illustration of this. But our practical treatment here is largely concerned with counseling because this is mainly what is and ought to be done in an ordinary religious setting. Yet we have also included psychotherapy because it too has many dimensions that are complicatedly interwoven with religious issues.

Depending also on what we mean by "psychotherapy," we could still see it as a necessary aid to a "sick" human condition.

Sinfulness itself can be involved in sickness because, in a modern psychosomatic concept of illness, we realize that a person can be responsible in some measure for illness as he can for sin. In this sense, then, the use of the term "therapy" or "psychotherapy" approaches closer to the modern meaning of its Latin equivalent, "cura animarum."

On a continuum based on the analogy of health and sickness, we can place counseling on the "healthy" or normal side and psychotherapy over in the direction of the "sickness" side. But these distinctions in reality often break down, so that in any practical situation one is really doing both counseling and therapy at the same time.

For this reason, except where the terms counseling or psychotherapy are clearly called for in order to make a precise distinction, we have used the term "counseling-therapy." Generally speaking too, while for the sake of simplicity we usually refer only to "counselor" and "client," what is said could be equally applied to "therapist" and "patient" if one preferred.

Our main consideration here, however, is not so much to consider counseling and psychotherapy in themselves, but rather to adapt and pattern effective relationships from them in order to further the mature growth in the engagement and commitment to religious values. We will, therefore, most often treat counseling and psychotherapy, and the personality awarenesses and skills they have contributed, somewhat as the convex-concave components of the same personality dynamics and design. So considered, each might be said to extend and fill out the other, depending on whether one focuses on the concave or the convex side of the perceptual field.

NOT PANACEA

By juxtaposing in our title, counseling, psychotherapy and religious values we do not imply they are in the same order of relationship. Obviously religion is both wider in extension than counseling or psychotherapy and fundamentally different in intent and purpose. We are aware, too, of the limited efficacy of both counseling and psychotherapy as judged by modern psychological research methods. We do not, therefore, want to suggest some kind of panacea for the human condition that religion could borrow from counseling and psychotherapy.

On the contrary, genuine religious issues and concerns cannot be supplanted by methods of counseling and psychotherapy, as is sometimes popularly suggested. Such a point of view, aside from its misunderstanding of religion, vastly exaggerates the significance and achievement of modern methods of counseling and psychotherapy.

TOTAL PERSON INVOLVEMENT

But while in both personal relationships and group dynamics we have yet much to learn, there can be little doubt that this century has seen the emergence of a new and exciting understanding of man. With all the inadequacies of methods of counseling and psychotherapy and with all the research yet to be done and knowledge still to be gained, there already exists much freshness and richness in what has been acquired.

This is not to say that everything in our modern understanding of man is completely new. Any educated person can see in both western and oriental thought, traces that are, no doubt, the origin of present concepts of human dynamics. One can see too that in recent centuries, owing to the impact of mechanistic views of man and matter, we have been somewhat in a dichotomy in our view of man.

What is especially fresh and pertinent in modern counseling and psychotherapy is the way it sees man, not ideally or abstractly, but engaged in living with the totality of his being. The concept of the human person has, in this way, assumed a whole new existential dimension. This is what is particularly stimulating in our present view.

NEW PSYCHOLOGICAL LIGHT

Religion and the religious encounter have not yet profited from this modern psychological development to the degree that they could and should. For one of the intriguing things about present trends in psychological dynamics is that they often parallel many fundamental concepts in theology. In this way they can throw new light on these familiar concepts and bring them alive again to a modern age and for a modern mentality. Too long familiarity has staled and even deadened the original excitement and relevance of the biblical messages. Without distorting, therefore, the essential qualities and uniqueness of religious belief and commitment, such psychological consideration can bring to religious encounters the freshness, intensity and enthusiasm found in this area of research and practice.

But this parallel is not really strange, because, among many other things, the Old and the New Testament are significant psychological documents. They describe a psychological process and experience. They are records of human existence: what happens there, can or does happen to us. With a slight change in circumstance and living conditions, these people are ourselves. Their dilemmas are our own. Their hopes and joys, sorrows and discouragements, their anxieties and assurances, are the story of our lives too. This quality of the existent human condition permeates their message. It is *good news* because it has the human relevancy of news. It has significance for us because it can affect and change our lives.

In this sense, then, the message and witness of the Old and the New Testament intervene in our lives, can interrupt them by confronting us and challenging us to greater significance and value. However else we may describe this intervention, it is a psychological process as well that is initiated here. This includes all the subtleties and complexities, conscious and unconscious, that any psychological intervention in a person's life is apt to call forth.

Here especially we see the importance of relating counseling and psychotherapy to religion. In counseling and psychotherapy—granting many inadequacies and unproved assumptions—we have an approach to this same psychological process of the seeking of greater personal significance and value. In this context—"Know you not that you were bought with a great price?"—is the common convalidating language that all three are trying to speak to the anxious, alienated and confused person. This is likewise their common challenge to love and respectful regard of oneself and the other.

ENGAGEMENT

Religion's main aim, moreover, does not consist in theory or discussion. Its main aim is in engagement and encounter. It is not finally concerned simply with intellectual exchange. It concerns intense and involved experience. In attempting to face and embrace the world, religion can still impede its own purpose by becoming lost in abstract and theoretical discussion. It is probably this tendency more than any other that has made religion often seem irrelevent to many.

In this effort at authentic personal relationship, religion parallels aspects of counseling and psychotherapy. Counselors and therapists engage themselves deeply and intensely with others. This engagement involves their whole psychosomatic person: it is not simply intellectual. This is also the point of the religious encounter. Over and over, the Psalms and the Gospel incidents stress the risk and threat of leaving the state of comfort and security, and yet hold them to be essential ingredients of a truly religious experience with another person. In the Psalms and other parts of the Old Testament, the religious man often runs the risk of being lost or bogged down in the mire of misunderstanding and confusion, rejected by his friends and attacked by his enemies. In the New Testament, he must launch out into the deep, search in the wilderness and face the ravening wolves, anxiously but with courage, if he is to be a good shepherd. "Into the depths" and "into the wilderness" dominate the religious theme as they dominate many aspects of present-day psychological encounters.

In this kind of experience in the intense and hidden conflicts and confusion of the human condition, counseling and psychotherapy can offer their richest yield to religion. They can provide skilled understanding and an immediate sense of engagement with the human condition. Their contribution has been that they have entered into man and his depths and so provided us with increasing skill and understanding of many of the conditions by which genuine relationship is made possible.

COMMITTED MATURITY

We are not speaking here, therefore, of loose, unanalyzed and sentimental attachments in an effort to help others. Rather we see a sensitive and delicate art and skill which demands a high kind of maturity on the part of the counselor and therapist if it is to be a genuinely helpful concern and engagement for the welfare of the other person. These aspects of art and skill constitute one of the major contributions of counseling and psychotherapy. Treatment of various phases of this art and skill, therefore, occupies a central section of our earlier book.

Religious commitment, to be relevant, also demands psychological maturity and integration. By making religion appear too safe and cautious we may also have made it seem childish and regressive. Moreover, if love is the gift of self, one must genuinely possess oneself and respect oneself before one can give oneself as a valuable gift. One must, in other words, first be greatly and genuinely invested in oneself if one is to have real meaning as a gift to others. We have therefore defined one aspect of maturity as man's capacity to love. We have attempted to show that philosophical as well as religious conceptions of love and maturity need to be genuinely understood in order to aid in clarifying and implementing a modern psychological dynamic of loving.

UNIFIED PERSON

The old axiom "Whatever is received, is received according to the manner of the one receiving" suggests the subtle personality characteristics which seem involved in the recipient of knowledge of any kind. Counseling and psychotherapy concern themselves primarily with the manner or modus of the one receiving or experiencing. Human experience, in this way, is a psychosomatic experience relating soma, instincts, emotions, cognition and choice in a complicated and interrelated series of unified functions. It is not simply—as one is apt to think in the tendency to lecture or give advice—an intellectual experience.

The experience of religion, considered psychologically, seems to have much of this same psychosomatic unity about it. It too, like the process of counseling and psychotherapy, is not simply an intellectual experience from which certain choices may emerge. But it is, or should be, also a profound commitment of the whole person in a religious engagement. This kind of religious engagement is something different from the intellectual consent to doctrine. But doctrine must certainly be the beginning of this process. One must believe in something that one is at the same time trying to experience and in some measure to understand—the *fides quaerens intellectum*. But faith is more than an intellectual engagement. It is also, and more profoundly, the commitment of self to a process which should lead to both hope and love. In striving to love, we are engaged in a total experience, not simply in an intellectual exercise.

RECIPROCAL RELATIONSHIP

This parallel, then, between the religious and counseling-therapeutic experience is one of the main points of this book. We use the word "parallel" because, while the psychological aspects may be similar or even the same, religion itself introduces a new and different dimension. But counseling and psychotherapeutic research and awareness can enlighten and facilitate phases of religious encounter, particularly in the light of the personality factors of the one "receiving" or undergoing this experience.

At the same time, we hope to make clearer the reciprocal values religion can offer counseling therapy and indeed the whole field of personality dynamics. In this we support the view of Pruyser, who, in extending the field of psychology, remarks that William James left us with too constricted a view:

My thesis is that James set up too narrow boundaries to the field of the psychology of religion and that many of his successors held to those limits without giving the matter much thought. . . . Perhaps they found the limitation tactically useful. . . .

Religious life involves images, intuitions, concepts, and the human history of all these about God. But, above all, it involves an object relation with God, and psychology must be interested in all these aspects. I am not sure whether psychology can or should waive the ontological question, as, by the way, some theological systems do, but

I am sure that it cannot stop short of man's thinking about God and the forming and obtaining of his image. Besides the feelingful renditions of religious feelings stand the thoughtful renditions of religious thinking.[3]

This interrelationship of religion and psychology is very evident in any effort to study the factors that facilitate personal change. This is perhaps why, as counseling and psychotherapy have come forward in this century, the increased awareness of the relevance of religion to personality dynamics has also begun to be proposed and recognized.

COMMUNITY AND COMMUNION

But, as we have said, personal change needs a sustaining and aiding social structure. It needs, in other words, community. Our idea of community, however, and in particular our idea of the Church as a religious community, is in a complicated state of ambiguity. In contrast to the closely knit sense of warm and understanding family community that the early Christians and the Jews so highly prized, the Church for many centuries has been seen more in the model of a *city*, albeit a "City of God."

Within the framework of any modality—even a word—and behind it, there is a psychological structure. This structure contains an implicit and often unconscious value system that can predetermine large areas of our activity. We can become so bound up in the modality of these structures that we are unable to see that we are enveloped in one elaborate package, that much of what we are doing is part of this package from which we cannot free ourselves without starting all over with a new package. People often see this about themselves in counseling therapy. Extricating themselves often hinges on seeing clearly the unconscious and implicit values these models actually contain.

THE CITY

Our present views of the Church and much of our present religious conflict seem to involve a similar value package. In the value package as expressed by the title of the Church as "The City of God," the focus is not on the "of God" but on the values implied when we say the Church is a "city."

Obviously the title goes back to St. Augustine's famous book. Like many things in our personal lives or in the history of any organization structure, the initiating of this lengthy and monumental work of Augustine seems to have come about somewhat by chance. The chance factor is that Augustine did not plan to write this book in the way he had written learnedly on "the person," giving new richness and depth to the meaning of the person and its application to the Trinity. He began to write it in response to a letter saying that Roman politicians and others were blaming Christians for the existing decadence. His intent was to contrast the living "good" Christian City with the dying city of the secular world.

We do no mean here to imply that such an enormous work was the result of chance. We agree with Brown in this.[4] But as we will develop more fully later, if one accepts Gilson's version,[5] the sack of Rome did color the catastrophic tone of the work and the note of estrangement from the world.

From the Middle Ages to the present time, however, the Augustinian concept increasingly lost its original meaning; but the Church never lost its modality of the city. One effect has been increasingly to produce, in the work of the Church, a tendency towards a managerial relationship among us and in relation to others—a relationship that implicitly imitates and rivals the secular city.

This value package of the Church as a city now leaves us with a certain emptiness. The Greek and Roman model of the city is that it is a place of law and order. At best, then, we can define this idea of a city only as a rational structure. There is no place for love in such a concept. We do not expect a policeman, as a policeman, to love anyone. He is a representative of the *polis* and its managerial law and order.

Because we have been increasingly caught up in the awareness of the Church as a city, we are also caught up in the rival aspects of the other city, which—contrary to Augustine's presentiments—did not die but has grown, so that now we may say that the city is everywhere.

INNER-CITY BELONGING

By contrast to this rivalry and opposition implication, the earlier conceptualization of the pre-Augustinian period does not give the notion of the rival cities—the City of God and the "evil" secular city, as Augustine saw it. Nor is there any suggestion of imitating the secular city. Rather we have simpler images, such as that of salt which savors meat. Salt gives meat a special quality that makes it pleasing to one who tastes it. Like the leaven that permeates bread, enhancing its taste and value, salt does not destroy the meat—it improves its flavor and desirability. There is no dichotomy in those earlier scriptural images.

When Christ sent the disciples out, He sent them in pairs, not to set up a rival city or establish a power structure that would be equal to or greater than the city, but just to enter the city. If the people offered them understanding and acceptance and a sense of belonging, they were to stay. If there were no clusters of people within the city who would offer them such acceptance, they were to go on to other cities, without guilt, bitterness, hostility or cynicism. They were to search for an inner-city belonging and sharing. This was Christ's original commission. When some people handed Him a coin and asked, "Do we pay tribute to Caesar?" because this would represent submission to a rival city, He dismissed the issue.

COMMUNION AND COMMUNICATION

The modality in the early Church was that of a "cohesive community." Although we still need aspects of the city model in the Church, we certainly now need much more. While the "community" can be a city, it is far more understandable as a place of both communion and communication. If we think not only of a city as the model of the community, but of communion and communication as validating community, then we have no Christian community, or even no community of religious people in the inner city, unless we also have deep and intense communion and communication convalidating the worth and dignity of each member.

This is the profound need of our time. We are in difficulty with some of the implications of a modern city and its power-structure model and tone because, with its implied focus only on law and order in the Greek and Roman idea, we are in danger of having relationships of political power and not really of open freedom. Abandonment to "will to community" requires each of us to give up some aspects of power and control and to trust others. Not only broad Church structures but the parish, the classroom, small organizations and even our personal relations are affected by this power tendency to manipulate and control others. It has always been a heady and self-aggrandizing wine.

If we could define in one word the savor of a deeply meaningful experience, it would be the word "genuine." This genuineness would be experienced whenever people openly gave themselves to one another in a trusting communication. The yearning of our time is for such authentic communication. There are alienated and lonely people in religious life, in the priesthood and ministry and in married life. The issue is not to be resolved by jumping from one of these conditions to the other. The core of the loneliness and alienation lies in the difficulty of genuine communication and communion among people.

HORIZONTAL MODEL: VALUE OF PERSON

If we defined the model of the religious community as more than the image of a city, it would not be confined by the vertical modality of power and political structure. In addition we would seek the horizontality of the meaning and value of each person. This has never been absent, of course, from the image of the Church. But in the concept of the dignity and convalidation of each person experiencing another, we have a fresh modality of this more personal image of community.

While there were other reasons, no doubt, for the success of the early Church, one important factor was that, to the faceless mass of the large cities, particularly Jerusalem and Rome, it offered people convalidation of their worth. It gave them a sense of incarnate redemption, a feeling of having value in and of themselves. By comparison, our danger now is that in following the present modality of the city, we are caught up in the managerial manipulation of one another, and this situation impedes authentic relationship.

Our need is to bring the concept of community back to the human richness that it had in the early Christian Church. We need to establish again the kind of intensity of experience, one with another, that so convalidates us that we are incarnately redeemed. This would be communion and communication in a human as well as a divine way.

If the important issue in religion, as we have said, is not simply knowing but engaging oneself, then this involves self-investment. A major religious concern, therefore, is how to bring about this human self-investment in religious values. Assuming that the religious person believes, in what way can his actual living of the things in which he believes be facilitated from a human point of view?

Psychologically, by being loved first, a person seems able to grow in worth and towards the mature capacity for self-investment. In a religious atmosphere and with religious "mimesis," such experience should convalidate the person in religious worth and significance. As a result, his genuine self-investment and commitment to those religious concepts, convictions and actions in which he believes should be furthered, deepened and made more mature.

LEARNING: REDEMPTIVE PROCESS

This same kind of reflected worth and redemption seems also true of learning. If I feel myself an "ignoramus" in the pejorative sense, I am not likely to feel constructive courage to learn. If I learn in this condition, it may only be to defend myself from humiliation. For learning to be effective, *mimesis* or representation must become incarnate, it must *be,* and so convey redemptive worth and identification on the "one receiving." It can no longer simply "represent." Or, stated another way, it must involve the "one receiving" not only in passive meaning; it must engage him in value, in active and committed self-investment. To do this, the one representing must himself be genuinely invested in what he represents.

An operational model of this process from meaning to value and from a divided self to a more integrated one, we will call the *incarnate-redemptive* process. This model—in addition to its obvious application to religious values—will be here used in relation to the personality dynamics involved in the process of maturity, in that of counseling therapy and in the elements which relate and integrate meaning to value. This will be one of our main themes whose variations will extend throughout the book.

OPERATIONAL MODEL

What we will attempt to clarify is that counseling and psychotherapy give us an operational model of how mimesis or representation through incarnation can be both redeeming and a source of identification. Moreover, this incarnation-redemption-identification process is itself the path of maturity. The child, divided with himself and often self-rejecting, substitutes the representation of the parent-figure for his own inadequacy. In this state, the parent represents power, excellence and removal, far above and beyond the child. As the child grows in his own sense of adequacy, maturity, self-meaning and fulfillment, he comes increasingly to accept more aspects of his total human self and to recognize his own unique worth.

We have described this as a process of incarnation-redemption through which a person grows to accept and live with his total humanity, or, for want of a better term, his psychosomatic unity. As a mature adult, he no longer sees parents or parent-figures as representing superior excellence in an ideal and superhuman form. In real maturity, he sees such figures as incarnate like himself in what they represent. He can hold out to them the warm, sympathetic sharing of the human condition that is the heart of friendship.

VERTICALITY STILL NECESSARY

We are not implying, then, any loss of necessary authority, or that the organizational structure of the Church as a community would cease to be. Obviously, any formal organization must have structure and authority, and the Church is such an organization. We are proposing rather that richer and more personalized relationships need to be added to the inner structure of this organization. Its organization would become more person-centered. If it is simply managerial and authoritarian in the vertical sense, it will fail to reach and convalidate the meaning of persons. That is what we mean by adding the concept of horizontality to the vertical organization structure.

Verticality is needed too in any kind of educational learning. There must be a knower or teacher who is equipped through knowledge, training and experience. An authentic teacher understands a certain area of knowledge in far greater depth and extension than do his students. In fact, the vertical word "authority" and the word "author" are especially related here, since the author's assumed greater knowledge of his work gives him "authority." He therefore is vertically related to the students, who are themselves horizontal to one another.

But even here, as we will try to develop, real learning seems to involve the incarnate-redemptive process through which the knower strives to become like the learners. They can then gain through this redemptive experience a sense of their own capacity to know and so to become like the knower. In this sense, the norm of teaching might readily be that "he (the student) must increase and I must decrease." Later we will develop in greater detail this notion of learning by which the verticality of the knower becomes more engaged in, and reflective of, the person of the learner. Insofar as such a learning process encourages and depends on the personal dignity and worth of the learner, it may be said to be horizontal as well as vertical.

CREATIVE COMMUNICATION

It might be said that the relationship of love among men is the best thing we can offer as a modality of the relationship with God. Even the communion service, then, should have a completion in some sense of Godliness given, received and shared in the relationship of persons, acted out in communion and communication in the believing community. Only in this way will the Sacraments and the Liturgy—as an expression of Community—really come alive.

Throughout this book, therefore, we will attempt to show ways by which authentic relationships and creative communication may be furthered. To achieve them fully will certainly demand noticeable changes in our present structures. But even without dramatic changes, skilled awarenesses drawn from counseling and psychotherapy could have significant results.

PRACTICAL EXAMPLE

Let us suppose, for example, that one person—the pastoral priest or minister in this case—sets aside a forty-hour week, each hour of which will be spent with a different group of ten people. He begins each group session by playing back to them the sermon recording—no more than five to ten minutes—which was the central witness to the Word that he gave on the previous Sunday. This would imply, of course, a special kind of counseling-oriented sermon that would be "open" and not closed. It would attempt not so much to give "answers" to "problems" as to open out to the human situation and unfold the Gospel awareness and its present relevance to the condition of each hearer.

After hearing the sermon recording again, the leader's intent would be to enable these ten people to interrelate and counsel themselves and one another around the issue of what this Word means to them. Using group-counseling skills, his aim would be to help them integrate these ideas, invest in them personally and relate them to one another and the broader community. Other activities, sacramental, organizational and educational, would, of course, be carried out by others. We are describing here simply what one person might do.

If we accept the distinction between meaning and value, in the sense that intellectual meaning is only the beginning of a relationship, then what really finally matters for religious values is the meanings in which one invests himself. In this sense value engages meaning as salt savors meat and yeast penetrates dough.

The essential concern of the believing community and its communication would then center on those conditions which further investment in the meaning of the Gospel Message. These ten people—in the counseling process, with the sensitivities coming from the skills we now have at hand—could be helped to give themselves freely to one another and commit themselves to this religious witness. This could be done in repeated sessions of an hour's duration. In a forty-hour week, then, one person could relate to four hundred people every week, in groups of ten for an hour. And he would have them all together for common worship and witness once each week. Yet each one of this large community could feel himself joined to the others through the personalized relationship to the leader and the intimate communion and trust received and given in his own small group.

If such a counseling-skilled person is then also willing to spend fifteen more hours in half-hour personal interview sessions, he would be able to relate each week from thirty to fifty more individual children, adults, married couples or families in intimate personal counseling engagements.

COUNSELING AND GUIDANCE

Later we will discuss in greater detail some of these concepts of a religious communion-communication-dynamic. But one conclusion seems already evident, namely, far greater emphasis would be put on developing counseling and guidance centers under religious sponsorship and on occasions for personal encounters in small groups. There would be, therefore, much more concern for more personalized integration of religious knowledge, especially, into religious values.

This view would affect and extend the relationship of religion to education. In this we imply no misunderstanding of the paramount importance and necessity of education. But the purpose of education is to give meaning to our experience. This does not finally determine our lives. What determines our lives is the moment when we make an investment in a particular meaning, the moment when we take an empirical situation and plunge into it, the moment when we affirm ourselves as engaging in that meaning. If this is true, then, education as such is not a final concern of religion. Religion's stake is rather in values, in what people invest in, in the personal choices they make from the wide variety of knowledge that is afforded them.

The whole community of learning persons and the manner by which they learn can be affected by this. As we will discuss in detail, the conveying of worth and meaning to a person—the sense that he has value—furthers the atmosphere of learning, not only religious topics but any learning. Consequently, an educative process that is permeated by an incarnate-redemptive engagement between students and teacher and students themselves, while it would not in itself be necessarily religious, would incorporate a profoundly religious tone and atmosphere. It might be called a religious humanism. Such an atmosphere would not only further, say, the learning of English as a "second language" for underprivileged children, or the learning of a foreign language, or mathematics, it would also further in the learners a genuine regard for themselves and one another. But it could, in this context under the right condition, be a genuinely religious encounter too.

People now have vast options of self-investment from things they learn. And learning is everywhere. People learn not only in school but from television and radio, magazines, newspapers, and from immeasurable sources of meaning that we could not have conceived of even fifty years ago. Religion cannot handle this simply by setting up a wall in the manner of the walled rival city of long ago—a kind of an idealized "City of God." The city of man is now with us twenty-four hours a day—it cannot be walled out. There is no safe place, removed and protected from "worldly contamination."

PERSONAL INTEGRATION

The moment of investment in meaning and the kind of meaning we give ourselves to and make part of our lives is also the moment of counsel and counseling, the moment of engagement. The practical focus of religion, then, would not be simply on schools and colleges but on counseling-guidance centers as well. Here the matter of education could be filtered and sifted by the *person* of the individual student. Religion would be concerned with preventing the student from merely being part of a mass in the education structure, as he often is now in a large school or university. With the aid of skilled discussion leaders and counselors, the student could be helped to be, and become, in his own unique excellence. The aim here would be to further the personal digestion and investment process of values rather than only amassing meanings. Rather than a mass education for "meaning"—adding more to what already is overwhelming and perhaps giving many a kind of personality indigestion—religion would be more interested in aiding the process of personal investment, integration and action.

Religion would be concerned then with initiating in every person, through the sermon and all other relationships and settings available, the warm, deep, genuine sense of belonging of one human person to another that Augustine used as his model for the Trinity. We can add to this the incarnate-redemptive sense of meaning and worth that each of us should have in our regard for ourselves and the other. It would be in such a communion of shared redemptive incarnation—in imitation of the communion of the Trinity and Christ's incarnation-redemption of us—that each one would make his most complete, sincere and effective investment in religious witness and living. Here could be fulfilled, with increasing effectiveness, whatever is genuine in the individual and group engagements of counseling and psychotherapy.

Since these ideas of the necessity of personal integration and investment and of community involving communion and communication are so basic, they will occupy a central theme in this book. The whole book will therefore be an extension of these issues as they are seen and applied from each chapter's special coign of vantage.

SCIENCE AND RELIGION

Evident in the title and throughout the book is an insistence upon the important and necessary assistance that science, and especially psychological science, can offer religion. There is, we hope, no need to perpetuate the tragedies of the past.

Whatever may have been true in the Galileo era and later, science, in its various branches, has now reached such an eminence that it has achieved its own identity and independence. Psychological science in particular can now cooperate with religion. This can be mutually beneficial and liberating. There need no longer be a special claim to a particular definition of man to the exclusion of all other definitions. Science's right to independent research and investigation is now unquestionably established and accepted. Nor need religion fear and oppose science any longer as a person might fear and oppose someone whom he sees only in a rebellious and destructive light. Rather both have gained, through painful historical experience, a greater mutual understanding and respect and so can come now to mature regard and cooperation.

THE PLAN OF THE BOOK

In summary, then, the basic plan of this book is conceived on the hypothesis that modern developments in individual and group counseling and psychotherapy, with all their evident weaknesses, yet offer religion one of the best approaches to modern man as he really is. Consequently the book's main aim is to demonstrate that certain awarenesses adapted from counseling therapeutic knowledge and applied to the religious situation can be significant and effective aids to religion.

The chapters in *Part One* consider man as he is and help clarify the purpose and place of counseling as it relates man to religion and to religious values. While there is no intent here to offer a detailed treatment of basic counseling therapeutic skills, some discussion and illustrations of the aim and purpose of counseling seems called for especially from the point of view of our concept of "value counseling and psychotherapy" and its relation to religion. This will not take the place, however, of the careful study of detailed works representing this and a variety of other viewpoints. It especially cannot be a substitute for a thorough course with practical training and supervision. Nonetheless, some initial awareness, at least, is necessary to an understanding of much of the discussion that follows. We are, however, presuming at the outset some general understanding of what counseling and psychotherapy stand for and the various skills and theories involved.

Part Two takes up some basic issues centering first around sin, guilt and anxiety. These are first considered in the negative, immature and distorted light in which they are often seen, especially in psychotherapy. Sin, guilt and anxiety are then considered positively in the way they relate to religious maturity.

One chapter treats the symbolization of masculinity and femininity and how this affects creative relationships. This chapter also discusses what constitutes the model of the union of persons and how best to facilitate such a constructive and creative union.

Invariably any treatment of human action related to religion must face, in some measure, the issues of God and man currently much alive. We have tried to treat these wherever they fit, but in particular under *Part Three*. Here we will especially consider some related questions about God, Grace and Mystery and yet man's need to struggle to know himself, others and the universe, and the necessity to "love himself loving," in place of to "love himself hating," as Aquinas puts it. This, of course, will constitute the central theoretical treatment of the book.

Defining man as a "being in correspondence beyond," we will attempt to explain in detail how religion and counseling therapy correspond and interrelate in the stages of psychological growth. This correspondence can be seen too as contributing toward maturity and independence in learning. We will try to make clear how such "correspondence" between religion, counseling therapy and learning implies a common and mutually shared concern for the human person in his pursuit of his own excellence and in his regard for others.

Part Four will focus on some special aspects of the religious relationship. There we will seek to show how counseling therapeutic awareness, extended and adapted to religious settings and functions, can aid in making religion relevant to the lives of individual men.

Part Five will consider some aspects of the Church—that is, the "cohesive community" of the people of God. In this, one of the main purposes will be to establish some conditions for authentic religious relationships so that they result in genuine communion and communication. Drawing upon counseling, psychotherapy and similar models, we will suggest ways by which religious encounter can become incarnate and redemptive and so be of real meaning and value for those involved.

The *Conclusion* will seek to sum up some of the fundamental attitudes towards self and others which creative communication and involvement seem to require of each person.

NOTES

[1] See, for example: Lewis R. Goldberg, "Some Research on Clinical Judgments," *American Psychologist,* American Psychological Association Washington, D.C., July, 1968, Vol. 23 (7), pp. 483–496.

See also: Charles Hersch, "The Discontent Explosion in Mental Health," *Ibid.,* pp. 497–510.

And: Irwin G. Surason and Victor J. Ganger, "Concerning the Medical Model," *Ibid.,* pp. 507–510.

[2] Charles A. Curran, *Counseling and Psychotherapy: The Pursuit of Values* (New York: Sheed and Ward, 1968).

[3] Paul W. Pruyser, *A Dynamic Psychology of Religion* (New York: Harper and Row, 1968), p. 5.

[4] Peter Brown, *Augustine of Hippo: A Biography* (Los Angeles: University of California Press, 1967), p. 312.

[5] St. Augustine, *City of God,* trans. Gerald G. Walsh, S.J., et al.; ed., with an Introduction, by Vernon J. Bourke; Foreword by Etienne Gilson (New York: Doubleday Image Books, 1958).

Creative and Therapeutic Counseling

PART ONE

Creative and Therapeutic
Counseling

1
Religion and Man as He Is

IN OUR APPROACH to man we are concerned with *man as he is*, that is, man in his unique, particularized, mysterious condition. But this is not to leave him without relationship and belonging. Rather his whole being seems to cry out for this. He is therefore a being beyond himself—reaching out in seeking to know and love the other as well as to be known and loved. He is existential in the condition of his particularized uniqueness. But he is essentialist in his reaching *beyond* himself. He demonstrates this in his capacity to communicate understanding to others, especially by symbols, and in his need and will to affirm and commit himself to others and to the reshaping of things.

We see man, then, as an existence that is unique and singular and yet is interwoven with a shared essence. In this sense we might speak of an essential existentialism. By this we would be defining man as an existence that goes beyond itself. This is both man's grandeur and his tragedy. Existing always at the point of the contingent moment of experience, he seeks a personal base that is somehow enduring, fulfilling and that enables him to reach beyond himself. This is at the heart of the conflict inherent in the human condition.

We seek therefore to understand man, not abstractly or ideally, and not simply as he ought to be, but

man as *he really is today:* loving man . . . man as the superman of yesterday and today, ever frail, unreal, selfish and savage; man unhappy with himself as he laughs and cries . . . man as he is, a creature who thinks and loves and toils and is always waiting for something. . . .[1]

29

REACHING BEYOND

This reaching-beyond need in man seems so basic that unless he firmly recognizes the limits of the other, he may tend, in his narcissism, to swallow up others and so finally defeat himself. This condition of man impelling him to vault beyond himself, and consequently his corresponding need for a maturity and therapy of limits, is seen continually in the dynamic of counseling and psychotherapy. A core difficulty that counseling therapy reveals is this human tendency to over-sight and over-reach which, at the same time, causes a person to fall short of and fail in what he really is and could be.[2] It may, of course, also reveal under-sight and under-reach. But even here, these often turn out to be the other side of the over-reach coin.

Because of this tendency, one might argue that without a *Total Other* to whom to commit himself finally, man seems destined to be left in a kind of "No Exit" condition. Discussing man as he is, Sartre, for example, says:

> The best way to conceive of the fundamental project of human reality is to say that man is the being whose project is to be God. Whatever may be the myths and rites of the religion considered, God is first "sensible to the heart" of man as the one who identifies and defines him in his ultimate and fundamental project. If man possesses a pre-ontological comprehension of the being of God, it is not the great wonders of nature nor the power of society which have conferred it upon him. God, value and supreme end of transcendence, represents the permanent limit in terms of which man makes known to himself what he is. To be man means to reach toward being God. Or if you prefer, man fundamentally is the desire to be God.[3]

This desire can be so self-aggrandizing that to control it one seems to require here not only the concept *other,* but indeed the concept *Total Other,* if man is to find himself in his limited real existence. Such a Total Other can be seen by the religious man as a God-awareness. Belief in the incarnation and redemption would introduce the possibility of a human belonging to this incarnate Total Other that has "become like unto man in all things except sin."

LIMITED PERSONAL SITUATION

Many reasons might be given why a person tends to this misapprehension and distortion of himself and his personal situation. Sartre touches on a fundamental basis for this when he proposes:

> It may be asked, if man on coming into the world is borne toward God as toward his limit, if he can choose only to be God, what becomes of freedom? For freedom is nothing other than a choice which creates for itself its own possibilities, but it appears here that the initial project of being God, which "defines" man, comes close to being the same as a human "nature" or an "essence." The answer is that while the *meaning* of the desire is ultimately the project of being God, the desire is never *constituted* by this meaning; on the contrary, it always represents a particular discovery of its ends. These ends in fact are pursued in terms of a particular empirical situation, and it is this very pursuit which constitutes the surroundings *as a situation*. The desire of being is always realized as the desire of a mode of being. And this desire of a mode of being expresses itself in turn as the meaning of the myriads of concrete desires which constitute the web of our conscious life.[4]

That is, a man's actual condition here and now forces him to some containment of his self-affirmation or will to power if he is not finally to delude himself. He must act and choose always within the confines of his *limited personal* situation. This is all he really has in any particular act, whether it be loving or otherwise. Speaking conatively, he must temper and contain his basic desires within the confines of what is here and now possible to him.

This is evident in the client in counseling therapy. It is usually a main factor behind many of his personal conflicts. One of his "insightful" achievements in counseling therapy is to redefine and limit this "over-reach." But this can be equally true of the counselor. He too through over-sight and over-reach can have been using others for himself under the guise of loving or helping them.

SENSE OF THE OTHER

People undergoing training in the art and skill of counseling therapy often comment on the dawning new sense of the *other* that a counseling relationship brings them. Sometimes they feel that, for the first time in their lives, they have genuinely regarded another person for himself. The following is one such comment from a student in training:

At this moment in time occurred genuine, honest communicability, a feeling that the other person is "coming across" as a person, a person with feelings, attitudes and emotional responses. The communication was felt to be between us alone, as personalities aware not only of each other's words, thought and ideas, but also of moods, feelings and emotions. It is interesting to note here a significant response that the client made, "I can feel you—not only a physical presence—but you as you." The empathy, the togetherness we experienced resulted, I believe, from the mutual recognition that each of us is an individual, total and separate. It appears a contradiction to state that a thing that is separate can be together, but it is the awareness and acceptance psychosomatically, of the separateness in the individual that unifies.

One becomes keenly aware that one's self is being looked at and not just the words, actions and outward manifestations, I know you and you know me, not know *about* you and me. . . .

Prior to this "moment of truth," this total acceptance of each other, the interview hardly got off the ground.

FEAR OF OTHERS

There is, though, not only a tendency to manipulate, control and so absorb others. There is also a certain primitive fear of others which must be seen and overcome in the process of truly "going out" to the other in his unique and enigmatic self. Elsewhere we have pointed out the way in which giving advice to others, or any kind of intellectual discussion, can in fact sometimes be a subtle and even unconscious expression of our own urge to self-defense.[5] Or, stated another way, unconsciously we seem to see others as somewhat *inimical* to us, as threatening in some way our status, our self-affirmation and our values. This seems to come from the confused awareness that any encounter with the other puts limits on ourselves. We meet his border or frontier and we sense his unique difference from us. In this context, it is interesting to note that the word "defense" and the word "fence" or "barrier" are apparently related.

On the reverse side of this, many people are reluctant to engage in a relationship with us for fear of "bothering" us or appearing to be a nuisance. They are, in this way, already seeing themselves as, in turn, inimical to us, so that they hesitate to approach for fear we may reject them. We might say, then, in reference to the biblical injunction to love "our enemies," that we reach out to others and approach them as friends by controlling our self-defense urges and so being open. Otherwise our primitive reactions might cause us to close in the face of an initial sense of threat or disturbance to ourselves.

We discussed in detail an experiment with the eye-reflex in which a crucial moment occurs after one has trusted the experimenter and so does not blink his eyes or pull his head back from the experimenter's hand coming towards him. If, however, at a second phase of the experiment, the experimenter touches the person's face even lightly, it is then quite difficult for the subject to remain open and nondefensive on the third trial, even though he is assured it is not likely that he will be touched or "slapped" again. Here we see, psychologically, a way of understanding the difficulty of being open and "turning the other cheek" in the face of something that might appear to threaten or hurt me.

Interestingly too, in the Parable of the Talents, it is the man who is afraid to take the risk that the story rejects because he is unwilling to make an investment and commitment in the face of what he projects to be the threatening father-figure of a master. As we stated elsewhere:

We are afraid to love apparently because we fear to run the risk of losing some valuable part of ourselves. It is much safer to keep distance and avoid getting close to others so as not to risk the danger of jeopardizing ourselves. But this is a self-defeating paradox like the person who is afraid to enter water until he learns to swim. Christ expressed this with the penetrating phrase, "He that shall save his life shall lose it, and he that shall lose his life shall save it." By giving in to my protective urges to avoid risk, I never can know open human communion.[6]

TO GOD THROUGH OTHERS

It is necessary to add here the realization that our age especially has seen emerging the focus on the person—any person. Each person in himself is becoming the central locus for meaning and value in the human condition. We have, as we said, changed our model of the human condition from a vertical to a horizontal design. Previously we wrote:

> The heavens indeed still beckon with beauty and allure. But they can be seen too in the horizon where heaven and earth meet. This horizontal model has us seeking across the faces of the earth and the faces of one another as well as looking up, for the vision, beauty, meaning and mystery.

In the model of the horizontal line where the heavens are in the beyond, then, we move toward heaven by moving across the face of the earth, experiencing persons and things. One way we experience the unknown and the mysterious is when we give ourselves over to and accept the unique in other persons. In this enigmatic relationship we begin to know and love them. If we trust in them only what is like ourselves and so is familiar and reassuring, we have never really reached them. We have only a narcissistic reflection of ourselves. To reach others is to love and trust them in what is mysterious and unique and therefore unknown. Seen this way, we must trust and love others in order to begin to know them in their unique and special, and so "personal" selves.[7]

This, then, would also be a way of approaching God as Total Other. In experiencing this kind of regarding love from others and in being able also to give it, we would have some foreshadowing and elemental human model of the love of God.

One can see an implication of this in the Biblical text: "For he that loves not his brother whom he sees, how can he love God whom he sees not?" (I John 4:20). Beyond the way a person reflects and is like me, to love him, I must plunge myself into his uniqueness—that unknown and unresolved part of himself that is totally his. Yet in a certain sense one might say that I have never really known this person; I have only known myself, until I permitted myself this experience of what is unknown, unique and mysterious in him. Only in abandoning myself to this in him can I begin to love him. Through such trusting enigmatic love of another whom I see, I can then begin to have some correspondent love with an ultimate enigmatic and mysterious Total Other. This would be a way of seeing and regarding a God-image in each person that I know and reaching God through loving this unique image in him.[8]

EXPERIENCED CONVALIDATION

Whether we are speaking theologically or psychologically then, it is not enough that a person *hear* that he is redeemed or that he has worth. This can be repeated to him endlessly and he can even believe it, and yet it may not really "come off" in him. It may not really be conative. To have value he must *experience* his unique worth in the manner in which he is regarded by others. Here he is not simply looked at—in the original meaning of "gard"—but *re*-garded, that is *re*-spected for his real value—looked at again and again in all that he is and stands for. As a result of such reflective regard he is respectfully considered and treated. By such convalidation he grows, in turn, to respect himself and others.

There is, then, a basic affirmation to self-excellence that one needs to achieve in oneself and see reflected and confirmed by others. It is therefore an affirmation-confirmation personality need. Tempered and contained within the insightful awareness of a man's realization of his own limits, this, apparently, is his strongest source of meaning and value. It is at the heart of his courage to be and become. This is basic also to the way he regards others, since he tends to love them or disregard them according to the model of his attitudes towards himself.

THE URGE TO KNOW

Besides the necessity of containment of a man's self-affirmation by a sense of the other and his need of having his unique worth convalidated by others, there is also his basic urge to know. This urge to learn, to gain accurate facts, to see relationships, to grasp significance, is obviously one of the characteristics of man. It is, as the Greeks knew, a kind of becoming, and thus an enlarging of self. By a process of symbolization, things known become signs, and so enter significantly into the meaning world of the knower. They remain there for him to feed upon, and so grow in knowledge of himself and others. In this meaning way man makes the issue of knowledge some part of himself. He takes it to himself. Werner and Kaplan explain:

. . . Among the novel ends immanent in the nature of the developing human being—and most central in the context of the present discussion —is that of *knowing* about his world. This end plays an intrinsic role in man's transformation of his milieus into objects to be cognized and conceptualized. Indeed this end is so strong in man that even in the absence of certain normally employed instrumentalities of cognition (for example, sight and hearing), man may use alternative, compensatory means for attaining knowledge.[9]

This constitutes a "basic directiveness" and a special orientation to which man's behavior can be guided:

. . . with the emergence of a basic directiveness towards knowing, man's hand and man's brain participate in the construction of tangible tools out of the properties of the environment and the construction of cognitive objects (percepts and concepts) which mediate between man and his physical milieu: it is primarily toward these objects that man's distinctive behavior is oriented. It is in this context, as we shall attempt to show, that the most significant of man's instrumentalities, the *symbol,* is formed.[10]

Werner and Kaplan describe this developmental process by which the person not only reacts to and acts upon his milieu but cognizes it, or so directs his activities as means to these "recognized" goals:

. . . with development . . . local activities become more and more interrelated and integrated, that is, come more and more under the control of and the determination by the focal, goal-directed activities of the organism. Concurrently, the nature of the organism-environment transactions undergoes marked changes. . . . Finally and most characteristically and elaborately at the human level—the environment is not only reacted to and acted upon but is cognized, or "known," in the form of perceptualized and conceptualized *objects*.[11]

DISTORTION BY ABSTRACTION

One further and most important point in this consideration of man as he is concerns how we understand this cognizing process. Rogers, for example, suggests that in counseling and psychotherapy he witnesses a basic reasonableness in man, a reasonableness so evident that only his own confusion and conflict prevent him from taking advantage of it. Accordingly, one of the aims of therapy is to free man to make more adequate use of his own reasonable self-awareness.[12]

This stress on reasonableness might suggest Aristotle's concept of "rational animal." But this brings up the danger of distortion by abstraction. If we grant this Aristotelian affinity, then, it is necessary to point out one profound, basic and most important difference: the contrast between the reality of man's actual condition—caught up in a mosaic of conscious and unconscious motivation from soma, instincts, emotions as well as reason and volition—and the Aristotelian concept of a "reasonable" man. While undoubtedly, after Descartes, we tend to read into the word "reasonable" a kind of cold abstractive "rational number" implication that was not Aristotle's unified-person meaning, this concept still implies an ideal and a norm. It is not a totally human reality. Consequently such abstracted conceptions may be seriously misleading, particularly when applied, without cautious discrimination, to man.

Gilson makes this clear:

It would be a fruitful subject of reflection to consider the dreadful consequences of what might be called "the spirit of abstraction." In speculative matters, it invites the substitution of the definition for the defined, which is a sure way to render definitions sterile. It also invites the illusion that one can increase knowledge by merely deducing consequences from already coined definitions, instead of frequently returning to the very things from which essences and definitions were first abstracted. In the practical order, the spirit of abstraction probably is the greatest single source of political and social disorders, of intolerance and of fanaticism. Nothing is more uncompromising than an essence, its quiddity and its definition.[13]

The very nature of an abstraction process runs the danger of deformation because it is withdrawing from individual, contingent, concrete experience in order to find and distil what is common and so can be shared. As Gilson says:

... the characteristics of the abstract are exactly opposed to those of the concrete. Now reality is concrete, and this is the reason that abstract descriptions of it are liable to deform it.

Abstractions are mutually exclusive, because "to abstract" is "to set apart." ...[14]

Gendlin has discussed in detail this difference between an abstract and a concrete, individual human experience of meaning. As he points out:

Besides the logical dimension and the operational dimension of knowledge, there is also a directly felt, experiential dimension. *Meaning* is not only *about things* and it is not only a certain *logical* structure, but it also involves *felt* experiencing. Any concept, thing, or behavior is meaningful only as some noise, thing, or event interacts with felt experiencing. Meanings are formed and had through an interaction between experiencing and symbols or things.[15]

Consequently man experiences meaning through his total person, not simply intellectually. His "reasonableness" then consists in a kind of inner informing of his total person or, as we shall see, an affect-cognition intercommunication or intercourse with himself at all levels of his being.

ABSTRACT OR INCARNATE

There are, in other words, two ways of looking at reasonableness. There is a cold, abstractive, ideal, impersonal reasonableness which can act like a norm or ideal goal, or a most desired good—like the score three hundred in bowling—an ideal seldom if ever achieved. This is a nonincarnate reasonableness.

But there is another kind of reasonableness that permeates this person, that is incarnate in him, that forms and integrates his emotions, instincts and soma so that, in a particular act, they are responsive to reasonableness. It is incorporated and conative and so effective in determining his action. When he sees this kind of action clearly in the broad complex of its meaning, this can be truly insightful reasonableness.

The first reasonableness is necessary to offer possible goals and to spur one on to greater possible achievement. Without it, man might be listless and unmotivated. Such goals offer targets or ideals to shoot at and means to measure one's present position and accomplishment.

But the second reasonableness—incarnate and conative—makes one's real life. It is the reasonableness we must live with, day by day. Such reasonableness "informs" the personality and thus redeems it, so that it performs worthily. It is this kind of reasonableness that builds up self-approval and permanent self-regard as a result of those acts where, afterwards, a person may say, "I am really pleased with myself today."

This is the positive self-concept equation where the "I" relates to my own realistic reasonableness and "myself" performed up to it. It *"performed"* but it was adequately *"informed"* not merely in the modern sense of "information"—though this may sometimes be necessary—but more through conative integration of the whole self.

It is this second reasonableness that enables a man to be content, in some measure, with his "empirical situation," in Sartre's phrase, and with the unique, particular conditions of his self-investment. The first reasonableness, if not circumscribed by the potentiality of his particular condition, can lead a person to God-like postures and goals that are inefficacious and finally insane. It produces the fanatic and the cold, inconsiderate and unsympathetic man. It lacks the warmth of human kindness, of redeeming incarnation.

Applied to the community or to what could be called the "common good," it is the second reasonableness that slowly and tortuously, like a person in counseling, works out practical norms of common living. No ideal solutions work here, in the well-known sense that diplomacy and law—however ideal the reasonable norm

—must accommodate themselves finally to the possible in the here-and-now condition of men concerned. But reasonableness as an ideal still affords the goal and the target. Maturity in community, like maturity in one person, is a slow striving for betterment, for a realistic fulfillment of what is genuinely realizable.

VALUES

But, in addition to the process of *taking* or absorbing meaning and significance in experience, there is also an urge in man to *give,* to invest in other persons and things. In giving there is first of all the giving of himself. In a way different from knowing which *takes* into himself, there is the investment of self, the giving of self in a complete way to what is somehow known. This is a personal introsusception involving the whole self—soma, instincts, emotions, as well as the knowing and choosing functions. It is to stand committed to some aspect of what one knows by the singular investment of the whole self of the knower. This is the pursuit of value—this is to make knowledge a personal value. This is to go beyond knowing to loving.

Among many things and persons a man knows, he chooses some and makes a special commitment of his whole self in some way to them. This is meaning plus degree of self-investment. Basically it is the message of the parable of the talents and the launching out into the depths and the wilderness of the mysteries of love.

Understandably, then, such value-charged relationships often show themselves in positive and negative emotional states, arouse defenses and even somatic disturbance. When a person *cares* for something or someone, he has invested his *whole* person, not simply his conscious awareness.

MOTIVATIONAL EMOTIONAL FIELD

This notion of value and the motivational field it implies, resulting as it often does in emotional states, might be expressed by the popular phrase "vested interests." "Investing" signifies, of course, putting on clothes. In this sense, then, one has taken on "interests";

that is, one has set up goals and achievements which one wants with some degree of intensity. This is a creative tension. Emotions result from and are interwoven with such "invested interests." As Arnold explains:

To arouse an emotion, the object must be appraised as affecting me in some way, affecting me personally as an individual with my particular experience and my particular aims. . . . Since emotion has an objective, something to be gained or avoided that is appraised as good or harmful, desirable or undesirable, the question arises whether this appraisal itself could be the emotion. . . . Emotion seems to include not only the appraisal of how this thing or person will affect me but also a definite pull toward or away from it. In fact, does not the emotional *quale* consist precisely in that unreasoning involuntary attraction or repulsion? If I merely know things or persons as they are apart from me, there is no emotion. If I know them and judge them theoretically and abstractly to be good for me, there may still be no emotion. But if I think something is good for me *here and now,* and *feel myself drawn toward it,* sometimes even against my better judgment, then my experience is, properly speaking, nonrational; it is other than just cold reason; it is an addition to knowledge: it is *emotional.*[16]

It is to be expected, therefore, that people often begin counseling in some state of emotion. This does not need to be so, however. As we shall see later, counseling can also be significant in positive anticipation as a preparation for future experience. Counseling can be an exercise in what John Dewey described as man's capacity to "pre-think" an experience and so plan for a subsequent experience.

But since emotional states can be indices to values in conflict, the psychological pain of such conflict is often indicated by a degree of negative emotion. The person begins his communication, therefore, in a state of being angry or depressed or frustrated or disappointed, or a combination of these and other negative feelings. It is the release and clarification of these feelings and the uncovering and resorting of the values they contain that constitutes the counseling process. Since we have discussed this process and its art and skill in a previous book, we will describe it here more as it relates to man as he is. We will also consider later how this applies to religious counseling. Our intent here, however, is to show how man seems to need some sort of affective-cognitive reflection if he is to understand himself.

AFFECT-COGNITION REFLECTION

A person cognizes himself and others especially as he reflects upon his experience. Moments of experience themselves are usually so complicated that little is really understood here. Understanding comes more at the moment of reflection where conscious awareness symbolizes some part of what was experienced and so makes it part of one's conscious memory. This then makes later reflection possible.

This process of cognizing the self and the environment might be said, among other aspects, to include three phases:

I. Signification—giving symbols to moments of experience and so making reflection possible;

II. Evaluation—sorting out the different value packages or systems involved;

III. Conation—reorganization of whole organism goal-system and desire-motivation.

One reason why the counseling therapy process seems helpful is that it provides a person with a skilled aid which facilitates his own reflection upon himself. He can and often must do this by himself, of course. But he can be especially assisted to free himself from the binds of confusion and conflict about himself and others by the sensitive understanding and skilled awareness of another person. In this sense we can say that the counselor helps the person "re-cognize" himself.

This assistance that the counselor offers begins even with the first efforts of the client to explain himself. This initiates a complicated communication that we have described as a "language of affect–language of cognition" exchange. Through this, the steady growth in self-awareness and the untangling of emotions and values are made possible.

The sketch gives a rough illustration of what takes place.

The Process of Understanding in the Counselor-Client Relationship

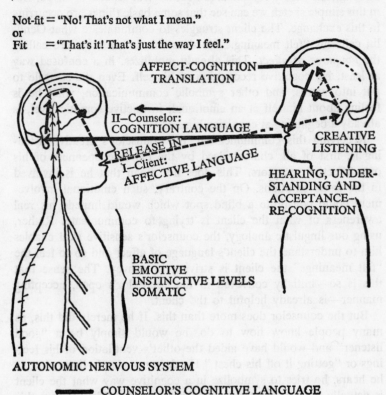

CLIENT   COUNSELOR

Not-fit = "No! That's not what I mean."
or
Fit   = "That's it! That's just the way I feel."

AFFECT-COGNITION TRANSLATION

II—Counselor: COGNITION LANGUAGE

RELEASE IN

I—Client: AFFECTIVE LANGUAGE

CREATIVE LISTENING

HEARING, UNDER-STANDING AND ACCEPTANCE-RE-COGNITION

BASIC
EMOTIVE
INSTINCTIVE LEVELS
SOMATIC

AUTONOMIC NERVOUS SYSTEM

■■■■ COUNSELOR'S COGNITIVE LANGUAGE
- - - - CLIENT'S AFFECTIVE LANGUAGE
═══ PARA-SYMPATHETIC
─── SYMPATHETIC

CLIENT	COUNSELOR
COMMITMENT	COMMITMENT
SECURITY	WARMTH
FREEDOM	TRUST
RESPONSIBILITY	AUXILIARY REASONING-POWER
HOPE	

© Copyright, 1968, C. A. Curran

AFFECT-COGNITION LANGUAGE EXCHANGE

We are obviously not attempting by this rough design to indicate, in detail, the highly complicated neurological aspects involved. But in this simple sketch we can see that some basic things are occurring in this exchange. The client struggles to communicate what Gendlin calls his "felt meaning." He does this in what we are calling the *language of affect*. This already mobilizes, in a confused way at least, his cognitive recognition of himself. Even the struggle to put into words, and other symbolic communication, what he is feeling about himself at an emotional, instinctive somatic level, is already a beginning at cognizing himself.

Receiving this communication, the counselor's creative listening is, first of all, characterized by the extreme openness of his own affective receptors. This does not mean that he is involved in the same emotions. On the contrary, such emotional involvement could constitute a blind spot which would impede his real awareness of what the client is trying to communicate. Rather, using our linguistic analogy, the counselor's sensitive skill enables him to understand the client's language of affect and so to feel the "felt meanings" the client is striving to convey. The sense that this is so—initially conveyed in the counselor's open, accepting manner—is already helpful to the client.

But the counselor does more than this. If he merely did this, as many people know how to do, he would simply be a "good listener" and would have aided the other's ventilation of his feelings or "getting it off his chest." He does not simply listen, but as he hears, he tries to symbolize in a cognitive way what the client is actually feeling. He then puts this in words which convey this meaning but disentangled now from its confusing, particularized affect.

Let us take only one example, for now, of what seems a simple exchange between two persons. Notice the following, in which a student intends to role-play an ordinary conversation but suddenly begins to talk personally of himself after only one response:

Client: Last night was terrible because we looked at the television and I'm a Senator fan and I was just hoping that the Senators would win, but the Sox won. The Sox don't win many games but when they do they have to beat the Senators—that was really bad news!

Counselor: Yes, it's disappointing, isn't it.

Cl: Yes, it sure is! . . . (*pause*) I guess that's not what I really wanted to talk about when I came in. The problem I have or one of the things I would like to talk about is the fact that I'm having a great deal of difficulty adjusting to and working with the fellow who is my boss.

Discussing this after the interview, he commented:

Well, I didn't follow through with the role playing the way I thought I was going to do. The thing that was surprising and almost shook me off the seat was this: "It's disappointing"—right at the beginning. That initially indicated that it was my "disappointment" that was the important thing in my comment and not the fact that the Senators lost. . . . That was terrific because . . . it was a total concern not for the objective topic but for my individual feelings about the objective fact.

"Disappointing" conveys the exact emotional tone that the client feels at the moment. So much so that he disregards the baseball topic and goes immediately into a complicated personal conflict. We will reproduce this interview later and discuss it in detail.

But in addition to the counselor's response, a central and most important point in the verbal exchange is the moment immediately after the client has heard the response. The rough diagram indicates this by the "fit" or "not-fit" arrow. At this moment, the client is fitting the counselor's verbal cognition of his affect-state down on the affects themselves and comparing the two. If they are comparatively congruent, there is, as in this case, a spontaneous and relieving agreement like, "That's it!" He may continue with, "That's just the way I feel," or "That sure does fit." In this case, the client said: "Yes, it sure is!"

Contrariwise, if the counselor misunderstands, minimizes or exaggerates emotional tones, or makes some similar distortion, the client seems often to react negatively even by showing visible pain. This misunderstanding of the affective state he was trying to have understood is frustrating and disturbing. Here is the nub of the feeling that he has not been heard. As a result, he can be left feeling alienated and alone with no one to share his confusion and conflict.

When he has been understood, however, he seems to be redeemed and freed from the heaviness and burden of the negative affect. This enables him to move on to the discharge of other confusing and conflicting feelings and to begin to pursue them to their basic causes.

This leads to a steady unfolding of the personal values that have resulted in the charged affects. Personal goals and relationships are in some way distorted or in conflict with one another, or the negative affects would not be there. The counseling process consists in uncovering these values. There is then a gradual re-organization and re-sorting of them. This is accompanied by the devising of better and more adequate operational systems. Its purpose is now to facilitate the achievement of those values that are still desired after they have become consciously recognized and clearly discriminated. Other values can be discarded.

EDUCATION-GUIDANCE-COUNSELING

If we assume that education is the area of more general knowledge and information, and guidance is the more particularized application of knowledge to the person's own situation, then it becomes apparent that counseling interrelates with these two sources of knowledge. Often a person has received much knowledge applicable to himself, and he may even have been advised in detail on what best to do. But until now, without counseling, he could not make use of the knowledge. It remained in an undigested or non-absorbed state.

As a result of the process initiated by counseling, he can slowly begin to digest and absorb what he knows as he reflects on himself and so lessens his narrow defensiveness and resistance. As he begins to see himself and his situation more clearly and less defensively, he can bring to bear on the devising of a more adequate solution whatever pertinent knowledge and advice he has previously received. Therefore he is now more open to the personal investment of himself in what he has learned, or at least has been told.

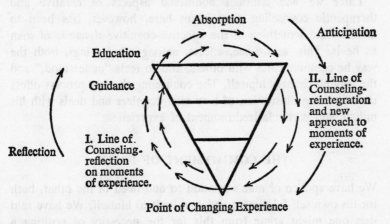

Education-Guidance-Counseling Process

Absorption

Anticipation

Education

II. Line of
Counseling-
reintegration
and new
approach to
moments of
experience.

Guidance

I. Line of.
Counseling-
reflection
on moments
of experience.

Reflection

Point of Changing Experience

© Copyright, 1968, C. A. Curran

The reflection-absorption-anticipation counseling process is demonstrated by the circular arrows. Line I indicates the *reflection* upon particular experience. This facilitates the gradual acquiring of a broader and more integrated self-awareness which includes a more extensive realization of one's personal situation. More general information, gained from Guidance and Education and from one's own observations, can be put to use here as the client becomes less defensive and narrow and so begins to understand and accept himself and his situation.

By repeated reflection on the details of a particular situation, a person can often see how knowledge he already has can be applied in ways previously not evident to him. He is made more open by counseling to the use of knowledge gained both from his own experiences and from the guidance and teaching of others. Previously he was too closed or discouraged to take advantage of this knowledge. But now, as a result, he can plan better approaches to his personal situation, having the added assets of his reflection on himself and others and the integration of what he has learned.

This circular line indicates a continuing process. We see then how each client statement and each counselor response adds to the extension and continuation of this movement of reflection, absorption, integration and planning.

Later we will consider additional aspects of creative and therapeutic counseling. Our intent here, however, has been to demonstrate something of the affective-cognitive dynamic of man as he is. This, as we see, affects, among other things, both the way he communicates with others, and so feels "understood," and the way he changes himself. The counseling therapy process offers an interesting illustration of how man cognizes and deals with his unique and particularized moment of experience.

THE COMMITMENT OF FAITH

We have spoken of man's relation to and need of the other, both for his own self-fulfillment and as a limit to himself. We have said that one might argue from this for the necessity of positing a Total Other whose being is behind and beyond all others. We might then say that man needs not only to be other-centered but, in a basic way, God-centered. How one realizes this need, or even whether one admits and accepts it, depends on one's religious faith commitment.

One can approach God, of course, by a kind of negation process, as Gilson explains:

Hence, in proceeding toward God by way of negation, we successively deny of Him all the properties, corporeal or incorporeal, that are found in creatures; for, even though God really is the highest among such properties as goodness, science, wisdom, and the like, we do not know what they are in God. Only one notion, then, remains in our intellect; namely, that God is, and nothing more. But it is for us all but impossible to think of a being *that it is,* being completely ignorant of *what* it is. Having reached this point, therefore, our mind finds itself in a state of confusion. . . .[17]

While we may affirm then a Total Other, it is by a faith commitment and the gift of self that genuine religious experience is made possible. We have seen that such acceptance of and abandonment to the enigmatic in another is basic to any real human commitment and relationship. This seems also true of divine belonging.

The religious man not only makes a "leap" into faith, he also "falls"—as a person is said to "fall in love." A diving-board analogy suggests both the plunge forward and the abandonment in God which the religious person experiences—as the swimmer feels himself surrounded by and submerged in water at the end of his dive. A prelude to this can be the experience of the enigmatic in others and the sense of their convalidation of his worth and meaning as a person.

Kierkegaard likened the condition of dread or *angst* in man to "dizziness":

He whose eye chances to look down into the yawning abyss becomes dizzy. But the reason for it is just as much in his eye as it is the precipice. For suppose he had not looked down.[18]

This dizziness of anxiety comes, according to Kierkegaard, from man's basic awareness of freedom and responsibility.

But a free and responsible commitment to God requires religious faith in order to give oneself to the plunge. The agency of this abandonment and the means for this responsible faith commitment is usually an historical doctrine of revelation which constitutes the creed of a person's faith, the structure of his "leap." In the analogy of the diver, this would be the diving board itself which lifts him up and makes his "leap" into faith, hope and love possible. The religious man usually believes in a God who has communicated with man in some defined manner—granting a wide variety of versions of this communication and its meaning.

But even at its most "other" or mystic level, there still seems to be some relationship to the human condition. As Gilson says:

There is continuity of order from the elementary judgment of existence formulated in matters of practical life and the highest of judgments formed by the contemplative affirming in darkness the existence of HE WHO IS.[19]

This leads us to the concept of "correspondence" and to the idea of man as a "being in correspondence beyond," a conception which, in varying forms, will occupy the remainder of the book. But first we need to consider, in some measure, the creative and therapeutic counseling process itself and some of the basic issues it raises about the condition of man as he is. We can then take up some resulting psychological aspects for a theology of human belonging and some practical applications and conclusions about man in himself and in community with others.

NOTES

[1] Pope Paul VI, "Closing Address to Vatican II," *Newsweek,* December 20, 1965, p. 41. (Italics mine.)

[2] See: B. J. F. Lonergan, *Insight: A Study of Human Understanding* (New York: Philosophical Library, 1957).

[3] Jean-Paul Sartre, *Existentialism and Human Emotions* (New York: Philosophical Library, 1957), p. 63.

[4] *Ibid.*, pp. 63–64.

[5] Curran, *Counseling and Psychotherapy: The Pursuit of Values* (New York: Sheed and Ward, 1968).

[6] *Ibid.*

[7] *Ibid.*

[8] *Ibid.*

[9] H. Werner and B. Kaplan, *Symbol Formation* (New York: John Wiley & Sons, 1963), pp. 10–11.

[10] *Ibid.*

[11] *Ibid.*, pp. 8–9.

[12] Carl Rogers, *On Becoming a Person* (Boston: Houghton Mifflin, 1961).

[13] Etienne Gilson, *The Elements of Christian Philosophy* (New York: The New American Library, 1960), pp. 251–252.

[14] *Ibid.*, p. 252.

[15] Eugene T. Gendlin, *Experiencing and the Creation of Meaning: A Philosophical and Psychological Approach to the Subjective* (New York: The Free Press of Glencoe, 1962), p. 1. Reprinted with permission of the Macmillan Company. Copyright The Free Press of Glencoe, a Division of the Macmillan Company, 1962.

[16] Magda B. Arnold, *Emotion and Personality, I: Psychological Aspects* (New York: Columbia University Press, 1960), pp. 171–172. For detailed discussion see *ibid.*, pp. 95–100.

[17] Gilson, *op. cit.,* p. 257.

[18] Sören Kierkegaard, *The Concept of Dread,* trans. Walter Lowrie (Princeton: Princeton University Press, 1946), p. 55. See also Seward Hiltner, "Some Theories of Anxiety: Theological," in *Constructive Aspects of Anxiety,* ed. Seward Hiltner and Karl Menninger (Nashville, Tenn.: Abingdon Press, 1963), pp. 53–58.

[19] Gilson, *op. cit.,* p. 257.

1 Gibson, *Ibid.*, p. 25.

14??? .... an .... From *content of Dewey*, p. 75. *Waser Loofie Pedawosee, Prac ... Co-rectiy Press, 1966 ... p. 55. See also Bernad Photer: "Some Blemat of ... mosity" *T logic*," in *Contribution slopey ed. ...? et al, Edward Hilton and Cecsl. ...lentine, *Education Hume:
Abegdoo Press? Velo. 99. 98 ...

Ilison, *op. cit.*, p. 257.

2

Brief Encounter

Man, then, considered not simply as a "human being" but as a "being-becoming" and a "being-beyond," is constantly engaged with himself in the confusion and conflict of his own dynamic tension. He is therefore always in need of taking counsel with himself about issues both in and beyond himself. Insofar as counseling or counseling therapy can help in this process, it can be seen as a normal necessity rather than something exceptional.

In this context of normality, we can think of both creative counseling, whose aim is the more adequate fulfillment of one's positive aspirations and ideals, and therapeutic counseling for the purpose of removing blocks which impede personality growth and achievement.

EMPIRICAL SITUATION

The human person functions, as we have seen, not only at a physico-chemical level, or by responding to stimuli, but also by directly acting on himself and his environment through a cognitive process. This cognitive process is usually thought of as relating and interpreting reality in abstract symbolization. This by itself, however, is not the same as the adequate understanding of a particular contingent experience.

A person needs to understand himself, others and his environment in the individual, concrete, empirical situation that occurs in his life from day to day. This often meets with mystery. Understanding here can be much more difficult than abstract symbolization or even the knowledge of what one "ought" to do. It is the familiar issue of "If to do were as easy as to know what were good to do." Such adequate resolution and action can be quite complex, involving one's past as well as one's present. This also engages a person in values and goals that are unconscious and implicit as well as explicit. This world of the singular contingent, where each man actually "lives and has his being," involves the total self and not simply intellectual awareness.

These conflicts and confusions may be practically settled, as we have said, by the person's taking counsel with himself. But in many instances they can be more efficiently and thoroughly resolved through the aid of the counseling skill of another. Moreover, many personal issues still in the class of ordinary life conflicts can yet be so complicated that such counseling aid seems essential to any adequate solution.

NORMAL PROCESS

Consequently, in this chapter we will discuss and illustrate the use of the counseling process in ordinary life situations. We will also attempt to demonstrate that counseling need not always be long-term and time-consuming, as is often thought. Counseling can in fact prove helpful—judged from the person's comments afterwards—even with a very limited use of time. A short-term counseling process, even of five or ten minutes, is therefore possible and can be of significant personal assistance.

Until recently it has been customary to think that the counseling interview had to be a half-hour or, preferably, an hour. It was thought, too, that the process must extend over a number of interviews—ten, twenty or more. Obviously, with this idea in mind, some of the first difficulties that the question of counseling raised were those of time and expense. While it is still true that much counseling is concerned with half-hour or hour individual sessions, and does extend over twenty interviews or more, it is becoming more evident, as we will attempt to show, that counseling skill can be used in very short-term relationships as well.

In general we can say that what might be called a "brief-encounter interview" can be seen in two ways: one, as a means to a long-term appointment and series; and two, as an end in itself.

MEANS TO LONGER RELATIONSHIP

To conceive of a short counseling encounter of five or ten minutes as preparing the way for a later relationship can be a way of avoiding some of the difficulties which a somewhat chance meeting can involve. Since, in this case, the counselor is usually on his way to some other activity, he will have the urge to say that he does not have time to talk to the person, and to ask, "Would you care to see or call me later?" This seems, under the circumstances, a quite good-mannered question. One could not normally expect anything further of the counselor, since he has been approached without notice. In fact, however, this can leave much to be desired.

To see this as a counseling situation, and not simply one of ordinary good manners, we need to consider all the vectors, positive and negative, which can be working together and which finally result in this somewhat insecure and hesitant approach to the counselor. In this light, the counselor's polite indication that he does not have time now may place an added, and perhaps too grave, impediment to the person's ever trying again. So, his "Thank you, I will call you soon," or "I will come to see you soon," may in fact remain a promise unfulfilled. It, too, was a polite response, but the person may actually have felt that his initial attempt to arrive at a real relationship with the counselor failed, and so he is too discouraged to make any further attempt.

Oddly enough, the counselor, on his side, under the tension of his embarrassment at being unable to see the person immediately, may take as much time apologizing and explaining the reason for his lack of time as he needed for a five- or ten-minute counseling communication.

If, in place of what the person might feel to be a polite "brush-off," the counselor begins immediately with counseling understanding and sensitive and penetrating kinds of responses, the relationship can become deep and real. Once such a secure relationship has been established, even after only a few minutes, it is a great deal easier for the person to make and keep an appointment for a later, longer meeting and, if necessary, continue a counseling series.

Sometimes a person can be made to feel genuinely understood

and accepted in two or three responses. Consequently, since the counselor has told him that he has only five or ten minutes for this initial relationship, a person does not feel rejected when the counselor soon must leave. He is already firmly secure in the counselor's acceptance and has some evidence that he will be understood. This brief counseling encounter would then be the means to a longer relationship.

END IN ITSELF

Another and perhaps even more important way of looking at this brief encounter, however, is to see it not as a means but as an end in itself. It aims at an immediate engagement in understanding the feelings and in clarifying the confused motives behind the person's approach. Recognizing the convergence of need-vectors that produced this moment of openness, the counselor immediately announces his limited time of five or ten minutes and then puts himself genuinely and concentratedly into the counseling relationship. Rather than seeing this initial moment as too isolated to be significant, the counselor's attitude is that this can represent an intensity of communication which may never be repeated again or for which, at least, one might have to wait through a series of interviews. In this sense, he sees the person's approach to him as possibly the climax of a long, hidden struggle and consequently as something it may have taken special courage for the person even to attempt.

Taking advantage of the intensity of the moment, rather than delaying the counseling relationship in order to see the person later for a longer time, the counselor's purpose is to crowd as much awareness as possible into his responses. For this reason he tries to pick up every nuance in the person's initial expressions. In this he seeks both to recognize the feeling components expressed and to clarify and reinforce the unfolding of whatever values, goals or purposes may be revealed.

COUNSELING CONTINUUM

Counseling, then, could be said to extend along the lines of a continuum. At one end it is seen as related to therapy and to complicated personality difficulties of people who, however, would still be considered psychologically normal. Involved marriage counseling, for example, where people have already applied for divorce, might be seen at this end. Difficulties of this sort, many of them of long duration, are not going to be resolved quickly and simply, no matter how skilled the counseling. They therefore will demand half-hour or hour sessions, and these sessions will, of necessity, have to extend over periods of time.

But at the other end of this continuum, we are now seeing that counseling skill can also be valuably used for short sessions of a half-hour, fifteen, ten or even five minutes. These may require only one, two or a limited number of sessions. In some instances, the immediately pressing issues may be settled in a comparatively short time. But even when no issues are apparently resolved, short-term counseling can prove helpful to people and so be well worth the time expended.

An essential ingredient for the effectiveness of such short-term counseling, however, is the quick and clear formulation of adequate counseling responses. In a way, the long-term interview allows greater counselor luxury. The counselor can make mistakes and still have time to see their effects and gradually correct them. But in a brief relationship, miscues may never be recovered. As a result, the attempted communication may end in a polite stalemate or produce covered or open hostility. Ordinarily no opportunity will ever occur for the counselor to correct this.

Of course the counselor can dismiss such failures as a function of the shortness of time. Hence, it is an enticing rationalization simply to say, "One cannot accomplish anything in five or ten minutes anyway, so what could you expect?" Even more commonly, one can dismiss such counseling as a waste of time and never even attempt it.

BRIEF ENCOUNTER: "SCOTT"

Let us consider now a ten-minute interview that occurred in a seminar of twelve people. One of the members, Scott, volunteered to do what he thought was going to be role-playing. But it quickly became personal counseling. He announced his role to be that of a person who seemed determined to waste the counselor's time with "shooting the breeze," as he expressed it.

The role-playing idea resulted from a question Scott had posed earlier about how to "handle" a person who insists on only "chatting" rather than having a serious relationship. In place of attempting an answer, the seminar leader suggested that Scott might wish to play this role, and the leader would be the counselor in the relationship.

Scott began with this role but did not choose to hold it beyond the first response. Immediately he switched to his own real personal situation—a minister in conflict with the pastor of the particular church where he is associate pastor. We will break up the recorded ten minutes to allow for comments on the process itself and certain elements in the skill of the counselor's responses. Later, using an "Interview Content Analysis," we will diagram what seemed to transpire and comment on the diagrams. Throughout this discussion we will be especially concerned with the way the client's developing insights also brought forward personal *value options*. This is one of the reasons for calling this "Value Counseling."

"Scott" Brief Encounter

Counselor: Hi, how are you?

Scott: Real fine. I was kind of . . . last night was terrible because we looked at the television and I'm a Senator fan and I was just hoping that the Senators would win but the Sox won. They don't win many games but they have to beat the Senators when they do win—that's really bad news.

Co: Yes, that's disappointing, isn't it?

Scott: Yes, it sure is.

Co: You were looking forward to the Senators winning . . . . I think I told you that I only had ten minutes now because I have to get to class. If you like, we could set something up for later. Yes, the old Sox are kind of kicking us all around again. We thought they were going to lose and now they are winning.

The counselor here, of course, is in the role-playing situation. He announces the ten-minute interview in which Scott is supposed to be in the role of a student who has just stopped by for a "chatty" visit. Notice that the counselor does what might be called a "sandwich response," in the sense that he repeats the feeling-tone and then puts the announced time in the center and repeats the tone of disappointment again.

It is important to announce the time at the beginning in this way. It offers a frame of reference to both counselor and client. As we will see in Scott's comments at the end of the ten minutes, it also gave a tone of seriousness and dignity to the relationship. It conveys the sense that both are people whose time is valuable.

1   *Scott:* Yes, they are . . . (*pause*) . . . I guess that's not what I really wanted to come in and talk about. The problem I have, or one of the things I would like to talk about, is the—I'm having a greal deal of difficulty adjusting to and working with the fellow who is my boss in the parish whom I affectionately call my "superboss" or my "father-image." I find some difficulty in working with him because he is such a controlling individual. My freedom feels—I feel cramped in with him to the point that I really have to just scream about it sometimes. Sometimes I would like to be free of, you know, "Why don't you do this?" or "Why don't you do that, Scott?"

  Co: Yes, he has you strapped in.

After the first response Scott immediately gave up his role-playing and started to talk directly about himself. We notice, however, that he begins with the statement—"Yes, they are," indicating the "fit" of the "disappointing" response. We have already seen, from an excerpt of his comments after the interview given in the preceding chapter, how striking it was for him to feel so completely understood in his disappointment. It was so striking, in fact, that he moved on to talk about what disappointed him in his real situation rather than in the symbolic role.

The counselor's responses here are brief: "disappointing," "strapped in." He is catching, in a sharp analogy, the basic feeling and emotional charge of the client's communication. This might be considered a language of cognition translation of the client's affective communication.

2 *Scott:* Yes, it's a very strapping kind of thing where you would just like to break off. I guess that's where baseball actually does come in because it's a chance to break away because he can't play ball. At least he doesn't seem like he can and that's a time, a free time, that I am unencumbered by him, because he has no interest here. Anywhere he is interested in I feel constricted—I mean, it's that generalized kind of thing.

Co: Yes, oddly enough this reference to baseball seems to help. It has a symbolization of freedom. It's the one thing among others, but at least it's one where you can break this tight. . . .

3 *Scott* (*breaks in*): Right, that's very true. That's a relationship I hadn't really thought about when we sat down and it's odd that the two came together at that point—but it's very interesting. I can work well with him depending upon how many freeing experiences I have. You know, if I have a number of experiences where I am on my own, where I am free, when I can operate on my own way without having to be responsible to him, then I can take a whole lot more of his constrictions.

Co: This is one way that you've learned to handle it, isn't it? If you get free with baseball or otherwise, but at least some freeing experience, then the constrictions are not quite so suffocating, if I can use that word.

INITIAL INSIGHT

The "fit" of the phrase "strapped in" is accepted and repeated. Then an insight emerges in the need of the kind of freedom which baseball symbolizes and Scott's realization that he can operate better whenever there are any occasions or elements of freedom.

The client himself is surprised to see that his passing role-playing remark about baseball carried a hidden significance when he had a chance to reflect upon it. This leads to a clearer awareness of one means of better operational relationship; namely, whenever he can take responsibility and have some freedom to make his own determinations, he can accept much more pastoral constriction.

The counselor responds directly to this insight, pulling it together. The counselor ends with the precise choice of the word "suffocating." This word is particularly helpful and Scott holds onto it. Later, in his comments, he refers to this as one of the important clarifying words the counselor used.

Scott: Right.

Co: But if you don't get some free air you're pretty suffocated in a short time by him.

4 *Scott:* Right, if I didn't come down here to school, I probably couldn't last two weeks up there because it's just the business of getting away, being free, being non-suffocating. I think "suffocating" is a good word for that because it is so stifling, you feel you can't breathe again, in terms of personal freedom—which leads into my own sense of worth. Because if I have to be told what to do and can't be creative on my own, even in a parish setting, I tend to think less of myself as being an errand boy or a flunky as opposed to being some kind of creative functioning individual.

Co: In our previous term, it is "anti-redeeming."

Scott: Yes.

Co: Just the opposite of redeeming. It is "de-deeming" or "demeaning," so to speak, as an experience. So baseball—but now on a more serious level—coming to school here are both outs and they are free air.

Scott: Right. Precisely! Which makes existence tolerable at least in the parish setting.

Co: Like a swimmer you can put your head up and breathe and stick your head back.

Scott: Right. Right. Right! And I do have to go back.

[to be continued]

SATISFYING AND FREEING

The reflective insight about freedom and the necessity of it is reinforced. These responses are deeply satisfying to the client as he responds with "Right. Precisely!" Having accepted the notion of his need for air like the swimmer, he turns again to look at the fact that he does, however, have to return. We will see that the rest of his statement here concerns this question of returning.

One of the most effective aspects of a clear response to feeling or a response to an insightful relationship is that it moves the client forward, so that he is free to continue to think through other phases of his situation. Less adequate responses tend to tie him up and leave him focused on only one area.

Responses that would not fit would be, for example, an effort to defend the pastor in this case, or a response that would not catch exactly Scott's disappointment and suffocated feeling but would only reach his more general discontent. These, and similar "misses," would tend to make the client have to speak in much greater detail about his feelings and his situation. Part of the efficiency of this ten-minute interview is due to the exact way the responses understand the client, and so free him to go on precisely because he feels so completely understood.

ALTERNATIVES TO ESCAPE

As a result of the counselor's clear responses thus far, Scott is now free to look at possible alternatives, namely, what else he might do.

Scott: Right, right, right! and I do have to go back. I try to figure out ways to get out completely but there are problems there because what would I do for money then if I don't work? But this is not the real problem. My concern is in relating to him. It's a great deal of frustration for me but there have been three guys before me who have apparently experienced the same kind of thing. I wish I could be "redeeming" to him. That's part of my guilt. Part of it is my own frustration, my own personal thing, but it is also a feeling of guilt that I can't be more freeing to him and give him an opportunity of being open and not so constricted so that he has to control everything, be at every committee meeting. You know, you can't buy a candle without his okay or something like that.

Co: Yes, there is your feeling, "Well, why not get out of it?" But you need some money and you need a job and the practical things we all face. But there is a more subtle thing and it is your own self-regard. I suppose as a phrase, in which you are saying to yourself, "Well, here I ought to be able to do something for this man. Other guys have probably failed him" and, "Do I just go down the same trail or do I come up with something that helps him out of his bind? He binds me but he is also bound himself."

Scott: Right. Precisely.

Co: You would like to do something to untie him.

Scott: Right—and in certain outward things I have.

PERSONAL VALUE

In going further into why Scott has to continue in this position, he looks first at practical things, the need for money and a job. Beyond this, however, there emerges a stronger personal value;

namely, his desire to do something significant for the other man. Here we see how insights lead directly into statements of personal values. This desire to help the other man both motivates him to stay in his present position as associate pastor and, at the same time, makes him conscious of his failing to do what he feels he ought to be able to do and, in a way, wants to do.

The counselor, realizing that together they have arrived at a basic value, states it clearly: "You would like to do something to untie him." We notice Scott's complete acceptance of this value and a further movement in his reflection; namely, exploring ways in which he has already been able to help the other man.

Middle

1   *Scott:* Right. And in certain outward things I have. He has, in a sense, become an imitator of a number of things that I do in terms of teaching techniques and being able to free up with people and being able to work with committees and everything. But that seems so superficial when it really comes down to the essentials. I guess it's true that my own self-worth is tied into being restricted by him and therefore I'm not able to do the things that I think are worthwhile. But it's also tied up with "Why can I not be redeeming for him and make him a freer person?" I hadn't thought of that. That's very good because I think that really pinpoints part of the bind.

   Co: Part of the bind is that you would like to help him.

The value insight is stated again by the counselor, and upon reflection the client himself recognizes that this "pinpoints part of the bind." This clarification allows him to explore further ways of relating.

2   *Scott:* Right, but I don't think confrontation is the answer. To say, "Well, now look here, you're controlling." I tried that once when I was really angry and that was helpful for maybe two days, but that's not a meaningful kind of exchange except that he knows that I resent a certain amount of control. But that's not really helping him.

   Co: That just defends you and gives you a little space.

   Scott: Right, right.

   Co: Let's see if I can pull this together. It's clear that it is not just a question of a job; that's there, but that's minor now as you look at it. The second more basic thing is you need freedom and you can function better if you have some freedom, so coming to school here is sensible as you see it because you function better with him then. Beyond this there is the realization that in some ways he has imitated you, so there is some break there. There is some contact, there is some give. You've tried confrontation and, except for just giving you a little space. . . .

Scott (*breaks in*): Yes, breathing space. . . .

Co: You don't see that as effective. It simply tightens him all the more or at least cautions him or warns him about limits to you. What you are asking now is "What could I do to further what I have done that gives evidence of change in him? How could I reach him in some way, reach one another, so to speak?"

Scott: Right, and this is the bind. . . .

SUMMARY RESPONSE

Here the summarizing response is demonstrated. In the summarizing response, the counselor attempts to pull together the awarenesses of the client up to this point. One might use the analogy here of a jigsaw puzzle: some pieces make an ear, some others make a nose, others make an eye or a chin. The counselor, in pulling them together, helps the client see that they perhaps make a face or even that they may make Lincoln's face. The counselor does not go beyond what the client has said but simply relates, in one statement, what was the client's own awareness up to this point.

Scott accepts this as "fitting" also. Immediately a strong feeling-tone emerges:

Scott: Right, and this is the bind. I guess the one that I feel the most keenly.

Co: You'd like to reach him.

Scott: Yes. And the question how that is possible is another one. The imitation is certainly a good beginning.

Co: This is positive and hopeful, isn't it? It's not much, but it clearly indicates a "give."

Scott: Right, which could mean that my freedom and openness might also become something that might be attractive to him as opposed to his uncomfortableness in having to control everything. I imagine that is quite a constricting thing for him and gives him headaches.

Co: If you could enter him and see him from out of his shell, he is probably somewhat uncomfortable seeing a guy more free and more relaxed who does get breathing space by going to school and so on. What you are saying is that conceivably if you could see this more clearly, he does have needs to imitate you.

Scott: Yes, that's a possibility I had not thought about.

BROADER AWARENESS

A broader series of insights and further possibilities are emerging as the client grows more empathetic to the other man's position in relation to himself.

Scott: Yes, that's a possibility I had not thought about. But in a small measure it is already being done, so why couldn't it be, if I were willing to take the risk with him? But that raises the question of my own resentment against him. I'm not sure I'd be able to do that.

Co: You have enough piled up hostility that you're not sure how open you could be. What you see is that if you could be open and let him learn from you, take somewhat the role of letting him imitate you, maybe it would work more.

Scott: Uh-huh.

Co: But you've got a real bind of resentment toward him too.

Scott: Right.

Co: We have a minute or so in our time.

The counselor catches both the positive desire for openness toward the other man and, at the same time, Scott's clear resentment.

ANNOUNCING TIME

The counselor's indication of the time left is usually a good procedure, similar to announcing the time at the beginning of the interview. It prepares both counselor and client and so makes the ending less abrupt. It also may act as an agent for some final clarifying push by the client. The possibility of this has often been discussed in counseling theory. There is certainly some evidence for this at least in some interviews or with certain kinds of clients.

End

1 *Scott:* Yes, and I guess that's the question. So ultimately it becomes a question of my own ability to resolve my hostility and resentment. That's the question, as to whether or not I can be of some benefit to him.

Co: It comes back to Scott.

2 *Scott:* Yes . . . (*pause*) . . . and that's very disconcerting, because as long as I can push it off and say, "Yes, he's an old fuddy duddy, he's been in the ministry thirty years and he hasn't learned more than two years' worth of the ministry"—that kind of thing—that's easy. Then I can push it off and say that it is his fault. But now it has come back to me again—and that's tough!

Co: It's difficult to accept yourself as a possibly redeeming person for him, isn't it?

3 *Scott:* Yes, yes, very much so. Yet certainly the possibility has been opened up—the possibility of a personal redeemingness.

Co (summarizing response): You have to do something about yourself to take on this. As you see it, it's a far bigger role, with regard to him, than just being angry at him and projecting hostility towards him.

Scott: Right.

Co: Far more difficult to do this other, if you take this option.

4 *Scott:* Right, right. And the question is still what option do I take. But that's got some possibilities that I hadn't realized. Very interesting.

Co: Well, let's call it off.

MATURE PERSONAL RESPONSIBILITY

What began as a confused feeling about someone else ends as a basic issue with regard to Scott himself. He now has clearly before him the option of fulfilling his value role of trying to be a genuinely helpful person to the other man and truly trying to understand him, or of continuing to function on resentment and hostility. He sees that he has this resentment and that it stands against his ability to accept the pastor.

In the Introduction we pointed out that one of the main aims of this book was to aid the internalization of religious values using skills and relationships patterned from counseling and psychotherapy. We see here a demonstration of how, in ten minutes, this process could begin to come about. In the beginning, Scott is projecting blame on the situation and the other person. A second phase of this was the possibility of leaving the position or of ways of manipulating the other person to a better relationship.

In the third phase, however, we notice the internalization and realization of direct responsibility on Scott himself to carry out his own values in his relationships. This involves having a genuine, positive regard or "redeeming" relationship with the other person. It is a movement from a less mature to a more mature sense of religious values. It is also a movement away from a parent-figure, as the client expressed it in the beginning image. By not merely claiming the freedom of an adult but actually recognizing the inner responsibilities which such a state puts on the person himself, the client moves to an adult relationship.

At the end of the ten minutes the client is more consciously aware of his own religious values, and how they can operate in this situation, than he was at the beginning. He is also clearly facing his inner resentment and the way it is acting as a barrier to a good relationship.

It is interesting to note, too, that this change in the internalization of religious values is also a change from a negative emotion, resistance and a defensive state of conflict, to a more positive and insightful awareness, with more precise choices now available. This we will see in a later diagram.

POST-INTERVIEW REACTION

In this type of counseling demonstration, we usually ask three questions immediately after the interview. The intention is to get something of the reactions a person might have just after he has left the counselor's office. The first is a general question like "Could you give us your reactions?" The second focuses on the reactions to the counselor's manner and responses. The third is again more general, such as "Any further comments?"

Let us look now at Scott's comments made immediately after the ten-minute interview:

Scott: Well, I didn't follow through with the role-playing the way I thought that I was going to do. The thing that was surprising and almost shook me off the seat was this: "It's disappointing"—right at the beginning. That initially indicated that it was my disappointment that was the important thing in my comment and not the fact that the Senators lost. . . .

(*Pause*) . . . Yes, that was terrific. Because that's the answer to my original question of how to counsel a person who seems just intent on chatting or "shooting the breeze." It was a total concern not for the objective topic but for my individual feelings about the objective fact. Then when you had done that and when you told me we only had ten minutes, then I had to make the choice right there. . . .

(*Pause*) . . . It forced me into a choice that I was willing to make because of the one statement that was made first reflecting my own feelings.

Co: Anything about the counselor's responses that you noticed?

Scott: Well, the things that I'll remember—I'll remember "suffocation." That's a good word to describe the feeling. And I'll remember the freedom of being able to "breathe" in the different illustrations used. But "suffocation" is a good way to crystallize what I'm feeling, and that was good in the recognition of feelings. But I also like the alternatives I got in ten minutes.

Co: You're pleased.

Scott: Yes, because I don't think of myself as a redeeming individual over and against a senior pastor, father-image person. That's a little hard for me to imagine. Yet that's a real live alternative and I was pleased with that.

Co: The difficulty in a father-figure image is the difficulty of a new generation seeing themselves in a different perspective from the old.

Scott: Right. So the suffocating, breathing and the movement towards new alternatives, I think, were very helpful. I think that was possible because there was a point before you called the one-minute shot, where you re-did the whole package. . . .

Co: The Gestalt.

Scott: Yes, and it was that which I think enabled me to move from that to another alternative . . . (*pause*). . . . It was pretty terrific.

Co: Anything else you would like to comment on?

Scott: From a counseling point of view, I really don't want to talk about a counseling point of view—it meant a lot to me personally. . . . But I can say that's a good approach in terms of personal worth. . . . I'll just say that the way you do it is to be concerned about the individual's reaction to the objective facts rather than just to shoot the breeze about the objective facts, so to speak, that is a really meaningful kind of experience . . . (*pause*). . . . As soon as you are understood

as having a feeling, then it does not matter how you get on with it—
you can talk about baseball or anything.

OBSERVERS

Since this occurred in the presence of twelve other people in a
seminar, we will reproduce some of their comments:

Man #1: I was very surprised. It seemed as though when you became one with him this gave you the freedom to go beyond him.

Co: I resist the idea of "going beyond him." If I had gone beyond
him, he would have been negative. I tried to stay right with him but
not go beyond him.

Scott: I think I said the germinal form of everything each time. But
each time he was doing a bit of clarification. But I was encouraged
to make the most of my desire to come to a greater significance in the
redeeming feature. So in that sense that was the counselor's doing. I
remember it as starting out with a little seed on my part.

Co: In that sense we watered it together.

Man #2: Well, take in a parish. There are many times when you
are not deliberately in a counseling role. For example, one of my
parishioners and myself go out every Saturday and shoot a couple
rounds of golf. And in this casual conversation you sense there is
something on the line, how do you switch from this purely recreational
role to the counseling role?

Co: You do it just the way I did with Scott. You give the person
the option to be in a brief counseling relationship by responding to a
basic attitude.

Man #2: And you think you can do this without putting any strings
onto it?

Scott: Yes, because it was always my option to pull out of it. The
option was given to me. If he had kept just talking about the Sox then
I never would really have been able to overcome that bind. But he
gave me that option.

A WEEK LATER: HOPE

The question might be raised, how much remains of such short,
ten-minute counseling? A week later, to explore this further, Scott
was asked to give his reactions:

SCOTT INTERVIEW

	N_1	N_2	N_3	N_4	N_5	N_s	P_1	P_2	P_3	P_4	P_5	P_s	I_1	I_2	I_3	I_4	I_5	I_s	C_1	C_2	C_3	C_4	C_5	C_s
First Four Client Statements of 10 minute interview																								
1		16	42	116	50	224	3					3	7	8	3			18						
2		28	51	72	20	171	3	10	3			16	9	10	9			28			9			9
3	3	6	6			15	4	24	39	16		83	9	36	51	16	5	117						
4	7	12	36	56	15	126	3	10	21	8		42	10	22	18	40	20	110						
Totals:	10	62	135	244	85	536	13	44	63	24		144	35	76	81	56	25	273			9			9
Middle Two Client Statements																								
1	3					3	6	18	24	12		60	9	12	63	52	15	151						
2	18	24	21	16		79	7	8	12	4		31	9	22	42	28	5	106		6	8			14
Totals:	21	24	21	16		82	13	26	36	16		91	18	34	105	80	20	257		6	8			14
Last Four Client Statements																								
1	1	2	6	4		13	5	10	9	12		36	11	14	30	56	55	166		3	3	4		10
2	10	22	24	16		72	6	4	6	16		32	9	20	45	24	30	128	2	3	3	8	5	21
3							9	8	39	28	40	124	11	8	18	44	45	126						
4	2	4				6	6	10	12	32	20	80	11	10	18	44	50	133	2	6	9	4	10	31
Totals:	13	28	30	20		91	26	32	66	88	60	272	42	52	111	168	180	553	4	12	15	16	15	62

N = Negative Emotions   P = Positive Emotions   I = Insight   C = Choice

Scott: Actually it's made life a bit more difficult in the sense that I was okay as long as I could place blame and responsibility onto someone else—then I could exist without worry about my own responsibility. But as soon as I came to the realization that—in terms of your own theoretical structure that we had on the board—the only thing I can do about it is to do something about my own reaction, that's still a little disconcerting. It's disconcerting because I know that's what I have to deal with. And, if I am going to make any change, I can no longer be content to project the blame, or just to project anger or hostility out. I've got a responsibility myself which I am attempting to work toward.

Co: This sort of fits Carl Rogers' comment, "The only people we can change are ourselves," and maybe by changing ourselves this may affect someone else.

Scott: Right, and this makes it more difficult for me because I guess I was happier not acknowledging my own responsibilities, at least in that sense.

Co: So what you are saying is that the insights into this added a certain amount of discomfort, disequilibrium, because there is a much sharper realization that the pressure is on you. It was more comfortable in that other state.

Scott: But lacked hope. But this way, if it's something that I can do in myself, then, knowing myself, I have more hope that the situation is resolvable—by the very fact that it is my responsibility. So it is disconcerting on the one hand but much more hopeful on the other.

Co: So it's an ambiguity. It's uncomfortable but hopeful.

Scott: So that's about where I am as far as the week later . . . (*pause*). . . . The thing that comes to mind is that it is going to be hard but the challenge is exciting enough to try it.

INTERVIEW CONTENT ANALYSIS

The Scott Interview rating chart is a composite of the ratings made by sixty persons who scored this ten-minute interview.[1] (The ratings were made on a scale from 0 to 5, 5 being considered extremely high.) The judging persons could give one or a number of scores to each client statement. Only the beginning, middle and end statements were scored. The role-playing statement was not scored. The first four scored statements are given on pages 58–60. The two middle statements on page 62. The last four on page 65.

The following is a graph of the combined totals. While insight remained the same in the middle two statements, negative emotion

Scott Interview

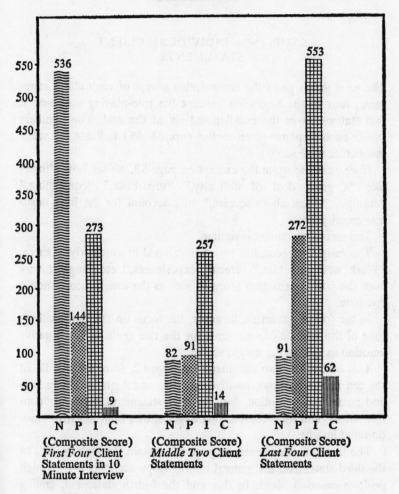

	N = Negative Emotion
	P = Positive Emotion
	I = Insight
	C = Choice

First Four Client Statements in 10 Minute Interview — (Composite Score)
Middle Two Client Statements — (Composite Score)
Last Four Client Statements — (Composite Score)

content had noticeably decreased. In the last six statements, while negative emotion stays near the middle score and below the beginning, insight and choice scores are notably higher.

SAMPLING: INDIVIDUAL CLIENT
STATEMENTS

The next graph gives the comparative scores of each client statement, four in the beginning (except the role-playing statement); two statements in the middle; and six at the end. The numbers beside each response given earlier (pp. 58–65) indicate the statements that were scored.

If we examine again the excerpt on page 58, we see how phrases like "a great deal of difficulty," "superboss," "controlling," "cramped," "just about scream," etc., account for the high negative emotion score.

The second statement is similar.

The insight suggested in two is developed more clearly in three. "Work well with him," "freeing experiences," etc., suggest why both the positive emotion score as well as the insight score should rise here.

In the fourth statement, however, the focus on the "suffocating" tone of the relationship accounts for the rise again of the negative emotion as well as the insight scores.

This first of the two statements on page 62, from the middle of the ten minutes, shows positive emotion and high insight ratings and no negative emotion. But the next statement involving "confrontation" and its accompanying anger shows both negative emotion and insight.

The last four statements, on page 65, sustain the high insight. In the third statement, the general tone of hope accounts for the high positive emotion score. In this and the fourth statement, ending the interview, the positive emotion score is associated with a rise in choice rating.

and six — one forward. Other commendations to the ten educated hearten over which I take no place, one since, I was approaching the one of the close, the counseling of the one that one should last only five minute.

Scott Interview

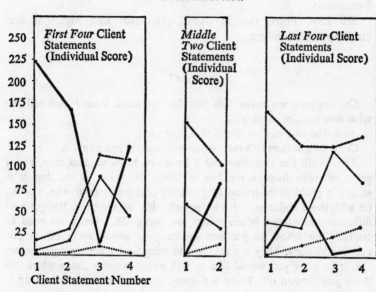

First Four Client Statements (Individual Score)

Middle Two Client Statements (Individual Score)

Last Four Client Statements (Individual Score)

Client Statement Number

— Negative Emotion
— Positive Emotion
---- Insight
...... Choice

ILLUSTRATION: FIVE-MINUTE INTERVIEW

Our second consideration will be a five-minute recorded interview also reproduced verbatim as it occurred. In the light of the assumption that a private and special place is always necessary for counseling, it is interesting that this took place in an ordinary classroom in the presence of sixty other people.

This occurred in the following manner: client volunteers were requested to take part in a demonstration of counseling skill, and among others this graduate student—a mother of two boys, nine and six—came forward. Other demonstrations, lasting ten minutes, had previously taken place. But since it was approaching the end of the class, the counselor suggested that this one should last only five minutes.

We have noted certain "key" responses that highlight and clarify personal values:

"Ann"

Co: Suppose we make this just five minutes. Would you tell me what role you are playing?

Ann: The role of a mother—that is, myself.

Co: All right then let's talk about yourself for five minutes.

Ann: Well, I'm a mother and I have two boys, six and nine, and I get upset with them a number of times. It seems to me that it is mostly a problem of trying to go along and understand what's going on with these children and with myself most of the time. We get into difficulty sometimes. When things are going OK, there's no need to quarrel, but when we get into difficulty, it seems we're off in our communications. They are saying one thing and I am saying another.

Co: So what you would like to talk about is those times when this thing gets thrown off. There are many times when this relationship is good. But what you see is that when you get sort of hung up in one of these difficulties, it has something to do with a breakdown in communication.

Ann: Yes, a breakdown in feelings. Perhaps they are going through something that I don't understand. I'm not understanding what they are feeling at the time and they might respond in a way that throws me way off base. And then I'm not understanding myself either. There are times when I just kind of have to pull out of the situation and try to understand what has gone on. I try to understand something of why they have been lashing out at me and to come back into the situation with a little more perspective as to what has been going on.

(VALUE):

Co: If I get it, you would really like to be able to stay in and not pull out and still be observant of what is going on and share their feelings. But what you do, often doesn't show any kind of understanding of their feelings. Yet your own reaction is that this is what you would like to be able to do better: understand their feelings. So that what you do in return would be more congruent with them, so to speak. But your present reaction is that in some way you are missing this.

Ann: Yes, and this feeling of being a parent to a child, to me it is like being in two different worlds. To me this understanding is the important thing as far as children are concerned, and I suppose my interest in psychology has made me very conscious of this. I want to be a person to them as well as a parent. But it's more when we are opening up a feeling, when things are opening up for us sort of accidentally, that I, as a parent and as a person, and these boys seem to run into difficulties. I would like to have more of those times when we are persons together.

(VALUE CLARIFIED):

Co: It is sort of sharp for you that you are aware of their communication to you as a parent, but you feel it should be to you as a person. There is some sort of distinction, as I get it, when your feelings are involved. When these three can come together, parent, person and the children on the level of personal feelings and a sense of unity or simply feeling together, emerges—this is the best relationship. Your interest in psychology may make you more reflective on it, but in your experience this is the best type of relationship. As I get it, you would like to have more of this. You don't seem to get enough and you would like to get sharper clues as to how to do more of this with them.

Ann: Yes, I would like to be able to be with them in a constant communication as persons and stop putting them in this category of children who are going through some kind of stage that I don't understand, because when it comes right down to it, I do understand and see what it is. Of course, I know what they are going through. It's getting out of this category of "problems with adults." It kind of makes me happier to know that the older they get, the more I seem to be able to understand them, and I keep thinking I'll be a great teenage mother or something. But getting them out of this category which, in the past, has been for me a frightening and threatening category. It has only become a more comfortable one, in this role of parent, as I have been able to see them less as things called "children" and more as persons.

(VALUE INSIGHT):

Co: So what you are saying is that, adult to adult, you are more comfortable. The more they get toward adulthood, the more hopeful you can be that you are also going to get some kind of real personal feelings toward them as they are and not necessarily be caught in this bind that somehow, as children, they are going to be removed from your understanding. But you would like to relate to them as children, not just wait around until they are adults or even teenagers, even though that is hopeful. But you would like to get at it directly now.

Ann: That's not enough—waiting around. . . . I don't think I realized what has happened . . . but that's exactly it and I feel better to know that's what it is.

Co: Yes, that summation did do something for you. Well our time is up . . . (*pause*).

The following are the three questions and the person's reactions immediately after the interview:

Co: Could I ask you to give your reactions?

Ann: It's been a very productive five minutes. And I'm glad I took something personal because I really got something out of it. I feel it was insightful.

Co: Any comments on the counselor's response?

Ann: I think the one thing that I felt constantly was that you were aware and understanding about everything I was telling you. You weren't just taking some piece of information, you were really going from point to point.

Co: Anything else?

Ann: Well, at the beginning I was aware of everyone else in the class, but as we got further along and you were focused so intensely on what I was saying, I forgot about everyone else and it seemed as if just the two of us were here.

ANALYSIS OF SKILL

In the light of this person's comments on how "productive" five minutes was for her, her feeling of its being "insightful," as well as her sense of being "understood" and the counselor's being "focused so intensely" on what she was saying, let us look at how this was accomplished.

AUTHENTIC CONCERN

We must stress again that the counselor's tone, manner and regard towards the other person must be one of deep warmth, openness and genuineness. This cannot be shown simply by the words. But here, for example, if the counselor had let himself be too much concerned about whether or not he would succeed or fail before the sixty graduate students, or if, in any way, he had been trying to manipulate or direct the interview, then it is unlikely that this person would have felt the security, closeness and concentration that she, in fact, quickly felt. Consequently, purely verbal proficiency in counseling responses will not be effective if a relationship seems wooden, cold and distant. There must be the sincerity and authenticity of one human being deeply concerned about another at the level of an important life issue.

AFFECT-COGNITION

But it is also essential that the counselor recognize the feeling-world of the person as he or she tries to communicate this. It is, as we have said, basic to our theory that values show themselves in emotional statements of conflict and confusion. The ability to both recognize and respond to feelings, therefore, is an important factor in initiating the counseling process.

This would be a different focus from that of an information-centered relationship, say, of personal guidance. Here our concern is to allow the person to begin to explore a world which is somatic, instinctive and emotional. He gets relief by trying to put his conflicts and confusions into words, and he gains security when he feels understood at this deeper and more personal level.

The counselor in turn hears, as we have said, a language of affect from the person. He hears the person's confused efforts to describe his inner world of disturbance and conflict that he is experiencing. As a part of his counseling skill, his ear is sensitively attuned to catch, in the words that are used, the feelings conveyed.

RE-COGNIZED VALUES

What are contained here, hidden behind the emotional confusion and the conflict situation, are somewhat obscure and unrecognized personal values. A person seems greatly helped when he sees these values become explicit and clarified in the counselor's response.

This is what the person meant when she described the five minutes as "insightful." She is suggesting this, too, in the way the discussion did not simply stay on the periphery of information— "You weren't just taking some piece of information." It moved in a cognitive way, relating one point to the other, in a manner that was finally clarifying and helpful.

We do not mean that such a five-minute interview would solve serious parent-child conflicts. We simply mean that if one has five minutes to use in this way, and it is used skillfully, it is not a waste of time but can be significantly helpful.

A week later in her comments to the class, about the value of the five-minute experience, Ann said:

Observing the children fighting yesterday, I had to laugh at how much more relaxed I was . . . I could see they were pretty good children after all . . . and I was a pretty good mother.

ACCURATE REFLECTION

Let us now look at the first counselor responses. We notice that the counselor does not exaggerate the negative situation Ann presented. He said, "There are many times when this relationship is good." It is just sometimes that she gets "hung up" with the boys because of, as she sees it, "a breakdown in communication."

Later, in a discussion with the class, Ann made the point that it was this distinction which relieved her and made her want, as she said, to really plunge deeply into the issue of herself and the children. Because the counselor neither exaggerated her difficulties with the children nor minimized them, she felt that he truly understood her in just the way the situation was, in her inner feelings about it. It is evident, however, how easy it would have been to overlook the positive aspect and heighten out of proportion the conflict she was feeling with the children. This, as she said afterwards, would have thrown her off completely and made it difficult for her to continue.

In reverse, we can also see that if the mother had really felt within herself that the children constituted a grave difficulty for her and the counselor failed to respond to her deep negative feeling here, she would also have felt rejected and misunderstood. Simply trying to soften feelings could be just as distorting, just as much a misunderstanding of the person, as the opposite error of exaggerating them.

Moreover, even if the counselor, from other knowledge, might know the children to be quite normal in their behavior, this would still produce a misunderstanding if he tried to force this awareness at this moment. The counselor is genuinely trying to understand the feelings of the mother, at the moment of expression, even granting that such feelings might be exaggerated. Later Ann seemed better able to see that they were exaggerated.

The point of counseling as distinct from other kinds of relationships, which can often also be necessary, is to help the person understand and explore his world of feelings even when they are distorted. Only when the distortions have been expressed, explored and understood can they be made cognitive, and so be reduced to their more normal reality dimension. The counselor, as we see here, neither exaggerated nor minimized the mother's concern but tried to understand it with something of the exact tones that she had communicated. It was this first response (as in the "disappointing" response of Scott) that, as she said, made her take the option to give herself deeply for the five minutes.

SHORT-TERM CONFLICT

This seems to add up to the concept that counseling, in addition to its use for troubled and upset persons, can be an effective aid in ordinary short-term conflict situations. The fundamental need to be understood and to be aided in the search to fulfill personal values and goals is shared by everyone. The counseling relationship seemed here to bring a special sense of meaning, security and clarification that these two persons, Scott and Ann, had not known before. It brought a kind of sharing and fulfillment that, despite the obvious limitations of time, made the experience significant and worthwhile. It is this that we mean when we speak of counseling as a normal process and of the "brief encounter" as an end in itself. To be deeply understood is to be helped.

Moreover, while neither of these people thought of this counseling as religious or moral as such, each was concerned in some way with obligations and with behavior according to a value ideal. In this way counseling, as a normal process, can be especially helpful in the daily discharge of responsibilities that a religious life-commitment especially demands. Such basic religious values, like other values, are often hidden behind even minor emotional conflict. They emerge, as we saw here, when, in a secure relationship of skilled understanding and clarification, people are given a chance to reflect on themselves and redefine their value commitments.

NOTES

[1] The method of scoring was first developed and explained in: Charles A. Curran, *Personality Factors in Counseling* (New York: Grune and Stratton, Inc., 1945), pp. 61–88.

3

Confessional and Personal Counseling

BY THE TERM "confessional counseling" we would mean, first of all, what is implied in sacramental confession, particularly as it is practiced in Roman Catholicism. It is evident, however, that what is stated here would also be applicable to any kind of confession of personal sin and guilt. So, while our discussion is directly related to sacramental confessional practice as it has been traditionally carried out by Catholics, we mean it to have these general implications as well.

NO EXTREME CHANGE

The idea sometimes expressed that we now have a special knowledge of personality which should radically change the confessional and confessional practice is at present without adequate support from research findings in counseling and psychotherapy. In psychological literature it has been stressed that we need much more counseling and psychotherapeutic research and new methods for such research. The report of the Conference on Research in Psychotherapy, sponsored by the Division of Clinical Psychology of the American Psychological Association, comments:

. . . Much research has been done . . . but there has been relatively little progress in establishing a firm and substantial body of evidence to support very many research hypotheses.[1]

So the suggestion that somehow methods from counseling and psychotherapy should entirely supplant the traditional methods in the administration of sacramental confession seems unwarranted. Some changes will and should be made. But anything that has been

81

in existence for a long time usually has had valid reasons for exist-ing and perhaps for continuing to exist. Often we do not entirely know all these reasons, and sometimes only when something has been removed is there a clear understanding of the special need it supplied. If we did away with the traditional practice of confession, we might slowly discover that we missed the notable things which this confessional practice had been supplying for a very long time.

This having been said—namely, that we do not intend any radical suggestions here—we can yet recognize some genuine contributions which modern counseling therapy might offer. These would still be considered, however, within the framework of present confessional procedures and practice.

CONFESSIONAL PROCESS

Traditionally we speak of five steps to confession: (1) examina-tion of conscience, (2) sorrow for sin, (3) purpose of amendment, (4) the telling of sins, (5) the acceptance of the penance. From the point of view of psychological awareness, then, we can think of a number of distinct psychological processes in this five-step delineation. The first would be the confession itself. This results psychologically from a sense of guilt. It includes the discrimination of particular aspects of guilt, the questioning of the self around this and the symbolic verbalization, release and communication of this guilt in a precise way as a result of such self-examination.

DISCRIMINATED GUILT

A person comes to confession because he feels guilty, but usually this guilt is somewhat undefined. The examination of conscience is intended to define the sin aspect of this feeling of guilt: "I feel guilty. How can I reduce this to particular sins? How will I say it?" Guilt then is released in a discriminated way as a result of such self-questioning by adequate verbalization and communica-tion with the confessor.

A list of sins would be the means, or "mechanism," of doing this. This is not simply a list like a grocery list, or even a list of medical complaints; it is a psychological process whose purpose is some kind of discriminated awareness of guilt and some communication of this awareness. In other words, I do not merely say I am guilty of sin. I say that in the "Our Father" and other prayers. What is added to this is the minute discrimination of "how" or "why" I am guilty in a communication with another person. Psychologically it is the discrimination and communication of guilt in terms of sin and the reasons for sins, rather than a vague and general *sense* of guilt, that constitutes the process of confession of sins.

UNDERSTANDING GUILTY PERSON

The second aspect would be the absolution of the confessor. But prior to this is his human understanding of what is confessed. This we usually use to justify, for example, the priest's asking certain basic questions which, in his judgment, are necessary to evaluate the meaning and significance of the sins and the state of guilt symbolized by the penitent.

But this understanding of the confessor can be interpreted in terms of a kind of Cartesian intellectualism and Kantian legalism. In this sense, to understand the details of "why," "when," "how many times," would become the only meaning of "understanding." Such a categorization of sin is not necessarily an adequate communication of guilt. On the contrary, it can leave the person uncommunicated in his guilt because the list itself is so depersonalized. Granting that there is a personal and even embarrassing element here, yet "I told four lies; I got angry six times" can, in certain ways, be as remote from the person as any other list. This is especially so after long practice and frequent repetition. Depending on how this communication is made, it can simply be an "I-it" relationship, as Buber calls it. The coldness and rigidity of the categorization seen simply in its Cartesian quality of a focus on "things" and "number of times" can tend to depersonalize the relationship between priest and penitent.

PERSONALIZED COMMUNICATION

We need, therefore, to personalize this communication and not assume that this category sin-list of discriminations is the end of the confessional communication of guilt. This can be achieved by an additional personal identification with one's guilt and sinfulness and a correspondingly personal response on the part of the confessor.

The confessor does not always need to ask questions, or, if he does, his manner need not be so depersonalized that he has constituted himself in an "I-it" relationship with the penitent. The relationship can become personal. That is, for the penitent, guilt is a personal anxiety and concern. Its singular circumstances mark it with his own uniquely personal identity. In this sense, his sins are not simply a list to be gone through as a fetishistic ritual. This will not psychologically discharge his guilt but tend to suppress it, and so it may only appear again in more complicated disguised and self-defeating forms.

The purpose here is obviously not this, but rather to make guilt constructive and positive as a force for personal change. But perhaps this is the psychological reason why the confession of a list of sins may sometimes leave the penitent still feeling psychologically guilty. Granting that he truly believes in the forgiveness of sins, psychologically he may still feel "unredeemed" because he has not communicated himself clearly as far as his guilt is concerned.

In the Old Testament, Solomon, we are told, prayed to God for an "understanding heart," and this was the essential quality of his remarkable wisdom and effectiveness with people. If we reinterpret the "understanding" of the confessor in the sense of Solomon's prayer, then we reinterpret the human agency of the confessor. In a counseling way, then, the confessor is understanding the guilty *person*, not simply understanding details of the sin or the number of times.

To understand the guilty person means to come to some sense of belonging together, "to become like man" in the sense that God first loved us and became like us in all things save sin. In that two human beings are becoming "like" one another in shared humanity, the one who stands for God would most completely represent an incarnate and human Christ in this process. This redeeming sense of human sharing, not the intellectual remoteness of a questioning judge who seems far removed in his "I-it" relationship, would constitute the deep psychological sense of "understanding" that we put into the phrase "He was a very *understanding* person."

This will not be achieved by a simple list of sins and details which, taken alone, tend to depersonalize the relationship and inhibit real understanding. If you ask me questions and I answer them, we are getting farther and farther away from one another. We are not genuinely relating by such cold interrogation.

SKILLED RESPONSE

A simple skilled counseling response could help this and yet would not have to take a long time. We do not need a lengthy exchange. Even if we limit the time of the confessional relationship to five minutes at the most, an exchange that could be deeply personal might still be effected. Since the confessor's response would predictably center on guilt, a number of somewhat routine counseling responses might be anticipated. By routine we do not mean that they become artificial. They must be filled with genuine warmth and spontaneity. Nevertheless we might foresee some of the kinds of responses which might be made to help the person's guilt feelings to emerge in his communication.

ILLUSTRATION

What the priest would be seeking is a "living" communication of guilt rather than a "dead" list of sins. And so a response might break down the list by selecting a particular category for consideration. For example, "You mentioned being quite angry with your wife. Would you care to talk a little bit about that?" This is simply an exploratory type of response, but it is exploratory in a living sense. In other words, it breaks into the set list with which the person came and loosens the communication in order to make it more spontaneous. The person is more likely to begin to speak in an unprepared, spontaneous way. He may, for example, even blurt out something about his relationship with his wife. It is possible that he will be at least slightly surprised by this break in the depersonalized structure of the list of sins. He may even become momentarily "threatened." It was safer to have a cemented list, and he feels threatened by having to make it a living communication. His comment might be "Well, I don't know what to say."

(This is quite understandable since he came with a list.) "I just . . . get angry with her. . . . I don't know whether it is her problem or mine. I guess it is mostly about the kids, although it is not just that. I don't know what to say."

This is the beginning of counseling. It expresses confusion and conflict. It no longer has the clarity and discrimination of a distinct list of sins. The human condition from moment to moment is far more confusing and disordered than that.

Therefore the second, somewhat predictable, response would be in that direction. Having made the exploratory one, one could expect some type of confused response in return. Or, if the atmosphere now seems slightly threatening to the person, a partly defensive question might follow: "What do you mean, talk more about it?" He may have been made momentarily defensive by this personalization when he is used to a depersonalized relationship.

COUNSELING RELATIONSHIP

Feeling defensive, threatened and confused are obviously counseling situations. The movement from depersonalization to personalization establishes this counseling relationship.

A person might say, "Well, I don't know what you want. I told you that I just get angry with her." The priest might respond: "It is hard for you to know how to describe this any further." This would be different from the confessor saying: "Well, you can surely give me some details, can't you?" In this case, the confessor himself is now defensive. This is not counseling but two people in open conflict. In the first situation the priest understands and is prepared for the penitent's defense and sense of threat and so is able to respond to it. This would make it counseling.

The penitent, now less threatened because his defense is understood, may then say:

Well, I don't know what to say. I guess the big thing is about the car. We seem to be quarreling about the car quite a bit lately. She has to have the car for the kids at school and I . . . I just think she makes herself a servant. She is chasing around after them everywhere and

they have bicycles. They can walk since they need exercise. But no
. . . if one of the kids says that he has to go to visit a friend down
the street, out comes the car. I think she uses that automobile everywhere and makes herself a slave.

This is now clearly a counseling situation concerning a husband-
wife tension over the issue of the children.

MARRIAGE CONFLICT

This moved quickly from a category of "angry six times" to a
common marriage conflict. The response would now be a broad
one, catching his feeling and its stated causes:

Co: One of the big sources of tension between you and your wife is
the children and the use of the car. You feel she should not be a
servant to them and you resent it.

The counselor-confessor hit the emotion clearly with, "You resent
it."

Well, yes, I do resent it. In fact, I just feel she sells herself out to
the children.

We notice that this is broader and deeper. It has left the car now.
This is the way counseling goes. What started as a list of sins is
now a clear and deep cleavage between husband and wife. This
happened in two responses.

The priest-counselor responds:

Co: You resent her losing herself in the children.
Husband: Yes. I just resent the whole situation. When we were
first married I felt deeply related to her. I mean I am glad we have
the children that we have, but . . . I just think we have lost part of
our marriage over the children. I guess I have not said this to her
exactly this way, but I've been thinking about it. But I suppose that's
why I resent it so much when I see her chasing after the kids. We
never have any time together. I need her too and I've told her that
a few times, but I don't think she pays any attention to it. I suppose

many men feel this way if you could judge from articles—I read an article in the *Reader's Digest* the other day, and that is exactly the way I feel—I am just being used at home.

We are in a counseling relationship in three responses of this reconstructed and simulated communication.

REACHING SOURCES OF GUILT

This is what we mean by moving from a list of sins to a broad communication of feelings and "why." Guilt may be a disguise of personal confusion and conflict not clearly understood or resolved. Here is a man in the confused state of needing to talk about a painful psychological tension he is under, and perhaps not knowing where else to go, he comes and confesses sins. He also wants to go to confession, of course—the two are interwoven. But it is obvious that just confessing "being angry six times" is not remotely going to reach this alienated feeling that his anger contains.

In the light of the idea that there should be a human understanding between the confessor representing Christ and the penitent, this is a deeper and more understanding relationship than merely giving more minute details about the precise circumstances of a particular sin even when this may be necessary. These details are often not nearly as significant as what could be arrived at in perhaps only three skilled counseling responses.

Now that the man's anger has been communicated at this understanding level, one might even question whether his anger was a sin or a kind of justifiable indignation. At this point the person might be given an option such as

I don't want to keep you too long. Would you care perhaps to discuss this further, say, at your next confession, or, if you wish, I could see you in the rectory? You might perhaps even want to have your wife come with you.

People often take such an option, and it can become a secure counseling relationship with one or both. At least the person now knows he can speak further of this, if he chooses, at his next confession. He always has a later option to come to the rectory himself or with his wife.

WHOLE PERSON

Human understanding of the state of guilt or sinfulness between confessor and penitent would not change the traditional idea of a list of sins and their details. The change would rather be that which, to some degree, has a parallel in medicine. In place of the physician's concern merely for "Where does it hurt you and at what time does it hurt you?" we have the psychosomatic notion that the *whole person* is hurting. It is now the doctor's effort to understand the whole person in pain. In a similar way, the confessor's effort to understand the *whole person* in sin and guilt would lead to a relationship quite different from that which is concerned with the categories and details of sins. It would rather engage confessor and penitent in a deeply understanding commitment of mutual trust; in a communion arising from the sense of belonging together and sharing the pains, conflicts and confusions of being human. The end product of the confession, the sins a person commits, would be simply the starting place for this kind of healing, forgiving dialogue.

SORROW AMBIGUITY

A second phase of confession we might now consider is usually called "sorrow for sin." While such sorrow can be obvious, it sometimes contains subtleties. There is often a kind of ambiguity here. The person rejects the wrongness of the action, on the one side, but he is still strongly pulled, or in some sense attached, to the person or the circumstances involved in the action. So, sorrow may be mixed with satisfaction and even a partial sense of fulfillment.

A person may say: "I'm not sure about sorrow. I guess I regret the sin, but I don't regret a lot of the things that went with it. In fact, the whole experience meant a great deal to me." Since such ambiguity reactions are common in counseling, we are therefore in a counseling relationship. The confessor-counselor might respond by holding up both sides of the ambiguity:

The wrongness of the sin, as I get it, you regret, but other aspects you see in a very positive light, they had real meaning for you.

Cl: Yes, they did. I never felt so respected before, and I had some wonderful experiences. I really do feel badly about the sin though, and I don't want that.

Here one can see a counseling process emerging. It can be discussed further in this or later confessions or, more directly, in a separate counseling relationship with the priest-counselor or another skilled counselor. The sin, however, and sorrow for it, are now already being distinguished from other complex personal fulfillments, real or hoped-for, which are also intertwined here. Most human situations are, in fact, similarly complicated. Sin and sorrow for sin are usually parts of a complicated motivational fabric of good and evil. Even brief counseling can often help people, in some measure, to distinguish the two more clearly and so define their sorrow.

FORGIVENESS

Related to sorrow is the sense of forgiveness or, more exactly for our purpose here, the psychological issue of *accepting* forgiveness. It is sometimes said that, of all phases of the penitent's state, the most important is "sorrow for sin." To determine this, one would have to look carefully at what is meant by "sorrow."

If by sorrow we mean simply self-condemnation, then we are up against the very serious issue of Judas and Peter—an issue which we will discuss repeatedly throughout this book. This basic question of forgiving oneself recurs because it is tied up with the possibility—also recurring—of how we can love to hate ourselves in place of loving to love ourselves. Both themes will reappear, in a variety of ways, in later discussions.

For our purpose here, however, there seems to be no question that Judas was overwhelmingly sorry for his sin, judged by the way he acted it out: he went to the high priest; he threw the money at his feet; he said, "I am guilty of the blood of a just man." This is heroic sorrow, as far as human sorrow is concerned, and heroic penance as well. This was risking all the danger and harm these powerful persons could invoke.

In contrast to this, we have the pusillanimous fear and anxiety of Peter, afraid even of a servant girl in the courtyard. By comparison to the heroic acting out of sorrow of Judas, Peter seems an inferior and even a shameful figure. Judas seemed far more sorrowful and penitential. How much more could he have done? In this sense, Judas even appears more honest. We do not hear of Peter's going back to tell people that he had lied.

FORGIVENESS OF SELF

The real issue seems rather to center on the forgiveness of self. This can be overlooked if we simply focus on external evidence of "sorrow." The difference between Peter and Judas is that, in the Gospel report on Peter, no stress is laid on any kind of dramatic penance. The only record that we have of Peter is that he seems to have forgiven himself enough to come and face Christ. This is what Judas could not do. The facing of Christ seems to follow from Peter's forgiveness of himself. How did he get to the place where he could look at Christ's face? The answer seems to be that he had enough faith, self-respect and trust to go there.

Judas, in a hatred of self, could not go to Christ, and so was caught in a masochistic bind. In Aquinas's terms, he loved to hate himself in place of loving to love himself, as we said. We recognize a similar masochism in some people who come to confession—centered only on self-condemnation. But simply to pour out self-condemnation as a symbol of sorrow for sin can be a distortion. It can be the use of confession to scourge oneself. In such a masochistic bind, sorrowful as Judas was, he yet could not forgive himself, and so he remained bitterly hateful of himself. The issue here is the psychological movement from hatred of self to forgiveness of self. This in turn leads to approaching Christ in faith and trust and accepting His redemptive forgiveness.

PETER-JUDAS COMPLEX

Consequently, another tone that might lead to a counseling exchange would be the confessor's ear for this Peter-Judas conflict. That is, while the person has confessed his sins, he may still be faced with the issue of forgiving himself.

Let us consider the situation where the confessor routinely says, after the confession of sins, something like "You feel genuinely sorry for these sins, don't you?" The person replies,

I don't know. I'm just disgusted with myself. I never thought I would strike a woman, and most of all I never thought I would strike my wife.

He is explaining how in the upheaval of a quarrel he struck his wife and is now caught up in self-rejection for this action. The counselor's aim then would be to understand his difficulty in forgiving himself and reflect or re-cognize it in his response.

The understanding of the priest would have to reach out beyond the feeling of sorrow to the hatred of self that may also be involved. Certain types of sins, then, as well as certain types of relationships, can have a counterpart of self-hatred. In fact, one might propose that sin itself is often an acting out of a masochistic self-hatred. Until such self-hatred is itself understood and worked through, sin is simply going to continue to be the agent and expression of that self-hatred. To be reprimanded, corrected and warned—even if this could be seen as the function of the confessor—might feed this psychological state of self-hatred into which the penitent has already got himself. This would seem to fix him more completely in the state of Judas. It might not help at all in leading him to the penitential state of Peter—the forgiving of self and the facing of Christ. Despite his sin, Peter was somehow restored to a state of dignity and self-respect. Otherwise he could not have accepted later the position of head of the Apostles, with all its responsibilities. He would have done something like what Judas did.

In this sense, then, the understanding of the counselor-confessor would be aimed at the forgiveness of self. The goal would be to restore friendship and love between Christ and Peter. Experiencing the friendship of the confessor, in the sense of his warm, accepting understanding, allows the penitent to begin to experience the counterpart of the divine-human relationship between Peter and Christ. In other words, the priest himself first convalidates the forgiveness. The respectful quality of his understanding can make possible, then, the feeling of truly relating to Christ in a self-forgiving way.

To achieve this, the confessor-counselor might respond to the person's self-rejection with

Co: You are just very ashamed, and it is very difficult to forgive yourself for having struck your wife.

Cl: Father, you just don't know what it is. Even telling you this way about it I feel better already. I'm just awfully relieved even to be able to tell you about it. I said I was just angry before, but I guess I was just too ashamed to tell you about it. I wasn't sure I could.

As in the previous option, the issue might then become counseling in the rectory at some later hour or day.

FAITH MAKES WHOLE

The process of forgiveness, then, involves the sense of accepting forgiveness, the belief and inner security that one's sins have been removed, that one no longer needs to be in a state of self-attack and condemnation, that one is freed of sin, that one is now truly a "freer" man in the Pauline sense, and no longer under sin.

Basic to these elements is the quality which permeates and interrelates them, the conviction of faith. Beyond the psychological experience, the symbolic, verbal communication and exchange, and the deep sense of the communion and communication with another person is the relationship with the Total Other, God, which the priest and the sacrament represent. Through this faith, sacramental communication and friendship with God, if lost, has been restored; if impeded, it has had the impediments removed. The confessor and the sacrament, then, stand for friendship with God and the sense of restoration, renewed healing and redemption in this God relationship. But since these are also often difficult psychological experiences, skill coming from counseling awareness may noticeably aid the degree to which the confessor's words, manner and actions achieve not only their natural and psychological purpose but, more fundamentally, their intent as human acts and instruments of the Divine.

PERSONAL COUNSELING

Let us look now at what can happen as the result of such a counseling-confessional encounter when a person chooses to continue the discussion in a regular counseling interview of an hour.

The following recorded excerpts are taken from such an interview with a middle-aged businessman, Adam, who had previously confessed "uncharitable" feelings and attitudes towards his wife. Asked by the confessor to discuss this a little further, he began to release feelings of guilt and confusion about this comparatively recent attitude toward his wife, whom he had previously considered a model mother and wife. He did not know why he had these negative feelings now, and at first sight he felt they were wrong and quite unjustified. He accepted the confessor's offers to discuss this further in a later counseling interview outside the confessional. When he arrived for the interview, he readily agreed to having it recorded, saying that he felt it would help them both to have such a record of what was said.

In the following excerpt, taken from the middle of the hour-long counseling interview, Adam has arrived at the realization that his earlier notions of his "perfect" wife and their "ideal" marriage were partly due to his own self-deception. He sees that a great deal of his present guilt and conflict is the result of a confused but growing awareness that he and she had never openly faced one another as they really were.

VERBATIM RECORD

It is interesting to note that Adam refers to the tape almost as if it were the presence of another person adding veracity and integrity to the relationship. This reaction is, of course, not that of everyone, and hence a person should not feel forced to consent to the recording. But a surprising number of people do appreciate the counselor's efforts at such integrity and accuracy. The person should be informed, however, of the possibility of the tape, if this is the counselor's intent, so that he is prepared for the option of whether he wishes his interview to be taped or not. Often, a person not only consents but, as in the present case, even considers the tape an added assurance of skill, accuracy, respect and thoroughness. However, taping an interview should obviously not be suggested in any circumstances in which the purpose might be misunderstood by the person interviewed or the recording misinterpreted by others. It is not, in itself, necessary to counseling effectiveness.

Adam is speaking about the difficulty of facing his own self-deception:

Adam: It's extremely unpleasant from the standpoint of my own self-deception. It's not very palatable to admit to myself, or to you, or to the tape here, that I've been wrong. (*Pause.*)

Co: Yes.

Adam: Through a long period of time, and that I've been wrong as a (*pause*) self-defense, and I've been wrong in a most unusual way—what you might say in a justifiable way. It's very unusual.

Co: Yes.

(INSIGHT):

Adam: I saw clearly this jealousy while we were courting, and I recognized it as such. I resolved that when we decided to get married, or rather after I had thought the whole thing through and we had talked about marriage, that I had a job on my hands.

Co: In other words, as you see it, before marriage you saw this problem clearly. What you see now is that it really did continue to exist, but in a much more disguised and subtle form.

(UNFAIR TO WIFE):

Adam: Right. That's exactly it. Possibly I built my own self up by—how could I explain it?—by being so thrilled, by being so happy and pleased that it did not exist in the form that I had previously seen it—was I thrown by this? I recognized it in that phase and that phase disappeared. Complete trust and confidence was placed in me, so that I was completely blind to this. As a result of this I can see that I was responsible, to that extent, for a very unpleasant life for my wife insofar as I was even going on patting myself on the back that it wasn't going on. This was unquestionably unfair to her.

Co: If I could catch what I see here . . . that having expected it to turn up in the form of open and obvious jealousy, and it not turning up that way at all, you just dismissed the whole thing. What you see now is that you expected the wrong thing, that is to say, that it was still operating but it was operating in a different form than you expected. This is where you see your own failure—it was the failure to see that although it wasn't operating in the form you expected, it was still operating very strongly.

(INSIGHT):

Adam: Yes. And I was on the fringe of it for a long while, at least previous to last fall. However I never got through. I could get to a high point once in a while, but I could sort of sense a low one coming, which is entirely different. (*Pause.*) . . . You begin to go back for a moment, and then you bridge over. As I see the picture now, I was extremely conscious of my recognizing that jealousy. I—as I am very apt to do—was sold a bill of goods. She went completely the other way and reassured me that under these circumstances it would not show up—and not by her words, not at all, but by her actions. No matter whatever came up. (*Pause.*) . . . However, as I see the picture now, it took a completely different turn-about in many respects.

Here we have a situation that might be likened to what medically would be called "false healing." A real personal difficulty that was apparent even in their courtship was artificially resolved, and so in fact lay dormant in the early years of marriage. But as Adam is aware now, it really expressed itself in repressed forms during these years.

PERIPHERAL TO CENTRAL

Here the analogy of peripheral and central vision may be helpful. An object on the side of one's eyes is distracting and disturbing, particularly because one is vaguely aware of it but does not clearly know what it is. One arrives at a greater state of security when one has the object in front of the eye in central vision. Even though it may still be disturbing, it is less distracting when seen clearly.

One at least has the security of knowing more exactly what it is. It is something of this kind of feeling that Adam is describing.

This kind of movement from peripheral to central vision is very common in counseling and is one of the first positive securities that can occur. Nothing has changed, and one may in fact be no better off; yet one has definitely gained in security and positive feeling simply by the fact of coming to a counseling interview. Forces can now be activated which focus a person's perception, so that issues are at least beginning to be faced and looked at clearly, in contrast to the repressed and distorted forms they took previously.

In the courtship and early in marriage, many difficulties can occur because of this kind of false view of the other partner. This false view then crystallizes itself and affects not only husband and wife but the children as well. As the years go by, so much has been invested in this view that it seems to take a painful crisis of awareness, such as happened here, to help the person begin to question it.

Perception studies can be of some use in illustrating what seems to occur here. Perception ambiguities can result in a person's getting a fixed view which is difficult to change, even though an alternate view is equally possible.

In a somewhat similar way, when people have crystallized their views of one another and operate on such views, as for example, in marriage, it seems extremely difficult for them to break this view and see any alternatives. Counseling is one of the rare occasions offering people an opportunity to change fixed views of themselves and others in this way.

SUCCESS FAÇADE

Toward the last part of the hour interview, Adam, continuing to talk about his relationship with his wife, feels caught up in what he calls "false notions of our duty" and "false notions of charity toward one another." He refers to this as a "religious sham." What he now feels more strongly about is that under the guise of "false notions of charity toward one another" and their "marriage duty" they have failed to be honest and genuine. They have, in his view, done one another a small good, but covered over a great harm.

The following excerpt is from the last third of the hour. By this time, we notice, the client has become increasingly insightful. We notice, too, how the counselor's responses, catching and bringing the insights together, help the client to move on to new facets of self-awareness and understanding of his marriage relationship. In this excerpt he has returned to talking about needing to have a very successful marriage and selling himself and his wife a rosy picture of something quite artificial. As a result, the two of them were unable really to look at themselves and one another. The counselor is summarizing previous insights:

Co: The fact that she sort of covered all this over so that you quickly sold yourself a bill of goods that you got the jackpot, that you were quite different from other men in all this, and then as the years went by you were reluctant to admit that it wasn't so, and she continued to carry this façade, so to speak, of non-jealousy, you could never get through to this real person whom you feel you did know before you were married.

Adam: Yes, that's right. And I think, the more I look back at it, the more I am convinced that, that it's—all a religious sham on both of our parts. She did, as I see the picture, a terrific job of overcoming her jealousy toward the other girls, and I'll say justly so, because I never did look at one. That threw me. Then, she did a terrific job of looking at duty as she saw it. I feel as though I did also. I would say that we hid behind *false notions of our duty, false notions of charity toward one another,* under the guise of our obligation to one another. Completely false.

Co: You used the phrase "religious sham." Now this is a pretty powerful expression, isn't it? That is, that you feel something terribly deep here. Under the pretense of a sort of superficial, ideal religious family life kind of thing, you really were carrying on a very dishonest relationship with each other and, as you see it now, a very unreligious relationship.

INTENSITY OF RESPONSE

The reader could be somewhat surprised here at the intensity of the counselor's last response. To accuse someone of a "religious sham" in his marriage is certainly strong. If we did not have at hand the client's accepting reaction, we might theorize that this response would have been too strong for him to accept. We notice, however, that he does accept it and gives added meaning to it in his later responses.

This raises the important point, applicable not only to negative and positive emotion but, even more, to insightful responses. When a person has struggled to say a deep and complex thing about himself, albeit very negative, there is implicit in this a deep trust in the counselor's acceptance and understanding of this intense feeling. This is even more true when a feeling contains a penetrating insight, as in the present case.

Consequently, for the counselor to have softened and diminished the intensity of the insight would have been to betray something of the trust that enabled the person to say it in the first place. It would be as if the counselor said: "Look, I can't quite take your having this extreme view about your marriage after all this time." Or, stated another way, the counselor would be saying that the client is not really free to be profoundly insightful about himself or his marriage if these insights take an extreme negative turn.

We see that this would be a serious infringement on the client's freedom. It would tend to narrow the margin of communication possible between client and counselor. It would diminish the trust the client had in saying this and force him, to some degree at least, to be more positive. But as we can see, this would be an artificial attitude brought about in response to the counselor and not really any genuine gain in self-awareness. On the contrary, Adam might even be made guilty and embarrassed for having said as much as he did.

What would appear to be a kindness, at first sight, encouraging the client not to be so negative, in fact, severely restricts him in the real insights he might be gaining. The insight process would then be handicapped for what might appear to be a counselor consideration.

A little later the counselor responds:

Co: In other words, as I get your perception of this, if it were a truly religious reason that would have been all right, but what you see now is that it was just reaching into religion for a rationalization, an artificial defense or pretense. You just sort of covered the thing over and didn't look at it because you could give a pat answer, or you could give some sort of an artificial religious reason to justify it.

Adam: Yes, exactly so. And therefore the word, the use of the word "sham." It is surprising how that did put more healing ointment on the festering wound. And I put another layer on top of that which was already healed.

Co: Yes, you had a lot of digging to do when you tried to get down to the fester you had covered with so much superficial layers that appeared to be religious motives.

We notice that the counselor matches the word "sham" with a strong analogy of medical false healing. Unless one studies the statement carefully, again one might question if the analogy were not too strong, and, in fact, might be resisted. We notice, however, that it was not and that the phrase "religious sham" and the "festering" analogy are interwoven in the client's own evaluation.

ANALOGIES

Analogies can be extremely helpful, as we see here and elsewhere, as counseling responses. They run the risk, however, of either missing the feeling by being too strong or too weak or by being disproportionate to the insights expressed. When an analogy such as this one truly fits, however, it can often give the client a vivid and very clear tapestry or context into which he can weave a variety of separate insights. It is, too, something that he can remember and keep with him a long time.

We have already commented how negative emotions unfolded, released and explored in counseling seem to lead to positive awarenesses. Or, stated another way, negative emotions seem to have their most disturbing and distorting effect when they are covered over, suppressed and not faced. When they are looked at, talked about, examined and organized in terms of the values and awarenesses they represent, the whole feeling tone can change. This can happen in an individual interview or over a series of interviews.

CONSTRUCTIVE SELF-BLAME

In the following excerpt from the end of the hour counseling interview, Adam has now reorganized his attitude toward his wife and, at the same time, is taking blame on himself for the failure to communicate and his lack of adequate and genuine regard. His feelings are now constructive and positive in place of the earlier resistance and hostility as he first began to face their mutual self-deception.

We notice how the counselor announces the approaching end of the interview and then continues on with his response:

Adam: What I get out of this whole thing, aside from a deep understanding of it and a realization of it, is a deep feeling of gratification. And surprising as it might appear—aside from enabling me to make contact with my wife, it gives me a feeling of deeper understanding and love for her. There's just no comparison. Instead of getting all excited and peeved and mad and blaming her for the whole mess, I could no more do that than jump out of the window.

Co: It's quite surprising in a certain sense, isn't it, that you are really facing this woman as you did when you chose to marry her—as being a rather jealous woman, among many other things, with her background and peculiar orphan life. Now you are coming back to that again after many years and honestly facing her again in all this jealousy and inadequacy. You have a sense of love for her now, in a way that in this pretense and artificiality, you didn't have.

Adam: Definitely.

(VALUE INSIGHT):

Co: So, by truly knowing her as best you can, in her weakness and her inadequacies, as you see it now, it's a truer kind of love.

Adam: Yes. It's a real love. It's an understanding love. It's, well it's. . . . (*Pause.*)

Co: I have the impression that this real relationship was a little bit surprising to you.

Adam: Yes it was. It was surprising but not for too long, sort of a quick surprise. But it's this realization of this new love, new understanding in love. What was surprising was the fact that even after our short talk I didn't tend to fly off the handle. That sitting alone, thinking things through, I did not say "Damn it, what is she pulling on me now?" and look for some means of condemning her. Not at all, exactly the opposite. It makes me realize what a damn fool I was, and I just can't understand how I could have been that way. It makes me realize what a, what a . . . I'm sort of at a loss for words! My mind is working but my tongue isn't! It makes me love her all the more because of the injustice I've perpetrated on her. In other words, had I not been so blind, she would not have had to go through a lot of the doubt, in-decision, worry and fear that she did. Yes, so instead of she coming out the culprit and me lily-white, it's exactly the opposite. That's the way it is. That's the way it is . . . and I'm satisfied to face it . . . happy to face it.

Co: Well, just a few minutes yet in our time. It's pretty clear to you, and satisfying now too, that as you look back you could see her inadequacies, whereas you had been mounting this false picture of her. What you are doing in the end is blaming yourself for mounting the false picture and recognizing that this false picture, through all these years, has been an injustice to her. The real just picture of her was the one you had before you were married.

(INSIGHT):

Adam: Absolutely, absolutely. Had I been—to use charitable in its true sense—living it, I certainly would not have acted this way. I would have recognized what I saw before we were married and dealt with it as such—the simple, plain fact that it was and not looked for a million and one excuses and alibis to not face it.

(SUMMARIZING RESPONSE):

Co: In other words, this is a weak woman, like most of the other women that men talked about when you were first married. The only difference was—and this was to build up your ego and you tripped yourself with it—her weaknesses were not so obvious as those of these other men's wives. The problems she created were not so obvious. Now that you can truly accept her in herself with her weaknesses, you have a kind of relaxed sense of more truly loving her.

Adam: Right. Also a realization that this religious background which she had, left her with a lot of strong points—real strong points accord-ing to my old way of thinking, which in reality are not strong points any more than my religious sham points are.

Co: Yes, well our time is about up. If you wish we can set up another session—say the same time next week?

Adam: Well, I have a lot to digest out of this. Why don't I call you? I feel real good about this and maybe that's all I need for the present.

Co: Okay—as you wish.

Here we see the counselor's trust in the client. This applies even to leaving with him the decision whether to continue or end counseling at this point.

By this time, still holding onto the concept of religious sham and artificiality, Adam has, at the same time, come forth with new awarenesses of a different kind of love for his wife. This love, he now feels, has been made more genuine by the fact that he has been allowed to face her real inadequacies and talk about them. He has, at least, been able to see this, whatever else he may not yet be able to see.

RATIONALIZATIONS

This represents a common awareness that is particularly applicable in marriage and family life. People often find themselves using, manipulating and controlling one another, for purely personal motives and needs. Yet in the beginning of counseling, they are usually unable to face such attitudes in themselves or others.

Rationalizations built up through many years can make such motives and attitudes actually appear altruistic and genuine. There is throughout this period, however, as this excerpt indicates, always a peripheral awareness of suppressed guilt and unrest. There is still a submerged feeling that all is not the way it appears and the way one is claiming it to be. Consequently a person never feels secure and genuine, despite his endless contention to himself, his wife and others that he has, as this man said, "hit the jackpot."

ACCEPTING HUMAN LIMITS

The end effect of counseling insight is surprisingly similar in many different interviews: the acceptance of the human condition in oneself or others. Obvious as this may seem when it applies to someone else, it is a difficult realization for a person to arrive at about himself or about someone intimately associated with him. Since a person has to live with and face in others all their weaknesses and inadequacies as well as his own, it is hard to arrive at a clear view of himself and others.

People rarely, if ever, arrive at awarenesses that human wisdom has not long since uncovered in some way already. Yet, as this wisdom applies to the unique circumstances of each person's life, it is often startlingly new and fresh. So that, while insights reproduce ancient wisdoms, they do so in a personal pursuit that demands courage, honesty and trust in oneself and others.

The counselor, before and while these insights are being acquired, must trust this process of arriving at human wisdom. Only with such trust in the deeply reasonable integrity of the client, when he is allowed to face himself openly and honestly through the counselor's skill, can the personal flowering of such reasoning come about.

LIMITED GOAL

We are not implying here that as a result of the counseling hour all of Adam's marriage conflicts will be resolved. His wife is part of this too. The next step might be for Adam to persuade her to join him for marriage counseling as a couple.[2]

But Adam at least has a clearer grasp of his situation than when he originally confessed his changing attitude toward his wife. He now knows something of the origin of his negative feelings and his guilt and some of the personal values that are involved here. To achieve this in some measure would be the limited goal of the hour interview.

We see here an illustration of how an hour counseling session, coming from an understanding confessional relationship, seems to have proved, in some measure, effective and so produced the beginning awareness of a more mature religious regard toward oneself and others.

NOTES

[1] "Epilogue," in *Research in Psychotherapy*, ed. E. A. Rubinstein and M. B. Parloff (Washington: American Psychological Association, 1959), p. 292.

[2] See Charles A. Curran, "Marriage Counseling," in *Counseling and Psychotherapy: The Pursuit of Values*, *op. cit.*

4
Longer Counseling Awareness

UNTIL NOW we have been considering "brief encounter" and short-term counseling. Longer counseling, however, is as necessary in religious values as in other forms of personal concern. We therefore need to look, with more precise scrutiny, into a counseling process where the personal situation is more complex than the concerns we have just considered.

Consequently, we will now analyze in some detail a more complicated situation of anxiety which shows itself—among other things—in "scruples"; that is, an exaggerated concern for "sin" especially in minute and apparently unimportant issues or details. This same person we will also consider later under "Religious Maturity and Positive Anxiety." By staying with one person in this way, we will have greater consistency. But the skill involved is still generally applicable, since the issues here are typical of those often encountered in counseling where religious values are concerned.

ILLUSTRATION

This person, Martha, a woman twenty-five years old and an unmarried teacher, is professionally engaged in helping other people. The excerpts that we will study in detail here are taken from the last of six half-hour interviews which were held once a week. Later we will consider her comments after the twelfth interview. As she says in the interview, she feels herself quite capable, responsible and successful in her professional work and in many aspects of living. She is, however, anxiety-ridden in some other areas.

105

One form that this anxiety has taken over a period of fourteen years has been to show itself in various religious and moral "scruples." That is, Martha had an exaggerated moral concern and an excessive fear of doing the "wrong" thing. Such anxiety often causes people intense preoccupation with "sin." For Catholics, for example, as in the case of this woman, it can be a source of great difficulty both when they are trying to examine their conscience before they go to confession and in the actual confession. In typical instances, such examination can occupy a person for days in advance of confession. Afterwards, they can worry about not having given the exact details.

HEART OF GUILT

In considering a person involved in "scrupulousness," we are, according to Ricoeur, also engaging in a personal situation that is at the very heart of guilt. It is symptomatic of an immature and external dependence on the law through striving simply to fulfill minute prescriptions of it and harassing and rejecting one's self in one's failure to do this. This is "the curse of the law."

So Ricoeur says:

. . . Guilt, we have said, is the completed internalization of sin. With guilt, "conscience" is born; a responsible agent appears, to face the prophetic call and its demand for holiness. But with the factor of "conscience" man the measure likewise comes into being; the realism of sin, measured by the eye of God, is absorbed into the phenomenalism of the guilty conscience, which is the measure of itself. If this analysis is brought to the light of the Pauline experience of justification by the works of the law, it appears that the promotion of guilt—with its acute sense of individual responsibility, its taste for degrees and nuances in imputation, its moral tact—is at the same time the advent of self-righteousness and the curse attached thereto. Simultaneously, the experience of scrupulousness itself undergoes a radical re-interpretation: that in it which had not been felt as fault, becomes fault; the attempt to reduce sin by observance becomes sin. That is the real meaning of the curse of the law.

The curse is twofold: it affects the structure of the accusation and that of the accused conscience.[1]

As a result, a vicious circle is set up that keeps the person bound by its recurring demands. The person wearies himself with self-punitive measures which, at best, alleviate the anxiety of guilt momentarily. So Ricoeur continues:

The two curses give impetus to each other unceasingly. The zealous penitent gives himself the infinite task of satisfying all the prescriptions of the law; the failure of this undertaking gives impetus to the feeling of guilt; the integral observance by which the conscience seeks to exculpate itself increases the indictment; and as the atomization of the law tends to shift moral vigilance and direct it towards isolated and sometimes minute prescriptions, conscience consumes its energy in single combats with each of them.[2]

This process is evident in the following excerpts even though, since it is now the sixth interview, Martha is already becoming more insightful about herself and her situation. As in earlier excerpts, we have indicated by headings and inserted comments particular value insights as they occur. The following excerpt is from the beginning of the interview. Martha has been telling how depressed she feels:

Martha: I don't know. I just don't know.
Co: You feel pretty low.
Martha: Yes, but it's not always like this. I mean I don't just feel constantly bad. I try to keep very busy just to keep my mind off it. So it's not a constant conscious state but it's just kind of in the background. I'm not happy about it because it has affected me so much, but, on the other hand, I don't know, it makes me unhappy. I try to make the best of it—it's here.
Co: Yes, you can distract yourself, and it's not always so obvious. There are times when it is less intense. From another point of view you just try to accept it and say, "Well, here it is." It seems sort of always there underneath and you have to live with this.

DEAD-CENTER STATE

These two responses are valuable in the way they illustrate two contrasting counseling aspects. The person's first comment implies a kind of a "dead center," where she seems to have nothing more to say. The counselor, we notice, does not try to encourage her to speak. He simply sums up the negative emotion tone of her previous statements with "You feel pretty low."

As a result of the counselor's simple acceptance of her "low" state, she can agree with it. But then she is freed to make comparisons about these "good" and "bad" feeling states.

This illustrates the point, repeatedly proposed, that negative emotions clearly accepted and responded to by the counselor often move the client to some positive statement. By contrast, had the counselor attempted to persuade her that things were not so bad and she should look at the brighter side, it might have only produced artificial agreement. It might have even pushed her, on the contrary, to a more detailed negative emphasis because she did not feel understood. She might have felt forced to try to convince the counselor of how bad things really were. Since, however, he simply accepted her language of negation, as we see, she began to move forward in analyzing herself.

The counselor, in the second response, recognizes and reinforces this self-awareness. A little later, the counselor is responding to a further clarification in relation to an earlier experience:

(*Awareness of exaggeration tendency*)

Co: You had an experience a year ago that kind of gives you a hold here, by way of comparison, didn't you? You know that you did build it all up and exaggerated it, and that the reality turned out to be quite different when you got there, and you're wondering if this same pattern has not happened again now.

(VALUE):

Martha: I really do. I would really like to think that is what it is and all I have to do is just get a hold of myself and say, "Now, listen, there's nothing wrong, you really have no symptoms outside of these feelings that come over you." I would like to be able to do that but I haven't tried often enough.

(VALUE RESPONSE):

Co: Sort of like to have it worked out. You'd like to be able to prove to yourself that you have exaggerated all this, and that if you did, you can solve it. You can do away with it by getting a hold of yourself, by working it through and getting a hold of this exaggeration. That's what you'd really like.

(INSIGHT AWARENESS):

Martha: And then to change this whole emphasis on exaggerating without being overconcerned over things which you should normally be concerned about but not to the point where you build up big worries. One thing that I think I've learned is the valuelessness of worrying. Why should a person worry? It doesn't change a thing.

(INSIGHT RESPONSE):

Co: What you are seeing is a tendency to overreact, to overdo your reactions. You see some point in being afraid of something but, as you see it, you are overreacting and exaggerating. It has become more and more apparent that worrying gets you nowhere. It is largely a meaningless activity, not constructive.

Martha: No, really not constructive. Oh, I don't know and I just wonder if this thing can be worked out through counseling. I hope it can.

Co: You don't quite trust this. You hope counseling will work it through but you're not too confident. You're hopeful but on the other side you're not quite sure.

Martha: No, I guess I'm really not quite sure that it will . . . . Really I just don't know.

Co: You haven't any security here. You've just got a very deep "I-don't-know" kind of feeling.

Martha: Yes, I just don't know what to do next.

Co: You're not really sure of anything, of what to do.

(CHOICE-ACTION):

Martha: You know all those other things we had talked about in the previous interviews about my relationship with my mother. Well, all those things have just kind of slipped, not into the background, but they just seem more manageable.

MORE MANAGEABLE

We can see here how the counseling process and the counselor's skill aid growth in value awareness. The insights and clarifications of personal goals and purposes which counseling provides seem especially helpful. They provide a sharper realization of what a person really wishes to achieve. This makes personal options more evident. Clearer cognition of motives seems to facilitate more adequate choice and action. We notice that conflicts with her mother, for example, are now "more manageable."

The following excerpt is taken from a later period in the interview:

(Scruples = Anxiety)

Martha: Well, I'm sure it is not from the outside. As I say, there is nothing in our family. I'm sure upon examination, this is all myself. In thinking of these problems and these scruples, I see how suggestible I am. I mean, how easily I am overtaken by an idea. Like if something may present itself to me as being a sin or an occasion of sin and I get . . . I can use my reason and say, "No, this isn't sin." Yet I'm not sure. (RESPONSE HEARD FROM COUNSELOR) As you said before, just to save peace of mind, I go along with my own idea and it works out okay.

REASONABLENESS VS. PEACE OF MIND

Here we note a growing self-realization with regard to "suggestibility" and how this plays into anxiety. Toward the end of the excerpt, there emerges a conflict between "reasonableness" on the one side and "peace of mind" on the other. Two basic values which we usually think of as going together are here disjointed and incongruent.

To be reasonable, for Martha in her present state of awareness, would seem not to mean having peace of mind. On the opposite side, she arrives at peace of mind not by being reasonable with herself but rather by succumbing to this suggestibility coming from her anxiety. This is a livable solution even though it obviously leaves her in conflict with the reasonable judgments of others and to some degree with her own reasonableness.

An interesting point here is Martha's repetition of what the counselor said in his response, "As you said before, just to save peace of mind, I go along with my own ideas." This illustrates a common situation in which a motive or self-value stated in the counselor's response seems clearer to the person. Even though she expressed it first in her own statement, it was apparently recognized only when she heard it in the counselor's response. People often remember and hold onto the counselor's phraseology and later repeat it. Sometimes this can be a sentence, a phrase—or even, as we have seen, a particular word that has proved especially clarifying. The following excerpt continues in the same vein:

(*Scruples = Instance of Anxiety Solution*)

Co: Let me put it this way, if this would be catching it. Out there, there are a series of ideas, and then there are your ideas and they don't coincide, as for example, in this case of scruples. (INSIGHT RESPONSE) For your own peace of mind, it is easier to follow your own ideas or your own reactions even though, from a reasoning point of view, the other would seem to be sound.

(INSIGHT):

Martha: Yes, and I know that it is sound.

Co: So you know the other is sound but it is more peaceful to follow your own version, so to speak.

(PAST VALUE):

Martha: And for all the years I've had them, that's how I've acted. And they didn't bother me as long as I knew that what I was doing was just kind of to satisfy my own scruples because I was never really following a priest's direction for any length of time. There were times that I was, but not over a period of years. So I just would figure out things to do to get rid of these scruples or to act in accordance with them. As long as I had peace of mind it didn't bother me too much.

Co: This was livable for a rather long time, in the sense that you knew you were following your own exaggerations, your own version. You knew the other solution was more reasonable in a way, but you could get along by following your own version and you didn't have to come to grips with putting the two together.

CHANGE IN VALUES

For this person, as we said, anxiety is attached to doing something "reasonable," not, as we would ordinarily expect, to doing something unreasonable. This is caught by the counselor's response:

"You know the other is sound, but it is more peaceful to follow your own version." The direction that the counseling process is taking is becoming evident. Only when what she accepts as "sound" is, at the same time, no longer threatening to her can she approve of it and truly invest herself in it.

Contrariwise, her own version which, in one sense, she sees as unsound and exaggerated, must cease to be seen as a source of security. She can then free herself to follow her "sound" solutions without being insecure and anxious.

This adult situation might be said to parallel the fetish need of small children. That is, certain adult actions, like dolls or other child objects and rituals, can be made sources of security and peace. By following this ritual of performance, "her own version" as Martha describes it, a person seems, for a long period, to be able to get along. Like the fetish of the small child which may seem amusing, odd or strange to others, these anxiety-charged actions somehow bring a kind of security to the person, even though they may seem senseless and unreasonable to others. They may even provoke others to negation and irritation. Consequently, it is usually safer and wiser for the person to conceal these fetish ritual actions and only reveal them in confidence. This explains why, in those instances where they cannot be kept covered, others are often surprised by them.

The interview continues:

(MISTRUST OF SELF):

Martha: I could follow what I knew was the right thing and just to forget about the scruples and yet there was always that doubt, I *never trusted myself*. Well, are you taking the easy way out? If I could think of something specific, it would probably help, but I just kind of always felt on the safer side. It was all too easy to just listen to the priest and forget about all these things as they would say in confession, "Just forget that kind of a sin and don't worry."

Co: You had to sort of make it harder on yourself. You were afraid that this was too easy if you gave in to that other side. You felt more secure taking the harder solution. Your version was always the safer.

(EASIEST WAY OUT):

Martha: No, actually, I think it was the easiest way out. It would have been harder for me to ignore these things and to go along with what I knew I should do. This would have been the harder way, but what I think I did was take the easy way out.

(VALUE PARADOX):

Co: So, for you it was easier to take what was extrinsically harder or at least safer because the other seemed just too easy if the priest just said don't worry about this. But really that would have been the harder for you to do. Sort of an upside down figure here. So what would have been harder objectively was easier for you to follow because in a way it was your version, your security. (LOSS OF SELF DIRECTION) What would have been easier objectively, would have been a lot harder for you to follow because it would have meant giving yourself over to someone else.

Martha: Um-huh, I just can't get . . .

Co: Some sort of basic mistrust here of yourself in being able to do this.

Martha: Yes. In the area of my own scruples I never trusted my own judgment, when it really came down to that, I don't think I ever did. It was always the same way with my confessions. All my confessions were, for the last fifteen years. I don't know if this was mortal sin but I'll confess it anyway. It always had to be prefaced by that. It was never definite and I just felt incapable of making a decision in a moral area, and I remember that we got on to this last week, about the two selves. (TWO SELVES) I trust my judgment at work in the area of working with my students and I feel that I operate fairly well in making judgments there. But when it gets into the moral area, then I'm really off the track in deciding what are sins and occasions of sin.

(SCRUPLES LESSENED BY CHANGE OF FOCUS):

But I really should point out that the scruples have really lessened a lot just even the past couple of weeks because I've been so bothered with this other thing that I can't be bothered with them to such an extent.

Co: Yes, you see a connection here, a kind of two selves, that is your ability to be objective and trust yourself in your work and yet not trust yourself in the moral order. This led to this two sides or two persons conception. What you also see is that because this deeper thing has been uncovered, the scruples seem not to be so disturbing. That has been less of a pressure on you.

TWO SELVES

As we have indicated in our inserted comment, Martha is growing to realize areas in which she mistrusts herself. In the light of this, her scrupulous solutions were the easiest way out for her as she sees it. The counselor catches the value paradox with "What would have been easier objectively, would have been a lot harder for you to follow." He recognizes, too, another basic value, namely, to follow the guidance of others, when she could not internalize it, seemed to threaten her with the loss of self-direction. From this emerges the realization that she is "two selves," one where she trusts her judgment in the area of work and professional responsibility; the second, in the moral area, where she mistrusts herself. She ends suggesting that, because of a change of focus and switch in inner concern, the scruples "have really lessened a lot just even in the past couple of weeks."

The interview continues with the following "surprising" incident:

Martha: As a matter of fact and what amazed me and I don't know what it was, the Grace of God or what—but last Saturday when I walked out of here I sailed over to Saint _____ as if I were going in to say "hello" to somebody, it was the easiest confession I've made in years. I have a lot of doubts about it because I spent much less time in preparation. But I wasn't so physically upset the way I get before every confession. All day long when I know I'm going to confession, I'm all upset and tense and nervous. But that day it was so easy for me to do it. I don't know how it was that I could do it that way.

Co: This is very surprising and, in a sense, positive that for the first time in many years you could go to confession rather easily and yet not feel disturbed. You could feel all right even though you had not made near the preparation you normally would.

(NEW OPERATIONAL VALUE):

Martha: Well, I was kind of disturbed about it because I didn't spend the kind of time I normally do, an hour or so just thinking up things, but that day I just didn't care. A few priests say not to spend that much time in making a preparation, so I didn't. I thought of all the things that were at the top of my head and just included everything else generally and the priest knew that, so it was okay.

Co: It was disturbing and yet you were able to do it. You were able to do more or less what priests say you should do rather than your own version which you had to follow before. In that sense it was positive.

(POSITIVE ACCEPTANCE OF NEW VALUE):

Martha: Yes it was.

Co: We have a minute or two in our time.

SURPRISE: NEW OPERATIONAL VALUES

Here we see how a shift in operational values seems to occur. It is usually first signified by a "surprise" reaction. In the comments of Ann, the mother discussed in the previous chapter, she also expressed surprise at not being disturbed at the noise of children playing in the basement. She was surprised too by her spontaneous approval of herself as a mother in contrast to the feeling of self-rejection that she might have had previously.

We notice a similar illustration here. In an action like that of going to confession which had for many years been filled with anxiety, Martha suddenly discovered that she had done this simply and without apparent concern. Her disturbance came afterwards as she reflected upon this simple action and its ease, in contrast to the heavy burdensome process that she was used to. It was an extension of the paradox stated earlier, that what was easy and simple in itself made her uncomfortable and disturbed her afterwards. Despite this, however, she could still agree that the surprise experience was positive. The growing release and insight and shift in focus of her concerns, resulting we can presume from the previous five interviews, had somehow freed her—without her conscious awareness—of her obsessional preoccupation before going to confession. She then, to her surprise, found herself not only in the confessional but finished before any of the accustomed anxieties began to occur.

The word "surprise" suggests a kind of twilight zone as new insights and values begin to appear. There is usually a certain "wonderment" at this, sometimes even astonishment. In a limited way, it can be compared to the surprise people have when they discover the other perception in an ambiguity picture. The difference here is one of action. It implies that new value perceptions were somewhat unconsciously accepted—so the surprise came in the ease of the new action itself.

COUNSELOR OVERRESPONSE

This excerpt also offers us an interesting and valuable example of a slight counselor mistake. We also see how he avoids a conflict.

In his first response, the counselor says, "You could feel all right, etc." Actually, if we look carefully at the previous excerpt, Martha did not "feel all right"—rather she began to worry, but only *after* the confession. What surprised and pleased her was the ease of preparation.

Martha, we see, resists this overpositive tone, with, "Well, I was kind of disturbed about it." The counselor wisely corrects himself at once by responding exactly, "It was disturbing and yet you were able to do it. . . . In that sense it was positive."

The client, Martha, can now accept this corrected version with "Yes, it was."

Done skillfully by an observant counselor, such corrections seem to pass easily with little apparent conflict. We use the word "apparent" because perhaps any distorted response, even though immediately corrected, as this one was, still does some harm to the sense of flow and understanding. One can feel this here.

This verifies and demonstrates our earlier statements about the counselor's failure to recognize a negative response at its real depth or, as in this case, being too positive. The client seems always to resist this, usually, as we see here, by an open disagreement. This is very different from the "fit" type of reaction that we see in the forthcoming excerpt, "Exactly!"

NEW LIFE PLAN

Reflecting on this experience, Martha can see that, by operating on this new set of values, she responded in a "positive" manner. As these values emerge with greater force and clarification, they should produce a growing preference on her part for achieving this kind of confessional experience. This could be accompanied by a similar freedom from anxiety in other "fetish" areas rather than the need to revert to these reassurances and securities. Previously, she saw that her self-responsibility expressed itself partly in her professional work and partly in a distorted need to resist the guidance of others. She is beginning to see now a positive security if she can herself guide and control these areas of anxiety. We will see that this is, in fact, what happened as a result of later interviews.

In the following excerpt, concluding the interview, Martha has returned to a discussion of her general anxiety state and to the notion that maybe someone could tell her what to do to get over it. It would be, as she said:

Martha: Yes, like taking medicine, kind of like a cure or a prescription.

Co: Kind of like doing it twice a day sort of thing.

(VALUE OF SELF-RESPONSIBILITY):

Martha: Exactly! But on the other hand, I certainly can see the value in my getting at this all by myself; it would be the first time, if it does come to that.

(TWO SIDES):

Co: Two sides here. You can see a prescription but you can also see that this prescription is not your doing. If you really get at this yourself and can resolve it, it would be the first time in your life and in that sense it would be a real achievement.

(POSITIVE ASSURANCE FOR SELF):

Martha: Yes, and I think of the value of something like this for the future, if something like this would ever come up again, I would be able to handle it by myself, and this is what I'm thinking. If this is just a run-away idea or something that has gone beyond itself, then I will have learned how to control it and it will be the same in the area of scruples too. This is what I would have achieved. . . .

Co: You sort of get an overall feeling that "If I could really do this, I would have accomplished something very significant in a sort of lifetime way for myself."

Martha: A lasting thing, yes.

Co: And this is sort of inviting if you could achieve it.

Martha: Yes, but on the other hand that idea of a prescription really. . . .

Co: Really appeals to you too. . . .

Martha: Yes, it certainly does, and I can see both, and they are sort of hitting at one another to see which would win out.

Co: Yes, you are tempted in both directions.

Martha: Oh, I sure am!

Co: A short-term prescription or the long-term security of being on your own. You don't know which will win.

Martha: Well, I have a pretty good idea which one is going to win. I doubt if I'm going to get any prescriptions from you. (*Laughs.*)

(COUNSELING VALUE SYMBOL):

Co: You have the feeling that I am structured in terms of the long-term solution and of your being your own security system. Well, suppose we call it off. (*Pause*) Thank you very much for allowing me to record your interview.

Martha is caught in the middle between a desire for some kind of prescription she could passively follow and the more difficult but long-term security that would put her on her own. They are, as she says, "sort of hitting at one another to see which would win out." At the end, however, it seems evident to her which value system she has implicitly chosen if she continues this kind of relationship with the counselor. As she says laughingly, "I doubt if I am going to get any prescriptions from you."

RESPECTFUL SELF-CONCEPT

In his description of this anxiety condition of scrupulousness, Ricoeur says:

. . . distrust, suspicion, and finally contempt for oneself and abjectness are substituted for the humble confession of the sinner.[3]

What we see here is a gradual transition in the opposite direction, to a different self-concept that is growing steadily more responsible and respectful of itself. With this has come, at first surprisingly, the ability to make a simple and direct confession of sin. We will return to this in our subsequent discussion of factors that constitute religious maturity and positive anxiety.

CREATIVE AND THERAPEUTIC COUNSELING

In comparison with the "brief encounter" excerpts, this was clearly an example of counseling therapy. The personal issues involved were fundamental and of long duration. This demands, of course, skilled counseling. It also illustrates some of the differences between the constructive, positive use of counseling, even for short relationships, and more complicated long-term involvement.

From the viewpoint of counseling as a normal process, we might emphasize this difference by using a term like "creative counseling" in contrast to therapeutic counseling. In *creative counseling* we would be concentrating on the positive value of counseling in aiding any constructive process or achievement. Rather than being centered on "problems" and personal conflicts and confusions, as in therapeutic counseling, the focus would be directly on furthering positive growth and development.

It is becoming increasingly evident that such a positive creative view of counseling would make it an effective asset to many relationships such as those in learning, marriage or work situations. In premarital creative counseling, for example, the focus would be on the aspirations and values the two people could develop and share together as they approach marriage. They would, therefore, counsel together to search for and unfold these common goals with the aid of the counselor's communication skills. Its aim would be to further the awareness and realization of common ideals and goals.

But even therapeutic counseling has its positive and creative side. A sense of sin and guilt, even in an anxious "scrupulous" person, is still not totally negative. As we see in these excerpts, counseling skill can aid the person's "negative will," as Otto Rank called it, to begin to become positive and constructive. We will return again to the person in this interview, to see, at later stages, her comments on this positive and constructive side.

This leads us in our present discussion, however, to a direct consideration of some basic issues beginning with the concept of sin and guilt.

NOTES

[1] Paul Ricoeur, *The Symbolism of Evil,* trans. Emerson Buchanan (New York: Harper and Row, 1967), p. 143.

[2] *Ibid.*

[3] *Ibid.,* p. 145.

PART TWO

Some Basic Issues

5

The Concept of Sin and Guilt

OUR TREATMENT of "sin and guilt" here is basically psychological and directly related only to counseling therapy. It treats peripherally some issues that are considered extensively elsewhere. The literature dealing with these questions in the spheres of ethics and moral theology is vast, and they are likewise dealt with in various forms of legal theory and juridical practice. Hence we mean only to touch on these questions as they relate to the counseling process.

To begin with, it might be said that the manner in which one reacts to any discussion of sin and guilt may depend on how one views their effects in one's own life or the lives of others. A person's reaction, therefore, can be determined by whether he sees this question in a positive, constructive light or in a negative, destructive one.

AMBIGUITY

Among the perceptual figures used in psychology, especially to illustrate Gestalt concepts, a familiar one is either an attractive young girl or an extremely ugly old hag, depending upon the perceptual clues on which a person is focused. If he sees the old hag first, it is sometimes extremely difficult for him to see the young girl. Alternately, if one has pleasantly focused on the young girl, one finds great difficulty in appreciating how others are reacting to the ugliness of the old hag.

This seems to fit something of the issue of guilt and sin. In counseling and psychotherapy the effects of sin and guilt are often seen in their ugly forms in the lives of disturbed people. And from this focus it can be difficult to see that these same concepts might

123

have, for others, a positive and constructive value. Alternately, one can see sin and guilt in a positive psychological or theological context. Here it would be the absence of desirable goodness for which one is, realistically, striving and the stimulation and urging on to greater efforts to acquire that goodness which a constructive and courageous self-ideal has produced. This viewpoint would be very different from one of destructive shame, self-rejection and ugliness which concepts of sin and guilt, distorted usually from early childhood, can produce in many people's lives.

FAILURE TO LOVE

Evil has been defined as turning completely to oneself and away from others, whereas virtue is seen as the consistent capacity to turn to others, not as rejecting or opposing oneself but as giving oneself in an act of love to others. This we have already briefly considered. This suggests a balanced integration between our own rights and duties to ourselves and our own self-meaning and the rights others have and their meaning as persons and our duty and love toward them.

Looked at in this way, sin is always a failure to love. "The sinner," said Aquinas, "does not love himself enough." That is, in not really loving and respecting himself adequately, he cannot give himself as something worthwhile to others in love or to God, and he does evil to himself in place of good.

It would, therefore, be a distortion to make sin synonymous with worthlessness. On the contrary, David in the Jewish tradition and Paul and Augustine in the Christian tradition could be held up as classic examples of people who admitted to having committed grave sins and yet, as sinners, recognized their own worth in God's forgiveness and redemption. Christ said, "Let him who is without sin cast the first stone," to the crowd around the adulterous woman, and no one dared and the crowd sheepishly and shamefully dispersed. Of Mary Magdalen he said only, "Because she has loved much, much is forgiven her." In fact, the classic image of Judas does not really involve his sin as such—Peter's, as we have seen, was probably as great—but his horrible and violent self-condemnation and his despair. This is the final temptation of guilt, to refuse the possibility of being made whole again and of being a decent person in one's own eyes, worthy of others' love and the love of God. The only basic threat is the fear of loving and of being loved. In the light of this, what sins a patient or client commits are not the real issue, but his willingness to love again and to let himself be forgiven and to forgive himself.

KNOW BUT NOT DO

In our discussion of man's anxieties we have already pointed out the tendency towards disorder, the lack of expected integration between what a man knows and is convinced he should do and what he actually does. So sin and guilt seem to follow from this basic conflict. That is, knowledge alone is not enough. When people change, as we saw, they have changed not simply because someone gave them knowledge but because they acquired a whole new view of themselves in the therapeutic experience of feeling and willing. This resulted in a change in some areas of values and in a different set of actions. These they choose as more desirable.

Until this occurs in some measure, we have guilt as a sign of alienation from the self and self-rejection. Raimy's early studies of the self caught this well.[1] In the beginning of counseling therapy, the person's predominant attitude was a negative self-reference. Only gradually, in the process of therapy, did it begin to become positive.

This alienation and conflict within the self—of knowing yet not doing—which St. Paul describes so well, is a kind of personality dualism.

Ricoeur comments:

This dualism is far from being a primordial ontological structure, it is rather a regime of existence issuing from the will to live under the law and to be justified by the law. This will is sufficiently enlightened to recognize the truth and the goodness of the law, but too weak to fulfill it: "To will the good is present with me, but not to accomplish it; for the good which I will, I do not; but the evil which I will not, that I do" (Rom 7:18–19). At the same time, by contrast, that which I do not wish to do and yet do, stands before me as an alienated part of myself. St. Paul expresses well, by the very hesitation of his language, this cleavage in the personal pronoun. There is the I which acknowledges itself: "but I am a being of flesh, sold into the power of sin" (7:14); but, acknowledging itself, it disowns itself: "it is no longer I who perform the action" (7:20); disowning itself, it establishes itself within: "I delight in the law of God after the inward man" (7:22); but honesty requires me to take both the I of reason and the I of flesh for myself: "It is, then, I myself who by reason serve a law of God and by the flesh a law of sin" (7:25). This cleavage in myself is the key to the Pauline concept of flesh. Far from being a primordially accursed part of myself—the bodily part, sexuality for example,—the flesh is myself alienated from itself, opposed to itself and projected outward: "Now if I do that which I will not, it is no more I that do it, but sin that dwelleth in me" (7:20).[2]

This disjunction is evident in the counseling therapeutic interview, where sin and guilt can be and often are distorted into intense self-condemnation. But sin is not really the central issue—since we are in fact all sinners in some form or other. Rather the excessive and unforgiving self-condemnation and rejection, so often appearing under the guise of a distorted notion of sin and guilt, are the basic issues appearing in counseling therapy.

MODELS OF ATONEMENT

This introduces the larger question of the nature of atonement itself and the various theories and models that have been used to explain it. Pruyser has pointed out that religious speculations about atonement have produced several models or theories, each with its own history, images, strengths and weaknesses. They fall into three main groupings: the ransom theory, the satisfaction theory, and the moral influence theory. These atonement theories constitute three thematic structures of thought regarding man's relationship to God.

These models tend to correspond, at least loosely, to certain growth stages in the life-process from childhood to that of an adult. Pruyser explains:

There are certain developmental stages and crises in life in which there is a special proneness to feelings of anxiety, guilt and shame.

The course of personality growth is determined by the ways one learns to cope with these, by the successes and failures in dealing with them. May this not imply that there is an appropriate and fitting ad hoc symbol system of the atonement for each age level, stage of development or personality type?[3]

. . . Thus far a close parallelism has been indicated between three typical intrapsychic conflict situations and three typical formulations of the atonement mystery. The parallelism raises some question for the religious educator who wants to know what difference it makes to stress one atonement theory over the other in the appropriation of the faith.[4]

Pruyser suggests the possibility of deriving other models of atonement, more suited perhaps to the adult life experience of today and to values and analogies more meaningful and relevant to modern experience. As one of these possible new models, he suggests a therapeutic concept of atonement:

If God is active love, as the fourth Gospel has it, and if loving and working are the essential ingredients of mental health, as Freud once said, in our pedagogy God's image as well as man's behavior must be purged of anything tending toward the contrary. The words and ideas used in teaching must set forth the enduring Christian qualities of mercy, charity and hopefulness. Adequate symbols must be located to stress grace in graceful ways, mercy in compassionate terms, bliss in joyous metaphors. The idea of God must be therapeutic and the language and imagery in which he is pondered, worshipped and proclaimed must also be therapeutic.[5]

ALERTING SIGNALS

But even without additional models of atonement, guilt can be seen as a positive and even necessary aid. We are familiar with the child who is, by a strange and rare exception of nature, born without any reaction to pain. We know that he is tragically handicapped because he has no capacity to feel the warnings of pain and thus to avoid or recoil from, or at least to face, situations that are physically very dangerous or injurious to him.

In something of the same way sin and guilt can be looked at in themselves in a positive light even if they are not the main point of the Judaeo-Christian theological tradition—even if the main point of that tradition is love. They warn us of the dangers to ourselves; they alert us to the necessity of facing issues when we wish to avoid facing them. But—like physical pain—while they are not desirable in themselves, or in excess, they are warning and alerting signals in our psychical, spiritual life; without something of the kind we would be seriously handicapped. This does not mean that we seek guilt and sin. As with regard to pain, we seek not to increase guilt but to remove it. If by drugs or neurosurgery we have removed a patient's feeling of pain, without in any way removing the causes of this pain, we have ultimately only done him grave harm. He is all the more gravely handicapped and his cure can be all the more difficult for him because he has been led to think that, feeling no pain, he is actually well when, as a matter of horrible fact, he still has all the symptoms and weaknesses of a serious disease.

Freud suggests this idea in regard to anxiety when he says:

Two possibilities with regard to the appearance of anxiety, therefore, may at once be distinguished: the one, inappropriate and inexpedient, in response to a new situation of danger; the other a useful one, as a means of giving warning of and adverting such a situation.[6]

Applied to guilt we could say that, in their destructive form, guilt feelings are "inappropriate and inexpedient" responses, but they can be a "useful . . . means of giving warning of and averting."

RESPONSIBILITY

Consequently, in the light of this function of the feeling of sin and guilt as alerting man psychologically and spiritually, one can wonder if anything could be accomplished by changing names. "A rose—and sin—by any other name" would both come out to be the same thing after all. They seem, in fact, intrinsically bound up with both man's freedom and his responsibility. Rank pointed this out:

Free will belongs to the idea of guilt or sin as inevitably as day to night, and even if there were none of the numerous proofs for the inner freedom of the conscious will, the fact of human consciousness of guilt alone would be sufficient to prove the freedom of the will as we understand it psychologically beyond a doubt. We say a man reacts *as if* he were guilty, but if he reacts so it is because he is guilty psychologically but feels himself *responsible;* consequently no psychoanalysis can relieve him of this guilt feeling by any reference to complexes however archaic.[7]

Looked at in this way, it would seem that—however desirable it might or might not be—we cannot separate a feeling of guilt and sin from the whole psychological process of personal and social responsibility. We only weaken the person psychologically otherwise.

REASONABLE CONSCIENCE

In the last century or so, conscience has sometimes been reduced to a kind of bundle of Kantian categorical imperatives coming from outside; from one's parents, family, or—what is even more threatening—from the state itself. Now, while no doubt all these things influence a person most deeply, it is becoming evident that the therapy process itself—no matter how it is brought about—is a process of rational self-awareness and personal responsibility. In a positive sense, this process might be said to be the effective work of a reasonable conscience.

The therapeutic process is a movement from a negative irresponsibility for oneself to the facing and changing of one's actions toward oneself and others. This, in fact, means a change in the perception of one's obligations and duties and one's positive capacity and willingness to fulfill them. It is in this sense a reasonable process of growing self-integration. This process is apparent in the following comment:

. . . I think, among other things that have transpired here, you have through your subtle processes stimulated my conscience gland. (*Laughs*) Before, I was a free agent. But now it is pleasant to think that before I wasn't immoral, but certainly amoral, and now I feel that I would like to be a moral person. There is overall a sort of healthy resolve on my part. I think it's healthy to walk in the paths of righteousness without being dramatic about it, simply because I can find life more worth living.[8]

Rogers[9] has remarked, describing his observations of the counseling therapeutic process, on the basic rationality that it reveals, once a person can get his perceptual awareness clarified and integrated with his actions.

SELF-DECEPTION

A major factor in personal conflict and unhappiness, as Aristotle pointed out, is this fact: that a person can seek an apparent good which satisfies one or the other of his needs but which is contrary to his overall good. A person's particular desires for particular personal, emotional, or sensual satisfactions can be directly opposed to broader reasonable goals. This is the source of his self-deception. He has the option to give in to particular urges toward objects and goals which he knows will not really satisfy him nor ultimately be to his good. This, then, seems to be a main source of guilt, the capacity of the self to reject and condemn while yet submitting to the narrow view. This kind of guilt and self-rejection gives rise to the negative self-reference, "I am disgusted with myself," and similar negative self-judgments, commonly heard in the beginning of counseling and psychotherapy.

ILLUSTRATION

This process of the changing perception of motivating personal values invariably involves a shift in focus and an increasingly broader realization of all the factors involved in a situation or personal relationship. This in turn results in a changing perception of what is really good, and choices and actions change. To illustrate this, we can consider excerpts from a second interview and contrast it with the insight stage of the tenth interview with the same person.

These data were drawn from a series of interviews of a married woman in a serious infatuation. In the second interview the only thing she considers beyond herself and John is one brief phrase:

"I've got people that I don't want to hurt either."[10] In the whole of the first and second interviews the above statement represents the only expression of consideration for any factors or persons except herself and John. However, if we contrast this limited viewpoint with the insight stage of the eleventh interview, we have a marked change in perception. The superimposed image of John and herself has given way to quite a different picture of the whole situation.

Interview II: **Interview X:**

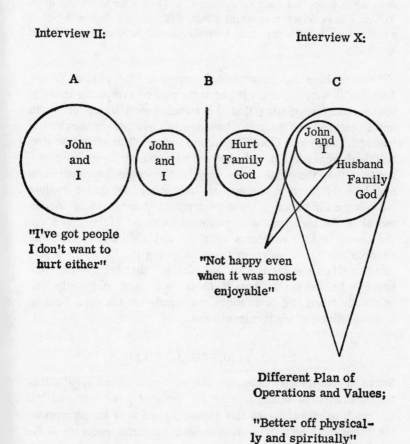

A   B   C

John and I

John and I

Hurt Family God

John and I

Husband Family God

"I've got people I don't want to hurt either"

"Not happy even when it was most enjoyable"

Different Plan of Operations and Values;

"Better off physically and spiritually"

When John and I were together it just sorta pushed everything into the background . . . But you just can't turn aside and say, "Well, I'm going back to where I was"—even though I, if I really wanted to—I couldn't do that. It's hard to give up John after all the good times we've had and the things we've done, but when you stop and think what could have happened, why you see things different. (*Long pause.*) . . . But I know even now, just by not seeing John, I'm better physically and spiritually too. . . . Yes, the way it was before I wasn't really happy, it was just a state of conflict and misery and fear of being found out and thinking of the kids and all—no, it really wasn't happy, even when it seemed most enjoyable. . . . There's no happiness in it. You're always under a constant strain. (*Pause.*) I'll lose a lot in a worldly way, but I'll gain too. I would gain more than I would lose spiritually.

Observe here the perceptual language in the phrase "When John and I were together, it just sorta pushed everything into the background," suggesting that the superimposed image of "John and I" blocked out the overall awareness of responsibilities to her husband, family and God. The second phrase, "But when you stop and think what could have happened, why you see things different," suggests that the thinking process of the counseling interviews also brought about a different self-perception. When we analyze what is the difference in these perceptions, it seems to be the removal of the superimposed, narrowed focus on "John and I" to the broad reality awareness of the responsibilities to husband, children and God. Now, even though giving up John is a severe sacrifice when she focuses on the pleasure that being with John brought her, she sees herself to be better off physically and spiritually when her perceptions are clearly on the total field of responsibilities, as distinct from John.

TOTAL PERCEPTUAL FIELD

Stated in goal-directed language, this viewpoint would suggest that the superimposed image is itself an apparent good and that the self tends to move toward this apparent good until its perceptions are broadened and the reasoning and insightful process of the personality, in this case brought about through counseling, brings out from the background the real good, the total perceptual field. This puts into its proper perceptual organization the immediate good, which in this case came from the relationship with John. When the immediate good is measured against the total perceptual field of all values involved, the self chooses and moves toward the relationship of husband, children and God in the total perceptual field, as the real good, and rejects the apparent good which previously was a narrow focus on "John and I."

It was this type of awareness of a change in self-perception as a major source of responsibility that caused Rogers to propose

that the self, under proper conditions, is capable of recognizing, to some extent, its own perceptual field, and of thus altering behavior . . .[11]

a point of view which he and others have increasingly stressed in writing and research.

Sin and guilt are, as seen in counseling therapy, the result of conscience. We see this too in David, Paul, and Augustine. But this is a different conception of conscience from a simple categorical imperative.

Conscience [says Aquinas, representing in this an older tradition], according to the very nature of the word, implies the relation of knowledge to something: for conscience may be resolved into *cum alio scientia,* i.e., knowledge applied to an individual case. But the application of knowledge to something is done by some act. Wherefore from this explanation of the name it is clear that conscience is an act . . .[12]

In a more recent definition, we have conscience defined as

the intellectual consciousness or reasoned awareness of right or wrong in a situation here and now to be judged . . .[13]

Earlier we quoted Ricoeur's definition:

Guilt, we have said, is the completed internalization of sin. With guilt, "conscience" is born; a responsible agent appears, to face the prophetic call and its demand for holiness. But with the factor of "conscience" man the measure likewise comes into being; the realism of sin, measured by the eye of God, is absorbed into the phenomenalism of the guilty conscience, which is the measure of itself.[14]

APPLICATION OF VALUES

Conscience then might also be considered the application of values, as we have defined them, to a particular immediate situation. This is accompanied by a judgment on the self and the act that is either approving or disapproving—the act being considered either right or wrong as measured by a set of values. One might then distinguish this from more general self-approval or disapproval as coming from parents, etc., by proposing that such attitudes are often, in fact, the result of unexamined value attitudes implicit in one's family and social matrix. When these are examined and consciously sifted and evaluated, they may or may not still be retained as part of a conscience value system.

Moreover, as we will treat in detail under "Pastoral Counseling," the conscience of a religious man would, in addition, be clearly related to his religious convictions coming from the Divine Revelation he believes in and the interpretations of his Church.

In this light one major aspect of counseling therapy is the furthering of this reasonable movement of conscience to a constructive and practical outcome.

Counseling therapy can aid in this process because, as the person mirrors himself and slowly sees all the factors that enter into a given series of actions, he grows more able to work out in detail the immediate means to carry out a reasonable solution. This seems to be the basic difference before and after counseling. Before counseling the individual may, and usually does, consider himself guilty of an unreasonable series of actions. Sometimes this feeling of guilt is excessive. In this case he must, and often does, slowly correct this excessive self-blame as he comes to a more adequate understanding of himself, his past influences and what he has done.

But counseling, as in the two excerpts cited, does not always do away with guilt. The person may still feel that his acts are truly wrong. In the beginning, however, while he recognizes the wrongness of his actions, he is glued to the immediate needs which are desirable and attractive. He feels himself unable to do without the things which fulfill these needs. Through counseling, he is able to see that, although these immediate needs are pleasurable, they ultimately lead to unhappiness and dissatisfaction. Moreover, he can now relate other factors which, in his focus on these immediate pleasures, he previously avoided considering. As he begins to act on these new insights, he finds that they bring him greater permanent happiness and self-approval. This, in turn, further stimulates him to follow his reasonable judgments.

SIN AS IMPOTENCE

But unless a person makes a conscious effort to reach out and grasp all the integrated factors that enter into a situation, he may find himself led quickly by a particular emotion to seek an immediate good which, while temporarily satisfying, is at variance with the integration of the whole good which he is seeking. It will, therefore, lead him away from his real purpose. He is responsible for having failed to make the integrated effort, since he had the basic capability of such integration. Kierkegaard remarks that sin is always an "impotence."[15] In the Aristotelian sense, it would be an "absence." In both it would be a failure to do what one could.

Consequently, it is not entirely an excuse for the person swept along by his emotions to say he could not help it. In many instances he actually could have controlled these impulses, provided he took the necessary means, particularly through the aid of a skilled counselor. He would then be more able to see all the factors which enter into his practical choices. As long as he fails to do this, he may be quickly conditioned by emotional tones such as hostility, threat, or anger which particular persons, places or things have for him. These emotions may be so strong that, unless an intense effort to prevent it is made, he will find himself swept along in the impetuosity of these impulses into a path of conduct which in the long run solves nothing.

But he is capable of broadening his perceptions so that he can combat this tendency to immediate reactions and precipitant judgments. Otherwise counseling would not be possible. He can arrive at those solutions which result in and from greater self-integration.

We see this taking place as we compare the early interview excerpts with later ones in which these attitudes become related and form themselves into more adequate solutions. These, in turn, give a more realistic evaluation of the complex aspects of the personal issues presented.

It is, therefore, difficult to know where responsibility lies in cases of this sort. We can consider any unreasonable act morally wrong. We cannot, however, always make the person performing that act completely responsible, since in particular instances his responsibility may be diminished, either by lack of knowledge which he had no opportunity or obligation to acquire or by the degree to which his emotions made him incapable of acting reasonably at that time.

A person's conscience (as a function of his own reasoning) can witness and retain evidence of past unreasonable conduct as well as give approval or disapproval to present actions and serve as a guide to the future. In this sense, if we were to do away with conscience—that is, the person's capacity to make a reasonable judgment about his conduct—we would do away with one of the main forces for therapy.

CONCEPT OF SUPEREGO

Here one might raise the question of the relationship of the idea of conscience with the more recent concept of "superego"— prominent now not only in formal psychoanalytic literature but in all other considerations of the psychodynamics of personality.

Brenner would tend to equate them, with some distinctions:

The superego corresponds in a general way to what we ordinarily call conscience. It comprises the moral functions of the personality. These functions include (1) the approval or disapproval of actions and wishes on the grounds of rectitude, (2) critical self-observation, (3) self-punishment, (4) the demand for reparation or repentance of wrongdoing, and (5) self-praise or self-love as a reward for virtuous or desirable thoughts and actions. Contrary to the ordinary meaning of "conscience," however, we understand that the functions of the superego are often largely or completely unconscious. It is thus true, as

Freud (1933) said, that while, on the one hand, psychoanalysis showed that human beings are less moral than they had believed themselves to be by demonstrating the existence of unconscious wishes in each individual which he consciously repudiates and denies, it has demonstrated on the other hand that there are more and stricter moral demands and prohibitions in each one of us than we have any conscious knowledge of.[16]

The moral demands and prohibitions of parents, or of the nursemaids, governesses, and teachers who may act as substitutes for the parents, begin to influence the mental life of the child very early. Certainly their influence is apparent by the end of the first year.[17]

Regarding Freud's concept of conscience, Hartmann comments:

About the "necessity" of moral codes, however, he repeatedly and clearly expressed his opinion. He realized the integrative function that such codes and standards have for the individual. "Conscience" was, for him, "a necessity: [its] omission the source of severe conflicts and dangers." But, impartially, he also emphasized that in one's relations to one's fellow man "it is by no means the rule that virtue is rewarded and wickedness punished." More than once, he traced the "necessity" of moral codes to the fact that human society could not live without them. He called the superego a highly valuable possession for human society. In another connection, he showed how the development of the superego can lead to a reduction of the external means of coercion used by society. He noticed "with surprise and dismay" that "so many people obey only outer pressures," instead of developing their own moral standards. He was obviously very far from being a moral nihilist.[18]

MATURE CONSCIENCE

Menninger, among others, prefers the term "archaic conscience" for the superego, thus clearly distinguishing it from "mature conscience."[19] This seems to correspond to the mature action of the person's reasonable conscience, as we have described it, as it relates to personal change towards greater responsibility and broader perception and regard of self and others. This can often involve constricting limits on the self out of genuine regard for the other.

LOVE

There are therefore some difficulties in the position of Fletcher: "Only one thing is intrinsically good, namely, love: nothing else."[20] At first sight, nothing could be more appealing to the counselor than the concept of the law of love. He represents the warmth and openness of a healing, understanding and accepting relationship. He seeks the fulfillment of Solomon's prayer for an understanding or listening heart. Consequently the general position of Fletcher, representing deep concern for each person's unique situation, speaks directly to the atmosphere of counseling.

NARCISSISM

There are some complexities here, however, that go beyond the question of accepting and understanding the individual. When one looks carefully at narcissism, one has to consider the extremely complex forms it can take in the manipulation and control of others, under the appearance of caring for them. The question of the degree of a self-determined type of ethics which seems ultimately implied would need to undergo careful scrutiny.

Where does a therapy of limits and a maturity of limits emerge here? We are increasingly considering now, in counseling and psychotherapy, not just the self, the self-concept and its self-actualizing potential, but the community as well. This involves the relationship of the self to the *other*, with the other's own unique limits and worth and urges to self-affirmation and fulfillment. This is making us aware that the limits of the self are basic to any movement out of narcissism. In this sense, only when the old definition of justice, "to each his own," is fulfilled, can one even begin to talk of love. There is a difficulty in speaking of a law of love— even if we clearly define it—without a clear knowledge of one's own narcissistic tendencies. One runs the risk of deceiving oneself by appearing to be loving the other, when one is loving only a reflection of oneself. One might argue, then, that it is in the painful submission of the self to one's own limits and the beginning of the boundaries of the other that a movement out of narcissism is possible and the beginning of love occurs. Valid ethical imperatives should, it seems, aid this, sometimes even by painful confrontation, in order to make one aware of one's disguised narcissism.

Ethics must certainly consider unique rights to self-fulfillment. But we can still conceive of ethical principles as aiding the person in his own community fulfillment with and through others rather than necessarily seeing them only as repressing and inimical. There are not, in this sense, simply imperatives but, more fundamentally, the expression of a genuine reasonableness. These would not seem to be in conflict with a mature conscience.

Areas that remain unresolved are part of the growth of this mature conscience, a growth for which the individual's action and commitments can often be the initial catalytic agent. But for this to be so eventually, there needs to be a genuine "otherness" in the person's motives. This is often difficult to achieve.

EDUCATED CONSCIENCE

Considered in this light, conscience needs education. It does not function adequately on complex issues without education and guidance. It has its own wisdom, to be sure, but additional awareness can be necessary to enlighten and broaden a man's perception of himself and others. Such awareness comes from others, both in the traditional realizations of mankind and in immediate observation. Counseling, as we have seen, is often required to aid a person to assimilate and absorb the richness of this educational knowledge. Without it, a man can be the victim of his own ignorance or resistance.

CREATIVE TENSION

The difficult and painful processes, then, by which moral and legal determinants are arrived at are often the here-and-now possibilities of a particular culture and people. Like a person in counseling, the law too can be improved. For this to take place, there needs to be a straining kind of tension and discontent similar to that which accompanies a person taking counsel. Such creative tension produces a better realistic fulfillment in the direction of the ideal norms of law and reasonableness. The religious impulse of love can be a catalytic agent here too. In this sense, it is always straining against, and even at war with, what is. But such impulses need the cautions of the Old and New Testament and the inherent respect for law, with all its inadequacies, that the Judaeo-Christian tradition has maintained.

To cylinder this creative tension so that its explosions accomplish a forward movement in community and personal benefit, in place of futile destructive explosions that can be suicidal, is the main goal. Incarnate and realistic community reasonableness is finally measured, then, not by the law alone but by a common, growing, educated awareness in each man's conscience.

CONSTRUCTIVE CONFRONTATION

Permissiveness is not always loving; it can, in fact, simply be not caring enough to intervene. So confrontation is not necessarily rejecting, even though it may have these initial tones. It can genuinely convey an honest regard for the person and a true concern that he live up to a better self. It of course opens the way for projecting hostility and guilt under the guise of "fraternal correction," but this does not have to be so.

Constructive confrontation[21] is possible and can be effective if the attitudes involved are ones of authentic consideration for the person confronted and his better self-fulfillment. He himself can, upon reflection, know and realize this. In such reflection after confrontation, a counseling relationship can often be efficacious.

The analogy of firewood might fit here. The warm, inviting fire and the readily burning logs could be the insightful counseling process and relationship. But, at an earlier time, these logs had to be cut down and let dry out. Only then was the easily burning firewood produced. This "cutting down" aspect might be constructively understood as a kind of confronting experience which starts a painful self-awareness process and begins to move a person out of his particular narcissism. But this may take time before it can become even the beginning of counseling or a sense of the need to take self-counsel and so finally to change one's values and actions.

In the counseling process itself, a person often refers to comments of others—parents, relatives, friends, work associates—made sometime before, that have only now begun to be accepted and assimilated. These remembered comments can be the source of rich, insightful self-realization and the developing of new self-concepts, ideals, and values. This was initially made possible because these people cared enough, even in constructive anger, to offer the person these confronting but basically respectful challenges to his better self-fulfillment.

THEOLOGICAL DIMENSION

But in a special sense we could say that sin, as distinct from guilt generally considered, implies some at least implicit acceptance of, and relation to, a religious code and to God. In this, sin is not only against ourselves and/or our neighbor; the same sin is also against God.

In fact, it seems that to leave sin unrelated to a personal God and the possibility of forgiveness is to be the victim of a far greater dread—potentially unlimited in its anxiety and threat and with no hope of remedy.

Ricoeur makes this point:

It is enough that the sense of sin as being before God be abolished for guilt to work its havoc; at the limit it is an accusation without an accuser, a tribunal without a judge, and a verdict without an author. To be accused without being cursed is the highest degree of accursedness, as Kafka shows. By the semblance of intention that remains in a radically anonymous condemnation, the verdict is hardened into fate. There is no longer any place for that astonishing reversal that the Jews called God's repentance, or for the conversion of Erinyes into Eumenides, celebrated in Greek tragedy; God's repentance is the counterpart of our own advance from discovering God in wrath to encountering him as mercy. To become oneself the tribunal of oneself is to be alienated.[22]

The Pauline version of man's conflict within himself is, according to Ricoeur, behind all the more recent conceptions of man's alienation:

. . . this alienation, upon which we have been attempting to throw light through the notion of justification by works, can also be understood after the fashion of Hegel, Marx, Nietzsche, Freud, Sartre; but the Pauline stratum underlies all these stratifications of our ethical history.[23]

Here, certainly, sin and guilt cannot be separated from love. "God is love," says the Fourth Gospel, "and he who dwells in love, dwells in God and God dwells in him." One must, in a special and unique way, fall into God's love by believing in it and by abandoning oneself in faith, hope and utter trust to the divine mystery. "Thus Faith becomes the existential attitude of man in the state of grace, man living in Christ—even should the communal life with Christ and God be disturbed by sin."[24]

Sin is, therefore, in some way an impediment to this love between God and man in much the way that the insensitive, inconsiderate and selfish person withdraws and prevents the love of others from reaching him. Consequently the sinner, by his sin, hurts essentially himself in his love relationship with God. A line in the Psalms says, "He who commits sin is the enemy of his own soul."

This idea that sin is ultimately against God has implications for another important point—using sin as a reason for condemning others as worthless and inferior. Psychologically we know this is most often, if not always, a compensationism for refusing to face one's own guilt and sense of sin and a vicarious satisfaction through trying to make someone else more sinful. This reveals the psychological subtlety in Christ's warning, "Judge not, that you be not judged." This way of making others worthless is not only psychologically injurious but is directly against the core concept of the Judaeo-Christian tradition. This tradition is one of sincere and realistic humility before God in the face of another's sin and the intense self-awareness expressed in "There but for the grace of God, go I."

CONSTRUCTIVE GUILT

Psychological guilt, however, can be separated from sin in the sense that it can be considered that kind of judgment which hindsight and a greater comprehension produce. One might call this constructive guilt when the regrets it invokes are preventive of a repetition of the same action or judgment. Yet, under the circumstances, knowledge and impulses of the moment when the original judgment was made, one would have repeated the same action without the advantages of hindsight. Here often a false or destructive guilt must be displaced by one that is constructive. We see this illustrated in an after-interview comment when the person says, about a counselor response, that "just being able to distinguish this much made me feel much less guilty. I had just about half as much to be guilty about because I could understand and readily forgive myself for that much anyway."

Religious and personal values often seem to produce this kind of constructive guilt in that they urge a person on to a greater self-fulfillment and meaning. This is the opposite of a state of "impotence," as Kierkegaard called it, which simply "gives in." In the wake of this positive drive, there is often regret and sadness when one fails. This kind of guilt seems simply the other side of an intense positive urge and so is itself positive in that it constitutes a strong vector against repeating the failure.

Such constructive guilt seems a basic part of the value structure of maturity. This is clearly different from guilt that is a destructive self-hatred which corrodes and defeats and so constitutes a vicious circle. Constructive guilt, on the contrary, like positive religious anxiety which we will now dicuss, seems involved in any kind of serious striving for ideals and goals. Man, as we see him and know him, is always in some conflict and turmoil. For each achievement brings rewards, satisfactions, meaning and value, but it also poses new goals yet to be achieved. Conflict, frustration and confusion reoccur as new goals and ideals emerge to supplant those either discarded or fulfilled or no longer meaningful. In this sense man never entirely "is but always will be blessed." Constructive guilt is part of his mature push to ever greater becoming and being himself and the creative tension of striving and longing that this involves.

NOTES

[1] Victor C. Raimy, "The Self-Concept as a Factor in Counseling and Personality Organization," Ph.D. thesis, Ohio State University, Columbus, Ohio, 1943.

[2] Ricoeur, *The Symbolism of Evil,* pp. 142–3.

[3] Paul Pruyser, "Anxiety, Guilt and Shame in the Atonement," *Theology Digest,* XIV, 3 (Autumn 1966), p. 187.

[4] *Ibid.,* p. 185.

[5] *Ibid.,* p. 186. See also the same author's *A Dynamic Psychology of Religion* (New York: Harper and Row, 1968), pp. 317–328.

[6] Sigmund Freud, *The Problem of Anxiety,* trans. H. A. Bonker (New York: The Psychoanalytic Quarterly Press and W. W. Norton Co., 1936), p. 173.

[7] Otto Rank, *Truth and Reality* (New York: Alfred A. Knopf, 1936), p. 62.

[8] William U. Snyder, *Casebook of Non-Directive Counseling* (Boston: Houghton Mifflin Co., 1947), pp. 243–262.

[9] Rogers, *On Becoming a Person,* pp. 194–195.

[10] *Ibid.,* p. 55.

[11] Carl R. Rogers, "Presidential Address," *The American Psychologist,* 2, No. 9 (September 1947).

[12] Thomas Aquinas, *Summa Theologica,* trans. Dominican Fathers (New York: Benziger Brothers, Inc., 1947), I, Q. 79, a. 13. Excerpts from this work included in our text are quoted from this edition.

[13] Paul J. Glenn, *Psychology* (St. Louis: B. Herder Book Co., 1936), p. 294.

[14] Ricoeur, *op. cit.,* p. 143.

[15] Kierkegaard, *op. cit.,* p. 55.

[16] Charles Brenner, *An Elementary Textbook of Psychoanalysis* (New York: Doubleday & Co., Inc., 1955), p. 125.

[17] *Ibid.*

[18] Heinz Hartmann, *Psychoanalysis and Moral Values* (New York: International Universities Press, Inc., 1960), pp. 15–16.

[19] Karl A. Menninger, M.D., *A Manual for Psychiatric Case Study,* 2d ed. (New York: Grune and Stratton, 1962), p. 76.

[20] Joseph Fletcher, *Moral Responsibility* (Philadelphia: Westminster Press, 1952), Introduction.

[21] See Curran (1968) *op. cit.*

[22] Ricoeur, *op. cit.,* p. 144.

[23] *Ibid.,* p. 145.

[24] Rudolf Schnackenburg, *The Truth Will Make You Free* (New York: Herder and Herder, 1966), p. 117.

6

Religious Maturity and Positive Anxiety

IN BOTH a psychological and religious sense, therefore, there seems to be a destructive guilt that is immature, impeding, distorted and self-defeating, and a constructive guilt that is positive, strengthening and mature. In counseling therapy one can sometimes trace this process on a continuum. It begins in a negative self-attitude which includes an immature resistance to others and yet a dependence on them. Slowly the person acquires both a more positive self-regard and a more genuine courage to be independent and responsible.

In a religious context, one can see reflections of this continuum in the way people relate to religious concepts of sin and guilt. Actually, though, these religious attitudes seem no different from other life attitudes. They are, however, sometimes brought more sharply into focus through a person's concentrating on a specifically religious kind of conflict.

LATER COUNSELING COMMENT

To illustrate this and discuss it further, we have drawn from comments made by the person (Martha) whose interview we studied earlier. In the excerpt that follows, she is commenting on the effects of a series of twelve interviews on herself and her earlier difficulties. We can see here how religious and psychological factors and experiences are intimately interwoven.

This commentary was made at the end of twelve half-hour counseling interviews. This is *not* a counseling interview but a *direct discussion* after the twelfth interview. The interviewer's manner is, however, somewhat that of counseling insofar as he helps the person explore her reactions by both understanding what she is trying to say and at the same time synthesizing and clarifying her meaning. Its success is indicated by the way the client relaxedly and securely moves forward in her analysis of herself and her reactions—showing that she feels genuinely understood.

PERSONALITY DISTORTION

As the interview indicates, the anxieties about sin began about fourteen years before. While this excerpt does not give an adequate picture of all the personality dynamics involved, it does show one important point, namely, that "scruples" or anxieties of this sort about sin, are part of a whole personality profile and not simply an isolated moral phenomenon. This point is especially important for clergymen and others who may see such people only in a moral or religious context and relationship and consequently often do not have the chance to see the other ramifications of these personality distortions. The present excerpt shows how the "scruples" are only an end-product of a broader personality conflict state.

We previously noted how surprised Martha was that confession had become so much easier, although she did not discuss her confessional difficulties in the counseling interviews. This comment is repeated here again, after a longer period. The counseling process itself, as it often does, aided the anxiety without the sins being directly talked about. Work situation, home problems and similar areas often improve for the client as a result of counseling, even though they are not directly discussed and analyzed. These improvements come about rather because of basic changes in the client's attitude toward himself. As these attitudes change, many indirect changes seem to follow.

The commentary is given as it occurred. Brief observations are interjected on points of special significance.

Martha: Well, first of all, I have found it quite amazing myself that instead of spending this lengthy time preparing and trying to think of everything that I had done—uh—that I'm now able to go into the confessional and get it over with and it not be such a laborious task.

Co: It's a great deal easier and a great deal quicker now than it was.

Martha: And out of it, I think I have become aware that maybe even these scruples were a form of self-attack, too. In other words, accusing myself of sinning all the time. And now I don't feel as guilty in not trying to remember everything that I thought was sinful. And I think this was a thing that compelled me just to rack over things—uh—and try and remember everything because if I didn't, even though I could leave them out, I was afraid of feeling guilty. And now I don't feel that I have to. And I feel just as content.

Co: Now you don't feel guilty, so you just say what you remember, and you seem to be more at ease.

Martha: Yes. And leave all the other stuff, the way other people do.

ACTING OUT

Self-attack and rejection is one of the basic attitudes found in most people who come for counseling. Confessional scruples would apparently be one way for a Catholic to "act out" this sense of worthlessness by being unable to accept forgiveness of ordinary human failings. One's sense of worthlessness demands that one be worse than everyone else. In the light of this, it is interesting to note our earlier emphasis on the need for a genuine love of oneself as an important aspect of responsible maturity. The interview continues:

Martha: And then this, in turn, helps in another area. Before because confession was so distasteful, I wouldn't go for long periods. And then in between there was a self-disgust, because—uh—I had been away from confession for—you know—a month or two, or three months. And I'd know that I'd have to go back and I wouldn't go. This would generate more self-disgust. And usually I wouldn't be able to go to daily Mass. It was just one big circle.

Co: Again it was self-defeating, wasn't it? It turned it into a sort of vicious circle. You kept putting off confession, because you found it so difficult to go, and then you felt all the more guilty and self-attacking because you didn't go. And now that you can go regularly, without all those overtones, it makes you feel a lot better. So the whole picture, as I get it, is a great deal more positive, in your relationship to confession.

(NO CONSCIOUS EFFORT):

Martha: Umh-hm. But I must confess that there was no conscious effort on my part. That's just the way it happened to turn out.

Co: Uhm-hm. Yes, it seemed to follow the counseling process some way, but it wasn't something you were focused on.

Martha: No, I wasn't.

Co: This is very surprising to you since you weren't focused on it.

(PREVIOUS ANXIETY VALUE):

Martha: Yes, it's something that happened without my directing it that way. (*Laughs.*) You know, that there could be such a thing (*pause*), that I didn't have a hand in, directly.

Co: You're quite astonished that the counseling process itself would bring about this change. All other things you had to control or do something about, to bring about this change.

Martha: Yes, and the thing that I do notice is that I seem to have more will power, too. For instance, just to say: "We're not going to re-hash all that, and try to think of every-minute-thing that happened."

Co: You seem to have more control now to stop yourself. Before it was sort of automatic—you couldn't stop yourself.

Martha: Always with this wanting to spare myself of any guilt feeling of having left something out.

GROWING MATURITY

This self-defeating mechanism is also quite characteristic of people in the beginning of counseling interviews. One can see how, without skilled help, they can remain in this situation for even a lifetime. We notice too this person's surprise at the ease and suddenness with which the confessional agony seemed to have disappeared. This is always one of the surprising effects of a skilled counseling relationship, when areas not discussed at all seem to improve. What really happens, apparently, is that as a person assumes a more generally responsible and adult life-role, particular areas—in this case that of confession—begin to show the effects of this growing psychological maturity. The interview continues:

(BROADENED CHANGE):

Co: You're building up sort of positive attitudes that make it easier and easier for you to do it.

Martha: Uhm-hm. And I see this in other areas—it's not just this confession business.

Co: Uhm-hm. It's broadened out to be a whole series of positive developments and confession's just one of them.

Martha: Yes, but none so big as that . . . it's quite nice.

Co: You're very pleased with the change.

Martha: Yes, because when I consider how tortuous confession has been for such a long time—I know that it's hard for everybody to go. But it's senseless with the things that I had to tell—why I should make it such a big issue, when there's nothing that big that I ever have to say.

Co: It might be helpful if you would say how long you had this disturbance of scruples.

Martha: I think it started about in 1946.

Co: Fourteen years then. When did you notice this change now, would you say?

Martha: Last December.

Co: And how long had you been coming for counseling then?

Martha: Just a month.

Co: Just a month—and yet it's held now for three or four months.

Martha: Well, December was the time that it first struck me—then I had been away from confession about three months. But the experience itself wasn't enough to push me back to going to confession again (*laugh*) 'till recently. So it was another period of three months. And the experience repeated itself and seemed even much better. In the meantime, since that confession, things just don't bother me. Even as far as going to Communion in the morning. I mean I don't have to run through everything and figure out if I'm in the state of grace. So that these two weeks since my last confession, nothing has happened which will prevent me from going to confession anytime I want to now—which is usually the reason I push it off, you know.

Co: So you're just a lot freer to go to confession now. And you discovered this after putting it off for a while. Then you went back and you found it easy again. And so now you're encouraged to go more often, because it is easy. And you find each time that it holds up—that you can do it without all this worry or guilt.

(INSIGHT):

Martha: Yes, and it's been just recently that I kind of tied up the scruples with the self-attack business, and so that I seem to be able to settle things more. If there's a question of something being a sin, it seems that I can settle it one way or the other, without always trying to take the benefit of the doubt—I just seem to be able to do this better.

Co: You have more firmness of decision. You can discriminate better—and make the judgment on the spot.

Martha: Yes, and then once having decided about it, just to let it go. Yes, it's easier to do that. I don't say that I do it all the time, but it certainly seems to me a lot easier than it used to be. . . . And, as a matter of fact, not that many things even bother me, that I would even have to question.

Co: You're much more able to apply what you know now and judge on what you know, rather than doubting and making everything a sin.

Martha: Umh-hm. Yes, much better. But I'm not expecting a miracle —that this thing is really going to disappear overnight. But it seems to be moving better.

Co: Umh-hm. Yes. It's not a total overnight change, but it's better.

Martha: Umh-hm. And I like the practice—(*laughing*).

GAIN IN SELF-CONFIDENCE

Here the pattern of change begins to unfold. As she breaks into the self-defeating circle of self-attack and worthlessness she begins, among other things, to gain respect for her own judgments. Consequently there is less swaying and vacillating. We can see here how this affects her approach to confession. The interview continues:

Martha: It seems to me that there have been many good things and good changes—uh—but I seem to take them in stride. They're not maybe outstanding, but—well, for instance, at home, which was one of the trouble spots. Just this whole thing of being so irritable at home or not communicating when I felt that I was being dominated by my mother, *made to be the little girl,* then I'd pull back from this. I don't know if I can really judge this too well, because it seems like in the past couple months there haven't been too many times when I've even been inclined to be this way. And I don't know if that's positive, but it seems as though I can pass them off easier now, than if I'm inclined to be moody or to sulk about something, or made to feel the child.

Co: You aren't doing the things that cause it, as you were before, and you don't seem to be getting so moody or so disturbed.

Martha: Umh-hm. Umh-hm. Because it's the initial set-off. I mean if I let myself—

Co: You seem again to be able to control this now, more, rather than letting it happen to you. So home's a lot better, too, in that sense that somehow you can control these reactions in yourself.

Martha: Umh-hm. And then, too, I think the thing that bothered me so much was this feeling of being dominated and being a little girl at home. I don't have this feeling so much anymore.

Co: You feel more like an adult at home.

Martha: Yes, I do. I really do and I think that's probably why that other situation is keeping away—because the feeling is gone.

Co: You're beginning to feel *really* like an adult, aren't you? Even at home.

Martha: I do! I even feel it at work . . . .

(VALUE CHANGE):

Co: So you're actually an adult now, even in your own feeling system, whereas before you were always feeling a little girl.

Martha: Umh-hm. You remember how much I wanted to feel that I was grown up—I just at least had that feeling about myself. Whether these things will come back, I don't know. But I'm, you know, just recounting this much.

Co: Yes. This is the way it is. You're always (*client begins to laugh*) vaguely thinking it might all come back again, but as of now it's quite noticeably changed, hm?

Martha: Umh-hm. But as I say, it seems that the changes are so much a part of everything else that they are always imperceptible. You know, that they come (*pause*)—

Co: Piece by piece.

Martha: Yes, exactly. And this confession, because it is (*pause*)—

Co: A focal point.

ADULT SELF-CONCEPT

Basically this feeling of being a little girl would appear to be one of the core self-concepts behind Martha's more general immaturity and, indirectly, her confessional irresponsibility. Obviously, before counseling, she resented intensely this attitude in herself, but it was an unconstructive and frustrated resentment. It apparently brought no real maturing changes. Rather she projected her resentment outward, blaming her mother and the home. Now while these factors no doubt influenced the development of this arrested maturity, we notice that as Martha herself assumes more responsible attitudes, the mother and the other people in the home accept and cooperate with these changes. This, too, is surprising to her.

This often happens in counseling. As the person himself changes in his own self-attitudes, other people begin to treat him differently. Before, he often was blaming them for his situation. Now he is able to see more clearly that the responsibility for how others treat him lies with himself. The interview continues:

(WORK CHANGE):

Martha: Oh, and another thing: I go to bed regularly now! I don't stay up till twelve midnight, twelve-thirty, one o'clock every night. But I get to bed at a reasonable hour, and I get up feeling much better. And I've been on time for work for two months, which is for me a record. They have even noticed this at work, that I make a real effort to—that it's not a struggle, really, to start the day.

Co: So this too is a striking change, your whole life is more orderly now, and you can get to bed and get up. You couldn't do this before.

(INSIGHT):

Martha: No, I felt more the desire to stay up and read. I suppose this was compensating for not doing anything constructive during the evening. Umh-hm, but now I see it as part, too—as a health concern, too. You know that to try to live on five or six hours a night steadily for a couple years is no good.

Co: Now you have real motives for going to bed and you're actually able to do it now. And at work and everywhere else they notice that you're more able to control this and be on time. And you yourself feel better by getting more sleep.

Martha: Very definitely. I shouldn't take the credit really for this being all health-motivated, because recently I've had well, really since the beginning, I've had so much difficulty relaxing enough at night to go to sleep right away. So that, if I get in bed early enough, I will pretty well get the required number of hours of sleep. And—uh—there's another thing in here, too. Before, I was always the last one in the house to get to bed at night; now I'm not the first but usually about the second. So there's always, there's usually someone up. And it seems that—this may be not so good—but I feel better if—

Co: More secure.

Martha: Yes, I do. Umh-hm. Because I'm afraid that if I don't sleep and I become upset, that I'm there—quite alone in this thing. And that has happened several times. And it's—just not a pleasant experience.

Co: Yes, you're less anxious if you go to bed earlier.

Martha: Umh-hm. Umh-hm. And I think that probably as I get more relaxed and not as fearful, as night comes, about not being able to sleep, that I can go back to what it was before.

Co: Well, thank you very much for your comments.

BASIC ANXIETY

Here we see revealed a fundamental anxiety—an anxiety whose ramifications probably affect almost everything this woman does. This was and continued to be the main focus of subsequent interviews. As her confidence and acceptance of herself grew, this anxiety slowly, imperceptibly decreased. Some months later, for example, she was able to take a long trip to a large, strange city —a thing previously inconceivable to her. By such real-life achievements, mature self-reliance and responsible judgments increasingly assert themselves in the formation of those things which generally constitute a psychologically adult person. "Scruples" are apparently just one symptom of a generally arrested development. As psychological maturity is furthered, the "scruples" apparently decrease proportionately.

Distorted guilt, then, like the nightmare images of the small child, are immature in a religious as well as a psychological sense. Maturity involves, as we have seen, the pursuit of basic personal values that are in some way also shared by others. At the same time, maturity is the capacity both to love self and yet to offer oneself as a genuine gift to others.

STRIVING AND LONGING

Such conceptions are related to two main and continually recurring religious impulses or "thrusts" that the Judaeo-Christian tradition introduces. The *first* is the movement toward maturity: the "anxious striving" to be a mature and responsible religious person as well as a psychologically and physically mature person. The *second* is a profound sense of the transiency of all immediate goals, but not their rejection—and consequently an "anxious longing" for lasting fulfillment, and ultimate being and becoming in an increasing participation in the person and being of God. We might, therefore, summarize these two thrusts as an "anxious striving" to total maturity and an "anxious longing" for finally being oneself in Divine Being.

RELIGIOUS MATURITY

In proportion as a person in the counseling therapy process is religious, he often applies anxious concern to the rethinking of his relationship with God. In this rethinking process, he sees this relationship as more mature, responsible, honest, independent, and really "loving" in place of an artificial and self-protective fear of God or a childishly immature and often somewhat irresponsible dependency.

Although he may often not realize it, in this the person is in fact demonstrating the deepest concepts of Judaeo-Christian mature and responsible religious growth. This in no way contradicts becoming "as little children," as Christ directs. We can distinguish the childlikeness, the candor, the directness that is characteristic of a spiritually and psychologically mature person from the childishness of the infantile or pusillanimous person. There is, therefore, in the spiritual process the same anxious striving for religious maturity that one finds in the basic drives for other kinds of independent and responsible maturity. A religious dimension in the believer is interrelated to and interwoven with these common, positive, anxious concerns.

ILLUSTRATION

To demonstrate what we mean here, let us examine an excerpt from a recorded counseling interview with a woman graduate student (Fran). In this excerpt the woman is in the midst of an intense and thorough personal re-evaluation. In the previous interviews of this series, she had unfolded and clarified for herself that while college and graduate work were satisfying achievements, they still left her feeling that she had no value as a person. This was the same worthless feeling which she had had almost as long as she could remember. She was able to trace the origin of this to some of her earliest childhood experiences when, for a very short period only, she remembered herself as being accepted and loved. Then, with the coming of a younger sister and a switch in family circumstances, she became definitely a burden, particularly to her mother. From here on, in her home life, she could only remember veiled criticism and rejection coupled with adolescent antagonism from the younger sister because she, the elder, was physically more attractive and more socially acceptable. The mother, too, seemed to foster this antagonism because she preferred the younger sister.

In the interviews she has come finally to accept herself as a person of worth and meaning, and she now finds that she must establish a whole new personal plan of life. Her re-evaluation goes beyond her relationship to herself and others and penetrates through to her relationship with God:

Fran: I was thinking—as a result of that last interview, it was almost like a rebirth again. As I thought about it during the week, I realized that the same thing I had felt before in relation to all other people, I felt also in relation to God. *I don't think I could feel that God could really love me.* (CHANGE) But as a result of that interview and now here, I really see that very clearly.

I can go along so long and pray and then all of a sudden I'm back again to the very beginning and I feel as though I've never had anything in a spiritual way. And I think that's the reason, because I just can't feel that it can be so (*cries softly*), that I could have value in God's eyes.

MATURE BEING ONESELF

Later she says (NEW VALUE):

I guess I'm just glad to be able to face these things now. But, I'm afraid to talk about them too—because they are so meaningful that I don't want any of that artificiality (*pause*), which I am so capable of, to spoil them. (*She speaks very slowly, seemingly having difficulty controlling her voice.*)

What we see here is a growth of self—the new birth of a mature person—a true being oneself. This is a growth away from artificiality and withdrawal. It is motivated by a positive anxiety to be honest with oneself, to face and accept responsibility for oneself, to become a genuinely mature person who is at the same time a religiously mature person. Both strivings for maturity are interwoven and unified.

CORRESPONDENT BEYOND

Consequently, in this first religious thrust of anxious striving, we are not changing the nature of man's struggle for maturity in all its psychosomatic components as Selye[1] might describe them, nor in its id-ego-superego conflicts as Freud would see them. These issues still remain. The Judaeo-Christian tradition would simply add a further force and dimension.

This force and dimension is as strong and extensive as the person's faith in a Divine Being and his conviction of a particular religion as the voice of that Being. Put another way, intense and intelligent religious faith introduces another voice into the counseling or therapeutic dialogue and diagnosis because it introduces another—in this case supernatural or correspondent—Person into one's hope and love relationship. The intensity of a person's religious faith, his religious investment or commitment in other words, will determine how loudly or softly he hears this voice and how important its presence is to him. Assuming a strong religious faith, however, we have in this striving for a mature religious self an often untapped source for growth. This does not change the person's struggle and conflict in gaining maturity but adds—in proportion to his religious faith—a concomitant weak or strong new positive force and dimension to all his positive anxious concerns.

In his discussion of dreams Freud remarks, "Anxiety is only fastened onto the idea that accompanied it and is really derived from another source."[2] The Judaeo-Christian tradition would make this ultimate source of anxiety—whatever its more immediate sources might be—the intense desire to possess and to belong to a Divine Person who is Love itself.

That is to say, as the sun permeates the earth with its light, so Divine Love, in the Judaeo-Christian tradition, permeates every human love and relationship. Stated again in the words of John: "He that loveth not his brother whom he seeth, how can he love God whom he seeth not?"

If we put this in the Judaic analogy found in the Psalms, we have the religious man as the explorer, struggling through the complex underbrush or hot sands of daily living, or finding his footing, when he is sinking in mire, on the rock that is God, as the Psalmist says. But in this tortuous journey he always can see in the distance, as the sixty-eighth Psalm says, "the hill which God desireth to dwell in; yea, the Lord will dwell in . . . forever." This awareness encourages and guides him so that he is never wholly lost, and yet offers him a final goal and destiny that gives meaning to his journey and its joys and sorrows. Or, as in the Psalm that remains perhaps the most consoling and reassuring statement of the Judaeo-Christian faith, he has the Good Shepherd to lead him to green pastures.

Here, too, however, as with the first thrust of anxious striving, the second thrust of anxious longing is not separated from all other longings of an immediate and pressing nature, as we might see them, for example, in counseling and psychotherapy. Rather, all these immediate longings are intimately interwoven. There is no other-worldly removal or withdrawal. In the mainstream of the Judaeo-Christian tradition, the religious "anxious longing" is part of all the other positive anxious longings that make up the motivations of a man's strivings. As the sun permeates the earth and the traveler must go through the underbrush, mire and sand to the mountain, so the religious longing permeates and is integrated with all other human goals and purposes.

We thus find man in a transitional state. He is both being and becoming himself and straining painfully to get beyond the limits of himself. He has in this sense, as Sartre, quoted earlier, says, "the project to be God."[3] And this can be his suffering too. Every becoming, with all its achievement and sense of fulfillment, brings with it the corresponding threat and anxiety of its possible loss. He cannot of himself find any final security or non-transient Being. Thus the human counterpart seems to call out for its divine correspondent, if the anxiety and sense of loss built into man's existential state and threatening his every achievement are to be finally assuaged.

In a poem of Baudelaire aptly entitled "Correspondance," one gets a sense of this strange and anxious longing even in man's corruption:

> La Nature est un temple où de vivants piliers
> Laissent parfois sortir de confuses paroles;
> L'homme y passe à travers des forêts de symboles
> Qui l'observent avec des regards familiers.
>
> Comme de longs échos qui de loin se confondent
> Dans une ténébréuse et profonde unité,
> Vaste comme la nuit et comme la clarté,
> Les parfums, les couleurs et les sons se répondent.[4]

The potential of the counseling or psychotherapeutic relationship—significant as it is—is yet limited by this finite and transitory state of the human condition. In this sense it concerns "echoes from the beyond" as well as present sounds. Behind every striving to be and to become there seems to be the foreshadowing of a Being for which any becoming—implying an absence—has no meaning. As in Baudelaire's lines, it is as if one hears in every therapeutic dialogue mysterious words whose overtones extend beyond to the Eternal. Each human being and becoming then—in its fulfillment and its corruption—seems, in a way, to beckon to this beyond—to *choses infinies*. As Baudelaire concluded:

> Il est des parfums frais comme des chairs d'enfants,
> Doux comme les hautbois, verts comme les prairies,
> Et d'autres, corrompus, riches et triomphants.
>
> Ayant l'expansion des choses infinies,
> Comme l'ambre, le musc, le benjoin et l'encens,
> Qui chantent les transports de l'esprit et des sens.[5]

NOTES

[1] Hans Selye, *The Stress of Life* (New York: McGraw-Hill, 1956).
[2] Sigmund Freud, "The Interpretation of Dreams," *Standard Edition of*

the Complete Psychological Works of Sigmund Freud, 4, 5 (New York: Modern Library, 1950), p. 236.

³ Sartre, *op. cit.,* p. 63.

⁴   "All nature is a temple whose living pillars seem
      At times to babble confused words, half understood;
      Man journeys there through an obscure symbolic wood,
      Aware of eyes that peep with a familiar gleam.

   "Like endless echoes that from somewhere far beyond,
      Mingling, in one profound and cryptic whole unite,
      Vast as the twin immensities of night and light,
      So do all colours, sounds, and perfumes correspond."
—From *Flowers of Evil,* by Charles Baudelaire. Trans. George Dillon and Edna St. Vincent Millay. Copyright 1936, 1962, by George Dillon. Reprinted by permission of Harper and Row, pp. 160–161.

⁵   "Perfumes there are as fresh as children's bodies, springs
      Of fragrance sweet as oboes, green and full of peace
      As prairies. And there are others, proud, corrupt, intense,

   "Having the all-pervasiveness of infinite things,
      Like burning spice or resin, mush or ambergris,
      That sing the raptures of the spirit and the sense."
                                                —Ibid.

7

Masculinity, Femininity and Persons in Union

IN A PAPER entitled "The Impact of Psychotherapy on Theological Thought" Tillich says:

One can say that psychotherapy has replaced the emphasis on the demanding yet remote God by an emphasis on his self-giving nearness. It is the modification of the image of the threatening father—which was so important in Freud's attack on religion—by elements of the image of the embracing and supporting mother. If I were permitted to express a bold suggestion, I would say that psychotherapy and the experience of pastoral counseling have helped to re-introduce the female element, so conspicuously lacking in most Protestantism, into the idea of God. The impact of psychotherapy and the experiences of pastoral counseling on the idea of man and of God necessarily have consequences for an understanding of the relation between God and men.[1]

MASCULINITY AND FEMININITY

Tillich suggests that counseling, psychotherapy and religion share, in a sense, this quality of femininity—that is, beyond the masculine elements they obviously involve, they contain too, subtle feminine aspects we are only slowly growing to understand. The psychological complexities and the model implied here not only relate counseling, psychotherapy and religion but also involve the whole question of the mature and creative psychological and religious personality.

The feminine religious element, "this self-giving nearness . . . of the embracing and supporting mother," may suggest the Catholic concept of devotion to Mary. While Mary in this concept is obviously not to be identified with God, yet, in Tillich's terms, Catholicism would in this regard seem to have a greater "female element" than Protestantism. But the question is broader than this since it really involves a basic religious and psychological approach both to Woman and to God through woman. Consequently we will consider the religious feminine element as including those aspects in which the Woman, Mary, the Church and the People of God are biblically taken together as interrelated symbols or prophetic images and psychological models.

SUMMARY

We must first, however, consider in greater detail the psychological implications of masculine and feminine elements. We will then briefly discuss this biblical concept of woman. We will also examine some evidence that "creative" people seem to exhibit feminine as well as masculine components functioning constructively together in the same person. Similar to this, in marriage counseling, a continuum emerges which begins by emphasizing masculine and feminine differences and contrasts and moves toward a sense of unity, of persons and of mutual regard and respect.

This consideration will lead us finally to change our model from masculinity and femininity to a model based on the concept of the Trinity Itself—a model of Persons in Union. Psychological relationships of masculinity and femininity would, from this view, lead to the ultimate implication of an Augustinian Trinitarian concept-model: of unified loving Persons who are the complete fulfillment of their own personality and are at the same time perfectly related in a timeless love in perfect equality. This seems to be the goal toward which human relationships tend, granting that in themselves they can, of course, only remain in process.

PERSONALITY POLARITY

In recent psychological literature dealing with counseling, psychotherapy, personality assessment and related areas, the human person is not considered simply as either exclusively masculine or feminine, as his sex might designate. Rather qualities, tendencies and characteristics considered analogously as either masculine or feminine are now seen as interwoven in varying degrees in the same person, in himself and as he relates to others.

There is no implication here of homo- or heterosexual tendencies. Rather it is a model of two forces or trends in the same personality. So, relationships and attitudes can be regarded as masculine or feminine irrespective of whether they are exhibited by, or refer to, a man or a woman.

The nature of the creative personality, then, may in a certain sense be considered a combination of these masculine and feminine elements. In the agency of the self, the person's ability to use himself to his best capacity implies qualities from both categories. These same qualities seem also to be implicit in mature and creative relationships among people. As Tillich suggests, this has further implications too for the God-and-man relationship.

ACCEPTING FEMININITY

In the light of the fact that an adequate and positive self-concept is necessary in counseling therapy, in personal maturity and in a person's capacity to give himself to others in love, one can see the importance of the way a person has grown to regard masculinity and femininity through his past and present experience. His (or her) relationship with mother, sisters and others, for example, might in large measure predetermine how he relates psychologically to the feminine elements in himself, in his relationship to others and in his religious and prayer dialogue. A man or woman's attempting to function as a counselor in an understanding way, being a client in counseling or psychotherapy, or other similar relationship, could at first arouse deep resistance, which may in fact be elements of masculine protest and evidence of negative feminine relationships in his or her earlier life. Maximum creativity might also be impeded for similar reasons.

This might also lead to blockings in any kind of feminine psychological or religious conceptualization or modality. When religion is now considered to be "not a conquest but a service,"[2] this might suggest a feminine as well as a masculine element. That is, a mature person's view of religion would seem to involve feminine service elements, and not simply aggressive masculine aspects, if he is to function at the best level of himself and others.

To paraphrase Aristotle, one might say that the beginning of friendly relationships with feminine elements external to the self would consist in friendly relationship with the feminine element in the self. Attitudes like a man's psychological difficulty with woman figures or a woman's conscious or unconscious resistance to femininity in herself or others might seriously impede or distort any relationship which suggests a feminine element.

CHANGING VIEWPOINT

Applying this to counseling and psychotherapy, we might say that earlier ideas of helping people were, in a psychological sense, much more masculine; that is, they centered on instructing, lecturing, directing, guiding, reprimanding and similar confronting or advice-giving relationships. They told people what to do—in a somewhat masculinely oriented way. These kinds of relationships are, of course, of real value, and they therefore continue to be necessary in a wide variety of circumstances. But as we have seen, more recent research and development has added another relationship that has focused on words like "understanding," "sensitivity," "reflection"—words which in Tillich's sense suggest a more "feminine element."

To be deeply understood by another person in this feminine sense, not simply at the level of ideas but at the much deeper level of emotional, instinctive and somatic reactions, can be, as we are aware, a most salutary kind of communication. But this sense of being understood does not of itself imply that the counselor, therapist, or friend offered any solution, or even any advice. He did not suddenly rescue the person from his personal turmoil or even try to. It is here that the feminine element is most evident. What we see in counseling and psychotherapy and in the experience with an understanding friend is that somehow we are strengthened, encouraged and even profoundly helped by a sensitive kind of acceptance and sharing which, however, does not try to tell us what to do or even to change us. Yet this can enable us to begin to change ourselves, often more effectively than advice or reprimand—more masculine forms. These, on the contrary, may only make us more resistant and fix us more firmly in our state of conflict.

The person is better able to handle his situation as a result of this kind of understanding dialogue, is stronger and more perceptive of himself when he leaves. Much more could be said, of course, of the extremely complicated interweaving of masculine and feminine elements that inevitably enter into a counseling-psychotherapeutic process, just as they go into any significant friendship. But in these qualities of the loving acceptance, of "unconditional positive regard,"[3] at moments of deep and sometimes shameful communication, we have one of the most subtle demonstrations of how this feminine element operates to facilitate therapy and personality growth.

DIALOGUE WITH GOD

André Feuillet points out that

Man's greatness is focused by the Bible on the fact that he can enter into dialogue with God, as contrasted with the Greek stress upon his abstract reflection on what God is in Himself.[4]

Biblically, the figure of Woman, Mary and the Church enter into this dialogue as the feminine element. Speaking of the symbol of Woman used in the Fourth Gospel and the Apocalypse to represent the Church, Feuillet says:

In recent times much has been written about the woman in Apoc. 12. Some authors like to think that this symbol represents primarily or even exclusively the Virgin Mary. The references to the Old Testament (the Isaian texts of the glorified Sion giving birth: 66:7–8; 26:17–18; cf. Songs 6:10) show clearly, however, that the woman of this wonderfully enchanting vision is the ideal Sion of the prophets who, once she has given Christ to the world, becomes the Christian Church. Like the people of the old covenant, she lives in the desert protected and fed by God while awaiting the parousia (6:14). If the Virgin Mary is seen here secondarily (and we think She ought to be, at least in the first verses of the Chapter), this can be only as an incarnation of the people of God; in fact, it is through her that the Church has given the Messia to the world. As Mother of the Messia, Mary is simultaneously the image of the Christian Church through which her Son is daily given to souls through preaching and the sacraments . . .[5]

FEMININE ELEMENT

Biblically considered, then, we see the suggestion that God's dialogue with man introduces, as do other forms of deep psychological dialogue, a feminine as well as a masculine element. In this dialogue, biblical concepts of the Church as Woman could be said to present religious qualities of feminine sensitivity, understanding and love. These are the same qualities which modern psychological research is revealing as basic elements to any complete and profound human dialogue.

CREATIVE TENSION

This interweaving of masculine and feminine elements has some further implications. Recent studies in creativity suggest that creativity results from an inner blend of characteristics in the personality of each creative person. When we examine what these creative inner states are, it is interesting to note that they too are characterized by the same blend of masculinity and femininity that we notice in the successful counseling and psychotherapeutic relationships and see symbolized theologically in the relationship of the Church to God.

"All the highly creative male groups studied," one study concludes, "scored high on a femininity test. They were more open in their feelings and emotions, more sensitively aware of themselves and others, possessing a wide range of interests—traits which in our culture are considered feminine. On the other hand, most of them were not effeminate in manner or appearance but instead assertive, dominant and self-confident."[6]

We see here a balance between characteristics that are open, loving, accepting, and those that are closed, determined and definite; a contrast, in other words, between feminine and masculine characteristics. According to this study, in creative persons neither masculine nor feminine characteristics predominate but both exist in a subtle and balanced polarity. Possibly the tensions produced in such personalities by somewhat opposite characteristics are accountable for the creative achievements of such people.

As these tensions are resolved in the process of a significant achievement, the creative person's peaceful fulfillment, inner balance and outstanding accomplishment seem to result. "Other findings," the study continues, "support the hypothesis that creative individuals are more able than most to give expression to opposite sides of their nature, to achieve a reconciliation of the conscious and unconscious, reason and passion, rational and irrational, science and art."[7] We do not have, in other words, a simple picture of either a purely masculine, dominant personality or a feminine reflective one. It is rather the integration of these apparently conflicting attitudes that seems to characterize a creative person as seen by the data here.

COMPLETION

This relationship of masculinity and femininity has further implications for the relationship of men and women themselves. Biblically, St. Paul suggests that the relationship of the husband to the wife is as Christ's to the Church: the man should love the woman as he loves his own body. (Eph. 5:25–33)

The mature man is here seen as psychologically extending himself to the woman. At the highest level of the marriage relationship, for example, she is presented as in a sense the extension and completion of his own body. He loves her, not as something external to himself, but with the same intimate identification with which he loves his own members.

FEMININE CONVALIDATION

There is, too, a special kind of "consensual validation"[8] in the way Christ is said to sanctify the Church and in the way this is held up as the model whereby man is to relate to woman. Implied here, therefore, is the idea that the way a man sees a woman will determine the attitudes he radiates to her. She in turn, absorbing this attitude, will then also tend to look at herself in the same way. The feminine element is here seen as empathetic and reflective, as the highly sensitized response of the beloved to the lover. It was Juliet who, at the high point of her love, saw Romeo not simply as another man but as a kind of god capable of turning her into his image of her.

The image of woman thus presented reflects her at a high level of her state as a person. Such high regard of herself, especially when it is reflected to her by a man, could in turn be an effective element in elevating her own self-regard. Moreover, an increasing awareness of the religious feminine image in the relationship of the Church to God should have a significant influence on her attitude toward herself and her role as a woman.

MARRIAGE-COUNSELING PROCESS

The relationship of men and women as revealed in marriage counseling also has some more general implications around the concept of masculine and feminine elements. In marriage counseling one frequently observes a kind of continuum. Counseling begins with two people who feel quite distant from one another in a variety of ways. In this distance they are focused on the degree of difference between them. They seem to have comparatively little in common. Most often the focal point of these differences will consist in the highly accentuated masculinity of the one, contrasted with the evident femininity of the other. It may be sexual incompatibility that is one of the strongest differences they first emphasize. This may be evident in other ways if they insist on a strong sexual compatibility. Sometimes the sex difference may assume a reverse emphasis—the woman complaining that she is forced to be too masculine because of the man's passivity. Alternately, the man can resent the woman's aggressiveness, excessive sexual or affectionate demands, etc., which he feels threaten and thwart his normal masculinity. But whatever form such opening interviews take, they generally seem to center on this sense of difference and distance between man and wife.

REGARD AS PERSONS

As the counseling process continues, however, there can be a clearly marked line in the direction of quite different attitudes. There is often a decreasing emphasis on sexuality and sexual differences and a slow but steady movement toward attempts to regard one another as persons. They begin to see one another less superficially. With greater depth and subtlety they move from an "outer" to an "inner" view. From this, mutual respect begins to grow again, and with it comes a far greater sense of unity, belonging and mutual commitment. Marked differences still remain, but they are less differences of sexual masculinity and femininity and more differences of the uniqueness of two persons communicating themselves through their predominating masculine or feminine elements.

One may observe, too, a sensitivity beginning to develop between them. They speak of really "understanding" one another, sometimes for the first time. But this "understanding" cuts through exaggerated sex differences to become a mutually shared double language of personal commitment and communion as well as communication. The focus is no longer on the contrast between masculine and feminine elements but is now on a more unified image of their belongingness as persons. Yet this unity heightens rather than diminishes their sense of and respect for the unique qualities of each. Often they say they never realized this kind of uniqueness in one another before—they were too much focused on sexual differences. Yet interestingly—and even strangely—this increased recognition of themselves as unique persons does not separate them, as an earlier emphasis on sex-differences did, but brings a greater sense of unity, belonging and mutual commitment.

PERSON MODEL

In this process, we are shifting the model from masculine and feminine elements to a more unified model. These differing elements are fused together and their relationship now seems to have as its goal a unified love of self and of one another. At this level we have moved from a model centering on masculinity and femininity to one suggested by both the unity and the relationship of Persons

in the Trinity. We will consider this model in the next chapter
especially in its relationship to counseling and psychotherapy.

Eliade, interestingly, cites both scriptural and apocryphal writings to suggest that this convergence of man and woman to a
common sense of person was not strange to early Christians:

Doresse refers to some parallels in the New Testament (*John,* XVII,
II, 20–23; *Romans,* XII, 4–5; I *Corinthians,* XII, 27; etc.). Outstand-
ingly important is *Galatians* III, 28: "There is neither Jew nor Greek,
there is neither bond nor free, there is neither male nor female: for ye
are all one in Christ Jesus." This is the unity of primal creation, before
the making of Eve, when "man" was neither male nor female (Grant,
p. 144). According to the *Gospel of Philip* (codex X of Khenoboskion)
the division of the sexes—the creation of Eve taken from the body
of Adam—was the principle of death. "Christ came to re-establish
what was thus (divided) in the beginning and to reunite the two. Those
who died because they were in separation he will restore to life by re-
uniting them!" (Doresse, II, p. 157.)

Other writings contain similar passages on the reunion of the sexes
as an image of the Kingdom. When asked at what moment the Kingdom would come, the Lord himself replied: "When the two shall be
one, the outside like the inside, the male with the female neither male
nor female." (*Second Epistle of Clement,* quoted in Doresse, II, 157.)
The quotation from the *Epistle of Clement* probably derives from the
Gospel according to the Egyptians, of which Clement of Alexandria
has preserved this passage: "When Salome inquired when the things
concerning which she asked would be known, the Lord said, 'When
you have trampled on the garment of shame and when the two become one and the male with the female is neither male nor female.' "
(*Stromates,* III, 13, 92; Doresse, II, 158. Translation M. R. James,
The Apocryphal New Testament, p. 11.)[9]

So, counseling, psychotherapy, creativity and marriage as well
as the theological images of the dialogue between God and man,
all contain and transcend the contrasting differences that might be
considered masculine and feminine elements and point in the
direction of a unity that does not erase but embraces and harmo-
nizes these apparently opposite characteristics. Aristotle remarks
that God is what man is (and for our purpose we can add woman)
at his best, and that infinitely more. At their best, psychotherapy,

creativity and marriage, beginning in the tension of diversity, end in the direction of harmony and unity. But this movement toward unity does not diminish, but rather heightens, the uniqueness of each person.

DEMANDING CHALLENGE

It has already become apparent through our discussion that to allow for and realize feminine as well as masculine elements involves a highly complex process. To establish a genuine relationship in counseling, psychotherapy or friendship; to be a significant creative person; to achieve a successful marriage—all these pose real difficulties as well as exciting challenges.

It would not be surprising, then, that such a feminine religious element as Tillich proposes might also meet with some complicated psychological reactions in both men and women. As the psychological process of understanding and integrating the feminine element makes high demands on individuals and relationships, so the theological process must make equal, if not more exacting, demands. There is here, therefore, much more than simple sentiment or emotion. A purely sentimental devotion to the image of woman in the person of Mary or as the People of God, the Church, would only suggest the complicated psychological process we are treating here. It would, at best, probably be an early stage. This helps explain why the concept of Mary or the biblical image of the Church as Woman is often not easy for people to accept. Such a model, seen psychologically, calls into play at its deepest level a person's whole relationship with himself and with others. It would seem to imply not only the highest regard for femininity and some ease in regard to a feminine image but also a profound sense of persons in both man and woman. One would have to have this both toward himself and others for an adequate theological encounter with a feminine element.

Until this is reached, one could envision a conflict and tension—confronting the feminine religious element—somewhat similar to that which we witness in beginning counseling or psychotherapeutic relationships, in the initial stages of creativity, and in the early periods of marriage conflict and tension. We are describing, therefore, not a static state but a dynamic process involving factors which are the same as, or similar to, those which lead to psychological maturity and fulfillment in each individual person.

In this discussion, we are not pretending to resolve all the complexities which are introduced into counseling, psychotherapy and religion by the consideration of masculine and feminine elements. Rather, we have attempted to extend the implications of Tillich's comment and to explore the possibility that an exclusively masculine model does not fit either a counseling therapeutic dialogue or the characteristic integration of a creatively mature person or, biblically considered, the dialogue between God and man. All these seem also to call for feminine elements if constructive and mature relationships of the highest kind are to be established and maintained. Yet these contrasting elements do not work in the direction of diversity but point toward unity. The model of unified masculine and feminine elements also could be thought to suggest, at the highest level, the Augustinian model of a unity of Persons in God as an ideal toward which all human love relationships finally tend. We will consider this in greater detail in the next section.

NOTES

[1] Paul J. Tillich, "The Impact of Psychotherapy on Theological Thought," *Pastoral Psychology,* February 1960.

[2] Pope Paul VI, *Time,* June 28, 1963, p. 42.

[3] Rogers, *On Becoming a Person,* pp. 47–49.

[4] André Feuillet, S.S., "The Era of the Church in St. John," *Theology Digest,* 11 (1963), p. 4.

[5] *Ibid.*

[6] "Creativity," *Carnegie Corporation of New York Quarterly,* 9 (1961), p. 3.

[7] *Ibid.*

[8] Harry Stack Sullivan, *The Interpersonal Theory of Psychiatry* (New York: W. W. Norton Co., 1953), pp. 224–225.

[9] From *Mephistopheles and the Androgyne: Studies in Religious Myth and Symbol* by Mircea Eliade, © in the English translation of Harvill Press, London, and Sheed and Ward, Inc., New York, 1965, pp. 106–107.

Toward a Theology of Human Belonging

PART THREE

Toward a Theology of

Human Belonging

8
Man: A Being in Correspondence Beyond

IN OUR DISCUSSION thus far, we have made repeated reference to man's striving to be and become beyond himself. We have also spoken of a parallel or correspondence between man's psychological process toward maturity and an inner value system and the demands religion makes for a similar kind of "putting away the things of a child."

In this present section, we wish to look directly at these concepts and at their religious psychological implications. Like the drawing of the ambiguity staircase where one sees the stairs descending or ascending, depending on whether the blocks are seen as convex or concave, so one can see this concept of "correspondence" as theological or psychological depending on one's focus. Consequently, conceptions generally considered theological can also shed significant light on the nature of man himself and on the encounter between men.

This is evident in the personalist way in which man has regarded God and in the implication of the process of incarnation and redemption. That is, "correspondence" is shown in the manner in which the Trinity and incarnation-redemption can be viewed not only in a religious sense but also a description of a psychological relationship and process. This is demonstrated in counseling and psychotherapy, and one can pattern educative relationships from this model.

In this correspondence, while there is obviously a basic difference between the relationship of man with God and counseling therapy or educational relationships, these can nevertheless support and reinforce one another. Such psychological consideration brings

175

an added richness to the religious side of these concepts in that it invests them with a deeper and more intense involvement in the human condition. We might say that it gives the psychological substructure for a *theology of human belonging*.

It is not our intent here, then, to discuss these theological concepts in detail. They are, in themselves, well known. We wish rather to show that in the tradition of man's relationship to God, there is a corresponding theme that applies to man's relationship with himself and other men.

RELEVANT BEYOND

Religious values, then, are *in* but go *beyond* immediate human concerns. They involve being and becoming in God. Religious faith—and the hope and love that follow—is a present human commitment to and engagement in this divine potential and continuum made possible by a belief in a redeeming communication with God in all the richness that is implied in any deeply communicative friendship. In this sense, we might speak of a present or "relevant beyond."

This relationship is traditionally called "supernatural" to emphasize its total Otherness and the fact that such redemptive love could not be humanly merited but could come only from God. But the word "super" alone may seem to imply, in our present understanding of it, only a remote relationship. "Super" used between persons, for example, can suggest a state of nonbelonging and even alienation from the one considered to be inferior. Or it can give the tone of complete removal and contrast, as in the title "Man and Superman." It can also imply the confused and distorted directives of a "super" ego. "Supernatural" can now also be thought to mean a kind of magician's skill. Consequently the word "super" as reflecting man's relationship with God may need to be extended and clarified. We have therefore added the terms "correspondence" and "beyond" to extend and clarify the concept of "supernatural," so as not to suggest to modern sensibilities the notion of removal. In adding other terms we are emphasizing the divine relevance to man. In this, we are not intending to change its original, traditional meaning.

CORRESPONDENCE

Paintings, for example, that fuse sea and sky, off in the horizon, give this sense of both "correspondence" and the "beyond." Or as Tennant has remarked, in classic Dutch and Italian paintings it was the artists' practice to give a

drawing-room or kitchen in which there is a window open, through which you see the masts of ships, or a strip of grey sea, or vistas or colonnades or a balcony, a garden or a court. . . .

The experience afforded the viewer here

is essentially one of gazing *beyond the immediate scene* to a timeless sky or a timeless room, in which the future and the past, the unspoken and the unknown, forever beckon. . . .[1]

Like these paintings, religious values introduce this "gazing beyond the immediate scene." Religion then can be said to represent not only the vertical "supernatural" but also the horizontal "correspondence beyond" in that it always invokes in each experience resonances like "extended echoes that from the beyond mingle together in a confused and profound unity."[2] These "echoes from the beyond" correspond and fulfill each present experience, giving a sense of an extended continuum to each immediate meaning. They are relevant to any immediate experience. They give religious context to it.

Carnap and others have used the term "correspondence"[3] to relate the observable to the nonobservable:

But now we come up against a difficult problem. Our theoretical laws deal exclusively with the behavior of molecules, *which cannot be seen.* How, therefore, can we deduce from such laws a law about observable properties such as the pressure or temperature of a gas or properties of sound waves that pass through the gas? The theoretical laws contain only theoretical terms. What we seek are empirical laws containing observable terms. Obviously, such laws cannot be derived without having something else given in addition to the theoretical laws.

The *something else* that must be given is this: a set of rules connecting the theoretical terms with the observable terms. Scientists and philosophers of science have long recognized the need for such a set of rules, and their nature has been often discussed. An example of such a rule is: "If there is an electromagnetic oscillation of a specified frequency, then there is a visible greenish-blue color of a certain hue." Here something observable is connected with a nonobservable microprocess. . . .

Different writers have different names for these rules. I call them "correspondence rules."[4]

This is directly applicable to man in a scientific psychological sense. A consideration of religious values, however, would have to include not only this correspondence between what is observable and nonobservable but also that which leads *beyond* man and relates him to God.

JENSEITS

Freud, in a much-neglected observation, also suggested a concept of the "beyond" in present experience. We are indebted to Bakan for pointing out that Freud's own personal concern about death may have been involved in this:

My analysis of Freud's state of mind as he wrote about the death instinct and Eros also suggests an explanation of the meaning of the title *Beyond the Pleasure Principle*. In German this is *Jenseits des Lustprinzips,* which might be more literally translated as "the other side of the pleasure principle." "*Jenseits*" as a noun also means the other world or the life after death, and, according to Jones, Freud jocularly referred to this book as "The Hereafter." (Standard Edition, XIX, 54) The pleasure principle was for Freud one of the essential principles associated with his *individual* psychology. *Jenseits* is the other side of the individual, the place of the individual in the larger whole.[5]

The "beyond" is, in this sense then, the "jenseits" beyond egocentricity. It is the other side of each of us or, in a literal sense, that which leads us to "the other." In any relationship that we may call "loving," the narcissistic reflection of oneself is difficult to distinguish from a genuine loving gift of self to another.

For my relationship to be truly loving, as we have said, it must plunge out into the risk of another's mystery, into his or her uniqueness, into that aspect of him or her that I cannot calculate and where no discernible reflection of myself is evident.

But religion would go even further. For the religious man in his faith commitment, the beginning of loving would be a movement in the direction of that totally, mysteriously Other—the Jenseits—called God. This movement, however, would also be in and through other persons. Every human love, from this view, might be said to contain the love of God. One need not, therefore, so much teach the love of God as reveal and uncover it behind and beyond what one loves.

EXPANDING DYNAMIC

Any encounter with another, as Eliade has suggested, is a way of "experiencing an encounter with the unknown."[6] Now an encounter with the "totally other, whether conscious or unconscious, gives rise to an experience of a religious nature." For the religious man, there is then one final Other, totally, uniquely and mysteriously different from man, to whose image man is made—not the reverse.

By contrast, however we explain it, man seems to have a strong urge to re-create others to his own image. In the process of maturity one strives to control this urge by applying a therapy of limits to oneself. But this urge would help explain both narcissism and "will to power." Community comes with the identifying of and submission to the limits of the other—his unique "jenseits." This is evident in the painful struggle for communication and communion that is revealed, for example, in joint sessions of marriage counseling. These sessions may not result in love, but they can sometimes achieve a kind of "justice" in the ancient sense of "to each his own." Love may then be possible as a result of later peak moments of genuine sharing together.

Man might be said to represent not a static but an expanding dynamic correspondence of himself and the beyond. In this sense extension into the beyond would need to be considered as an aspect of the human entity itself and not something superadded.

Adequate means would accordingly need to be devised for the further development of this aspect in any complete theory of man. This theory should especially concern itself with human motivation, values and the learning process if we are to be open to all the data that is now apparently relevant to man.

INTRINSIC RELIGIOUS CONCERN

The evidence of the counseling therapeutic process and the personality dynamics it reveals about man is not, then, alienated from religious concerns but actually seems in many ways to correspond to them. Man's human yearnings seem inescapably bound up with a being and becoming not only himself but beyond himself. For in order really to become a fully functioning person, he seems to need to go beyond himself through love to others somewhat like himself—and for the religious man this means to one Other, totally and uniquely enigmatic and beyond.

Man is then a being in transition, or being-becoming. To capture in words this existential transitional state, we should not so much speak of "human beings" as of "human being-becomings." His existence should be described not simply with the verb "to be" but, more exactly, with the phrase "to be-beyond."

One may ask, too, which is sound and which is echo? In its concreteness and immediacy, "here" is reality and "after," the echo which corresponds. But in another sense, existence, in its transiency and ephemeral illusiveness, may indeed be quivering echo and "after" truly "hereafter" in the clarity and enduring tones of its reality. In this sense, as Bakan remarks, "the manifest is but the barest hint of reality, that beyond the manifest there exist the major portions of reality."[7]

CONCERNS HUMAN EXPERIENCE

Eliade carries this further when he explains the special existential value—or, as we have called it, "correspondence"—of religious symbolism:

Finally, we must stress the existential value of religious symbolism, that is to say the fact that a symbol always points to a reality or a situation concerning human existence. It is, above all, this existential dimension that distinguishes and divides symbols from concepts. Symbols preserve contact with the deep sources of life; they express, one might say, "the spiritual as life experience." This is why symbols have a kind of "numinous" aura: they reveal that the modalities of the spirit are at the same time manifestations of Life, and that consequently, they directly concern human existence. A religious symbol not only reveals a pattern of reality or a dimension of existence, it brings at the same time a meaning to human existence. This is why even symbols concerning ultimate reality also afford existential revelations to the man who deciphers their message.

A religious symbol translates a human situation into cosmological terms, and vice versa; to be more precise, it reveals the unity between human existence and the structure of the Cosmos. Man does not feel himself "isolated" in the Cosmos. He is open to a World which, thanks to the symbol, becomes "familiar." On the other hand the cosmological significances of a symbolism allow him to escape from a subjective situation and recognize the objectivity of his personal experiences.

It follows that the man who understands a symbol not only "opens himself" to the objective world, but at the same time succeeds in emerging from his personal situation and reaching a comprehension of the universal.[8]

In this vein, one might question the term, "ultimate concern." It, too, can fail to suggest adequate human resonances and belonging and imply that man is left in the alienation of immediacy while "ultimate" concern exists only in the boundary beyond. Bakan comments:

Paul Tillich has made a very significant advance in our thinking by giving emphasis to the term "ultimate concern" as a designation of our quest for meaning at its depth. "Our ultimate concern," he has written, "is that which determines our being or not-being. . . . Man is ultimately concerned about that which determines his ultimate destiny beyond all preliminary necessities and accidents."[9] For Tillich, ultimate concern is the region of theological investigation. He distinguishes between preliminary concerns, such as artistic creation, scientific and historical theory, healing, social reconstruction and politics, on the one hand, and ultimate concern, on the other. He asserts, "The first formal principle of theology (is) guarding the boundary line between ultimate concern and preliminary considerations."[10] Although my respect for

Tillich and his contributions is very great, I feel that thus drawing and guarding a boundary interferes with our pursuit of the very understanding which we are all interested in obtaining. Unfortunately, on the other side of the boundary there are those who guard it against the theological. On the one hand, such a boundary keeps the theological relatively impoverished; on the other hand, it prevents us from endowing our other concerns with context.[11]

MODELS OF CORRESPONDENCE

This brings up some special difficulties, however, of how God relates to man and if a human counterpart or "correspondence" is possible.

The highly personalized images of God in the Old and New Testament seem to raise no issue here. Nor do the analogies used. For example, in the model of salt giving meat its savor, we have the implication that while religious faith gives a new and special savor to human experience, it does not radically change its fundamental nature—the meat remains meat after it is salted.

Augustine, borrowing from the early Christians' experience of community, used the person and the personal relationship as the basis of his trinitarian concept of God. We will discuss later the relevance of this idea. Aquinas followed in this same humanistic tradition. He saw a continuity here, a continuity based in the Being of God and the shared being of man and reality. As Berthold says:

Thomas' treatise on grace makes it perfectly plain that he had no notion of teaching that the desire for God can be fulfilled without grace. But the grace which is needed to fulfill man's destined end completes rather than reverses the tendency which is natural even to fallen man.[12]

Aquinas proposes at least three models of the way God and man relate. The first is drawn from the nature of being itself and man's need and "desire . . . to be made like unto God"—a position that might be related to that of Sartre except that Aquinas held firmly to its possible fulfillment.

Another model, especially relevant to counseling, is the comparison of the human counsel process with that of the indwelling of God. This is in no way contrary to man's reasonable nature and freedom:

> ... it is proper to the rational creature to be moved through the research of reason to perform any particular action and this research is called counsel. Hence the Holy Spirit is said to move the rational creature by way of counsel.[13]

A third model, which is also fundamental to the counseling relationship as well as all aspects of religious community and communication, is that of "friendship." Aquinas sees the friendship of a man with himself and with others as the model par excellence in the religious calling to be friends.[14] This in a special way marks the nature of community and communication between God and man and men with themselves and one another.[15]

OPPOSITION

This humanistic view was never accepted without difficulties and objections, however. What has been called the "total depravity" view was based on the fear that any human analogy or counterpart might lessen the ultimate and unique Otherness of God: the initial and gratuitous love of God for man. Berthold maintains:

> The Protestant position on this matter came to be expressed in a doctrine of "total depravity." It remains clear in the writings of Luther and Calvin that this point of view, which had not yet hardened into a separate doctrine, was maintained for one very simple religious reason: to guard the conviction that God in Christ takes the initiative in salvation. Later, however, the doctrine was elaborated and made rigid by means of metaphysical definitions and distinctions.[16]

This question is, of course, quite complicated. A recent study of the influence of the Calvinistic tradition in America, for example, suggests a quite different view from what is often maintained:

> Calvinism did not divorce the salvational process from human conduct, but it did place Christian behavior in a new perspective. Its first and possibly most significant achievement, in this regard, lay in cutting

the confusion created by those ministers who, as Tennent complained, kept "Driving, Driving to Duty, Duty."[17]

Inherent in this tradition was a genuine regard for the meaning and worth of each person, not a preference for a special upper class. According to Heimert:

. . . What Calvinism asked—or rather demanded—was that no man use whatever worldly success he enjoyed as an occasion for looking on "the common people, with an Air of Disdain."[18]

Perhaps Barth has most clearly represented the modern expression of the difficulty. He states the issue sharply:

. . . a determination of man's existence by the Word of God . . . is not to be confused with any sort of determination which man can give to his own existence. . . . No determination which man can give himself is as such determination by the Word of God. But neither can there be room here for the other view, as if in this experience it were a case of cooperation between divine determination and human self-determination.[19]

On this, Berthold comments:

Nothing can be a flatter rejection of the notion that theology can gain anything of importance from an analysis of human experience for its concept of the relation between God and man. There is no structure of human experience which even discloses the possibility of a relation to God. The possibility of knowing God is created new in the moment in which God makes himself known.[20]

DARK NIGHT

Barth might be understood to mean, however, what Schnackenburg says is "the paramount meaning of revelation: the personal encounter of man with his God, which is brought about by God himself in his revelation and in his demand that man make a response."[21]

Barth emphasizes concepts that seem similar to those of St.

John of the Cross—self-projection in any form impedes relating to God. But Barth seems to hold that this affects both knowing and experiencing, that the two equate. St. John of the Cross rather proposes experiencing in unknowing. In abandonment to the total Other, the total Beyond, human knowing would experience, in darkness, a love God alone could give and could choose to give uniquely and in different ways to whom He chooses.

The experience of God, in this view, would always be in mystery. It would resemble but be essentially different from the unknown, the unique, the mystery one experiences in making any personal loving abandonment. The mystery of God, then, consists in darkness, in letting oneself fall into believing, hoping and trusting love —not in seeking to reduce the experience to human terms and so to re-create it according to a man's own self-image.

PURE REFLECTION

St. John of the Cross expresses, in the analogy of a window, the loving abandonment to trust in darkness:

The sun, with its rays, strikes a window; but if that window be stained and unclean, the sun cannot shine throughout nor transform it perfectly into itself, as it would have done, had it been clean and un-sullied. This depends not on the sun but on the window, so that if the latter were perfectly clean, the rays of the sun would so shine through it, and so transform it, as to make it seem identical with the rays and to give forth the light thereof, though in truth the window, while it appears one with the rays of the sun, preserves still its own separate and distinct substance. In this case we might say that the window is a ray, or light, by participation.[22]

One might transpose this image of the window and propose friendship as a similar image. Like the window, it is at its best the more completely it reflects the other. As the clean window reflects the sun, so, in a genuine relationship of friendship, the other person shines through in his own uniqueness. Both the sun shining through an unspotted window and the uniqueness of the person reflected in another's transparency and regard for him would offer models of the divine experience.

But while the reflection of the other may be clear in the personal "transparency" and genuineness of the friend or counselor, love itself is always an experience in abandonment, in letting oneself go in uncalculated and uncontrolled commitment. So faith and hope lead to obscurity, not clarity—darkness being the only means, for St. John of the Cross, by which one could experience Total Love:

And though the understanding derives certainty from faith, yet it does not derive clearness but rather obscurity.[23]

This is perhaps Barth's idea of the total otherness of God—in the realm of experiencing. One can accept this and still recognize a corresponding echo, a reflection of the image of God in man, and so experience faith, hope and love in commitment to what is unique in the other person. Here is a prologue and pre-experience of loving man in order to be able to love God. Only in this striving to reach and accept the unique in another do I really love him. Beyond this, then, would be the commitment of religious faith, hope, trust and love.

RICHNESS OF PERSON

This highly personal sense of God was, in fact, one of the sources of our present deep understanding of the meaning and value of the concept "person." Elsewhere[24] we have developed in detail how this modern, rich significance which the concept "person" has in psychology, and in our society generally, could not have come from its original meaning and usage as an empty mask. It is owed rather to its later development in the Judaeo-Christian tradition. This tradition was especially evident in the writings of Augustine when he applied the concept of *person* to God.

DYNAMIC HUMAN CONCEPT

The idea which Augustine applied to God of person and persons in union also represents a profound and dynamic human concept as well. It implies a positive, constructive development and unfolding of man's potential and destiny in contrast to the dead and static "fate" idea of man which dominated earlier Greek and Roman thought. Seen as a personality dynamic, we have a model which is applicable to counseling therapy, to education, to marriage and indeed to all human in-depth relationships.

Obviously, early trinitarian writings could not have envisioned all this. But we do see in these writings deep appreciation of the profundity and subtleties in human relationships, communication and commitment. In their attempts to apply these concepts to God minus their human limitations and inadequacies, they have, at the same time, left us with a rich human model of the dynamic process of persons, relationship and communion.

CREATIVE AFFILIATION

Consequently, the concept of the Trinity in unity applied by Augustine and others to God can be seen in its creative correspondence applied to man. Augustine looked closely at the human condition—his own and that of others—in his careful analysis of the person. His views of God and of Divine Persons can also be understood, therefore, in their original human dimensions without distorting Augustine's ultimate intent.

This creativity model is particularly applicable to the person himself and the forces necessary to generate his own creative fulfillment.

Looked at from the point of view of a creative affiliation in counseling therapy, one can consider the client as the first person, since he can be seen as central to the whole process. Without his commitment of himself, no other relationships are possible. The end of the process is his increasing recognition of and respect for himself. He thus strives to become and to be a person in the most creative sense of that concept.

Secondly, there is the counselor-therapist—in his understanding, reflective sensitivity that strives to be totally for the other, as much as is humanly possible. He might, in this sense, be called the "logos," because from him comes the receptivity and sensitive reflection that makes the dia-logos possible. In this dialogue, as we have said, he listens to and strives to grasp the meanings of the

client's or patient's language of affect. One of his main contributions is the manner in which his responses make these affects
cognitive. They can then be consciously recognized and understood by the person. By this turning of affect into cognition, he
furthers the person's understanding of himself and his more adequate control and constructive use of his emotions, instincts and
soma.

Thirdly, there is the communicating relationship itself and the
self-gnosis it produces. The atmosphere must be warm, secure and
intense—surrounding, permeating and suffusing the whole therapeutic process with a deep sense of trust, sharing and belonging.
This is the unifying force that brings person and counselor together
at an ever deeper level of communication and commitment. Out
of this related communication in love comes the client's self-understanding, his *gnosis*. This results from those responses which "fit,"
that is, which integrate and unify his soma, instincts and emotions
around his knowledge of himself and so make some coordinated
action possible. This is knowledge of himself which is unique and
personal and so implements and facilitates his ability to *act* on what
he knows and wants.

THE OTHER

If, however, we switch our focus to the manner—not of creativity
in the person himself and the forces he needs but of aiding
another—then our trinitarian model can take a different and somewhat reverse form. Here we are concerned with the process of
going out to the other, especially after one has achieved some
measure of one's own maturity and inner security.

Augustine also gave us a remarkable awareness and description
of this process of "going out" to *others* and how this fulfills the
maturity of love.

Let us consider, for example, the following résumé of Augustine's view:

> This leads Augustine to declare that a Divine Person is at one and
> the same time a) A Reality identical with Itself existing *in se,* and
> Absolute, and b) also a Reality *ad alium,* essentially directed toward
> another, and dynamically directed toward the others.[25]

If we remove the concept "absolute" from this description, we have, in a sense, an apt definition of "the fully functioning person."[26] This is first represented by the counselor, therapist or teacher in his role as a key figure and at the same time as one who gives himself to the client or student. Then, as a result, the client or student in turn moves increasingly to respect the reality in himself and his basic abilities. He grows in independence and courage "to be" and "to become." Through this he moves toward others as the expression of his own more complete person. He becomes "dynamically directed toward the others," as the therapist or teacher was so directed toward him. The profound relationship of genuine love has generated this intense and constructive personality dynamism. Through it the person becomes increasingly a "reality *in se*" and a "reality *ad alium*," in the process of his own self-becoming.

In Augustine's view, this reality *ad alium* was a basic explanation of the process of God's gratuitous intervention in the redemption of man. This was a description of the way in which Christ was "dynamically directed toward the others." But looking at this incarnation-redemption from a psychological focus, we can see more clearly its correspondence especially in the counseling therapy relationship and process.

TO GIVE ONESELF

This counseling therapeutic "going out" to the other person might, rightly understood, be called the counseling or therapeutic "mission" in the original meaning of that word with its special connotation that one must first *give himself*. The religious man gives himself in imitation of God. St. John described not only the Christian situation but the universal one of how love is possible between God and man: "In this is the love, not as though we had loved God, but because He has first loved us. . . . Beloved, if God has so loved us, we also ought to love one another." (1 Jn. 4:10–11; 12–21) This is a fundamental point in the religious man's approach to others. He loves first, in imitation of the way God loves him.

Psychologically, too, we are coming to see the profundity of this idea of loving first. It seems basic to any human relationship if that relationship is to produce a sense of meaning and worth for anyone. Somehow, before I can feel worth as a person or have faith and trust in myself, I must have encountered someone who, at some time, gave me an unqualified experience of being loved. Usually we assume that a person receives this as a child, especially from parents and others on whom a child must depend for love. What we are seeing in counseling and psychotherapy, however, is that a vast number of people have had no such experience of being loved. As a result, in their innermost view of themselves they appear alienated and without worth. For counseling and psychotherapy to be basically significant for such people it must first of all engage them in an encounter in which they are sure of being loved.

IMPLICATIONS OF LOVE

We must, however, define what we mean by this kind of effective love encounter. The word "love" has many different meanings. We obviously do not mean a narcissistic attachment with its misleading erotic or sentimental overtones. The cloying quality of popular songs has flooded us with descriptions of such relationships. Even at their best, such sentiments, however poetic and appealing they may sound, are usually not possible of fulfillment for the human condition. They rather suggest an intense and unfulfilled yearning for a love *beyond*. Such songs, in their extremes from euphoric joy to tragic sadness, suggest rather a love of unrecognized depth and intensity—a love indeed unaware of itself—and so finally confused, frustrated and lost. By comparison, the kind of human love that is possible can appear mundane and prosaic.

This may help explain why there is a kind of love that seems now to be encountered by many in what might often be considered a "professional" atmosphere. This seems so because such convalidating love demands a special kind of personal integrity, self-awareness, and control if it is to convey worth and regard to the other person. It must be genuinely other-centered. To love first in this way is made all the more demanding by the fact that many people, especially those encountered in counseling and psychotherapy, have succeeded in making themselves difficult to love. It is even difficult to persuade them that they could be lovable to anyone. Such a person's actions and attitudes, reprehensible to himself and others, are usually a kind of acting out of his hostility to himself. It is precisely this need that calls for so much giving of himself on the part of the counselor or therapist. Only then does any sign of reciprocal faith and trust slowly emerge in the therapeutic relationship.

COMMON HUMAN WEAKNESS

Contained in this acceptance and understanding of counseling therapy is another element, shared with religion—that of the weakness of everyone and yet the positive force, even more powerful, of his possible cure or "therapy." For the religious man as he relates to God, this conception is essentially one of the sinfulness of all men—and the possibility of each sharing in the divine redemption. Or, put another way, the religious outlook is optimistic: the mire of my own weakness and confusion can never be so deep—I can never be so bogged down—that I cannot find a firm footing on the rock that is God, to paraphrase a line from the Psalmist. Even Luther and Calvin, who might be considered among the more "sin-conscious" or "weakness-conscious" theologians, held firmly to the optimistic idea of man's redemption. Aquinas, as we have seen, emphasized strongly the natural capacity of man— even in his weakness—for a high degree of goodness and personal integration. This natural capacity would, according to Aquinas' view, be elevated, reinforced and completed by the effects of divine redemption.

In the counseling therapeutic relationship, we also see this same fundamental acceptance of common human weakness coupled with an optimistic view of man's capacities for self-betterment. Whether we think of it as a physical analogy like "maturity" or "growth," or from a medical concept of "therapy" as related to sickness, or as "integration" implying greater organizational completeness and functional capacity, we nonetheless imply a confidence in a person's inner capacity—activated or encouraged by counseling therapy— to be and become more truly or more completely himself and therefore to be a better self.

Here too is a further corollary. If all men are "weak" or "sinful" in the religious sense, there is, psychologically considered, an implication that, from the ideal point of view of what man should be, all men are somewhat abnormal. This is what Freud made psychology aware of—that behind all the apparent normalities there yet lie subtle depths which, if probed, show urges to disorder, confusion and even viciousness. Certainly this could be considered as similar to what theologians mean by the tendency to sin in man. We see in addition, of course, the more obvious and more extreme abnormalities not shared by all—the psychopathologies and similar states. Consequently, the theologian and the counselor-therapist might agree that, ideally considered, all men are abnormal, but some are normally abnormal and some—the more extreme—abnormally abnormal.

UNIQUE ASPECTS

But there are aspects of religious values which are unique. Religion is not a substitute for the counseling therapy relationship or vice versa. In fact, when counseling psychotherapy or any form of healing fails or is increasingly inadequate—as, for example, in the approach of death—it is precisely here that religious factors have their most significant power and meaning. Religion then suggests an added dimension in the psychosomatic relationship of the self and the other: the theological need in man.

FREUD TO AUGUSTINE

In a certain sense we might say that in detailing the religious aspect of psychological dynamics we are going from Freud to Augustine. It was Augustine who, in his own intense self-probing and questioning, anticipated Freud in finding at the deepest self-level an unpacified restlessness. Augustine concluded from this, however, that man has an intrinsic yearning, an abysmal need that he himself cannot fulfill, nor can others fulfill it for him. He is restless at the very core of his being for something beyond himself.

Moreover, man seems to live in a state of anxiety. Anxiety is inevitably behind every human goal or love. Behind every achievement or value seems to lurk the fear of loss and resultant misery and emptiness. Freud suggests a similar idea in considering the anxiety intrinsic to early childhood:

> I am forced to the conclusion that the earliest phobias of childhood do not permit of being directly traced to the impression made upon the child by the act of birth, and that they have thus far, in fact, defied all explanation. A certain predisposition to anxiety on the part of the infant is indubitable.[27]

The child uses his parents and parent-figures and fetish objects to secure himself temporarily against this anxiety. If we propose, however, with Augustine, that these and later adult objects, loves and achievements are, finally considered, simply surrogates for this God need—"idolatries," to use Tillich's term—then man could be considered, in his operational being, a God-centered animal.

FULFILLMENT IN GOD

For Augustine, only the possibility of achieving God and the quest of knowing and loving God could give final meaning and security to human goals and loves. These were, so to speak, reflections of Divine Goodness and Love, the becomings which would fuse into Divine Being—not a static state but a personal unfolding and fulfillment in God. This, Augustine felt, was what man was really made for, and no other person, achievement or value could satisfy and alleviate this need, except temporarily. A man's anxiety may be stilled for a time by such temporal meanings, but it comes back each time with even greater force when these are again threatened with loss.[28]

Outler comments:

> The simplest form of Augustine's explanation of how anxiety may be fruitful runs something like this. God, the Ground of being even for those creatures who deny or defy him, has revealed *himself* as loving and sustaining, as able and willing to satisfy man's hunger for happiness, as active in human history and destiny. This *self*-manifestation of God's love, as it affects our hearts and lives, Augustine termed *gratia*.

Without any close rival, this is the key word in the Augustinian vocabulary. It always connotes a divine action, for God's love is never inconsequential. Yet it is not a physical or palpable force. It works dynamic changes in human lives—there is a sense in which it is *irresistible*—but it is never impersonal and it does not abrogate human freedom. At least this is what Augustine says over and over again, and his disavowals should be seriously considered even by those who are unpersuaded by his arguments.[29]

Like Freud and Kierkegaard, Augustine studied anxiety most of all in himself. Outler describes Augustine's "therapy":

Augustine was not a placid man nor a faultless one nor exempt from acute *angustiae*. His childhood was unhealthy; his adolescence neurotic. His mature life was spent in a demoralized world and he died in an uproar, with the Vandals battering at the walls of Hippo. His conscious longing was for "peace" but he found precious little of it in his outward circumstances.[30] Yet this same man—with his swollen id and raucous super-ego—lived and died with an inner steadiness and productivity, as if he had found his rest on bedrock, beneath life's heaving surfaces. He had found a "cure" for his ontological anxiety and this made all the difference in turning a gifted dilettante into one of the church's greatest "doctors."[31]

PRIMAL ANXIETY

We are not implying in this discussion that religion's only purpose is to act as a kind of personal therapy. It is essentially a faith, hope and love commitment to a binding relationship with God. But its personal effects can be profoundly therapeutic, as the ancient term "cura animarum" suggests. This seemed to be so, in a striking way, in the personal life of Augustine.

Outler describes well the condition of the religious man in the face of the *anxst* of existence when he says:

In these and a multitude of other places Augustine makes plain that God's grace is God's therapy for man's *primal* anxiety. When it is recognized as *God's* grace and rightly acknowledged, it answers man's anxious longing for love and so changes what Dylan Thomas called "the weather of a man's heart." The quality or "feel" of our existence affects the way we perceive and value the events and relations in our experience. In an atmosphere of acute anxiety, a person will "decode" the anxiety signals that he perceives quite differently from one who feels upborne, accepted, beloved. Grace displaces one "atmosphere" (ontological anxiety) with another (ontological buoyancy). Whatever their "destructive" effects, our anxieties may also confront us with the question about the quality of our existence: is it, at last and at bottom, hostile, neutral, or "gracious"?[32]

Consequently, it is with special reference to man's existential transient condition and its correspondent God-centered need that religious factors and values aid counseling's therapeutic effectiveness and indeed strengthen all forces of healing and growth. This divine dimension, for the religious man, goes beyond the somatic world of pain and the psychological world of conflict and fear to a faith-love commitment mutually shared between God and man. In such a relationship and dialogue with the Divine, man places his confidence and security in a "being" and "becoming" in and beyond himself and others. This implies a most complete self-unfolding and fulfillment at the highest level of his own personality and his own unique pursuit of excellence. At the same time, it demands the commitment of himself to others, especially in what is mysteriously beyond him in them. Such self-regard and regard for others would, in a religious man, be suffused in a faith-love involvement with a correspondent Total Other: God.

We have here the Pauline religious conviction that "I can do all things in Him who strengthens me"—the religious man, in this sense, never feels ultimately helpless or alone; he is a committed man. He responds and so makes "correspondence" with the Divine.

NOTES

[1] Stephen Tennant in his Foreword to Willa Cather, *Willa Cather on Writing* (New York: Alfred A. Knopf, Inc., 1949).

[2] Baudelaire, *op. cit.*, p. 161.

[3] This concept of correspondence differs from, but has relation to, Bohr's famous "Korrespondenz-prinzip." See B. L. van der Waerden, ed., *Sources of Quantum Mechanics* (Amsterdam: North-Holland Publishing Co., 1967), pp. 5–18, 163, 203–219.

[4] Rudolf Carnap, *Philosophical Foundations of Physics,* ed. Martin Gard-

ner (New York: Basic Books, Inc., Publishers, 1966), p. 233. (Italics mine.)

5 David Bakan, *The Duality of Human Existence* (Chicago: Rand McNally and Co., 1966), p. 178.

6 Eliade, *op. cit.,* p. 11.

7 Bakan, *The Duality of Human Existence,* p. 5.

8 Eliade, *op. cit.,* pp. 206–207.

9 Paul Tillich, *Systematic Theology* (Chicago: University of Chicago Press, 1951), p. 14.

10 *Ibid.,* p. 12.

11 *The Duality of Human Existence,* pp. 1–3; a critique of Tillich's "ultimate concern" concept.

12 Fred Berthold, Jr., *The Fear of God: The Role of Anxiety in Contemporary Thought* (New York: Harper and Brothers, 1959), p. 79.

13 *Summa contra Gentiles,* trans. Vernon J. Bourke (Garden City, N.Y.: Doubleday, 1956), Book III, Pt. 1, Ch. 16.

14 *Summa Theologica,* II-II, Q. 52, a. 2.

15 *Ibid.,* II-II, Q. 23, a. 1.

16 Berthold, *op. cit.,* p. 85.

17 Alan Heimert, *Religion and the American Mind: From the Great Awakening to the Revolution* (Cambridge, Mass.: Harvard University Press, 1966), p. 55. Also Gilbert Tennent, *Uncoverted Ministry,* p. 9.

18 *Ibid.,* p. 55.

19 Karl Barth, *Church Dogmatics,* trans. G. T. Thomson, (New York: Scribner's, 1936), 1, Pt. 1, p. 227.

20 Berthold, *op. cit.,* p. 121.

21 Schnackenburg, *op. cit.,* p. 73.

22 St. John of the Cross, *The Ascent of Mount Carmel* (London: Thomas Baker, 1928), pp. 79–80.

23 *Ibid.,* pp. 83–84.

24 Curran (1968) *op. cit.*

25 Paul Henry, S.J., *St. Augustine on Personality* (New York: Macmillan, 1960), p. 9.

26 Rogers, *On Becoming a Person;* see pp. 183–184, 191.

27 Sigmund Freud, *The Problem of Anxiety,* p. 75.

28 St. Augustine, *Confessions* (New York: Modern Library, 1949).

29 Albert C. Outler, "Anxiety and Grace: An Augustinian Perspective," in *Constructive Aspects of Anxiety,* ed. Seward Hiltner and Karl Menninger (Nashville, Tenn.: Abingdon Press, 1963), pp. 95–96.

30 Cf. Albert C. Outler, "Augustine and the Transvaluation of the Classical Tradition," *The Classical Journal,* 54 (December 1957), p. 214.

31 Outler in *Constructive Aspects of Anxiety,* p. 95.

32 *Ibid.,* pp. 96–97.

9
The Incarnate-Redemptive Counseling Process

WE HAVE SEEN how Augustine's personalist conception of God could be paralleled by a correspondent application to a creative human dynamic. In this sense it could be a model for the relationship between client and counselor and, as was suggested earlier, of all creative relationships extending beyond masculine and feminine differences and polarities. We can now consider another theological concept which can also be a model of psychological and personal engagement and development. We might speak of an incarnate-redemptive dialogue and communication. That is, "correspondence" is here exemplified by the way counseling and psychotherapy echo, in their own order, an incarnate-redemptive process.

Theological incarnation may be described as God taking upon Himself the nature of a man and becoming like us. This theological incarnation penetrated man's alienation from God and his feeling of worthlessness in God's eyes and gave him the possibility of personal redemption, of achieving divine worth, meaning and belonging.

In counseling therapy both counselor and client, therapist and patient, begin their relationship in distance, in a nonincarnate intellectualism—the person often seeing the counselor or therapist as quite removed from his weak human condition. At the same time he can tend to regard his own emotional somatic self in a kind of "angelic" or nonincarnate way as something somewhat separated and apart, and he usually feels himself, to a degree at least, alienated from himself and others and often proportionately of less value in his own eyes and in the view of others. At this stage people can sometimes speak as if their instincts and emotions formed no part of the judgmental self that is condemning and rejecting their actions.

In the counseling therapy process, there seems to be a kind of correlation between the way the client or patient grows to accept his total self as having worth and meaning and the manner in which he begins to attribute value to himself as a person. A greater sense of both worth and personhood then appears concomitant with this psychological incarnate-redemptive process. At the same time he begins to relate to others with growing dignity and respect.

TOTAL UNIFIED SELF

The person in the human condition must undergo, then, as we have seen, an incarnate process of accepting his total self—soma, instincts, emotions, intellect, will—functioning together consciously and unconsciously. In this he seems to change from a prior state that is dichotomized and quasi-angelic in its acceptance only of conscious intellectual and voluntary functions.

This dichotomy may begin at the first dawn of consciousness with the experience of pain. In pain infants and small children seem to separate the "self" from the body or, at least, parts of the body. A child may say, "*It hurts,*" and then, "My leg hurts me," with the focus on an "it" that hurts "me." Pain is thus "ego-alienating," to use Bakan's phrase. There is, however, an interesting opposite urge in adult amputees to feel the pain of a removed limb apparently as a surrogate for still possessing the limb.[1]

In this dichotomized state a person often, in a removed and even negative manner, looks on other aspects of the self as if they were really unrelated. There is a disowning of and removal from one's whole self. Only when this whole incarnate self is admitted and its actions "owned up to" is one truly responding to life and therefore responsible. One is at the same time psychologically redeemed in feeling and accepting a reasonable and respectful self-love.

What we mean here, then, is that the incarnate-redemptive process is a means of describing what seems to be a normal and natural growth in the human person. A genuine sense of self-worth or psychological redemption does not seem possible until there has been some measure of acceptance of and commitment to a whole psychosomatic self. In his early situations a person is in a state of rebellion with this self. These forces, somewhat like Plato's concept of wild horses, must be in a measure controlled before a person has any basic feelings of security and self-value. As one cannot get much value out of horses running wild in a canyon and over the mountainside, so one cannot seem to get any sense of worth or value without some inner integration of these somatic, instinctive, emotional forces.

ENGAGEMENT AND DIALOGUE

To achieve this, counseling and psychotherapy have to establish a profound engagement between the self and another and an intensely searching and probing dialogue. Interwoven and mutually dependent are the understanding process itself—the dialogue—and the deepening relationship it produces—the commitment. Together, relationship and dialogue aim at greater self-understanding, orientation to more adequate goals and values and more complete operational integration and efficiency. The relationship is unquestionably one of deep emotional and somatic significance, but it is most of all a dynamism of the giving or withholding of the selves. The degree to which both "commit" themselves to this relationship seems to determine much of the relationship's ultimate significance.

Religious values imply a commitment of self that goes beyond this but corresponds to it. In religious literature this commitment is usually called "faith" or "love" or both. The religious man must give himself to the divine relationship and believe and trust in God's love, understanding and acceptance of him even at the deepest level of his own self-misery and inadequacy. The deepening counseling therapy process, producing a trusting of oneself to the relationship, can in a sense prepare the way for this relationship beyond. As one client remarked to the counselor after an interview:

You know, through this experience I can understand for the first time how God can really love me. You know me in a way I never thought I'd ever reveal myself to anyone; you know all my weaknesses and yet you still accept and respect me. I'm beginning to feel that God too is somewhat like that towards me.

This person, having communicated himself without reserve, discovered that the counselor's accepting understanding extended to all facets of himself, even to those he may have kept hidden from others and even from himself. This helped him to his first real understanding of how God could love and accept him at the same profound level.

This experience in shared humanity can lead, then, to a correspondent "beyond," something that in the darkness of faith touches on the divine. Such an incarnate belonging experience of being accepted in one's weakness and inadequacy carries with it, too, a growth in self-worth, and so is redeeming. This seems to aid in the acceptance of the self-worth and value conveyed by the belief in a correspondent divine redemption—St. Paul's contention that we are purchased at a great price.

Here we note another mutual term between counseling therapy and religion: "communion." The religious person "communes" with God; the client and the counselor "communicate" together. Even though the human communication in counseling and psychotherapy takes place by dialogue, much more than words go into what is really exchanged; the communication between man and the Divine goes beyond verbal prayers to an intense sense of belonging, of sharing and being understood and understanding. Through the counseling therapy dialogue, the client seeks to be understood and thus to understand himself. It is in a way the counselor's striving to understand him that intensifies the client's own efforts to understand himself and to communicate and share with the counselor what he slowly and sometimes tortuously is discovering about himself. As another client puts it:

Because you are trying so hard to understand me, I'm urged all the more to want to explain myself clearly to you and to myself.

We have, then, beyond this, the religious man's conviction that God's love and acceptance is both a deep understanding of him at the level of his weakness and a spur which produces in him an intense urge to "better" himself. This does not mean simply by external change or through some process of "positive" thinking; rather, he now longs to "become" more really himself, to "be" himself as God made him. But for the religious man this "being" and "becoming" oneself contains a real possibility of fulfillment that urges him on constructively. So, too, a person in counseling therapy is urged to movement and growth, not by being condemned or criticized. Rather by knowing that he is understood, he understands, and somehow is freer to become and to be himself in a more completely integrated way.

The client begins to trust both the counselor and the relationship because he feels the counselor's regard for him. This corresponds to the religious concept of the value of each person. The religious man, in faith, believes that God respects, loves and accepts him, and through this he can grope for self-respect, love and acceptance of himself. Here we have the theological concept of redemption and its fruits being extended to all men, depending only on their free and responsible cooperation. No man is so alone or so unworthy that these effects cannot reach him.

SEARCH FOR MEANING

Such a discussion of the relationship of persons involves us, as we have seen, in concepts of communication and communion. If we think of capital "C," we are obviously referring to the sacrament of Holy Communion that is so central in the religious belief and practice of many Christians. "Communion" with a small "c" interrelates with communication which makes communion and community possible.

Less commonly known is the dictionary definition of "sacrament" with a small "s": "Something regarded as having . . . mysterious meaning." In this definition, with "meaning" and "mystery" juxtaposed, we have another significant aspect of the counseling and psychotherapeutic correspondence. For they too are "sacraments" in this sense. They too are concerned in a special sense with something regarded as having mysterious meaning.

The special characteristic of this meaning seems evident in the respect that permeates the counselor-therapist's attitudes and actions and slowly initiates in the person a reciprocal regard for himself. It comes to a climax at those moments when the counselor's genuine communication of himself brings the person correspondingly deep moments of trust, security and self-awareness. Through such communion emerges the sacrament of human belonging, penetrating with redemption a man's sense of alienation and worthlessness.

PURSUIT OF VALUE

There is here a mutual search for meaning and value in mystery. This re-emergence of the "unique" in man has been one of the most significant developments in recent psychology. We are now becoming aware again of a uniquely personal aspect of existential man that has a kind of incommunicableness. It is incommunicable in the sense that he must seek it and find it by himself, because it is knowledge he alone can have about himself. To this kind of knowledge of a man about himself the Greeks, as we have seen, applied the word "gnosis" in contrast to "logos." We are treating, then, not only an incarnate dialogue but also an incarnate "diagnosis."

This "dia-gnosis" shares much with the usual meaning insofar as it is a relationship in which the knowledge, training and skill are essential. It puts greater emphasis, however, on the unique self-knowledge (gnosis) that is acquired through this "dia" process. The main exchange is certainly an affect-cognitive dialogue, which draws upon the expert's indispensable "psycho-*logical*" knowledge and skill. Yet, for this knowledge to become finally meaningful and operative, it must be digested and assimilated by the client or patient in a process of knowing himself. It must become not simply logical or insightful, but gnosistic with all the uniquely personal meanings and extensions implied in this kind of self-knowing in mystery. For man, with all his scientific knowledge, still remains in many ways a mystery to himself as well as to others. A "science of man" is daily impressing us with its rich and useful yield of knowledge. But more than this common understanding is necessary as each person faces the singular encounter, caught up as it is in the anxiety, threat and disorder of moment-to-moment experience. Here he must face and struggle with that conflict and confusion that is part of the mystery of self. His process of self-knowledge is the striving to find meaning and value in this mystery of himself. He can then grow to respect and appreciate the unique mystery of others. He thus recognizes in himself and others this sense of "sacrament," or "mysterious meaning."

MYSTERY

Without this idea of "sacrament" in the human condition, neither love, hope nor faith could flower. They come to full bloom only in mystery. To have people "all figured out" is probably neither to love nor trust them. To solve someone's "problem" is perhaps to demonstrate one's own logical acumen, but it usually leaves the person no better off than he was before. A human person is not reducible simply to a series of "problems" with its implication of answers in the back of the book. He is sacred—a sacrament—and so both mysterious and meaningful at the same time.

This mystery does not seem to be penetrable by any cold mathematical or scientific process alone—granting that these are valuable and even indispensable for one aspect of the science of man. For an individual man more is required. A person opens himself up and comes out of his encrustation of defense and withdrawal only when he is loved first in an open, trusting and hopeful relationship. This love does not propose predetermined solutions or answers, but embraces him in a mutual sense of mystery and of striving to understand and be understood. His growing faith, hope and love of himself leads him to open himself to others and slowly to begin to move out to them. He has thus found meaning and love in the mystery of himself and others in a communion of human belonging.

If, for example, a couple marry mainly because they "understand" one another, they may really mean that—in an escape from anxiety—they have one another "figured out" and so are secure because there will be no surprises. But such security could also be the boredom trap of a dead relationship. To have all the problems in a mathematics text "figured out" is to be secure and perfectly prepared for an examination and to be assured in advance of an "A." But to have to live for the rest of one's life with no new challenges or mysteries in a relationship with another person would be to be imprisoned in a narrow and unstimulating personal environment. This seems a high price to pay for the narcissistic security of having the person calculated and controlled. One has, in a sense, only one's own image and little of the truly *other* in such a relationship.

Alternately, to sum up the nature of love, we could say that it seeks—in what Abraham Maslow calls "peak experiences"—to be an emptying out of self that is totally for the other. Looked at from a theological parallel, this is also a description of the love of God and of others in and for God—traditionally called *amor benevolentiae*—which also seeks to empty out itself and be totally for the other.

PERSONAL INTEGRITY

This quality suffuses the therapeutic relationship with a profound respect for the integrity of the person. In this way, a person's own growth in self-respect is made possible. Such a person has usually become accustomed to being manipulated and controlled by others for their own purposes. Counseling therapy does not do this. The person often finds this absence of manipulation so strange and unusual that he cannot believe in it for a long time. He waits suspiciously for some hidden maneuver, no matter how genuine the relationship may appear to him. Only after repeated testing of the counselor's trust and confidence in him and respect for him does the client reluctantly come to see himself as a person worthy of confidence and respect, and so begin to have trust in and hope for himself.

In fact one of the things that is apt to single out the counseling therapy experience for the person undergoing it and mark it as clearly different from thousands of other encounters is the overriding concern for him that emanates from it. It is this more than anything else, apparently, that initiates in him a new dynamic of self-regard and ultimately actualizes a self-potential that he vaguely knew existed but never really trusted as being possible of fulfillment.

MATURITY AND THERAPY OF LIMITS

We can see how much such a relationship, at the opposite pole from sentimentality, would demand not only commitment on the part of the counselor or therapist but a clear sense of limits as well. Here a very real concept of "to each his own" is necessary. One of the main advantages of a genuine training in counseling therapeutic skills is this sense of counselor limits. He can examine, from the vantage point of his own supervised training experiences, his own manipulatory and narcissistically centered urges to possess and control others. He therefore recognizes that commitment and involvement can be misleading unless they are truly other-centered. His relationship must be honestly oriented for the freedom and growth of the other person.[2]

CONFIDENCE AND TRUST

We have used the words "faith," "trust," and "confidence." This leads us to further concepts usually called the "theological virtues of faith, hope and love." In this context, however, we can see their *correspondence* with the relationship we have just described. Before reciprocal faith is even possible between counselor and client, therapist and patient, and, *a priori,* before any experience of hope and love can emerge, the person must be reached at the deepest level of his sense of worthlessness and alienation. Lacking faith in himself and faith that any relationship with another can be genuine and truly for him, the person is often at the farthest distance possible for any capacity to believe either in himself or in another. From childhood on, usually, his very psychological survival seems to have depended on mistrust and suspicion. In the exact opposite of the experience of the ideally mature and secure person, those upon whom he depended for love, understanding and acceptance somehow always managed to betray him and leave him unloved, without worth and alone. They managed to do this amidst sometimes astonishing displays of appearing to love and value him. But what he received from these experiences was finally the feeling of being "used," of never really being cared for, for himself.

In the light of this, it is quite evident that for any relationship to have genuine meaning to such a person, it would have to be characterized by the clearest kind of honesty and integrity. If it is to be, no shadow of duplicity or phoniness can mar its moments of significant communication. Rogers has used the word "transparency" to characterize the complete open "givingness" of the counselor at these moments. Because the client or patient is often so expertly armed against any surrogate use of himself, only the most genuine kind of commitment will penetrate him and make possible, sometimes for the first time, the beginning of a growing conviction that he is genuinely regarded for himself.

In the theological parallel of faith, the person must believe that God loves him and must submit himself to this love before he can draw personal strength and meaning from it. In a corresponding way, the client or patient must do this, too. He must believe in the counselor's unselfish concern for him. He must accept—and many people admit great difficulty in accepting this—that someone really cares about him. As a person remarked recently, "One of the most difficult things I have ever done in my life is to believe that someone can really love me for myself."

As in the religious experience, so, too, apparently, in the therapeutic experience, faith is a crucial issue upon which the whole subsequent process depends. Here, too, it can be said to the person at the end of successful therapy, "Thy faith hath made thee whole." We note that this is not simply faith in the counselor but much more subtly faith and trust in the relationship between the counselor and himself. As a result, we see the person beginning, almost imperceptibly, to believe and trust in himself. He shows this especially by committing himself with more openness and decreasing defensiveness.

HOPE

Somewhere here, isolated expressions of hopefulness and positive feelings begin to show themselves. Somewhere, too, in this delicate process, the first impulses of love, like the first green shoots of spring, appear above the morass of self-pity and self-rejection. The love that slowly emerges here is a genuine and respectful love of self. Later on, of course, there will be gratitude and appreciation. But basic to this is the person's conviction that he can be truly independent, that the counselor wants nothing more for him than his own best regard and use of himself. For the counselor, this is one of the finest tributes he can receive to the genuine unselfishness of his regard. For the client or patient, faith and hope come full circle in love and self-regard.

INCARNATE REDEMPTION

To sum up, then, we can say that man as we encounter him in the counseling therapeutic relationship, often feels alienated and worthless. This can be true not only in the obviously rejected and inadequate, but also in people whose extrinsic manner and achievements give the opposite impression. Men can be alienated, alone and without any sense of basic worth even in the midst of astonishing material possessions and intellectual accomplishments; and women, also, can feel profoundly unloved and unwanted even though they are models of physical allure and charm apparently surrounded by admirers.

For a relationship to be helpful in face of this sense of alienation and worthlessness, the counselor must penetrate this nonbelonging and somehow, by entering it, make redemption possible. For this psychological redemption—as in our theological correspondence—also depends on another. I cannot acquire initially a sense of worth by myself. It apparently depends on what Harry Stack Sullivan has called "consensual validation," in this case a reflected awareness of my own worth shown in another's actions toward me.[3]

For many who come for psychological help this need of "consensual validation" is fundamental. However full of meaning and accomplishment their lives seem, on the surface, to be, they remain at some psychological center unsure of themselves, self-rejecting and cut off in significant ways from communication with themselves and others. They are, in a sense, un-incarnate with themselves—afraid really to "be" themselves because they do not trust their total selves, that is, their incarnate selves. Whether we describe this as caused by an unrealistic ideal self-image, exaggerated perfectionism, or a disordered superego, such people seem somehow almost angelically unwilling to accept themselves in the human condition and to belong to it. In the sentence "I am disgusted with myself" with which they so often begin a discussion of themselves, they show a sort of disembodied hostility and intolerance toward themselves. In this state of negative self-concept, it is as if they themselves have never really taken upon themselves "the body of a man," with all the warmth, understanding and acceptance of themselves that such incarnation into the human condition would involve.

INCARNATE DIALOGUE

The counselor-therapist enters this conflict situation through what we have called an "incarnate dialogue." He does not simply talk as others do. His communication enters into the very incarnate being of the person—his animality as well as his rationality. As the person trusts more and communicates more with his emotions, instincts, and soma, as well as his rational process, the counselor sensitively helps him slowly to accept his incarnate self, to respect it as a fundamental part of himself, and to begin to understand it.

There is a significant change, too, in the way the person regards the counselor-therapist. From an ideal figure, perhaps even a projected father-figure—removed, aloof, and almost godlike—the counselor becomes man. He is experienced as someone genuinely and humanly warm, trustworthy, and honest. This becomes most evident to the person when, with growing confidence in the relationship, he dares to bring forth hidden unfaced, and hitherto unaccepted, aspects of himself. He yet remains sure of being understood, accepted and still respected as a person.

What makes this incarnate dialogue so significant is that the person, in talking to the counselor or therapist, is really talking to himself. He begins to face his whole self through this incarnate process with another. Freud understood well the importance of this kind of incarnate dialogue. As Vergote remarks:

Freud knew how to allow himself to be taken by surprise and had the openness to listen attentively to what the evidence had to tell him. If the talking cure had been able to cure Anna O. of paralysis of the left arm and of her anorexia, it must mean that the human body can express a concrete human meaning through its functional abnormalities as well as by its conscious actions. Allowing itself to become the

vehicle of thought in action, it itself becomes concrete speech . . .
If the subject's talking was able to free her body, it must be because
another talking, not spoken but lived, had in the first place bound it.[4]

In this manner, the person is made whole not only by his commitment to the counseling therapeutic relationship but also by
the incarnate dialogue that follows from and depends on this
commitment.

Before this kind of incarnate communication can really occur,
however, the person must have repeatedly experienced a profound
and sensitive understanding on the part of the counselor or
therapist. Here we are led back to some early Greek notions, found
especially in Plato and Aristotle, about how understanding is a
kind of becoming like the other. The Greek philosophers saw
understanding as a kind of motion, but a motion that did not
force, change or absorb the other, but rather sought to be a true
reflection of the other. In this sense, the counselor "becomes
like unto" the other—in the correspondent theological description.
For his understanding strives to penetrate into every level of the
person's affective as well as his cognitive communication. It is,
in fact, through this delicate and all-embracing unlimited quality
of the counselor's understanding that the person is slowly led to
put fewer conditions and restrictions on the way he opens up to
and accepts himself—now in an increasingly total state of incarnation.

GROWTH IN SELF-WORTH

From this incarnate process of self-exploration, evaluation, and
growing integration the client or patient increasingly becomes
aware of his own meaning and value as a person. By such slow and
often painful self-acceptance he comes to participate in his own
psychological redemption. Striving to understand and accept his
total self, he becomes increasingly "whole." His redemption depended on another, but it was also due to himself. Without the
counselor or therapist he could not have arrived at this point, yet it
is not the achievement of the counselor-therapist alone. The person himself has literally "fought a good fight" and achieved his

victory through his own efforts—granting that the counselor's gift of himself first was necessary to make this possible. Thus redemption follows upon incarnation. He can now change the self-negating sentence and say, as one person said, "You know, I can now respect myself and in a way trust myself the way God made me. I don't seem any more to be always thinking about changing myself or comparing myself unfavorably with others."

Something of this kind of respectful self-love seems to constitute psychological redemption as we have described it. At the opposite end of a narcissistic self-involvement and inversion which at the core contains self-hatred, this kind of maturing self-love begins to move out to others in a genuine attempt to give of one's self. The experience of the therapy process starts to bring forth its own fruit. The person can now begin to love others as well as himself with something of the fineness and integrity that he has experienced in being loved. He can begin now, however feebly, to love first instead of always demanding that he be the central love-object. He comes thus slowly to accept himself as moving in the direction of becoming an adult in place of being captive to his own defensive, inverted and self-defeating, infantile egotism. When he denied, because he was afraid to face, aspects of his incarnate self, he was often the slave to these impulses in all their subtle, repressed forms. When he grew to trust himself, through the counselor's or therapist's skilled aid and trust, he could accept truth about himself that made him free. In Plato's sense, he was "out of the cave"; or as Otto Rank might have put it, his "trauma of birth" was over. In a word, he was "redeemed"; he had acquired some basic sense of worth and value to himself and others.

NOTES

[1] See David Bakan, *Disease, Pain and Sacrifice: Toward a Psychology of Suffering* (Chicago: University of Chicago Press, 1968), pp. 73–78.

[2] See chapter "The Maturity and Therapy of Limits," in Curran (1968), *op. cit.*

[3] Sullivan, *op. cit.*, pp. 224–225, 300.

[4] A. Vergote, *Problems in Psychoanalysis—A Symposium* (Baltimore, Maryland: Helicon Press, 1961), p. 143.

10

An Incarnate-Redemptive Educative Process

HAVING DISCUSSED THE CONCEPT of incarnate and redemptive correspondence in some of its theological and psychological implications, particularly as exemplified in the counseling therapy relationship, we can now consider its application to education.

An incarnate-redemptive model of the educative process would stand out in sharp contrast to our present highly intellectualized, socially isolated and teacher-centered educational methods. Its aim would be to incorporate teachers and learners together in a deep relationship of human belonging, worth and sharing. While such an incarnate-redemptive learning process has direct implications for education and teaching, it would also offer fresh ways of viewing religious education as well as all aspects of learning in a religious environment and context.

TEACHER EMINENCE

Learning, somewhat like illness, seems to involve the learner in a temporary psychological return to the state of a small child with its concomitant sense of weakness, anxiety, inadequacy and dependency. With this there is both the exaggerated sense of the teacher's power to humiliate by knowledge and a resentment, often suppressed, on the learner's part of this inferiority to the one who knows. This can and usually does enhance, on the other side, the teacher's will-to-power needs and satisfactions. The retaining of this superiority position is thereby encouraged, because it is or can be, in this way, personally rewarding. Such teacher superiority can be rationalized as essential to learning and therefore to be maintained.

INCARNATE ENGAGEMENT

Present research in counseling and in the use of teaching machines and learning apparatus is beginning to reveal, however, that this godlike teacher stance—while of very ancient lineage—is not only not necessary to many forms of learning but may in fact impede them. On the contrary, what often seems to further learning is rather an incarnate engagement in an open and warm relationship between knower and learner which activates in the student a steady growth in the sense of self-worth and security. This seems to draw the student out of his anxiety that, unredeemed or worthless as he is, he cannot learn this task or language and assures him of his incarnate-redeemed learning worth and ability. In this the model of the mother and small child seems not only to represent our earliest learning experience but also to be one from which we derive much of our later learning potential. It is the mother's loving security conveyed to the child that gives him worth and the initial courage to learn. He may, of course, learn without this, but this is a basic aid.

We also have here a correspondent reflection, in the human learning process, of the way theological incarnation and redemption, by first communicating love by "becoming like" man, also drew man out of his sense of worthlessness and alienation. This gave him the possibility of gaining a sense of worth and redemption and of sharing in divine affiliation.

The learning process considered this way is not simply intellectual but also incarnate, involving not only an atmosphere of knowing but also an experience in open and warm belonging and sharing such as we have seen in counseling therapy. To achieve this in learning, we need to borrow from present counseling and psychotherapeutic research and skill and incorporate into the learning experience some of the features which mark a rich and effective counseling therapy relationship.

Consideration of an incarnate-redemptive learning experience patterned after the counseling relationship, and of the place of counseling itself in the educative process, must then start with the effects on learning of conflict, hostility, anxiety, defense and other basic emotional and instinctive psychosomatic reactions. It must also recognize the learning experience as a community experience oriented to the fulfillment of the need to belong, to work together and to grow in mature giving of self to others. Such learning experiences would not only be task-oriented and intellectual; they would include relations to others and involve the whole person of each learner.

PRESENT CARTESIAN TRADITION

In many of our present educational methods we are still victimized to a considerable degree by concepts that are fundamentally Cartesian. This Cartesian attitude, combined with models drawn apparently from economic "laissez-faire rugged individualism," has perhaps made most classroom learning both exaggeratedly intellectual and competitive. The "good" student is still presumed to be able to learn best in an intellectualized and individual way, with little or no consideration given to his emotional somatic involvement or his need for a community learning experience shared with other students.

In the Cartesian dichotomy, the psyche was conceived of as highly intellectual and removed from somatic and emotional tones. Although we have in large measure discarded this dichotomy, we still find in our culture, structures of thought that make it difficult for us to free ourselves from its persistent influence. This dichotomy has affected the development of counseling in the way that it is so often considered only as remedial and corrective rather than as an integral part of the educative process. If, however, we look at the educative process as something experienced by a total personality, instead of viewing it with the distortions of a Cartesian intellectualism, counseling therapy skills, relationships and models may have major roles and not simply auxiliary ones.

RESEARCH

To investigate this we have been doing research in learning through a counseling therapy type of relationship.[1] This research has made us increasingly aware of the interweaving of the whole personality process in learning. We wish here, not to make a complete report of the various phases of this research, but simply to draw on some experiences to illustrate and clarify our view. Elsewhere we have explained in detail the nature of this kind of learning and the various experiences and research already developed around these ideas:

CONSTRUCTIVE-DESTRUCTIVE

The complicated and subtle part which conflict, hostility, anxiety, defense and similar reactions play in learning recurred repeatedly in almost all aspects of our research. Up to a certain point we can call these positive factors, for they engage one in the learning experience; they are forms of commitment and involvement. Beyond that point, however, they seem to become destructive forces; they block the student, make him want to escape the whole experience, or arouse him to a defensive kind of learning. Such a defensive learner often tends to disregard what he has learned as soon as it has served its defensive purpose, apparently because the whole experience has been so painful. Many students, for example, spoke of the deep hostility they had toward foreign languages as a result of previous classroom experiences. In their negative anxiety and conflict, most had defended themselves against this threatening situation by getting a passing grade—some even a high one. But afterwards it was difficult and painful for them even to try to speak this particular language in our research group.[2]

INCARNATE-REDEMPTIVE

Here we will only discuss this briefly. What is more relevant for our present consideration is the manner in which this educative process breaks with an overintellectualized or "angelic" idea of education—after a Cartesian-Kantian model—and incorporates the learning experience into an incarnate relationship with the "teacher" and the other learners. This incorporated sense of belonging and sharing brings with it a sense of communication, communication and community in place of isolated competition that can be both alienating and rejecting.

As a consequence, a redemptive process emerges by which each one feels his growing worth in the achievement of learning. By this he is further encouraged to confidence and trust in his own learning capacity and self-worth as well as faith in and commitment to the other learners and the informed person, the teacher. Such faith and hope engender love and security in place of fear, anxiety and self-mistrust and attack. The student is therefore learning in an atmosphere of respectful love of self and others and the genuine regard this produces. Personal enthusiasm, self-affirmation and even competition, are not stifled by this but encouraged. These self-assertions do not, however, break the bonds of closeness and caring which each one shares with others. They rather engage each one in a process which is the reasonable pursuit of his own excellence without encroaching on others or manipulating them for his own needs and purposes.

A wide variety of relationships were devised, some involving various learning apparatus. But whatever the method or apparatus used, it was basically intended to further the sense of belonging and sharing between the one who knew and the group, and between group members themselves. The idea was to diminish the distance, isolation, anxious state and sense of inadequacy into which a person is placed by not knowing something. In this way, a gradual sense of incarnation between the knower—who tended initially to be seen in a non-incarnate divinized role—and the one who did not know was furthered and intensified. At the same time, the feelings of distance, strangeness, isolation, fear of failure and humiliation which competition might bring between the members of the group were also diminished by the increase in their own capacity to give worth and confidence to one another. In this fashion they could redeem or rescue one another from the initial anxiety-bound state.

COUNSELING THERAPY MODEL

The core model for this incarnate-redemptive educative process was the closeness, engagement and sense of loving first which counseling therapy represented. Consequently the knower—for example, the native Spanish person in a group learning Spanish—strove in every way to imitate the counselor in commitment, belonging and sensitive caring. He did not take advantage of the power and exhibitionist superiority which his expert knowing of Spanish gave him over Americans struggling to learn Spanish;

rather, his whole manner conveyed openness, worth and security. They could then begin to trust him, and through him gradually grow secure in Spanish. Conversations were initiated at the same personal level of group counseling and were carried on in that atmosphere. There was this additional element, however: they were carried out in Spanish with the Spanish expert's constant reassuring presence, support and skilled linguistic counseling aid.

APPARATUS

The various apparatus which were employed and the learning theory implied have also been explained in detail elsewhere.[3] These were all constructed for the purpose of initiating and furthering the kind of counseling community relationship which we have been discussing. For example, each one had a learning lantern with eight colors and keys he could push which enabled him to exercise minute discrimination as he listened to others speak in the foreign language. This was also adapted for the use of children and slow learners in order to improve their knowledge of English grammar and spelling.

With this apparatus, the student could follow the counselor's color-code analysis of the grammatical linguistics on the monitor lantern. At the same time, when he wished to speak himself, he had the reassuring closeness, support and warmth of the expert counselor to give him whatever words, phrases or corrections he needed. The fact that the conversations could be turned immediately into a written tape which was color-coded for linguistic analysis further reinforced the discriminatory learning necessary to personalize such grammar and other linguistic comprehension. Since simultaneous sound recordings were made, pronunciation was assisted. There was first the total trust of the client in the counselor which freed him from his anxiety bind. He could abandon his tongue to what he heard and so repeat it with more exactness. He then had the opportunity to hear himself and the counselor immediately afterwards, and so reinforce his grasp of the correct forms or recognize errors from the sound and visual tapes.

In addition, the group process was initiated and furthered both by the commitment which a personalized discussion in a foreign language demanded and the common group engagement in learning that was made possible by the combined use of the learning lanterns. The resultant sense of group encouragement, sharing, belonging and working together at common learning tasks and goals not only furthered the learning process but stimulated growth in increasing self-awareness, confidence, worth and group-belonging.

FIVE STAGES

We divided the growth process of this counseling learning into five stages, extending from total dependency, in Stage I, to total independence as the theoretical goal at the end of Stage V. The following diagram illustrates this.

The various phases of the design are intended to show how the person, beginning in embryonic dependency on the learning counselor, slowly emerges to his own independent ability to communicate, so that at the end of Stage V he no longer needs the language counselor's help. This, as we see, is a steady process. In proportion, for example, as he can carry on a conversation with few mistakes, and so needing corrections only in idioms and grammatical subtleties, he would have arrived at Stage IV.

INDIVIDUAL AND GROUP AGGRESSION

Interestingly, the learner seems to go through a gradual process of security until Stage III. Then he often experiences renewed discomfort and difficulty, especially in Stage IV. This seems to be so because he is now far more aware of his mistakes even though he can be easily understood. He is therefore much more demanding of himself and more self-critical.

In addition there is, at this stage, a much greater resurgence of open aggression and self-affirmation. This seems to go with more direct responsibility for learning and a stronger determination to overcome barriers in the way of learning achievement. Sometimes this shows itself in direct hostility to other group members, especially if their behavior or manner seems to impede the person's progress in learning.

Stages in Language Counselor-Client Relationship from Dependency to Independence

I

Total dependence on language counselor. Idea said in English, then said to group in foreign language, as counselor slowly and sensitively gives each word to the client.

II

Beginning courage to make some attempts to speak in the foreign language as words and phrases are picked up and retained.

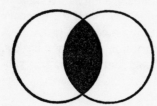

III

Growing independence with mistakes that are immediately corrected by counselor.

IV

Needing counselor now only for idioms and more subtle expressions and grammar.

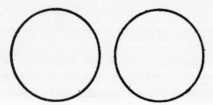

V

Independent and free communication in the foreign language. Counselor's *silent* presence reinforces correctness of grammar and pronunciation.

This can sometimes initiate intense periods of group confrontation and exchange. Since, however, the focus is still on the learning task, the tones and attitudes seem seldom to be carried over to outside relationships. Until people are used to this, they often express surprise at the relaxed tone of coffee breaks after such sessions. For some, it was a significant experience to be able to express this kind of constructive, task-oriented anger without any feeling of guilt or of a need to apologize afterwards. It was a great relief to be free to be angry and yet feel truly accepted by the group at the same time.

ADOLESCENT-ADULT

In some ways, these kinds of aggressive struggles in the group seemed to correspond to the adolescent's need for independent self-assertion. As the group grew more secure in language achievement and moved toward the end of Stage IV, much of this group aggression ceased. It became concentrated on the task itself rather than on group members. As the experiences in the group produced the rewards of successful language achievement and communication, the need for hostility and resistance among group members toward one another gradually decreased.

In these changes, one could observe a growing sense of maturity and security in the new language self. This seemed to be similar to the kind of secure self-affirmation that a young adult begins to exhibit as he arrives at a clearer delineation of himself. Stage V therefore, while concentrated in its effort for the most exact linguistic expression, was usually less tense and more relaxed. Easy personal exchanges could occur, anger could be expressed and quickly evaporate. Group members in Stage V were much more at ease with themselves and one another. They had, in other words, the ease of established adult relationships that were firm and secure.

EXPLANATION MATERIAL

The following material explaining these five stages was given to each participant:

Stages in Language Counselor-Client Relationship
from Dependency to Independence

Stage I

The client is completely dependent on the language counselor.

1. First (turning his head to the counselor), he expresses *only* to the counselor and *in English* what he wishes to say to the group. Each group member *overhears* this English exchange, but is not involved in it.

2. The counselor then reflects these ideas back to the client *in the foreign language* in a warm, accepting tone, in simple language especially of cognates, in phrases of five or six words.

3. The client *turns to the group* and presents his ideas *in the foreign language.* He has the counselor's aid if he mispronounces or hesitates on a word or phrase.

This is the client's *maximum dependency and security stage.*

Stage II

1. Same as above.

2. The client turns and begins to speak the *foreign language* directly to the group.

3. The counselor aids only as the client hesitates or turns for help. These small independent steps are signs of positive confidence and hope.

Stage III

1. The client speaks directly to the group *in the foreign language.* This presumes that the group has now acquired the ability to understand his simple phrases.

2. Same as #3 above. This presumes the client's greater confidence, independence and proportionate insight into the relationship of phrases, grammar and ideas. Translation is given only when a group member desires it.

Stage IV

1. The client is now speaking freely and complexly *in the foreign language.* Presumes group's understanding.

2. The counselor directly intervenes in case of grammatical error or mispronunciation, or where aid in complex expression is needed. The client is sufficiently secure to take correction.

Stage V

1. Same as IV.
2. Counselor intervenes not only to offer correction but to add idioms and more elegant constructions. This is the client's maximum independency and security stage.
3. At this stage the client can become counselor to group in Stages I, II and III.

The expert only aids the counselors—when help is needed; they, in turn, directly relate to the clients. The expert's presence, however, is reinforcing and reassuring, especially in his silence.

INTERRELATED DYNAMICS

These stages are, however, not only a description of a learning process and a person's growing competence and independent knowledge in a foreign language, mathematics, history, science or some other field. They are also descriptive of other interrelated dynamics. They can be seen, for example, as defining the growth of a child from embryo to independent adulthood, passing through childhood and adolescence, which might be considered Stages III and IV.

These five steps can also, in a special way, illustrate the process of counseling therapy. A person is anxious and insecure at the beginning of the interviews because he is in confusion and conflict about at least one area of his life. Gradually he is helped to reflect upon and see himself and his situation more clearly and so make more adequate independent judgments.

Stage I can also represent the dependent, inadequate person, unsure of himself and huddling in a group or behind others in defensiveness and fear. We can see him grow in successive stages to trust himself and allow himself to emerge in his own self-worth, as he begins to see himself as having value to himself and others. By Stages IV and V he has grown to where he can take security, satisfaction and confidence in being and becoming himself. Illustrated here then would be the emergence of Tillich's "courage to be."

But this process demonstrates at the same time a growth in self-unity in contrast to a self-rejecting dichotomy of loving to hate oneself. A person at the end would therefore be more accepting of his whole self—soma, instincts and emotions as well as knowing and choice functions. These would all form a part of his new sense of incarnate self-worth. These five stages, then, would also show the process of growth in self-incarnate redemption. This is first achieved through the concerned understanding and knowledge of someone who consciously loved first and on whom the person can depend. This convalidates the person's own self-worth and enables him freely to grow in his own redemptive sense; that is, in his own independent convalidation of himself in the learning process.

TEACHER COMMITMENT

What is needed in an educative process, then, is the same kind of willingness on the part of the knower, the "teacher," to give up his eminence and dominance in knowing. In this he needs to abandon himself to the meaning and value of the student somewhat in imitation of what the religious man should do towards God. The words "I must decrease, he must increase" describe the commitment that enables another person to learn from me. Starting in the ignorant dependency of not-knowing, he is free to develop into the independence of knowing. But to be needed can be self-aggrandizing for the "teacher," and to show off knowledge has an exhibitionist reward that can be very satisfying. For these reasons such a commitment is in fact most difficult.

As theological incarnation-redemption has Christ abandoning himself to man for each man's redemption, by correspondent convalidation the knower enables the learner to grow in the redeemed worth of knowing. By feeling himself loved and approved not only when he is in need or depends on the teacher but also when he seeks to be free of the teacher, a student is best aided to grow in this way.

LEARNING AS NEW LIFE

This would be *living learning*. By contrast we often have a dead structure which demands simply that the learner reflect the knower in order to please him and so protect himself from a poor grade or a classroom group humiliation. Anyone associated with, and observant of, a small child learning something new cannot help being caught up in the excitement, enthusiasm and coming-alive feeling which the child reveals in each new learning experience. One of the frequent consequences of our present socially isolated and information-centered educational methods is to deaden learning and to take away from it all the excitement and fresh bloom of coming to new life.

But the aim of counseling therapy, as we have seen, is to encourage and aid the independent coming to life or "resurrection" of the client. He often experiences this as a movement from a dead "old" self to an exciting "new" self-birth. In the counseling therapy process, it is not uncommon for a person to describe this "new life" feeling as he struggles, with the skilled counselor's help, for a new and more integrated understanding of himself and his situation. The following excerpt indicates this:

Co: It's a new way of evaluating yourself, and therefore it needs a great deal more delineation.

Cl: Uh-huh. This is the first time I've felt free to do this.

Co: It's your first real acceptance of a positive worthwhile self in a, shall we say, a fundamentally realistic sense.

Cl: Uh-huh. (*Pause.*)

Co: Quite pleased at all that, aren't you?

Cl: Yes, and it's deep. I think I'm going to cry again. I mean, it's like a, a new baby. You're afraid its skin or something is fragile. (*Sobbing softly. Pause.*)

Co: It's a very delicate bringing something into being in yourself that you sort of see you have produced? (*The counselor, in turn, speaks very slowly and quietly.*)

Cl: And forcing it to come out this way is the only way to do it.

Co: It's one of the final stages of getting born.

Cl: Yes.

Similarly, the dead learning methods—isolated and exaggeratedly impersonal—must be brought to life through a warm, personal and engaged living experience between expert knower and learner. The deadness of learning must be resurrected and restored to the natural joy and enthusiasim it once had for the learner when the learning experience was young and fresh.

Evident here are echoes of the recurrent religious theme of putting on the "new man," the redeemed and resurrected sense of personal self-worth. This comes psychologically to be a genuine and confident self-regard when, having been achieved in and through another, it finally reaches a state of independent meaning and value. At its best, the goal of the educative process should be the same. It should be the conscious realization of the learner that he now knows, and knows that he knows, and so can give his knowledge freely and without restraint to others.

INTERNALIZED KNOWLEDGE

St. Paul uses the analogy of the Law as a children's schoolmaster (Gal. 3:23). This may be applied to the expert counselor in a foreign language. He is someone who is needed in the dependency stages of growing to learn a foreign language. But a child or an adolescent, or an adult in the earlier stages, is both dependent on and yet struggling for independence of the counselor-expert. The ideal goal of such independence is when one has internalized all the linguistic knowledge of the expert and so oneself speaks the language expertly. One has in this sense cast off the teacher, as in a similar way one casts off the law. The mature religious person, having internalized all that the law means, has liberty not in contradiction to the law but above and beyond the law. In a linguistic sense, the laws of grammar are still basic to good speech, but when one has internalized this structure and uses the language easily, one is free because he need no longer be obsessionally concentrated on the law.

Something of this is implied by Ricoeur in his concept of the progression from scrupulosity, as an obsession with the law and its minutiae, to freedom.[4] Persons who are learning a foreign language tend to be obsessed with the minutiae of the grammatical construction. They may, in fact, learn the laws of grammar and be able to analyze a sentence and yet never really arrive at the freedom to speak. But representation has come into being when, in a certain sense, the law is cast off by being internalized into a living reality. In the Pauline sense of "Christ now lives in me," representation and being have come together in an integrity of internal meaning and value. In language learning, the person speaks correctly but without any consciousness of rules. In both senses, representation has become a living reality in the person himself.

This progression will then work against the tendency in the one who knows, who is a teacher, to hold the eminence of "pedagogue"; that is, to be a teacher of "dependent" children only. Instead, the knower must regard each person, child or adult, as having his own unique and personal learning potential. This is known only to the learner himself, and only he can unfold and activate it. In this process the "pedagogue" must decrease. He becomes rather Plato's "midwife," so that the new independent self—let us say it is a "French" self if the learner is studying French—can be born and grow in his own mysterious uniqueness.

Montaigne catches the mature relationship necessary to genuine total-person learning when he says, "To do well, learning must not be merely installed in the house but married."[5] He goes on to say of the teacher's relationship with the learner:

At the very outset he should put the pupil on his own mettle. Let him taste things for himself, and choose and determine between them. . . . this is one of the hardest things I know of. Only the most disciplined and finely tempered souls know how to slacken and stoop to the gait of children. I walk firmer and surer uphill than down. . . .[6]

MIMESIS

In the mimesic quality necessary to any learning situation, however, we have a clear distinction from counseling therapy. In this mimesic sense, the learning relationship would be determined by what the knower stands for or *re-presents*. It is the learner's awareness of this which brought him in the first place. In turn, it is the teacher's knowledge in a particular area which validates his position and determines the nature of his mimesis. In this the learning relationship between teacher and student clearly differs from the relationship of counseling or therapy. There the client is studying himself. He projects this study of himself in and through the counselor-therapist. In the mimesic relationship, the student is studying what the teacher knows, stands for and re-presents. Consequently, his study and learning through the teacher extend to a field or block of knowledge beyond both himself and the teacher. Here the symbolic, more universal quality of learning appears. For in its more universalizing symbolization, as Eliade, quoted earlier, pointed out, education frees both teacher and learner to go beyond their immediate selves to the broad vistas of the whole field of knowledge.

RELIGIOUS EDUCATION

This incarnate-redemptive process has special significance for religious education. Here above all knowledge should be given in such a clean, uncontaminated way as to stimulate real and unique religious experience in each learner. Here especially, the combination of mimesic and counseling relationships would be most significant since, of all the areas of learning, the one *par excellence* which involves and requires value investment as well as meaning would be the area of religion itself. Religious knowledge alone, so that one might readily say, "Lord, Lord," without doing, is not enough. As à Kempis put it, "I would rather feel compunction than know its definition." Here significance and meaning must most surely give way to genuinely invested religious experience and commitment if religious education is to have any final effectiveness and validation. Here too, especially, the knower must truly represent and, having presented, decrease steadily, so that the learner may move from a diet of milk to the strong meat of adults. Only in this way can he experience the mature growth and genuine investment of an incarnate-redemptive educative process.

NOTES

[1] This research has been supported since 1959 by a yearly grant from the Society for Human Relations Research. It has been carried on with groups at Loyola University, Mendel High School, Chicago, and Woodstock Central High School, Woodstock, Ill.

"Counseling Skills Adapted to the Learning of Foreign Languages," a report on the plan of this research and some earlier findings given in the *Menninger Bulletin,* March 1961. A later report was published at Loyola

University, Chicago, in February, 1965, entitled "A Counseling-Psychotherapeutic Methodology and Associated Learning Apparatus."

See also: Daniel D. Tranel, "Teaching Latin by Use of the Chromacord Machine," *The Classical Journal,* December 1967. This contains a detailed report of the methods described here related to a specially devised group learning apparatus.

Demonstrations and theoretical discussions have been presented at a variety of meetings, among them: The Kansas State Language Teachers' Assn., April 1960; the Spanish Language Teachers' Assn., February 1963, Chicago Teachers' College; The Midwest Psychological Assn., May 1963; and two National Defense Education Act Teacher Training Institutes at Rosary College, June of 1962, and Mundelein College, July of 1963; at a Fordham University Forum, May 1965, and at Barry College, February 1968.

See also "Total Involvement" A Picture description by *Jubilee* Magazine, May 1968.

[2] Curran, *Counseling and Psychotherapy: The Pursuit of Values,* p. 298.

[3] *Ibid.,* Chapters XIV ("A Counseling Model in Learning") and XV ("Counseling, Teaching Apparatus, and Learning"), pp. 295–338.

[4] Ricoeur, *op. cit.,* p. 149.

[5] Marvin Lowenthal, ed., *The Autobiography of Michel de Montaigne* (New York: Vintage Books, 1956), p. 18.

[6] *Ibid.,* p. 23.

PART FOUR
General Application

11

The Sermon as Self-Counseling

A CENTRAL PART of religious commitment, determining its nature, is the "Word of God." Discussing this, Barth says:

. . . Faith means seeking not noise but quiet, and letting God speak within—the righteous God, for there is no other. And then God works in us. Then begins in us, as from a seed, but an unfailing seed, the new basic something which overcomes unrighteousness. Where faith is, in the midst of the old world of war and money and death, there is born a new spirit out of which grows a new world, the world of the righteousness of God. The need and anxiety in which we live are done away when this new beginning comes. The old fetters are broken, the false idols begin to totter. For now something real has happened—the only real thing that can happen: God has now taken His own work in hand.[1]

This is the indwelling voice of Counsel, counseling each person in those things special and unique to himself. In this sense one can say, with Barth's title, that the Word of God must become the word of man—in each man as he takes counsel with himself and contemplates the areas of belief and action that constitute the force of his own religious investment. This would be the main aim and intent of a sermon modelled off the counseling process and relationship.

ANSWER OR SOLUTION

We have already referred to the way in which Cartesian intellectualism has affected our culture in leaving us with the assumption that to know is sufficient. This idea of figuring out people's problems and giving them "answers" seems to follow from a mathematical model of the learning process. From the Kantian influence in our culture, the failure to carry these "answers" into practice was attributed to "bad will" or a "bad" character.

These same cultural elements are evident in the manner of preparing and presenting a sermon. A sermon which aims at giving "answers to problems" is closed—allowing almost no room for the hearer to extend the sermon to his own area of personal concern. He simply has seen a problem presented and solved.

It is interesting to note in this context that the word "answer" means "something one swears to," indicating its precise and exact quality. What the sermon aims for might be rather considered a "solution," to suggest its *loosening* and freeing catalytic process while it yet offers the hearer the assurances coming from religious faith, hope and love. So considered, the sermon experience should be a freeing one, suggesting to the hearer release from the bind of his anxieties and frustrations. If Revelation is not simply a monologue from God but a divine dialogue, then the sermon should provide each person with liberating insights about those things uniquely important to him. It should invite him to personal commitment as well as assure him of God's genuine engagement in his anxieties and concerns.

There are, of course, a variety of types of sermons, each with its own purpose. The purpose here is to create a favorable state in each hearer for personal application and, if possible, as a first stage of a counseling discussion. There can be an instructional sermon, for example, one that is especially aimed at giving information. But even here, as we said in our discussion of the incarnate-redemptive educative process, the personal investment of the one receiving is still desirable. Klink puts it this way:

Worship and preaching are collective experiences in which individuals may experience the relevance of a universal gospel to their situation. They can, through hearing of proper preaching of the Word, come to feel that the gospel or the liturgy is properly expressive of their personal experiences. But there is an encountering aspect to preaching and worship. Worship can permit the individuals in a congregation to deepen their sense of peculiar individuality and, in that uniqueness, to be addressed by the gospel. Thus, not all preaching is encounter but all preaching may be.[2]

FOOD ANALOGY

In this sense, the sermon can be considered in terms of food. While a good piece of steak or similar basic food-stuff is essential, much of the effectiveness of the meal is yet determined by the skill of the cooking and serving. This involves adapting the meal to each person. The absence or presence of even small details can sometimes destroy the pleasure and assimilation of what was basically good food. It is not only the food itself that is important, therefore, but also the uniquely personal reactions of each participant in the meal.

As proteins, carbohydrates, etc., are necessary in one's basic diet, so doctrine is necessary to a sermon. But this is not enough. In fact it may be inadequate, much as an excellent piece of steak poorly cooked, or salted too much, can be a disappointment to everyone. The learned theologian, by the absence of other necessary qualities in his presentation, can fail to elicit an effective response in his hearers. He may not adapt his material to suit the tastes and needs of the audience. Excellent material will finally be determined in its effectiveness on its hearers by the way this material is received. It will not be assimilated if it is presented in a way that creates indifference, resistance or other negative reactions.

If the intent is to move the audience to some kind of personal involvement and action, then more than a cold, impersonal, intellectual presentation is necessary. There are some special complexities here. It is difficult to tell people what to do in such a way that they can readily do it. As we have seen, there is a vast difference between telling a person "what were good to do" and the process that brings about the internal, psychosomatic coordination and integration necessary to do this.

TRIANGLE

In counseling and psychotherapy, we have learned that people are most helped to make personal changes in conduct when they are aided to take counsel with themselves and interrelate the information they are receiving with their own inner world of personalized singularity. This would also seem to apply to the effects of a sermon. Each hearer has his own world of personal uniqueness.

Here we can return to the illustration of the triangle.[3] One can conceive of the base of the triangle as symbolizing the general theological knowledge that needs to be presented. This involves the basic tradition of religious faith and understanding.

The point of the triangle symbolizes each one's uniqueness. Applied here, the information presented will end in the unique world of each of the hearers. This unique world is not only that of intellectual understanding; it includes also those subtle qualities which involve emotions, instincts, soma, and the integration of these with reason and will. The results of the sermon must be finally to engage all levels of the self, if it is to make operationally effective anything that is heard.

HUMAN BELONGING

The expression "winning an argument and losing a friend" describes how one can be logically consistent without being truly effective. One can be convincing in the sense that one can conquer another person intellectually and thus silence him. Yet one has not really persuaded him. Persuasion fails if a person is not motivated to put into operation, in his own unique world of experience and action, the information presented to him.

In a passage of capital importance for the psychology of sermons, Aquinas illumines a well-known text from St. Paul. It is the familiar text in which St. Paul is describing the quality of charity. He says, among other things, "If I should speak with the tongues of men and of angels and have not charity . . . it profits me nothing" (I Cor. 13:1, 3). St. Paul then describes with a delicately fine discrimination the qualities of charity (4, 7).

Aquinas poses the question, "If I speak with the tongues of men and of angels—why would it profit nothing?" He answers, first, that "to speak with the tongues of men and of angels" is to be an outstanding intellectual. But, according to Aquinas, if I have all this knowledge, understanding and skill in exposition, yet lack these Pauline qualities of charity, my presentation will come to nothing, because no one would be effectively changed. Unless a presentation is permeated with a sense of human belonging and sharing, it will not move a person. More than cold analysis is needed. An intellectual appeal without some of the warm qualities of sharing and belonging that St. Paul describes would seem therefore insufficient to capture the personal commitment of the hearer. In relation to the audience, a sermon arrives at this when it moves from the cold skeleton of intellectual and theological structure to the warm flesh and blood of incarnate communication. It must go beyond the intellect to the emotions, instincts and soma.

EMPATHY AND SYMPATHY

In the counseling and psychotherapy relationships which attempt to achieve basic changes in self-understanding and action, there must be both empathy and sympathy. As we have seen, the word "sympathy," in contrast to "empathy," suggests a higher, more human and more directly conscious and rational sharing. Sympathy in this sense is not simply a kind of sharing in sorrow. It suggests people's conscious sharing of the human condition together. Counseling and psychotherapy seem most effective when the counselor has this "feeling with" others, this warm quality of commitment and belonging. If, in the sermon, the speaker takes a position of distance and puts himself on a height psychologically as well as physically because he is comfortable there, he is apt to remain unincarnate. This may help to explain some of religion's irrelevance and the present relevance of counseling and psychotherapy. They have reached people, whereas the sermon has remained removed and aloof.

A purely intellectual presentation then, however logical and well-structured, runs the danger of seeming to be impersonal and irrelevant. None of us are attracted to a skeleton. While it is a part of our humanity and we all know that we have a skeleton like the one we see, it still appears inhuman. It has none of the warmth of the living members that make a body. "Sympathy" is the giving of this warm human quality.

I-YOU DISTANCE

In a presentation especially of a somewhat abstract sort, there can be implied, too, a kind of condescending superiority, or at least a tone that seems to withdraw the speaker. This "I" passing judgment on "you" may be convincing in the intellectual sense, but it seems often to run the risk of leaving the other person "cold," as he may say. People are thus unable to assimilate and absorb what is said. "I" and "you" can be too far apart, too uncommitted, too removed. If "I" is a voice coming down from the Olympian heights, of course there is no humanity in that voice. It is not an incarnate-redemptive process. At best it treats of meaning and not values.

By contrast, we have St. John's conception that it was not that we first loved God but that God first loved us. In order to communicate this love, He took upon Himself a human nature and became like unto us. By "sympathy" we mean the capacity to become like our audience, to be one of them, to share the innermost sense of their human condition, to become incarnate with them and so help them feel a sense of worth.

THE PRODIGAL SON

How did Christ convey this deep sense of sharing the human condition? In the scene that reveals Christ's delicate love and forgiveness, the scene where Mary Magdalene falls at His feet, He said nothing. He knew the value of silent understanding. He let her act out all her deep emotions of sorrow and repentance as she washed His feet with her tears. He let her use her precious ointment to anoint Him lovingly. He only spoke when someone raised an objection. He said, to defend her: "Because she has loved much, much is forgiven her." Christ here gave us a classic statement of human "sympathy."

If one were to ask what was the most appealing sermon ever preached, many would refer to the sermon of "The Prodigal Son." Even for its literary quality, it has been called the most perfect short story ever written.

LOVE AND FREEDOM

The sermon begins with a common, deeply shared human experience: the conflicting feelings of a father who loves his son and yet wants his son to be free. Intrinsically bound up with the father's love is his sense of a young man's right and need to be free. This is the first thing that catches us, the psychological conflict of a loving father who nonetheless does not want to dominate or control his son. So when the son insists on his freedom, in loving kindness the father sadly agrees. The son is given his share of his inheritance, not only because the father loves him but also because the father knows that love is free, that it cannot be forced. The son must be allowed to be free. In just a few sentences, the whole basic condition of man—his freedom, his need to love and the interrelation of freedom and love—is revealed.

LONELINESS

The second deep human experience in this parable is that of loneliness. This comes after one has spent all one's goods and wasted oneself. Here we relive in ourselves this feeling. We feel that same sense of having wasted something and wasted it terribly. We too wanted to be free and on our own to do what we pleased. But we too come finally, at some turn in the road, to discover that we have been wrong—perhaps horribly foolish—and we are now caught in our own guilt and regrets. There is now only a sense of loss, of waste, and a gnawing sense of guilt.

GUILT

We have seen instances, in counseling therapy excerpts, of the way guilt digs into a person, often making him miserably unhappy. But all of us know guilt, and we all know this same sense of having wasted something selfishly. So here too we are caught up in this shared feeling, and we wander with this young man. We can walk with him because we know how he feels.

ANXIETY

We also can understand his fears about returning home. Logically he has no right to go home, because in a way he deserves only his father's rejection and hostility. He has no right to anything but to hear "I told you so. You were determined to make a fool of yourself and that is the end of it. I will have nothing more to do with you." From a certain point of view we can see that this could be. The other son has the right to everything. He was loyal and faithful. We share the fear and anxiety of the guilty one. We know this anxiety; we know it sometimes when we wake up in the middle of the night and these anxieties strike us; when our own guilts and fears come forward.

We know this young man in his innermost feelings. We know what it means to be alone; to feel guilty, anxious, distraught and fearful; even what it means to have no one. Now that he has spent his wealth, all the shallow superficial good-time friends of the past are gone. He is alone; alone with his misery, his sorrow; but most of all alone with his bitterness and self-attack.

LOVE AND FORGIVENESS

We all know finally the last profound human qualities that are touched in the parable: love and forgiveness. As we have seen, one of the most difficult issues for every person is not his sin or guilt alone—it is to be able to forgive himself. To return again to our discussion of the difference between Judas and Peter which seems to bear this out: Peter, in a sense, was more cowardly than Judas. Judas at least did something that had an element of manliness in it. He openly betrayed Christ. He betrayed Him for money, which money he later had the courage to throw back. But Peter, who boasted of his courage, became a cowardly figure in a courtyard, afraid of a servant girl. Peter's sin, because of his very display, would have been perhaps the more difficult one for him to forgive himself. Yet the core of the comparison of these two pivotal characters, as we see them in the Gospel, is not only their sin but what they did with their guilt. Peter was somehow able to first forgive himself for the cheap and shabby cowardice that he had displayed before a servant girl. He was then able to come back and face Christ again. He looked into Christ's eyes, and in that look he received forgiveness. The tragedy of Judas was apparently that he was so guilty he could do nothing but attack himself. He could act out his changed view in a very dramatic way. He could throw those coins at the feet of the men who had aided the betrayal of Christ and disavow what he had done. But he could not return and face Christ. On the contrary, in self-hatred, apparently, he hanged himself. Here, as we have seen, the sinner does not truly love himself but in fact, in his sin, hates and does evil to himself. In counseling and psychotherapeutic interviews one sees many people in similar psychological struggles not only because of the sin they committed but because they cannot forgive themselves. In vengeful self-attack it is extremely difficult for them to turn and face forgiveness.

SIMPLE SOLUTION

This is the struggle of this young man before he can start back home. We can imagine him violently attacking himself for his stupidity, his pride, his vanity, his selfishness, his inconsideration—like a person who attacks himself in a counseling interview. All these things the young man can say about himself because he knows himself better than anyone else and he is the best observer of everything he does. So there he is, standing in severe judgment of himself. The struggle, as he turns to walk the long, long way home, is: can he forgive himself? Can he, who deserves only rejection, take a chance at throwing himself on his father's mercy?

He finally resolves this agonizing dilemma in a very simple way. People in violent psychological states of guilt and anxiety often seek such simple solutions. The simple solution for this young man was that his father would hire servants, and did from time to time. Many times he had seen men wander in, profligates of various sorts, and his father had been kind to them, had clothed them and fed them. So he said to himself, "I am no different from any of those weak or drunken, disordered, inadequate men that I have seen come and go in my childhood. I will present myself that way at the servants' door and I will beg to be taken in just as they did."

It is in this human condition of complete degradation, of having "hit bottom" as the Alcoholics Anonymous describe it, that he is able to think of forgiving himself. He finds one condition no lower than his own, and this one condition is his pathway back to his father.

COMING HOME

All the time the father had been going, night after night, up a hill to watch for him in loving concern and anxiety. The father from afar thus sees him coming and is overcome by joy. All know and share the human condition of being forgiven and of coming home. This is the final, sensitively delicate touch in Our Lord's parable. By contrast to the anxiety and the fear of being unwilling to forgive ourselves for a horrible act against someone who loves us and whom we love, there is—when one is able to forgive oneself at least to the extent of returning—the indescribably overwhelming relief of love and forgiveness. All of us know this and have in some way experienced it. We know that mercy "is twice blessed," that it blesses him who gives and him who receives. So the father in mercy and love is blessed and the son in receiving mercy and love is blessed. The conclusion of Christ's sermon: through this father-image we can begin to understand something of the profundity of Divine Love.

PERSONAL IDENTIFICATION

To apply this concept of sharing the human condition so profoundly illustrated in "The Prodigal Son": we want to arrive at the hearer's own identification and involvement with what he hears. This is the way we feel as Christ is giving his sermon. We are involved, committed and intensely participant.

In sharing the human condition, then, we do not mean any extremely emotional or revivalist quality—this would be something else and could have quite a different purpose. What we mean—and what we find effective in counseling and psychotherapy—could be described by words like "warmth," "commitment" or "belonging." *We suggest to our audience some deeply human as well as theologi-*

cal theme and allow each one's own introspection to develop his uniquely personal variations and details. The analogy of a symphony theme with its many different variations for each instrument might be helpful here. Once this personal identification and involvement has been achieved in each hearer, the speaker can then enlarge on the theological points implied. These will then have personal meaning and application for each hearer. They will not remain simply impersonal and be only general information. Having assimilated and made personal the basic human theme, each hearer is now—like the hearers of Christ's sermon—taking counsel with himself in his own unique condition.

SPEAKER'S MANNER

This warmth and sense of sharing is communicated primarily in the material of the sermon. The speaker's manner will vary with the accustomed style and personality of each speaker. However, this kind of material would, it seems, tend to call for a calm, conversational tone. The speaker depends on the electronic speaking system to carry his words into the ear of the hearer. The speaker avoids those mannerisms that would perhaps take the hearer away from his own self-involved pondering on what the speaker is saying. For the purpose we have in mind, the hearer is rather talking to himself, counseling himself through the voice of the speaker. The speaker therefore strives rather to lead and direct this deep personal meditation than to attract attention to himself. His appeal, insofar as it is emotional, has a suppressed, and therefore intense quality, as compared with a more directly dramatic expression. It is more like the warm tone of deep sharing and understanding in the voice of a sensitive counselor.

PERSONAL MATERIAL

Personal material, of course, can be helpful and important here, provided that it can be really shared in such a way that people become personally empathetic to it. Something of this was evident in the explanations just given. The difficulty with material that is *too personal* is that it can embarrass an audience and also distract and alienate it; or be so egotistical that it does not move others to participate but rather makes them resistant or indifferent. Personal material has to avoid these extremes. One study in group counseling suggests in fact that the counselor's personal delineation runs the risk of appearing somewhat "phony."

The results of this study do not support the use of self-experience in group counseling relationships. There are no demonstrated advantages and one significant disadvantage. The counseling atmosphere was perceived as less genuine when self-experience was used than in similar counseling situations where it was not used.[4]

The same "less genuine" tone could result from the use of too personal material in a sermon.

ILLUSTRATION

Let us explore how one might introduce the idea of wandering away from home, of loneliness, of being lost, so poignantly suggested in "The Prodigal Son." In the next chapter we can see excerpts of recorded comments, illustrating how this presentation reached people in their own unique lives even though it refers to personal experiences of the speaker. The speaker begins:

Most little children have been lost at some time or other. I was lost one time when I was three or four. It was my own fault. I wandered off in disobedience and I had that same fear of going back home. I expected to be spanked because I knew I had deliberately disobeyed. And this theme ought to touch something in you too. You must have been lost sometime. You must have been terribly afraid when you were lost. And if so, we have touched on a common sharing of our uniqueness. You know what it is to be afraid to go home and so do I. This would again be the kind of common human touch that is in The Prodigal Son.

I can think of adults who have felt lost and alone. I recall one time being terribly lonely in a foreign country, and I suspect this too will touch you somewhere. You too must know the loneliness of being in a strange land, or a strange city. This feeling is particularly poignant if people are speaking a foreign tongue. This adds to the ostracized feeling. This kind of loneliness can be really devastating sometimes. There is a real truth in the fact of being homesick—it is a terrible sickness—like being seasick. You cannot believe, after it is over, that you were as sick as you were. But literally one can almost want to die of homesickness, just as one can nearly want to die of seasickness, even though both may pass in a comparatively short time and, in a sense, there is nothing physically wrong with us in either sickness. Yet loneliness can be a terrible suffering. All of us at one time or another must have known some kind of homesickness or loneliness. If so, we know how the Prodigal Son felt. We know too how he longed to be back home. We know how strange he felt in a foreign land, or unknown city, and how little he belonged there, how little any of it was part of himself. This we can all share.

We surely share deeply, too, the sense of coming home. Perhaps even the great appeal of Christmas to the world each year owes something to this strong human feeling of wanting to be home. There is something about the light and warmth around the crib shining in the darkness that tells us we are nearing home—nearing the place where we will always belong. It is not unlike the Prodigal Son's beginning to see lights in the familiar houses of his own village. He knows he is near his father and his family and all those who love him. He belongs again. Christmas somehow seems to lead us all back to some similar kind of belonging, to a sense of coming home to God. If, at no one other time, at least at Christmas the world seems permeated with this tone and mood of a return to the God who loves and forgives.

All of us then like the Prodigal Son have wandered off. And all of us have returned home and experienced great joy and peace in being there. We know too what it means to be forgiven. Few human experiences are as intense as to have carried around anxiety and guilt for a long, long time and then to discover that it was nothing, that all we had to do was to return home and face the issue and it all disappeared! To the relief of forgiveness is added the indescribable joy of an atmosphere that is suffused with mercy, kindness and understanding; all those tones that St. Paul lists as the qualities of charity.

This discussion of "the Prodigal Son" and its implications for ourselves should at some point have gone beyond what was said. The psychology of the sermon on the Prodigal Son is to lead us from the human love of a father, which we can feel, understand and share, to the plenitude of Divine Love beyond us. How can we love God, whom we see not, if we do not experience love from and to our neighbor, whom we see? If we cannot share love in the human condition, we will apparently have grave difficulty believing in it in the divine. Christ gives us this parallel of human love at one of its deepest and most delicate levels, so we could use this as a scaffolding or ladder to God. If we understand a loving father, we understand something of God's love.

ESSENTIAL THINGS

An English essayist has said:

> Primitive and essential things have great power to touch the heart of the beholder. I mean such things as a man ploughing a field, or sowing or reaping; a girl filling a pitcher from a spring; a young mother with her child; a fisherman mending his nets; a light from a lonely hut on a dark night . . .[5]

These are the human elements of a sermon—the common condition of life we all share. The Gospel gives us many of these. The Psalms are filled with this same kind of image: God's love covering us as a bird covers its brood with its wings or—a sharper image —protecting us as we protect the pupil of our eye. Deep basic protective mechanisms in animals and man are implied here that unfold both empathy and sympathy. Or again the frustration and helplessness that is suggested in the sinner being lost in a mire— and the sudden surge of hope and confidence when he can stand solidly or spring forward on the rock that is God. All of us have been "stuck in the mud" literally and psychologically, and we know this frustrating feeling very well indeed. We know too the freeing joy of a solid foothold.

LINGUISTIC VALUE-ANALYSIS

We are, in this way, tracing a word or phrase down to its basic meaning, which also then contains a value-scheme implication as well. This usually constitutes its theme or message. The process might be called a "linguistic value-analysis." That is, each word has a basic value hidden behind the myriad of more complex conscious and unconscious values it conveys to us. This basic value may be, and in fact usually is, totally forgotten, so that often the present various meanings of the word now appear to have no relation to this value. But there is a real and deep relationship still, a relationship in *experience*. This can offer a simple but profound clue to why the word was coined or first adapted for this particular use.

The Old and New Testament abound in such words. One way of approaching a sermon is to seek out the basic value of the word and offer this in an experience that holds the hearer. On this experience, then, the application of both meaning and personal value can follow.

Earlier we discussed the concept of implicit values in a word or phrase which already involved a certain kind of cultural investment. We pointed out, for example, that the phrase "figuring people out" seems to imply a mathematical Cartesian set of values that leaves one uninvolved and in a depersonalized relationship. Or as we saw, and will consider later in detail, the word "city" applied to the Church as the "City of God" contains the structure of implicit values quite different from the concept of salt savoring meat or leaven penetrating dough. One discovers this kind of basic value implication by tracing the sophisticated overlay of a word or phrase down to its basic origin. Often in the basic origin of a word there is a kind of experienced awareness that can be shared, and at the same time it reveals the total significance, conscious and unconscious, of the word or phrase.

EXAMPLES

This process of "linguistic value-analysis" can be helpful in preparing a sermon so that it can be a shared experience with the audience. Consider, for example, the word, "spirit." Let us assume that the overall intent of the sermon in this case is to describe, and involve the hearer in, an experience awareness that could lead to the belief in or greater consciousness of the indwelling of the Holy Spirit.

If one traces the origin of the word "spiritus," it comes from the word "breath." It could even be thought to imitate the process of breathing, especially in the French form of "esprit," apparently onomatopoeic for the effort to breathe. Obviously the experience of breathing is one of the most fundamental and primitive of experiences. It is evidence of a living thing. One can quickly become panicked when one feels unable to breathe. The experience of "holding one's breath" dramatically reveals how desperately we need air and must breathe.

This kind of primitive need for breathing can be an experiential substructure upon which to base the awareness of the religious need of spiritual indwelling. Just as life itself may be seen as a form of divine breathing upon us, so in the concept of the "indwelling," God can be conceived as aiding us to breathe spiritually. The same basic need, therefore, and the same panicked and anxious helplessness which breathing involves, can speak to us at the experiential level of the mysterious, enigmatic need of divine indwelling which the Bible promises us. The simple experience of breathing, then, can lead us to an awareness of the significance of the indwelling of the Holy Spirit through which divine life is shared in faith.

FELT MEANING

The tracing of a word from its theological or cultural meaning to its basic experiential origin can therefore help bring about a common shared experience. This can then lead to a better appreciation of its theological significance. It can be done with a wide variety of words and phrases used continually in religious discourse. What is important here is not simply that the word be explained in its origin or by way of analogy, or that it be a good example. It should somehow engage each hearer in a personalized experience, even if he were simply—momentarily, say—to hold his breath. He would have "felt" the urge to breathe and so experienced a need of "spiritus." His faith, then, and the sermon's subsequent theological development could lead him to greater awareness of the Holy Spirit.

To place ourselves "in God's hands" is an analogy of dependency and confidence in God. The experience, however, could be best brought about, for example, by thinking out ways in which a child is picked up and carried by his father, or a child who can walk is led across the street by taking the hand of an older person. One might illustrate the dependency relationship of adults on God by explaining that blind people, contrary to what is popularly done, would prefer to take your arm in such a way that they can guide themselves with your help. In making this distinction one catches the realization of how God treats adults differently than he treats the dependent child. Like the blind person, we too need to guide ourselves, but in the hands of God. God may be said to lead us in those things in which our own limited ability is inadequate. In a similar way the blind person prefers to be led by one who can see, but he needs and wants to act from his own efforts too.

In following this conceptualization of "hand," one has a common experience that can be incarnately shared by the hearer, his own experience equates it. It becomes congruent with it. It is not isolated and removed as a logical analysis might be. To hold up a book in one's hand and show how it falls when one takes one's hand away, in order to demonstrate the notion of existence and being in God and dependence on God, is not intended as such simply to convince a person intellectually about existential dependency. If he can feel himself held up like the book and falling as the book falls, perhaps the experience-expression of being in God's hands might then become personal. To feel oneself in the hands of a parent might be an even richer and more personal sense of God's hands. Such a concept of "hand" has personal significance when a person can share it at conscious and unconscious levels of himself. This could then be a possible substructure for the doctrinal effect of the sermon. Incarnately shared, such an experience could aid in making the exposition both effective and affective.

INCARNATE-REDEMPTIVE EXPERIENCE

Basic human themes can lead to, and should be designed to convey, a warm and rich sharing with each participant of the incarnate redemptive process of being a man beloved of God. Unless one communicates some kind of "understanding heart," as we have seen, one does not seem effective in helping people change. This, then, must also be true of any kind of preaching, teaching or exposition. No matter how clear the presentation in an intellectual sense, unless it is suffused with something of the quality of Pauline charity, it does not seem to convey to another this sense of a deeply shared belonging. The speaker's words and manner, like a counseling response, must seek to reach inside the hearers and tap in them some human quality of love, joy, gladness, sorrow, weakness—some element shared together. From this core element, as in "The Prodigal Son," the theological structure emerges. But if it is anchored in their own experience in some way rather than being coldly or impersonally intellectual, people can feel and share it.

The speaker, therefore, must both represent and present God and religious values and, at the same time, be himself in a genuine communication of his own authentic person. The religious appeal must be to personal involvement with the concerns of each hearer. People are then led to assimilate religious values not simply by words but by the experience of human communication on issues of deep, personal concern. Through this kind of incarnate dialogue, the message of hope and redemption is communicated. If it is not permeated by such realistic human caring, it will remain cold, impersonal and skeletal—lacking the sense of the warmth of incarnation and of the worth of redemption.

NOTES

[1] Karl Barth, *The Word of God and The Word of Man* (New York: Harper and Row, 1957), pp. 25–26.

[2] Thomas W. Klink, *Depth Perspectives in Pastoral Work,* ed. Russell L. Dicks (Englewood Cliffs, N.J.: Prentice-Hall, Inc., 1965), p. 41.

[3] Diagram p. 47.

[4] See, for example, J. M. Branan, "Client Reaction to Counselor's Use of Self-Experience," *The Personnel and Guidance Journal,* 45, No. 6 (February 1967), p. 572.

[5] S. N. Behrman, *Portrait of Max: An Intimate Memoir of Sir Max Beerbohm* (New York: Random House, 1960), p. 172.

12
Religious Group Counseling

WHAT HAS BEEN SAID about sermons is applicable to all religious instructional relationships. The sermon or other instruction is completed only through the unique involvement of each person. If its religious challenge and reassurance have reached down to the intimate experience level of the people who hear it, then it speaks to them in affective and somatic as well as cognitive language. It is conative. It becomes the *Word made flesh* dwelling in them, in their unique personhood.

While we have focused our treatment on sermons, what has been said, then, is equally relevant to any kind of religious education, guidance, marriage or personal instruction. Whenever possible, the person should have some feeling of option according to his personal taste and unique condition.

RELIGIOUS GUIDANCE

The term "guidance" is particularly apropos to the relationship of a religious faith commitment. The word "guide" suggests—like a mountain guide—someone of experience and knowledge who shares the condition of the one being guided. He goes up the mountain too. There is also implied a free commitment on the part of the one being guided to the goal or purpose of the guidance.

Guidance in a religious setting, then, presupposes the value solution the religious commitment stands for. People have already involved themselves with, or at least wish to "know more about," these religious values. The religious guide, therefore, both offers knowledge and shares experience of religious living. He runs the same risk and danger. This sharing of the human condition is quite

249

different from a "mystery-mastery complex"[1] relationship where one gains superiority by appearing to have "all the answers."

In summary, then, the sermon, or any similar presentation of religious guidance, becomes the catalytic agent for self-counseling when it has a unique content and meaning for each person. It initiates a counseling process that is channelled and directed toward the assurance of a religious solution. It gets its strength and support from the conviction and hope resident in religious faith. This demands more than that it be intellectually or logically convincing, however important this may be in itself. Values involve real and total assent, not merely intellectual agreement. To be a catalytic agent the sermon must finally reach a person at the level of concerns he alone understands. He is ultimately the best and most consistent observer and participant in his own way of life. The person is really value-engaged when the material of the sermon is filtered and personalized through events and thoughts unique to himself.

CONFLICT RESOLUTION

But the sermon and religious values not only assure people of religious solutions, they also challenge and urge them to greater and more mature religious striving. As religious catalytic agents, they sometimes initiate conflict as well as lead to peace. Religious peace follows after the resolution of such conflict. It is a state of positive anxiety; it is not the quiet, uninvolved security of the dead. Basic to a religious value process, then, would be the manner in which the *Word* is consensually validated in each hearer and so enters as a "solution" or freeing assurance and conviction of his religious faith in the demanding stress of each day's choices.

Consequently, one must expect and be prepared for the emotional conflicts and confusions which may sometimes emerge as basic personal and religious values are revealed and made conscious. The fact that this kind of conflict seems inherent in any genuine religious assent suggests why the clergy should be trained not only in individual counseling but also in group counseling and discussion as well as group dynamic skills. Such skills could aid in making relevant the personal and unique phases of religious meaning. Since religious engagement involves the whole self, the sermon or any presentation of religious knowledge, in order to achieve its ultimate purpose, could be helped by this kind of group encounter. While such religious discussions and counseling would center on religious values, they would yet allow and support a process of personal assimilation.

An open or value-centered sermon, then, is intended to lead the hearer to begin to think his own unique thoughts as he takes counsel with himself around the sermon theme. For a man to be thinking of his own son, for example, with the deep feelings of personal investment this involves, is to bring him far closer to the human intent of the "Prodigal Son" sermon than simply to analyze and grasp its theological import. As a result, the concern of God as a Father has all the intense personal impact of his own committed concern; it is not only understanding but loving and caring. When each person has found something that is his own and different from the sermon as heard by others, this is the area where religious meaning can come alive in personal values. These, believed in, can affect a person's conduct and his life.

GROUP COUNSELING DISCUSSION

To make this even more effective, however, group and individual counseling discussion is called for as well as a sensitively presented sermon. While the sermon alone can result in the person's taking counsel with himself, he may also need and be helped by a group or individual counseling discussion, especially after he has had time to ponder the sermon's value to him.

ILLUSTRATION

We will now therefore consider an excerpt from such a counseling discussion of a ten-minute sermon. The theme was similar to the sermon illustration given previously and was concentrated on the loneliness of the Prodigal Son. In this consideration, too, we will presume some knowledge of material treated elsewhere under group counseling and discussion.[2] Our special intent here is to demonstrate a group process in the personal assimilation of religious values.

The following is an edited version of the sermon they heard. The actual sermon was somewhat longer—it took ten minutes—with pauses and the repetitive manner and phraseology that go with a relaxed simple communication in a conversational tone. The speaker's voice was quiet, becoming intense only as his own feelings naturally moved him, but with no effort at dramatic effect. Dramatics focus attention on the speaker, whereas the intent here is to lead into each one's own personalized thoughts and feelings.

Speaker: Imagine a young man not when he decides to break with his father and leave home, but when he's lost his good-weather friends and is alone. His money is gone. He's isolated, bitter and particularly hostile toward his own foolishness. He wonders whether he's worthy of anything.

Suppose he comes to see you. He sits down and says something like "I feel rotten, I'm just no good, I've been on marijuana—I finally kicked that. But last night I was drinking. I don't know how or why, but I went down to the river and had the urge to jump in and get it over. I guess I didn't see much point anymore in trying to make it, in going on. I stood there for a long time.

"This morning I got the idea of coming to see you. You know, one thing I remember about my father—he always took care of people, even tramps. He gave them decent clothes and allowed them sometimes to stay around for a week. I got the idea that maybe I could just go back home and be like one of those drunks or junkies my father had taken in because maybe that's what I am now. If he could do that, maybe I could make it. I just couldn't face my father the way I am now, unless maybe I could think of myself as one of those guys."

As this young man talked, he sat with his head in his hands. For weeks now he's been pretty much alone. He says it's the same old story—he had friends as long as he had money. He doesn't know where it all went, but it sure went. During the last month he'd lost track of things. He didn't even know where he'd been. His one hope now was that somehow if he could hold onto the idea of going back to his father like the tramps he remembered his father caring for, he might be able to return. His biggest suffering now was guilt and loneliness.

Loneliness is a strange and even terrible suffering. As a child I remember getting lost and feeling extremely anxious and afraid. But at the same time I was almost afraid to go home because I felt guilty and thought I would be punished.

Another time when I was a student I remember while I was traveling at Christmas time I had a layover in Pittsburgh for an hour. I still see the Christmas decorations and feel the loneliness of being an outsider in a strange city. Walking around, I felt there was no place to go, so I returned to the drab and dirty railroad station which seemed to be the best place to be, because I felt so lonely anywhere else.

Similarly, American students at the American Center in Rome used to say that they could stand to be away from the Center for only two or three hours because elsewhere they had such a lonely feeling—a feeling of not belonging. As an adult I've experienced that horrible loneliness too in a foreign country, a loneliness that can really make you sick.

Thinking of this young man, I'm reminded of the terrible suffering of Judas and Peter. One of them caught in the violence of guilt with an intense awareness of the wrongness of his acts and his deep struggle to forgive himself. This seems to be why it's so hard to face and accept God's forgiving us.

Peter's story would reassure us of God's forgiveness. As with Judas and Peter, the issue is not even sorrow or guilt, though they were intensely sorry for what they had done. At these times a person needs to find some reason for respecting himself, if only a little, and to find justification for returning home. If he can hold onto this one idea of his father's kindness to others, perhaps this young man too can make it home.

Why was it that Peter worked it out, faced Christ again; whereas Judas didn't, but hanged himself? The core of the issue is somewhere here in how we regard ourselves and others. We can love, says Aquinas, to hate ourselves; and our return must be in some way to love ourselves again and so accept forgiveness. This is the struggle to love ourselves after the terrible loneliness of a guilt-ridden experience.

GROUP COMMENT

A group of ten people then began to discuss how they felt about what they had heard. A variety of religious affiliations were represented in the group and some had no religious commitment. This discussion lasted an hour. The following is an excerpt of the beginning of the hour discussion.

The discussion begins with the group counselor saying:

May I ask you to begin your comments on what the sermon meant to you personally? As we said, you may wish to speak in a general way or make a particular personal application—we will leave that up to you. Obviously what we say here implies our confidence and trust in the group and the leader. Each of us can gain much from each one's comments. (*Pause.*) Would anyone care to begin?

The counselor must be at ease with the pause that follows. This gives each one time to gather his thoughts.

Nancy: My primary feeling was that of hopefulness. I became aware that our greatest difficulty is to forgive ourselves. Other people are generally willing to forgive us, but first we must forgive ourselves. If we can forgive ourselves, then others can forgive us. But others can't forgive us unless we do it first. It leaves me with great hope because it focuses on forgiving the self. From that, I know where to start.

Co: You then got personal hopefulness in the direction of forgiving yourself. You can start there.

John: The sermon to me was very personal, not abstract. It wasn't the story of some guy who'd lived two thousand years ago and who'd had a hard time forgiving himself. But it was about me.

Co: You were caught up in it yourself—it was not just in the past.

Mary: When you started talking I had been thinking of other things. Then I was surprised that suddenly I began listening to you. I saw you standing there speaking of loneliness. You described how you had felt as a child and in a foreign country. You reminded me how I had felt when I left a city in another country and came here to live in a small town in a strange country. That made me reflect on how very lonely others must feel in a strange place.

Co: As you reflect on it, you were pulled into the sermon really by the child reference, and you too were involved in loneliness so you could begin to feel a real sympathy for other people in strange places.

Mary: Yes, I reflected on loneliness and forgiveness. In my discomfort in a strange place I must have done some strange things. But I don't feel so badly if I did, because I didn't then know better.

Co: Recalling your own loneliness now you recognize reasons for forgiving yourself, your own peculiar actions.

LEADER-COUNSELOR

If we examine what the counselor says, we can see his responses catch both *affect* and *cognition;* that is, he is both a discussion leader and a group counselor. He follows the person's reasoning process, summarizing it as he presents it to the group, and at the same time understands the feelings that accompany this reasoning as each one makes personal applications to himself and his own situation. In this manner, the counselor assists the person as he strives for incarnate understanding in himself.

The personal quality of the sermon is already evident in these comments. While it may have begun as an abstract discussion, it quickly reached each one in some unique way. This is noted also in the next comment and throughout the discussion, indicating that the manner of presenting the sermon achieved its purpose.

After each counselor response the person nodded agreement and there was a pause. Sometimes, as we see, the same person continued or another took up the personal discussion. The counselor sat quietly and peacefully during the pauses, giving no indication that he was anxious or uncomfortable. This, as we have seen, is most important for the group's security and ease.

PERSONAL INVOLVEMENT

The excerpt continues:

Bill: I was surprised at my change in feeling as you were giving the sermon. When you started, I was thinking of the Prodigal Son. Then shortly I was completely in myself, thinking about distance and wanting to go back to say I'm sorry. But I was caught in the complexity of returning and of asking forgiveness. Then I remember you said it is not so much getting back as it is having respect for yourself. I was relieved that you said that, because then the other difficulties seem as if they would take care of themselves if I could have respect for myself.

Co: You first experienced feelings of distance and removal, and then as you returned to the feeling of security and hopefulness, especially around the idea of really respecting yourself, what you could do would be to forgive and respect yourself.

Shirley: My thoughts seemed to go off on tangents. I'd like to have more time to reflect on each of them. First I felt myself wondering how I'd receive someone who'd left but now wanted to come back. I wondered if I could forgive myself for having driven this person away. And I wondered how would I be better able to accept the person back. Then I felt the loneliness which I've experienced in the past.

Co: You felt both a guilt in receiving someone back and a guilt resulting from what originally caused the person to leave. And you experienced a somewhat associated sense of loneliness.

Shirley: I don't know that I would have thought of these things before even though I've heard talks on the Prodigal Son many times. Your talk brought out of me a certain awareness of loneliness that caused me to imagine my own feelings in a similar situation and to examine them.

Co: As familiar as you are with the Prodigal Son theme, still it came through to you in a fresh and personal way.

Shirley: Yes, ordinarily I wouldn't have thought of it in this way and reacted to it personally. I never have before.

One sees here how rare, apparently, is an experience of personal involvement, even in a theme as warm and attractive as this theme. Familiarity "stales" the freshness. This reaction of deadness to sermons was repeated by a number of group members.

Ernie: While you were relating your childhood experience of guilt and loneliness, I was thinking of the guilt and loneliness that I felt once when I stole a cake from a neighborhood store. When my father found out about it, he called my four brothers and me in. "Did any of you steal the cake?" he asked. I said, "No"; I lied. I recalled the terrible loneliness that I felt at that time in being separated from my brothers by the lie. It's very hard to explain.

Co: Your guilt actually made you a prodigal. By lying you were shot off a distance from your brothers. The lying even more than the stealing gave you this feeling of loneliness and isolation.

Ernie: Then I remember the relief I felt afterwards when I got up enough courage to tell my father that I had lied.

Co: Tremendously relieving—kind of prodigal's return.

Joe: I am still trying to explore Peter and Judas' betrayal of Jesus and why Peter came back and Judas didn't. I wonder whether Peter really had a positive commitment before he betrayed Jesus or whether he became committed when he forgave himself that betrayal. But Judas, not realizing any commitment, couldn't forgive himself, and so he killed himself.

Co: You are still thinking through involvement and commitment. To you because Peter was the more committed, he could return. But because Judas lacked Peter's real engagement, he couldn't return.

John: During the early part of your talk, I was thinking of forecasting. I mean, I was trying to figure out where you were going. But then I found what you were saying was more important than my forecasting. Somehow I gave it up.

Co: So you stopped calculating.

John: Yes, I leaned back and experienced what you were saying at the moment.

Co: You got security in leaning on me. As a result you let your own thoughts and feelings flow with mine.

John: Yes, I quit forecasting and I liked it better. It had more meaning that way.

The contrast between Ernie and John's initial reaction points up the difference between a shared experience—the child stealing, lying and being guilty—and the abstract-observer position, taken up with the sermon's "mechanics." While John gave this up somewhat, it is evident that his is the least committed comment thus far.

By comparison with John, we notice the next person to comment was quite caught up in a personal sense:

Dolores: I was thrown back to two years ago when I was an anxious person. Now my hand isn't shaking. I just didn't know if it would.

I've heard inane sermons on the Prodigal Son so I wondered what you would do with it. I caught it more when you were talking about the man who was on marijuana and wondering where he was going to turn. I've never cried in this group but I was close to it. My anxiety used to separate me from people. But I've grown really, and the anxiety is much less. I'm out with people more too and, though I don't know how they are taking me, I'm having a wonderful time.

Co: You turned and came back to people, too, and it's very rewarding.

Dolores: Yes, I identified with those who take marijuana, drink, or shake. No matter what they do, I can accept them now.

Co: They usually do have the shakes, don't they?

Dolores: I had a big front. I still have it. I can't get rid of it. I'm an actress, but I think I'm communicating. I feel I belong now.

Co: So you deeply shared the young man's experience of loneliness and anxiety, but you also felt a sense of relief or security in feeling that you can really belong to people now. It's reassuring, isn't it?

Dolores: Uh-uh! (*and a long sigh*).

This person obviously finds it easy to communicate her personal feelings, and so perhaps does so for almost any reason. Yet even for such a verbal or oral person, the group communication and experience had apparently real meaning and efficacy.

The next person to comment speaks much more slowly and with greater difficulty as she probes herself:

Dorothy: I identify myself with two points in your story of the Prodigal Son. First with his isolation or loneliness. I was reminded of the many times in a crowd still feeling isolated because I was not relating to others. I was not interested in the group, but worse I could find no motivation to go back home.

Second point, was the Prodigal Son's motivation for the return. This point reminded me of the motivation to forgive myself and to go back home. Many times I've found myself in similar situations, and sometimes I've found the motivation but still the last step wouldn't come. So the isolation was more painful. He somehow found a way to return.

Co: You've struggled with both the loneliness of separation from others and the difficulty of forgiving yourself so you could begin to relate to them. You almost envied this young man's finding a clear reason for returning home.

Dorothy: His motivation must have been a strong one despite all he'd done wrong to himself and perhaps to others. I did envy him, his satisfaction in finding a motivation. It's his redemption. It's very difficult to find this. When people love you, you just feel more guilty.

Co: You sense not only the guilt and separation but equally the complexity of finding something that you can hold onto in order to bring about a return, a healing, a restoration, a re-belonging to others, to those who love us and therefore make us more guilty for what we have done.

The previous excerpts were taken from the beginning of the counseling discussion in the sequence as they occurred. They were edited to shorten them and remove too personal references. This may give them a cryptic quality they did not really have in the actual group session.

RANGE OF GROUP PROCESS

As people grew increasingly secure, this personal theme was applied in a wide variety of circumstances in their lives. The fact that the group had been meeting together for three months gave, of course, added security and no doubt aided in each one's freedom to say what he felt. Beginning groups usually need some time together before such security is achieved. But even here, deep and genuine discussion can occur especially after the group is assured of the leader-counselor's sensitive understanding and skill.

The following propositions, abstracted from the recorded hour discussion by a group process analysis, show the range and variety of the discussion:

1. Hope comes from learning that others feel as you do.
2. Returning home is difficult.
3. The lost child fears punishment when returned home.
4. Loneliness is sometimes an emotional sickness.
5. To forgive yourself in the face of guilt and wrongdoing is a hard struggle.
6. You need justification to respect yourself.
7. We love to hate ourselves, but also turn to love ourselves.
8. Forgiving the self is the greatest difficulty (Judas' problem).
9. Others are more willing to forgive us than we are willing to forgive ourselves.
10. We need to forgive ourselves so we can forgive others.
11. Hope comes from realizing that forgiving the self is basic, because it depends upon the self, not others.
12. Loneliness can lead to doing wrong to yourself and others.
13. We need to forgive ourselves for doing wrong when alone.
14. Guilt is both the cause and an effect of loneliness.
15. Guilt makes a person prodigal, creating distance between him and others.

16. We need to identify with others and to accept their differences.

17. Anxiety separates people.

18. We need to share the loneliness of the prodigal.

19. Relief and security come from belonging.

20. Failing to share yourself causes loneliness.

21. Sharing with others is a way of breaking out of loneliness.

22. One experiences pain in isolation and loneliness.

23. We need to find something to hold onto in order to bring about a return.

24. We need to stay open, not to resist others or want to change them.

25. Cutting yourself off from others leads to guilt.

26. Accepting others leads to positive feelings.

27. Letting yourself go, flowing with others, is a way to dispel nervousness.

28. Feeling for others dispels anxiety.

29. We keep from ourselves when we fail to make the return.

30. Hope remains no matter how low you sink.

31. Love always includes loneliness, anxiety, and isolation.

32. Love comes only after separation and conflict.

33. Closeness of the group provides courage for a return.

34. We need to trust others to share our guilt and need to belong.

35. We are freed by revealing our weaker sides.

36. We need more empathy for those who are lonely.

37. We should feel responsible for those who are lonely.

38. Overcoming loneliness results in inner strength.

39. We need to learn to live with loneliness.

40. We need to learn to keep loneliness in balance since we cannot do away with it.

41. Sometimes we are less alone when alone.

42. Breaking out can lead to guilt.

43. We all come from broken homes.

44. Breaking out is a form of maturity.

45. To encounter loneliness and belonging at the same time is to realize that life is not a "no-exit" situation.

END OF HOUR

Toward the end of the hour's exchange and sharing, the group is more free and growing secure with one another. They are sharing gratitude for the sense of communion. The counselor-leader, we notice, while holding to the gist of the response, now also feels free to add his own personal comments. He too has become more secure and at ease. The counselor is responding to a previous comment:

What I get from what you're saying—the prodigal design, so to speak—the prodigal configuration is a whole life and there could be no love really without some kind of prodigal hurt and distance and quarrel or removal. There isn't any clean line, in other words. The son who stayed home doesn't exist in real life. There's really nobody that really stays home in the human condition, and love comes after these other separation-disjunctive conflicts with ourselves and with others.

John: What I get too is when you want to go back and say that you're sorry—this is hard like it was for the Prodigal Son, but after having shared these feelings here, there's a kind of a bond of closeness in this group now that would give you courage. At least it would me in the sense that if you really got down you'd have someone who had heard this message here and you would almost trust that they would understand this same thing. This would then give me courage. Say, you tried to go back and say you were sorry to someone or you had tried to accept someone and couldn't quite do this, there would still be that sense it wouldn't be hopeless—on the contrary, well—there would be an almost endless hope, I would see.

Co: If I understand what you say now, you're talking about a trust in a community of persons aren't you? And the fact that there's a community of people here, it extends out because you could almost trust any one of them to share guilt or need for belonging or redemption or whatever the word might be. I mean, there would be someone else to go to if there would be one person who rejected you. There would be a community for you somewhere. You're saying this experience has produced in you a greater trust of this unity or this communion of people now because of the level of this kind of sharing, openness or sympathy.

John: I think it wouldn't take much for everyone to understand it.

We've all heard the same thing. While each of us have interpreted in our own ways we still know what we're talking about. When we say we feel lost from someone or from a situation—everyone understands it.

Co: You're reassured that these other people would understand you.

Dolores: This experience seems to be a culmination of what I've experienced previously in the group. I have been confronted. I have been wrong, but I've always felt accepted. I think this just culminates it—it's all here. I have trust in the group, even new people. When I trust, it works. I feel accepted. I think it's the way it's set up and I just see it now as a culmination of the experience I've had. People can be wonderful when you trust them. They can take an awful lot.

Co: This is reassuring because whatever happened—this community—you could trust them enough to plunge your own self. I mean the aspects of yourself that you were in conflict about and what has happened is they have received you—they didn't turn you away. Again the prodigal concept proved true. You're reassured that somehow trust is fulfilled in a community if it can be made rightly.

Tom: I felt at the moment when Dolores was talking—thinking back of the experience we have had together and I felt the same way. Once the people of the group knew me—good and bad aspects—the mask was off and it didn't make any sense to hide something. The opposite was true—I had the tendency to draw out many more things. The feeling was that I felt free.

Co: In some way then you're saying that community trust gives a kind of communion—to give all aspects of yourself, not just the protective aspects that make you look good in the way you protect yourself with others, but all aspects of yourself. This was freeing. Beyond whatever self-consciousness there was, the reward of freedom was far greater.

We have about a minute or so yet in our time. I'm saying this to give you a feeling of preparation that we're coming to a close.

Tom: This experience was so intense to me that it just occurred to me there were some people sitting around. (*He is referring to ten people who were observers—the discussion continued for another hour with this group as participants.*) And I'm concerned about them just now. Maybe they didn't experience this discussion in the intense way that we did.

Co: You're very struck then by how intense it has been for you and you're also wondering if the others on the periphery—have shared this with the same intensity.

Tom: I just presumed everybody here did, but I don't know if that's right or not.

Bill: Yes, that hit me too. I was wondering when you said there's a minute now. What's back there? It's been so intense, and I'm kind of anxious, really, about what they think. I forgot about them until now.

Co: Now that the closeness and support of this group is being removed, your perception is broadening as you realize there are eight or ten more people out there watching this. It's made you anxious.

Bill: Yes. It's another world out there right now. I have to go and talk to them.

Co: It's a world of distance. You know what's here but out there is distance. As I get it you have a need to communicate with them.

Rose: I think I'll take the rest of the minute with my comment. I just want to say just how pleased I am now to see there are three priests here because I was wondering how can a priest get some kind of communication with people beyond being in a great big church or hall. Even when you meet him personally you can't do this—you can't say these things to a priest individually because there just isn't time or it's not the appropriate thing to say. I'm just pleased that all these priests were here.

Co: Yes, it's reassuring and you're pleased they are sharing this too. Well, our hour is about up.

This group of twenty had been meeting together for three months. For small discussions, ten participated and ten observed and then they reversed positions. But this was the first experience with a sermon or similar presentation.

Even though they knew one another already, a deeper sense of group unity, sharing and belonging had emerged as a result of the sermon discussion. This would be one of the main effects of such sermon counseling relationships.

COUNSELING RELEVANCE

Seen this way, the sermon no longer would have simply an educational purpose and aim. The sermon, the liturgical service and worship, and similar functions, would seek to initiate a dynamic of communion, community and communication. The symbolism of religious belonging, trust and commitment would be carried out in small group pastoral relationships. The Word coming alive in each person would stimulate these kinds of counseling discussions. When necessary, individual counseling could follow. The congregation seen this way is very different from a mass of faces to be talked to from afar and educated in their "duties," in a Cartesian-Kantian sense. They rather become uniquely personal objects of pastoral concern and investment of which the sermon itself is a beginning phase.

In the light of present religious concern for greater relevance and for new approaches to the presentation of the Word and to worship participation, such small group methods of pastoral counseling and guidance would seem worthy of greater exploration and development. In this way especially religion would begin to reach people in the loneliness and isolation that seems to characterize so many in our age. Like the early Christian period, people seem again in special need not simply of knowledge but of sharing and belonging at the personal level of their own lives. This seems a means of approach to such a needed new sense of community and personal communion.

PRACTICAL APPLICATION

We have already suggested the practicality of this use of a short recorded sermon and then a counseling discussion, as a way of personalizing relations in a large congregation. A pastoral counselor could have this kind of intimate personal relationship with four hundred people a week and assuming each might be said to be the adult representative of one family, sixteen hundred families could be reached in a month. Let us propose that each family representative then meets for an hour with the members of his family, playing a tape of the sermon and leading the discussion in imitation of the pastoral counselor. Again a personalized communication and family sense of communion could emerge. In addition, if we assume that another pastoral counselor, especially trained in child counseling and guidance, were to meet sixteen hundred children every month in intimate groups of ten for an hour each, the Word could become personalized and living for them.

GUIDANCE AND COUNSELING

Religion is especially concerned, then, with group and individual guidance and counseling. That is, religion's concern is with those aspects of knowledge which become the object of a person's option of self-investment. The establishment of "guidance and counseling centers," working in cooperation with the public, private or religious schools, would therefore seem to be of major importance to religion. These centers could be professionally staffed and yet at the same time represent religious values.

Were Churches jointly to establish such guidance and counseling centers, the focus would be on personalized guidance information and discussion, group and individual counseling. Education functions in the centers would be related to this religious value focus. It would be positively oriented and not simply focused on counseling therapy. These centers could be adjacent to and work in cooperation with guidance and counseling programs of related grade and high schools or colleges and universities. This would not seem to involve difficulties now in effect from present legal traditions. A new working relationship could be legally established since they would be focused on personal guidance and counseling, not on education as such.

Moreover, in the light of the plans in many states for widely distributed out-patient mental health centers, parallel religious counseling and guidance centers—more directly therapeutic—could aid in the effectiveness of these centers and provide a professionally trained and sensitive religious personnel for pastoral and religious counseling and guidance.

The direct relationship of religion to counseling, psychotherapy and guidance would constitute the immediate religious concentration of forces here. Personal and financial investment could be more directly centered on affording aid through group and individual discussion, as well as religious guidance and pastoral counseling. At the point where religious values enter into the subject-matter studied in the schools or the treatment process in out-patient private and state clinics, religiously oriented discussion and counseling could be initiated. This could be the intercommunication center and link between the educational and therapeutic processes

sponsored by the state or private agencies and the pastoral, liturgical and sacramental action of the Church. Religiously sponsored
counseling and guidance centers might provide a much-needed
common ground here. They could, at the same time, be separated
from, but function in cooperation with, the formal religious functions of the Church as such while they directly aided the work of
schools, universities, hospitals and clinics.

NOTES

[1] David Bakan, "The Mystery-Mastery Complex in Contemporary Psychology," *The American Psychologist*, 20, 3 (March 1965).

[2] Curran (1968) *op. cit.*

13

Pastoral Counseling

FROM ALL that has been said, it is evident that the pastoral counselor needs the same basic skills and awareness as those we have previously described. These are as necessary to pastoral counseling as to other forms of counseling and psychotherapy. What D'Arcy and Kennedy say of "spiritual direction" is equally applicable to all aspects of religious relationships:

Recent psychological research has indicated that there are basic similarities in all good human relationships. That is to say, there is something that all good human relationships have in common. There is some quality that they must have if the relationships are to work at all. This shared characteristic may be far more important than the ways in which, on possibly accidental bases, we distinguish various kinds of human relationships. It is in this territory, in the realm of what happens between people in their most significant encounters with each other, that we need to grasp the root dynamics of interpersonal growth. We are saying, then, that what makes good spiritual direction effective is basically what makes good counseling effective. Spiritual direction works when there is a genuine interpersonal relationship between the people involved. There must be some real contact on a genuinely human level. This relationship implies real understanding and interest, and this arises when two people are related in the profound way that is possible only between human persons. This is far more important than techniques. In short, the conditions of healthy interpersonal exchange must be present or spiritual direction is a lifeless kind of enterprise.[1]

We will presume, then, that much of what has already been said applies to pastoral counseling as well as other religious educational, guidance and informational relationships. Our special intent

267

here is to search out reasons for a precise and perhaps unique designation of the pastoral counseling relationship.

ORDAINED PASTORAL MINISTRY

We are not discussing the traditionally established position of the clergyman as religious mentor, guide and counselor in the general sense nor his commonly accepted role of trusted confidant and friend. Nor, on the other hand, do we see pastoral counseling as a separate profession in the sense that Richard Cox apparently does "with reference to the minister who practices psychotherapy as a profession outside of the usual parish ministry."[2]

Moreover, it is apparent that, until now, we have been using the terms "religious counseling" and "pastoral counseling" as somewhat interchangeable. One might raise the question whether they are not in fact identical. If we were to make a distinction, we might say that religious counseling stems from and gets its source from pastoral counseling but is perhaps more general in its application. It might be the function of people not necessarily officially and ordained representatives of a religious belief. Here the concept "ordination," or of someone especially "being sent," might mark the difference between strict "pastoral" counseling and the more generally oriented "religious counseling."

We might say, then, that the ordained clergyman more exactly represents or is mimetic of a person's credal commitment. To relate to him in counseling, then, would be participating in a sacramental kind of relationship, since, in a sense, we do not exclude the word "sacramental," as we have seen, even from psychological counseling. Here we wish rather to sharpen its precise religious investment and focus as it occurs in the pastoral counseling engagement. We will come back again to the mimetic concept of one person as an ordained clergyman representing the faith commitment of the community, in our discussion of "representation and community."

RELIGIOUS GROWTH PROCESS

In our consideration, then, pastoral counseling would not be separated from the parish or pastoral ministry but would form a

basic and essential part of it. It would be called "counseling," however, in the way we have been considering counseling, namely as
a skilled, subtle and demanding relationship and so be distinguished but not separated from other pastoral functions. "Pastoral
counseling" would in some way relate to a person in those past
and present religious affects and cognitions—distorted or adequate
—which have influenced his present state of religious growth and
maturity.

THE WORD

If we accept the religious continuum, indicated earlier, that extends from the analogy of "milk for babies" to "strong meat for
grown men" or the implication of the Pauline affirmation that
when "I became a man, I put away the things of a child," we have
religious growth and development accompanying its physical and
psychological growth counterparts. Pastoral counseling then, as
distinct from religious guidance, support, reassurance, and similar
functions, would be directly related to the needs and stresses of
this religious personality growth process. Other forms of counseling and psychotherapy would involve this too, but not so directly.

The focus on the sermon and its relationship to the Word of
God seems to be essential to any definition of and approach to
pastoral counseling. Hiltner, for example, considers pastoral
counseling and the allied aspects of pastoral theology under "Shepherding," as a separate "perspective," but one that is related to
both "Communicating the Word" and "Organizing the Church."
Pastoral counseling implies the context of a credal commitment
to the Church.[3]

In searching for ways to define this function as distinct from
counseling and psychotherapy, we must then center our distinction
on the Word of God. It is the clergyman's belief and function,
centered on the Bible, and the person's corresponding belief and
acceptance of him as in some way God's representative and
agent, that together seem to single out the pastoral counseling
relationship and clearly distinguish it from other psychological
relationships. The common invocation of God through faith in
His Word, the teachings and practices shared by the clergyman and

his Church's adherents and the corresponding sacramental, liturgical and symbolic religious devotions, go together to form a
uniquely special bond—one meaning of the word "religion"—
between the participants in individual or group counseling and the
pastoral counselor.

In a similar way we can say that implicitly or explicitly, faith in
and loyalty to a medical tradition binds people to a psychiatrist or
physician, and a respect for and appreciation of a behavioral
scientific tradition binds people to a psychologist. This regard
seems to predetermine in large measure the nature of the medical
or psychological relationship. What people expect from the relationship and how they function in it follows from the frame of reference
they have formed.

In this sense, we can say with Allport:

> When we emphasize the importance of man's total orientation, we
> approach at long last the role of the religious counselor, for this is
> his specialty.[4]

It is precisely here, from the viewpoint of total life orientation
in time and beyond, that a person's faith commitment creates his
pastoral counseling engagement.

TOTAL ORIENTATION

We have proposed earlier that religious concerns are not something
"ultimate" in the sense of a removal from the immediate concerns
of daily existence. On the contrary, for the religious man, they
form the warp and woof of his daily commitments. What Schnackenburg says applies to every man of genuine religious conviction:

> As man perceives the intent and demand of the word of relevation in
> this way, he obtains a profound insight into his own human essence,
> which is most important for his self-comprehension. In faith, man's
> entire existence becomes illumined; he sees himself before God and
> can no longer envision himself in any other context save in this con-
> frontation with God. Here we have what is perhaps the paramount
> meaning of revelation: the personal encounter of man with his God,
> which is brought about by God himself in his revelation and in his

demands that man make a response. This we may call the "existential" character of revelation.[5]

Even though technical advance has created new questions in his life work and contemporary society presents additional complexities to be solved in the context of his membership in the community, the commitment of the religious man remains fundamentally the same:

These changes do not affect basically his behavior before the face of God as prescribed by the Bible. In fact, he must, conversely, apply the religious directives of revelation to his own historical condition, translate them corresponding to the altered situation, and make personal decisions in the spirit of the Bible.[6]

The religious man, through faith, hope and love, may be said to have acquired a new mode of existence. We have seen that something of this same sense of rebirth and the growth of a new and different self can take place in counseling and psychotherapy and also in a certain kind of learning. The religious man, however, feels himself "born again" in God and so sees himself in a new, unique mode of existence. His whole self is, in this sense, God-centered:

Now this new God-given existence shapes man's understanding of himself. . . . This fresh view of self in faith is therefore not merely a new recognition which man of himself wins through faith, but it is rather the result and fruit of the new God-given existence.[7]

UNIQUE PERSONHOOD

The word "pastoral," in addition to connoting this special religious faith-bind, and new mode of existence, as well as the psycho-theological values invested in the pastoral counseling relationship, also delineates another characteristic. It particularly implies reaching an individual person at the level of his unique self and personhood. To leave "the ninety-nine" in search of "the one" can be variously interpreted. But it certainly seems to characterize the difference between relating to a person simply as a member of a large group and the much more personal and invested involvement with an individual by himself or in a small group. Here his "oneness," in the sense of his uniqueness, emerges in all its delicate and subtle conscious and unconscious psychosomatic complexity.

Pastoral counseling is, then, for the person undergoing it, an individual experience in a re-presentation and re-examination of his God-centered convictions and belief. Its purpose is to aid him to sift and evaluate these for their present personal and unique meanings to him. In such a focus, it does not take the place of other forms of psychological counseling and psychotherapy. Rather, pastoral counseling and other religious relationships can work together with all forces for growth and change in the human personality.

GOD AS FATHER

But in the psychological factors of anxiety, in the search for meaning, in the pursuit of lasting values, and even in the nature of human existence itself, a Beyond seems constantly in correspondence with personal being and becoming. So, beyond the immediate and pressing life concerns that occupy the central focus of psychological counseling and psychotherapy, there is the "Jenseits," as Freud called it—the side beyond. For the religious believer, this "Jenseits" centers on his relationship with God. In the Old and New Testament, the concept of God as a Father suggests a parallel between the experience of a human father and this relationship with God. In the growth process, then, this Father-God-image could be subject to the same immature distortions and could demand the same correction as other psychological distortions if mature religious faith is to be achieved. We saw evidence of this in both the theoretical discussion and case material earlier considered, especially in destructive and immature guilt and in some phases of expert deification that seemed present in the beginning stages of learning.

Like parent relationships, childhood religious experiences, too, undergo inevitable distortions in the early developmental process; hence, if the person is to gain religious maturity, realignment and more adult models and values are necessary. If the need for God expresses itself in various real and distorted forms from the beginning of a person's existence, this has special relevance to pastoral counseling. This God-relationship would be a distinct aspect of personality growth and development in the Pauline continuum of "child" to "man," paralleling, but never being totally identified with, the other aspects of the psychological maturing process. This God-relationship would therefore constitute a central personality concern in its own order and so would mark an area of pastoral counseling—that is, the growth toward less distorted, less infantile God-attitudes.

MODELS OF PERSONALITY DYNAMICS

Various theories of personality dynamics might be used to delineate this concept further, each in a sense describing the same personality growth dynamics from its own viewpoint. We have chosen the "superego—transference" models, not because they are a final description of personality in this area, but mainly because they are now commonly used in psychology and widely understood. They constitute, therefore, a convenient hypothesis around which to express further this aspect of the special concern of pastoral counseling.

In using models like superego and transference, then, we are not presuming their ultimate psychological validity but simply taking advantage of the way they help us describe what seems to be part of a person's "actual experience." Referring to his speculations about the structure of the "mental apparatus," Freud wrote:

> Such ideas as these are part of a "speculative superstructure" of psychoanalysis, any portion of which can be abandoned or changed without loss or regret the moment its inadequacy has been proved. But there is still plenty to be described that lies closer to actual experience.[8]

We are also treating again, from a different view, some of those aspects of conscience we discussed earlier. Explaining the superego concept, Menninger says it comprises those unconscious determinants of prohibition and obligations that are rooted in infantile identifications, the "archaic conscience" as distinguished from conscience in the ordinary sense.[9]

Discussing "transference," Alexander and Selesnick explain:

Transference is based on the fact that during treatment the patient not only remembers his past experiences, but what is more important, transfers on to the therapist the feelings he had toward significant persons in his past life—mainly, his parents. He reacts to the therapist in a similar manner as he did toward his parents. Re-enacting and reliving the original neurotic responses permits the patient to correct them; his past maladaptive reactions are thus brought into the treatment. In reliving his past experiences, the adult patient has an opportunity to grapple again with unresolved childhood events and emotions; his adult strength helps him solve the emotional difficulties that as a child he had found insurmountable.

Nevertheless, Freud's principal thesis was that in order to achieve a cure, recollection of past events and insight into the meaning of these events must occur.

This thesis, upheld by fundamentalist psychoanalysis, has been challenged in recent times by those who emphasize not insight but the re-experiencing of emotions in relation to the therapist.[10]

Transference, Freud described as not bound to the father alone:

. . . but the transference is not bound to this prototype; it can also proceed from the mother—or brother-image, and so on. The peculiarity of the transference to the physician lies in its excess, in both character and degree, over what is rational and justifiable—a peculiarity which becomes comprehensible when we consider that in this situation the transference is effected not merely by the conscious ideas and expectations of the patient, but also by those that are under suppression, or unconscious.[11]

MATURITY OF HUMAN LIMITS

If we assume with Augustine, Sartre and others that the human condition can really be understood only if we accept the conception of man's project to be God, then there are built-in conflicts, stresses and distortions coming from a basic resistance to accepting his limited humanity and his actual state of incarnation. Here too, the maturity and therapy of limits is necessary in order for a person to accept that self-regard which is the "reasonable pursuit of his own human excellence" and its limitations. Religious connern and its components have their characterological and personality dimensions from this God-relationship conflict in man. In this they are interrelated with but distinct from other psychological factors. A person's probing of, searching out and re-evaluating his fundamental God-image and God-ego structure would involve discriminating a mature God-relationship from primitive or archaic infantile and childhood distortions about self and God. This would then be related to his developing an adult sense of religious worship and obligations and especially his acquiring an ability to distinguish these from more infantile symbols and immature anxieties.

In a sense one might say, then, that this is a process of transposing the God-image away from others—where the child in a distorted way tends to place it—to its real object in an adult faith commitment in and to a revealing God. Allport comments:

> It is probable that the sufferer who comes to the clergyman has some religious ideas to start with. Hence the task is to help him deepen and enlarge them, so that they more adequately embrace his present distress and groping. To employ my earlier terms, the task is to help him move from his relatively extrinsic religion, to a mature, all-embracing, intrinsic religion. This, I submit, is the primary assignment of every religious counselor.[12]

We are not, of course, implying that such concerns might never occur in psychological counseling and psychotherapy. On the contrary, as extensions of Father-image and superego, and indeed for many other reasons, we would expect them to emerge. But they would not be considered centrally but only peripherally. The central concern would be more immediate and confined.

FORMAL CREDAL COMMITMENT

Since this God-relationship would be believed in and shared with others in a formal credal community commitment and devotion, pastoral counseling would center on this faith commitment and the personal or group dynamics which such faith commitment engenders. The Word believed in and interpreted by credal commitments, liturgical devotion and sacramental reality and symbolism, would be the final determinants of the purpose and limits of the pastoral counseling relationship.

In the choice of pastoral counseling in conjunction with psychological counseling or psychotherapy or for itself alone, a person is evidently signifying and addressing himself to this special God-centered awareness for which he seeks both faith and self-clarification. Here "fides quaerens intellectum," and its conjoined struggle in this process of seeking to understand the self as a support and strength to faith, might be a way of describing the pastoral counseling experience. If the Father-image is often a distortion of the father, so the God-image could often also be distorted. The "God-ego" decrees following from this distortion could themselves be in need of realignment. The religious counsel necessary for this would be an area normally outside the focus, scope and competence of non-pastoral counselors or even of pastoral counselors of another religious faith.

Admittedly, then, the lines are not sharply drawn. Counseling and psychotherapy might be said to concern the self and the immediate other in persons and things. Pastoral counseling would begin here but go beyond, to the Other, to the Jenseits, to enter directly and entertain in central focus those issues which emerge from an implicit and explicit involvement with a God-concept and the nature and consequences of religious belief and commitment. This would center in oneself and be directly concerned with one's personal psychological distortions. But it would also reach out, in a faith, to God as a Unique Other Person. As Eliade, quoted earlier, says:

. . . an encounter with the "totally other," whether conscious or unconscious, gives rise to an experience of a religious nature.[13]

POSITIVE RELIGIOUS TRANSFER

A further consideration here would be the effects of positive religious transference. Wilmer has described how faith in large medical centers operates as a positive transference in medical healing:

> . . . it is possible to identify a common factor through which these powers are mediated: transference to a center . . .
>
> Positive transference permits physicians with widely varying levels of training, competence and experience to speak with the authority ordinarily invested only in the famous doctors themselves. . . . The patients have trust and confidence in all the physicians. . . . What was good enough for The Center was good enough for him.
>
> The very name of the institution is a cherished and sacred title, a powerful symbol to which much transference feeling is attached. The name not only brings heightened hopes to the patients but brings the physician himself to a greater expectancy of his own professional competence. And in this frame of mind, with reciprocal support from The Center, he commonly performs at a greater proficiency of therapeutic effectiveness than he would without "the symbol."[14]

Assuming the same kind of positive transference to a Church, one would have here another specification for pastoral counseling —it would function in and get its meaning from the religious faith context of such a positive religious transference. Transposed to a religious setting, a special trust and confidence—in specifically religious concerns—would be placed on all those associated with the Church and its credal interpretation of the Word. In this we mean to imply no lessening or disregard of the unique significance of religious faith in itself. Rather, we simply wish to show that it, too, can fit into the positive transference context from a psychological reference.

SYMBOLIC ACTION

Another means by which the function of pastoral counseling may be designated is to consider the way the symbolic aspects of the clergyman's garb, blessing, prayer, stole, Bible and various worshipful acts, convey and help define a particular faith relationship between himself and other persons.

Speaking of the importance of symbolic acts in defining the physician's relationship with a patient, Menninger says:

The physical examination . . . is not only a diagnostic procedure, but may constitute one of the most important steps in the therapy. Sometimes it is indeed the very keystone of the therapeutic relationship. It serves to identify the physician in his professional capacity, and to establish, by means of a now familiar and conventional procedure, a confidence in the examiner as a doctor. (A nurse or social worker, even a "friend," might take a history or make pertinent inquiries about the illness; only a doctor examines.) It disproves the common error that psychiatrists are only "talking doctors," not real, honest-to-goodness "touching doctors."

The "laying on of hands" has a deep and powerful significance to the patient.[15]

The fact that a religious analogy ends this description indicates how this same unique definition of relationship would follow upon what are the special acts of religious communication. If we see the person of the sacramental minister as directly involved in the sacramental relationship, we have an even stronger reason for recognizing a special meaning and bond when such a relationship leads to, or involves, counseling. This would be evident in the way, for example, the sacrament of marriage implies a relationship of both premarital and marital pastoral counseling.

LITURGY AND GROUP COUNSELING

But even more fundamentally, liturgical or symbolic worship, flowing from the Word of God and the believing community, would also significantly affect the nature and function of pastoral counseling.

If we understand with Eliade that "a religious symbol not only reveals a pattern of reality or a dimension of existence, it brings at the same time, a meaning to human existence,"[16] then religious symbolism and liturgical forms of worship would themselves engage people in deep personal quests for self-identity and relationship with one another. This would, for its most adequate fulfillment, invoke the skills especially of group pastoral counseling in order to arrive at the religious communication and communion which worship would require for its authenticity.

We would have in such personal liturgical participation a particular kind of "opening himself" through which each person could begin to "emerge from his personal situation" and not only "reach a comprehension" of, but really begin to feel how he belonged to, the Divine. Each person in such a group communication would be striving to regard himself and others in the special sense of *caritas*—seeking to fulfill his vocation to be "friends"—as a reflection of Divine Friendship. For this kind of profound self-engagement in worship to come about, the special skills of group and individual pastoral counseling, in addition to all other educational and guidance functions, would seem to be particularly necessary.

OTHER HELPING RELATIONSHIPS

Earlier we touched on how various views of man and his destiny affect one's approach to education, counseling, psychotherapy and, in fact, to any significant human relationship. These issues, while important for the whole nature of one's consideration of man's psycho-physico-theological dimensions, are also relevant to how one considers pastoral counseling. At its best, pastoral counseling would aid people, like the model of salt that savors meat, to bring the special flavor of religious convictions and values to their own unique existence. In so doing, it could be especially helpful in furthering the effectiveness of other forms of human healing and other forces for psychological growth and maturity. In this sense, religion and pastoral care could be said to support and enliven counseling and psychotherapy as salt supports and enlivens meat. Pastoral counseling, even if it may be said to have its own order and level, yet functions with and through other helping concerns related to the human condition.

GOD-CENTERED ENGAGEMENT

Pastoral counseling, then, may be considered a unique relationship which implies and recognizes God as a third party. The fact that it is actually counseling, and not religious education or pastoral guidance, demands the introduction of all known counseling skills.

Yet it is not counseling from exactly the same point of view as the professional counselor or psychotherapist might consider it. It is rather counseling within a Divine framework and perspective. This is why it has a unique quality that is particularly its own. Pastoral counseling can, therefore, use many of the same methods and skills of counseling therapy while, at the same time, it is always extending itself to "the Beyond" in the spirit of Paul's comment that we have not here "a lasting city."

Having received training and acquired skills in understanding another in his difficult struggle to understand and communicate himself, the pastoral counselor nevertheless uses counseling in a different perspective. This difference is evident both in the nature of the things discussed and considered important and in the scale of values by which judgments are made. Other professionals are not generally considered to have a concern for the basic questions and ultimate values for which people come to the pastoral counselor. Physicians and psychiatrists are concerned for health and its related psychosomatic and personality aspects; psychologists and others, with immediate personality reorganization and particularly pressing personal issues. Religious values may and do enter into these relationships, but this is not the main intent of the medical or psychological interview. It is to the pastoral counselor that one finally brings, for full-blown consideration, questions *that go beyond*—to values of "total orientation," even when they include these other issues.

In an early novel, *Royal Highness*—which we will treat later in more detail when we directly consider "representation"—Thomas Mann has the following remarks addressed to the Crown Prince by his tutor:

. . . representing is naturally something more and higher than simply being, Klaus Heinrich—and that's why people call you Highness.[17]

Pastoral counseling represents and incorporates a theological dimension. The person has come for personal help certainly. But he has come to reorganize his relationship with himself, others *and* God. This is implicit in his choice of a religious counselor who is ordained. It is implicit too in the whole perceptual field into which he places his immediate personal concerns and difficulties. The background is the Divine. He is looking at himself not only as he or others may see and judge him, but as he believes God sees and judges him. This significant additional force lies behind everything he says. Interwoven in the fabric of this pastoral counseling relationship is always a theological design. A relationship with a pastoral counselor extends beyond both counselor and client to this Divine dimension. It is not two but a Third as well Who, through a faith commitment, shares intimately in this pastoral dialogue and diagnosis.

PASTORAL NARCISSISM

The pastoral counselor, then, in addition to being aware of the capacity for reasonable self-responsibility in each person, would need to be especially conscious of the effect of the sense of God's presence in the relationship or, as traditional language might put it, in the work of *grace*. In other words, he must recognize his limited function in another's religious as well as psychological development. Chautard uses the phrase, "heresy of good works" to describe the religious counselor or teacher who tends to "overlook his secondary and subordinate role."

In his discussion of the "Pastoral Resolution of Transference" Godin comments:

Psychologically speaking, pastoral relations often emerge weighed down by the conscious or unconscious affective needs of the pastor and the counselee. Clearer thinking would reveal the enormous gap between what one hopes to do and what is actually achieved. The dispelling of a few illusions need not necessarily involve the slightest discouragement, provided that (1) we increase our trust in a strictly salutary action, the work of God alone. This supernaturally effective action is achieved by means of the most unworthy mediations without ever being intrinsically dependent upon them. Psychopastoral work has but one "dispositive" aim, which is to prepare the ground for the work of Grace; (2) we must remain faithful to the call of charity, which urges us to seek all available means for improving the quality and the flexibility of our pastoral relations, consistent with that supernatural mediation, the sole basis of our entire faith.[18]

Consequently, counseling understanding and skill, in addition to other qualities, can be a means by which the pastoral counselor checks his own narcissistic urges to possess and control. This is often rationalized as religious guidance and direction. In a too ready tendency to give "answers," for example, he may be in fact simply disguising his own use of the person for himself. He needs, therefore, to invoke on himself the same skillful self-discipline as that of the counselor-therapist. As Godin suggests, "by clearly revealing the underlying affective predispositions in pastoral work, psychology collaborates very closely with it in observing their development and, if necessary, in correcting them."[19]

The pastoral counselor does not therefore function in a "mystery-mastery complex"—to use Bakan's term—by which he pretends to special knowledge of the problem and the mystery of each one's human condition, and so has power over him. Rather, he too is enveloped in the mystery of evil and the mystery of grace. It is, as the foregoing indicates, in the sharing of the incarnate-redemptive process by counselor and client together that religious representation seems to be most effective in facilitating the client's gradual identification with, and assimilation of, what is represented. In this, the pastoral counselor must also recognize his own "too, too solid flesh" and human limitation. His pastoral religious commitment and faith call for him to give himself to others in such a way that God's grace and their own mature experience in insight, feeling and willing may be productive of a more adequate integration in time and beyond.

The pastoral counselor is, then, God-centered and not counselor-centered in his—as the older phrase described it—"cure of souls." This phrase, by an interesting historical development through Latin, could be considered the translation of the Greek meaning of the term "psychotherapy." These terms, of course, mean something different now. But they are not totally unrelated. In many instances, at least, they seem still not to be without need of one another.

PAIN, DEATH AND HOPE

But in addition, pastoral counseling represents a unique and particular kind of hope—a hope against all hoping. This hope, of course, permeates the whole of life. But it is especially evident in its religious God-centered dimensions when a person is faced with grave pain or death—either his own or that of others close to him.

All anxiety can finally be reduced to an anxiety about death, just as all courage can be reduced to a sustaining fortitude in the face of death. Death itself can be an ambiguity. For St. Paul it was highly positive, because it symbolized the final victory of the man of faith over death. Its sting had been removed by faith.

Existentially on the other hand, and perhaps primitively, the fearsome aspect of death follows from its being seen as annihilating, but also as threatening personal existence and the loss of being—like the basic anxiety of the child's nightmare fear. Such fear seems to threaten a person with the loss of all capacity to self-affirmation in the face of death.

Death, of course, can be passively endured, in the Greek sense of "fate"; but to be able to say "We shall overcome" in the face of death is to chant a religious cry. Only the man of religious values seems able to see death in this kind of victorious light.

Pain, in a measure, has the same kind of ambiguity and meaning as death. As Bakan says, "pain is simply too elusive to be grasped without taking the sense of annihilation into account."[20] Severe pain immediately suggests death. The little child or the adult may spontaneously say: "It hurt so much I thought I was going to die." Intense pain may be expressed by "It's killing me." Tribulation "dilates" a person, says Psalm Four. Indeed pain, hardship and, as it might be called, "evil fortune" can and do contribute to personal magnanimity. Like any basic life challenge, pain and misfortune can be stood up to and faced. In so doing, while one may not have achieved victory, he can grow in strength and confidence in himself and in sympathy for others. While pain and misfortune can defeat some and leave them traumatized, bitter and vengeful, they can also heighten courage, internalize fortitude and open the heart to the suffering of others. They can produce, in a word, a "grateful" life attitude.

SACRIFICIAL GIFT

One of the elements that make pain—in a constructive sense—also sacrificial and a gift of love is its non-narcissistic quality.

Even though a man may use pain and suffering for selfish manipulatory purposes, no man would wish for pain in and of itself.

Consequently, offered freely to God in a religious context, pain and death, with their inherent threat and anxiety, can be offered sacrificially in a loving way. In the darkness of faith, they are the submission to the loving will of God. Purpose and meaning are believed in, and so pain and misfortune, reprehensible in themselves, can still be lovingly accepted by the religious man as a faith-gift of himself and his destiny to God. The death of others can also be a source of great pain, particularly in the sense of loss and need of them. It too can constitute a faith-gift.

Clinically, according to Selye, one may face pain and death with attitudes that are finally reducible to either negative or positive feeling-tones. One can be—according to Selye's report on the large number of patients he studied—either *vengeful* in the sense of bitter, resentful and hostile to life, or *grateful* in the sense of looking positively at the past and hopefully to the future. Selye found that those patients whose attitudes were ultimately reducible to the word "grateful" met present life issues with more courage and hope.[21]

It is important to note, too, that concepts of death, and therefore the manner of reacting to death, change during childhood, adolescence, manhood and old age. Each views death differently and so fears it differently.[22]

In a certain sense, only religious values hold out any hope for the future in the face of incurable pain, illness and death. Menninger-Puyser *et al* point this out in their comparison of Greek passivity, stoicism and lack of hope with a religious man's firm affirmation of hopefulness in the face of pain and death.[23]

SPECIAL QUALITY

Pastoral counseling introduces a special mimetic quality here. In the person and presence of the ordained clergyman, and in the sacraments and rituals mutually believed in, there is a profound and penetrating faith-representation. Religious counseling—seen alone as distinct from this pastoral mimesis—psychological counseling or other forms of healing would not of themselves invoke this. Here we are in the realm, the very special realm, of uniquely pastoral values. As the reassuring presence of the medical doctor stands for the faith in the present powers of medical healing, so the clergyman stands for a salutary faith in the "beyond." Sacramentally, in addition, he represents and invokes, in God's name, the power, strength and hope of religious faith and divine commitment.

Here the "ontological buoyancy," as Outler calls it, in the face of the passing and transient, which the faith of Paul and Augustine so strongly proclaimed, permeates and penetrates the attitudes, feelings and actions of the religious man. In proportion as his religious faith is alive, he is sustained with a reassuring hope and love beyond pain and death. The mimetic person of the ordained clergyman and the salutary effects of his ministrations, important and basic in and of themselves, also draw strength from the person's own religious faith investment. In a special way, the religious confirmation, "Thy Faith hath made thee whole," reassures, strengthens and integrates in the face of death's final disintegrating threat.

In such a faith atmosphere of hope and love, in and beyond man's present condition, pastoral counseling—in the midst of sacraments and other religious ministrations centering on the word of God and its promise—would have its most central position and its most effective agency.

Thomas Mann describes an instance of this hope "out of the sheerly irremediable":

. . . It would be but a hope beyond hopelessness, the transcendence of despair—not betrayal to her, but the miracle that passes belief. For listen to the end, listen with me: one group of instruments after another retires, and what remains, as the work fades on the air, is the high G of a cello, the last word, the last fainting sound, slowly dying in the pianissimo-fermata. Then nothing more: silence, and night. But that tone which vibrates in the silence, which is no longer there, to which only the spirit hearkens, and which was the voice of mourning, is so no more. It changes its meaning; it abides as a light in the night.[24]

When all else fails, pastoral counseling gets its central focus, power and purpose from this fundamental faith conviction of a "light that shines in the darkness."

NOTES

[1] P. F. D'Arcy, M.M., and E. C. Kennedy, M.M., *The Genius of the Apostolate* (New York: Sheed and Ward, 1965), pp. 102–103.

[2] Richard H. Cox, "The Pastoral Counselor—Who is He?" *The Journal of Pastoral Care*, 19, 4 (Winter 1965), p. 203.

[3] Seward Hiltner, *Preface to Pastoral Theology: The Ministry and Theory of Shepherding* (Nashville, Tenn.: Abingdon Press, 1958).

[4] Gordon W. Allport, "Mental Health: A Generic Attitude," *Journal of Religion and Health*, 4, No. 1 (October 1964), p. 15.

[5] Rudolf Schnackenburg, *The Truth Will Make You Free* (New York: Herder and Herder, 1966), p. 73.

[6] *Ibid.*, p. 83.

[7] *Ibid.*, p. 77.

[8] Sigmund Freud, *An Autobiographical Study, The Standard Edition of the Complete Psychological Works of Sigmund Freud,* trans. James Strachey (London: The Hogarth Press, 1959), 20, pp. 32–33.

[9] Seward Hiltner and Karl Menninger, eds., *Constructive Aspects of Anxiety* (Nashville, Tenn.: Abingdon Press, 1963), p. 76.

[10] Franz G. Alexander, M.D., and Sheldon T. Selesnick, M.D., *The History of Psychiatry: An Evaluation of Psychiatric Thought and Practice from Prehistoric Times to the Present* (New York: Harper and Row), p. 199.

[11] Sigmund Freud, *Collected Papers,* ed. Ernest Jones (New York: Basic Books, Inc., Publishers, 1959), Vol. 2, p. 314.

[12] Allport, *op. cit.,* p. 17.

[13] Eliade, *op. cit.,* p. 11.

[14] Harry A. Wilmer, "Transference to a Medical Center," *California Medicine,* 96:1962, 173–180. Quoted in Karl Menninger, with M. Mayman and P. Pruyser, *The Vital Balance* (New York: The Viking Press, 1963), p. 362.

[15] *The Vital Balance,* pp. 48–49.

[16] Eliade, *op. cit.,* pp. 206–207.

[17] From *Royal Highness,* by Thomas Mann. Trans. by A. Cecil Curtis. Copyright 1939 by Alfred A. Knopf, Inc. and renewed 1967 by Frau Thomas Mann, Erika Mann, and Alfred A. Knopf, Inc. Reprinted by permission of the publisher. Pp. 76–77.

[18] André Godin, S.J., *The Pastor as Counselor,* trans. Bernard Phillips (New York: Holt, Rinehart and Winston, 1965), p. 95. Copyright © 1965.

[19] *Ibid.*, p. 96.

[20] Bakan, *Disease, Pain and Sacrifice,* p. 95.

[21] Selye, *op. cit.*

[22] See Herman Feifel, ed., *The Meaning of Death* (New York: McGraw-Hill, 1959).

[23] See *The Vital Balance,* chapter titled "The Intangibles."

[24] *Doctor Faustus* (New York: Alfred A. Knopf, 1948), p. 491.

PART FIVE

Creative Communication
and Religion

14

The Counseling Church

WE HAVE BEEN considering the way a large group encounter, such as a sermon, might be implemented so that it reaches each person and initiates a personal counseling process. But large groups themselves can undergo counseling either by being provided with smaller group-counseling relationships such as can be inaugurated around the sermon, or in individual pastoral counseling experiences, as we have seen.

But every large organization can also, through certain of its representatives, sometimes assume the form of a person taking counsel with himself. The process is, of course, complex and diffuse, but it can often result in significant organizational self-awarenesses and new and more vital ways of acting. In this sense it resembles the counseling process of an individual person.

We have witnessed such a worldwide organization taking counsel with itself and changing both its self-concept and its relations to others. Vatican II has given us a fascinating illustration of how this is possible. We might, therefore, consider some aspects of this Council, both from the point of view of the Church considered as a person in counsel with itself and as an illustration of how a counseling process, or one that in some ways resembles it, is possible even in an organization of millions of people.

This discussion is not intended to presume that the final fulfillment of this counseling process has already occurred. On the contrary, as Robert McNally, S.J., whom we shall quote more fully later, points out, many councils have completely failed in their purpose even when the need for change was most evident and the resolutions arrived at seemingly wise and necessary. We cannot, therefore, predict the final effects of Vatican II on Catholicism, Christianity, religion and the world. The extent of its implications is too vast. We can, however, study this Council as an organizational counseling process. Surveying its progress, especially in the comments of Popes John and Paul, we can perhaps learn something of how this kind of large organizational counseling process is possible.

THE CHURCH AS PERSON

This introduces us to a different concept and model of the Church, seen not as a walled city—impregnable, perhaps, but remote—but more as a person in humble counsel with himself, incarnate and human as we ourselves are.

The word "council" applied to Church Councils, as in the World Council of Churches and the Vatican Council, and the word "counsel" applied to personal counseling are from the same linguistic root. Webster's dictionary says: "Council: L. Concilium, group of people; Counsel: L. Concilium, com = together; sel = take, grasp." We could thus say that a council is a calling together so that a group might take counsel with itself and thus better grasp and understand its own various open and hidden aspects.

A large world body like the Church has many of the same characteristic psychological subtleties that constitute an individual human person. There should, therefore, be a psychological parallel between this process of the Church's taking counsel with itself in Vatican Council II and the way in which an individual person takes counsel with himself. Under certain conditions, any large organization might follow the same process. This consideration of the Church will lead, as in psychological counseling, to an evaluation of past issues and developments as they relate to the present state of the Church and to probable paths of future resolution and fulfillment as they seem implied in the growing awarenesses of the present.

PER CARITA CONFLICT

In a postscript added only for the Italian edition of *The Italians,*[1] Luigi Barzini discusses the difficulty inherent in a struggle for truth when that struggle seems to work against the fineness of feeling, the thoughtfulness and consideration that are due those to whom we owe loyalty and respect. Barzini applies this to respect for one's country. But the issue he raises of the apparent conflict between a rigorous pursuit of the truth and the demands of charitable consideration which tends to gloss over inadequacies can be applied more broadly.

One might substitute the "Church" for the "State" in the following quotation of Barzini, and we have one of the main difficulties which the calling of any ecumenical council must encounter:

Each time I wanted to face a very interesting problem, in which nobody seemed to be interested; or to write known things but illustrated by unknown, rare, unpublished, hard-to-discover details . . ., Someone told me, cryptically, that it was my citizen's duty to hide everything that might deform the public image of my country. The expression used to justify and to explain the decision was always the same, "Per carita di patria."[2]

This resembles the way a person comes finally to face himself in counseling and bring about changes as a result of this confrontation with himself. In the beginning, the same "per carita" conflict is involved in seeking the truth about oneself and others. In many life circumstances, in fact, it can seem better not to seek such truth too rigorously. Charity, which we usually call kindness and consideration of others and of ourselves, seems often to dictate a delicacy and refinement which rather holds to the more ideal image of oneself and of another since it seems more respectful and generous. Thoughtless truth is not always wise or efficacious. In the end it sometimes only hurts and sears when silence or a more gracious and good-mannered diplomacy would have spared such unnecessary and useless pain.

FACING SELF

There comes a time, however, for both individuals and organizations when such protective façades must give way—when, in a sense, one is paying far too high a price to keep up a picture of oneself that is increasingly at variance with reality. These are the beginning stages of change when, for example, a person sees at least vaguely that, as he will often say, "I cannot go on any longer continuing to live like this." Organizations too can come to a point of diminishing returns. They too must then face themselves in a painful reappraisal, like a person whose symptoms are now too serious and consistent to be disregarded.

So the Church in this case, facing itself in Vatican II, hopefully sought the means of normal change of this kind. Such change dependent as it is not only on grace but on human instrumentality, can never reach the divine ideal—this remains unchanged and above the men who compose the Church. But humanly speaking the Church can hope for and achieve a better-integrated inner life, as an individual can, and also a greater relevance to the world —the salt can again acquire more savor with which to flavor the meat of daily living. A margin of change is clearly possible between the divine transcendence of the Church of God and the human weakness of the Church of Men. This is not a Pelagianism which denies the necessity of grace but rather the affirmation that man freely cooperates with grace. The degree of his conscious and responsible cooperation measures his path from sickness and sin to health and holiness. As an individual man is not hopelessly lost in his confusions, but has strength within himself which grace augments and supernaturalizes, so the Church of Men must strive in manly fashion for greater integrity and clearer purpose.

RENEWAL

The announced intention of the Vatican Council was that it should be concerned with a renewal and rededication of the Church itself. It was not aimed at the discussion of outside conflicts and difficulties. This focus on internal renewal and self-study was one of the most basic attitudes relating it to the counseling process. A person enters into the psychological process of personal examination and probing into the self in order to arrive at greater internal harmony and integration. He does not intend to focus on others as such, even though a by-product of his self-examination is often better and more effective relationships with others.

In this process what a person does in the interviews themselves is often affected by what happens outside. So the very calling of a council activated forces within and without the Church which had significant effects on the Church's counseling process.

Moreover, comparatively small changes in a person during psychological counseling can cause positive changes in those around him. This in turn can set up a kind of chain reaction that sometimes has sustained and important results occurring long after the counseling itself is finished. Something of this sort appears to have happened as a result of the Church council. The issues which faced Vatican II were, in a sense, the problems of the whole Christian family. And as one part of that family cannot really evaluate and take counsel with itself without in some measure including the separated members, so too this council had of necessity to look at its separated Christian brethren as well as at itself. It had, of course, to go beyond this and consider other religions and, in fact, the whole of humanity. But in a special way, it had to consider its own Christian family.

FAMILY CONCEPTION

Using this kind of family conception, one might consider the history of the Church since the sixteenth century as a series of intense and sometimes even violent quarrels between a father and his sons. If we were to observe the psychological process in the relationship of a father and his sons after such a deep and agonizing break with one another, we might predict that it would go through a number of phases. There would be first of all, on both sides, a period of waiting in expectation of an apology and reunion. This would be particularly true on the father's side, since he, out of a sense of the respect due to him, would be likely to look for the first moves in any return or reunion as belonging to the sons.

The sons, on the other hand, determined to prove their own right to independence and to personal meaning, would be all the more aggressively resistant to such a return, seeing it as an admission of defeat and a loss of integrity. All that they individually stood for would appear to be put in jeopardy by the thought of such a reunion.

We can see that under these conditions, this state of confirmed rupture would last a long time and might even seem incapable of ever being healed.

There is at least a similarity between this conception and what actually took place in the Christian family at the time of the Reformation and after. The very fact that historians of one side tended to refer to a Protestant "Revolt," while the other side proudly insisted on a "Reformation" and restoration, indicates the negatively charged tones that gradually tended to fix both sides in adamantine resistance to one another. The endless repercussions of reproach and blame on both sides only fixed further this negative emotional state by adding ever-increasing distortions and misunderstandings to the original differences. The fact, too, that complicated political and social forces were involved, such as the rise of Nationalism and Industrialism—like property rights and political allegiances in a family quarrel—often only heightened the hostility and made all the firmer each group's resolution to resist the other. The actual historical ecclesiastical situation thus becomes psychologically understandable when we see it in the light of the factors that might readily have occurred in a deeply involved family conflict.

PRESENT AND FUTURE

It would not be unexpected, however, if at a much later period the brothers began to raise some questions about this rupture with their father, as well as their differences with one another. We can imagine then a particular brother coming to counseling in a somewhat confused and hostile state towards both his father and some or all of his brothers. Yet implicit in his coming for counseling would be the painful awareness that things were not all right in their present ruptured state.

We would expect that in a gradual reappraisal of the past in the light of the present, the brother would come to see that he and the other brothers were still their father's sons—despite all the bitterness and injustice that had gone before. We would expect him to see, too, with greater maturity and compassion now, something of the understandable human weakness that made the father feel and act as he had.

We could also predict that the father, too, as time passed and the sharpness of the quarrels lessened, would begin to feel, with increasing intensity, the pain of loss of his sons. Were the father then to come for counseling—most probably, at another place and to another person—we could yet predict that he, too, would follow the same path from negation, hostility and bitterness to a dawning awareness and appreciation that the blame was not entirely the sons'. The father, too, could begin to see something of their side. In the light of his present knowledge, he could now recognize wrong—or, at least, unwise—things he, too, had done. He would thus begin to concentrate more on the present and future and less on the past. As the counseling proceeded, predictably, he would show more concern about what he might do to change himself. His hope would then be that his sons, seeing the change in him, would themselves be won again at least to thoughts of some kind of family reunion.

BROTHERLY APPRAISAL

Certainly the World Council of Churches and other Protestant groups in their joint councils, here and in Europe, have begun this kind of brotherly reappraisal. The stated purpose of Vatican Council II to focus on the renewal and rejuvenation of the Church itself, while similar to the self-concentration of a person in counseling, would yet have overtones that would make it more acceptable and effective especially with other Christians. Before the Council began, Pope John voiced this spirit of self-reappraisal and even of taking blame when, in discussing the responsibility for the continued Christian rupture, he said:

> But it is to a large extent ours, because it is up to us to assuage the pain of those living in schism, through gestures, through words, through the example of our humility, of our charity.[3]

In the first session of the Council it became evident that the bishops were striving for an expression of doctrine "in charity, clarity, simplicity and gentleness," as one release put it. Another communique, in summarizing a discussion, said:

The point was made that each [Christian Church] must make clear exposition of its own doctrines in a calm, objective and clear manner, while taking care to respect the positions of the other and to seek a manner of expression which does not divide but unites.[4]

One of the first evidences of change in a psychological counseling process is that the person begins to see familiar persons and situations in a new and often more positive light. This new perception brings with it a new "plan of life," as Alfred Adler called it. That is, the person changes his whole approach to these same familiar persons and situations.

Something of his kind of change of operational plan was implied in the Church's process of taking counsel with itself. This was suggested by a remark of Pope John's in a radio address, "It is the Church that must bring Christ to the world." Here we see a different tone in contrast to the tendency to condemn the world for not responding to methods of approach which, while valid in past centuries, seem to many no longer pertinent or attractive. Pope John also reiterated an attitude voiced by many recent popes, that the Church welcomed genuine scientific research and progress in knowledge. An even more noticeable change of attitude was suggested in Pope John's repeated reference to other Christians as "brothers." This was highlighted by the presence of other Christian representatives in conspicuous places of honor during ceremonies and as observers and resource persons to the Council participants.

ENTHUSIASM

Such changes had the obvious consequences of winning Protestant enthusiasm. This enthusiasm, while directly centered on the simple and charming personality of Pope John, also radiated in hope and anxious, prayerful concern to the workings of the Council itself. Perhaps at no time since before the Reformation—if even then— had so many Christians been genuinely engaged in the careful following of almost daily reports of a Church council's activities and enthusiastically anticipating its outcome.

PASTORAL FOCUS

The pastoral emphasis repeatedly voiced by the Pope and the Council representatives introduced a further harmonizing note. While theoretical discussions can lead in many directions, pastoral considerations inevitably take their starting point from man as he is. This kind of existential confrontation of the human condition in its "here-and-now"-ness brings its own humbling and purifying element. When modern man and his needs are made the center of discussion, a core unity has already been established not only with other theological viewpoints and other churches but also with science, with culture, with governments, and in fact with every human endeavor. It is no wonder, then, that a Council with such an aim should gain both theological and secular sympathy. The human condition concerns everyone, and any sincere effort to improve it on a world scale is profoundly moving in its appeal.

NATURE OF CHANGE

One further point that seems significant in our parallel between the Council and an individual's counseling process refers to the nature of the change itself. In counseling we do not expect any basic personality changes. Persons after counseling remain fundamentally as they were before. Otherwise they might entirely lose their sense of personal continuity and meaning. They are therefore not usually dramatically different persons. We still know them as they were.

The change consists rather in a reorganization and reintegration of self resulting from a more profound self-knowledge. This increase in self-knowledge also includes a greater willingness to see that many present methods of coping with problems were drawn from much earlier periods in one's life. While these ways of operating may have been satisfactory then, they are now no longer adequate and they may even be self-defeating. A person, as he grows to see this, is also in a better position to devise more effective ways of fulfilling his present needs and purposes as he now realistically sees them.

Similarly, it would be unrealistic to expect any change in the basic nature of the Church as a result of the Vatican Council. As with an individual person, so also in the Church, there are strong forces for continuity and consistency. These could not be destroyed without destroying the whole fabric of the Church's personality.

The changes we could expect, however, as in individual counseling, could be nonetheless dramatic and significant. They could affect the whole nature of the way the Church relates to itself and others, particularly as it might change many things that for centuries have been its accustomed ways of operation. At an early stage in the Council, one bishop remarked that, in his opinion:

. . . some of the proposals which the Council will consider, and eventually adopt to be in keeping with modern pastoral needs, would have seemed radical, if not unthinkable, only a few years ago.[5]

REMOVE STEREOTYPES

To the observer of a counseling process, there often comes the realization that his own fixed views or stereotypes of the person taking counsel were astonishingly distorted and inaccurate. As one hears the person speak about himself in the unsparing realism and humility of the interview, one inevitably grows in respect and admiration for this kind of honest integrity, even when one might still not agree with the person's conclusions.

Something of this kind of respectful awareness seems already to have occurred with regard to the Church. The willingness of the Church to question herself under the scrutiny of the whole world broke many stereotypes. It became evident, for example, that the Church was not simply a monolithic structure fashioned entirely after the manner of an absolute monarchy. As Pope John remarked, apropos of a disagreement among the bishops, "We are not friars singing in a choir."[6]

SLOW IMPLEMENTATION

Moreover, a counseling process does not necessarily produce great changes in a person immediately. Rather, the beginnings of a new and more effective life-plan are laid down which are only slowly implemented and unfolded through subsequent years. We can hope this will be equally true of the Council, that its effects will continue to emerge now that its present work is finished. But even by the middle of the Council sessions, enough had apparently been accomplished to allow an editorial in a Catholic theological journal to say:

We already have much more in common with many "non-Catholics" than we realize, and relatively minor changes on our part can greatly broaden the areas of agreement.[7]

REACTION FORMATION

The open pursuit of truth, however, involves risks. In counseling it often removes one's defenses. One is psychologically naked before oneself and often before others as well. There is the fear of what others may do to us when they know these hitherto apparently secret weaknesses of ours. There is even the more disturbing fear of how one will live with and cope with oneself afterward. How does one handle the shame, guilt and recrimination that such relentless facing of oneself can bring about?

We are aware of the "reaction formation" kind of personality structures this can evoke. Truth once seen and then hidden and suppressed is not really stifled but is in danger of manifesting itself in other subtle and disguised forms. In an individual, endless compensation mechanisms that are basically self-defeating can emerge because of his fear of facing a truth, seen in counseling, which he has again made unconscious and buried even more deeply than before.

In the Church this pattern of reaction could take a variety of forms, each characterized by an escape into the peripheral issues and so avoiding the essential, central concerns. It could, for example, take the form of reforms and improvements, exemplary in their organizational efficiency and legal precision, which nevertheless left the basic issues untouched. So the Church might appear to change, and yet be growing more irrelevant to the world and more alienated and less loving in its members. Only the organizational structure would have really changed.

Pope Paul cautioned against this:

Conciliar renewal is not measured so much by changes in customs or in outward criteria as in a change of certain mental habits, of a certain interior inertia, of a certain resistance of the heart to the truly Christian spirit. The first change, and most important of all, is what is ordinarily called conversion of heart.[8]

ESCAPE

An individual person in this state often also projects all his difficulties outward—he blames other persons and circumstances as being their cause. By so doing, he can avoid the painful confrontation of himself and his own responsibility.

So the Church, too, can keep blaming the world and the failure of men to cooperate and obey it. Or it can look at itself in such a way that each Churchman and each Christian faces and responsibly evaluates himself. Vatican II, in its resolve not to condemn but to strive for inner renewal, held up this goal for every Churchman and every religious person. Each one is faced with a painful reappraisal of himself and his meaning as a religious man.

Another shape the Church's "reaction formation" could take would be wordy discussions and plans which wear themselves out in meetings and talks, build up an imaginary image of achievement and leave the reality untouched. Barzini describes this tendency as

the capacity to show the reality in a wonderful way, sometimes even to invent a reality more satisfying than the one that exists, to confuse finally the thing that is represented with the representation, the Saint's statue with the Saint himself. Edgar Quinet denounced, in 1851, the horrible contrast between the appearance of things, the "cult of beauty" and "la laideur infernale des institutions de choses."[9]

In either of these "reaction" states, "the last state of such a man" would be worse than the first. But it is a most difficult thing indeed, to look in a mirror and see what we really are and yet not go away and forget it. It can often, in self-deception, be far easier to suppress the unwanted and even hateful images we saw there and so defeat those moments of truth when we really knew "what manner of men" we were.

BASIC RISK

This, then, is perhaps the greatest risk involved in Vatican Council II: that it all really comes to nothing in the end. Such, apparently, has been the history of some councils. Writing of the century preceding the Reformation, McNally points out:

The remote origins of the Council of Trent go back to the decades before the Reformation. By the year 1400 it was clear to all thoughtful men that the Church was badly in need of renovation. Her external structure had become acutely lopsided through the accumulation and preservation of survivals of bygone ages. And in direct consequence her mobility in the changing world of the Late Middle Ages was greatly reduced. Liturgical and spiritual renewal, development of clerical and lay education, adaptation of administration to current needs, vernacular translations of the Bible and the liturgical books, a thorough reorganization of both the Roman Curia and the papal fiscal system were universal aspirations. A demand for renovation of the Church "in head and members" was voiced on all sides. In fact, *renovatio* is the theme, the leitmotif of the fifteenth century Church. Yet in this very century the Councils of Constance and Basle, and later the Lateran, failed totally in the work of reform. Centered in the peripheral and insignificant rather than in the great, pressing issues of the day, these councils were disasters. Their failure to renovate the Church is a significant warning that the character of the assistance which the Holy Spirit extends to the Church should be carefully evaluated before it is invoked as a panacea. For perhaps never before in history was *reformatio* so urgently needed in the Church; yet it is the tragedy of this historical moment that despite these reform councils *difformatio* prevailed.[10]

This fear on a person's part of facing himself and his awareness of the risk he is taking are commonly evident in the first stages of counseling. Hence it is usually only with great caution and hesitancy that he will begin to look clearly at himself and others. A basic and perhaps primitive anxiety and defense warns him that he is entering a danger zone, that the pursuit of this kind of personal truth can be a two-edged sword hurting himself and others. He usually remembers attempts at this in the past that have only ended in greater failure, frustration and depression. If he faces himself openly therefore, he does so because he sees this kind of self-truth not as a sword but as a scalpel which cuts, not to destroy, but to cure and bring health again. It is this hope and trust in the counselor and in himself which permeate the counseling sessions and bring about whatever good they achieve.

This too was the intent of Vatican II, not simply to make public confession of weakness, but to trust itself and its own powers of growth and to trust, too, to the understanding of other Christians and the world. Its intent was to begin a penetrating process of self-analysis and change which must extend beyond the Council sessions to perhaps the end of this century before all its positive and integrating consequences can be seen and judged.

MEETING PRESENT NEEDS

In the need for "aggiornamento," an expression used by Pope John, one sees revealed a basic cause of grave difficulties in the lives of persons as well as organizations: a too rigid fixation on past achievements and past ways of doing things. Psychological difficulties often involve a turning to the past long after it has ceased to have meaning. In this sense, positive psychological change too consists in a kind of "aggiornamento," a coming to grips with oneself in terms of present needs and purposes. Here one must certainly "let the dead bury the dead"—one must free oneself of the dead weight of a past age and past achievements which no longer serve a present purpose.

We often see a man, in examining himself deeply, come to the realization that his present failures and frustrations are due not so much to mistakes in his deliberate and conscious actions as to the fact that he is still living passively with judgments, values and ways of acting which were successful and productive when he first devised them. His present difficulties come from living too long on the capital of his past. He has drained his resources by failing to invest in more adequate ways of present action. So he comes to realize that he needs "aggiornamento." In the light of his present life circumstances, he must re-examine all those attitudes, judgments, and modes of action whose origins lie in his past and which have for a long time been taken for granted. He must renew himself in the existential meaning of today. For him, as for St. Paul, "Today is the day of salvation." He gains health and holiness by meeting and responding to today.

LIVING TODAY

In something of this same sense, the Council has brought "aggiornamento" to Christians. It has reminded them that salvation is of today, whatever the past may have been. In this the Church is not so much rejecting the past as simply saying that it is past, that, as with an individual person, many of its ways of operating are dead now, however valuable or justified they may have been at one time. The present need is to re-sort and re-group, discarding in the process what no longer is relevant. This, then, and not simply to raise issues or question the past, was the purpose of the Church's self-inquiry. As an individual cannot really know or judge well his present actions without re-examining his past, so the Church must not only reconsider its past actions but learn to what degree they still have relevance to its present concerns. Those that do not must be discarded or they block and stifle present living.

CONSTRUCTIVE GUILT

This brings us to a point previously considered, but applicable here in a special way, of the constructive use of guilt. When a person inaugurates such courageous facing himself and re-evaluating his past and present, he usually finds himself in a state of guilt and self-attack. But in place of the defenses and rationalizations that marked his previous handling of such guilt, he now openly accepts this guilt, turning it into a positive force which moves him to change.

By presenting the Church of God only as pure and spotless and perhaps minimizing the weakness of the Church of Men, we may have too easily overlooked this constructive aspect of guilt. To be mentally healthy a man must face his own guilt. If he suppresses guilt, he is only running the danger of seeing it crop up in many disguised forms to plague and obstruct him still more. Therapy in fact is the constructive admitting of guilt. In taking responsibility for guilty actions lies one of the strongest motives for change in the human personality.

In much the same way, if the Church as a human organization keeps suppressing those things for which it should feel truly guilty, it is not really helping itself, but hindering itself as an agent of the divine. For organizations like individuals can be victims of mass rationalizations and escapisms, as we have seen all too well in some of the mass tragedies of this century. The acceptance of guilt in a positive and constructive sense is both responsible and hopeful because it is a sign of a man's conscious willingness and capacity to change. Man is mentally sick indeed when he feels no guilt for those actions for which he should feel guilty.

Guilt in the psychological sense here considered is not simply a sense of sinfulness and penitence. It can be that, certainly. But it is often, upon careful analysis, the regrets and painful awareness which hindsight produces, when one sees with clarity and distinctness what, at the time of decision and action, was still in fog. Once the consequences of decisions are evident, one can readily judge, and regret as unwise, actions which at the moment of choice seemed propitious. Psychological guilt often includes this kind of regret and remorse as well as a conscious sense of sin.

Guilt that is purely negative and anxiety-ridden is, of course, not only valueless but destructive. It is simply masochistic and self-defeating. For a Christian, it would also be a denial of forgiveness and saving grace. We do not mean this kind of negative self-attack. This serves no purpose but to stagnate, by corrosive bitterness and disillusionment, whatever constructive forces might have been stirring in the person. What we mean is the normal guilt which accompanies and furthers honest and forthright self-appraisal and aids in more adequate self-decision and action.

CREATIVE TENSION

Perhaps an even better way of considering the operation of constructive guilt would be in terms of the creative tension between the Church's exalted self-ideal and its all too human and sinful reality. Pope Paul seems to be appealing to this kind of creative guilt when he asks, "In fact, is it not the strident comparison between holiness—which the Church preaches and which it ought to have—

and its actual condition which sustains irony, antipathy and scandal toward the Church?"[11] For in holding up this contrast, not negatively but hopefully, the Pope was indeed challenging the humanity of the Church into growth and reform. The kind of creativity that spurs an individual on to greatness is not an easy inner peace or static security. Rather it is a constant dynamic tension between a person's self-ideal and his acting self. As we saw earlier, "Other findings support the hypothesis that creative individuals are more able than most to give expression to opposite sides of their nature."[12]

So too, it would seem, when the humanity of the Church is deeply conscious of itself, what it is in contrast with what it can and ought to be, creative and constructive forces will be released through these contrasting inner tensions. Such forces should move it to significant new achievements. Peace-at-any-price can dull and stultify an organization as well as a person. There is a deceptive peace in a cemetery if the reality of death is forgotten. The dead cause no trouble, and never shock or scandalize. If it were not for the threat they pose to us, the living, the dead would disturb no one.

POSITIVE ANXIETY

By contrast with this kind of dead tranquility, the first stages of such change in both individuals and organizations can appear threatening and elicit anxiety. In the case of a person, feelings of confusion, conflict, guilt, hostility and similar negative emotions can swell in him and find expression in ways that often surprise and disturb him. As he trusts and gains confidence in himself, he also trusts his ability not only to handle these disordered states but also to look behind them for the significant values and self-revelation they contain. These were previously hidden by rationalizations and self-justifications.

So in organizations, and particularly in the Church, there must be a certain tolerance for the same kind of negative confusions and conflicts. If they are quickly stifled for fear of their consequences, they may in fact, as in an individual, simply become repressed again and show themselves in disguised but disrupting or impeding forms. Handled confidently and openly, they will perhaps more readily disperse themselves and reveal, upon analysis, the more basic and more valuable impulses that are hidden behind their confusion and negation.

For effective reorganization to come about in individuals, groups, or organizations, the change process must allow for the movement from a non-participant, hostile and protective withdrawal—the repressed states of organizational negation—through the conscious release and clarification of hostile feelings and resistant attitudes, to a more cooperative, responsible participation.

SELF-IDEAL

Involved and aiding the process of change at this stage is the defining of a realistic self-ideal. While the Church of God seen by the Christian in all its luminescent divine effulgence surpasses any possible human ideal, the Church of "the men who belong to it"[13] must, like an individual person, be rigorously realistic in deciding what it can achieve with the means at hand. Too great a preoccupation with the ideal rather than the real Church—a tendency to which Churchmen can be too prone—will simply be self-defeating. When a person proposes and tries to live by too high a practical self-ideal, he ends usually not only in failure but in self-demoralization that becomes passive and even cynical and bitter. A person prevents this through gaining a kind of self-awareness which lowers this ideal to a level which, with his best efforts, he can usually achieve.

In a similar way, a realistic self-awareness in the twentieth century, second half, is a practical necessity for the Church of Men, if men are to be genuinely effective in their work for God. Otherwise, with too transcendent a self-ideal, one fights against the human condition and inevitably discourages oneself and defeats one's cause.

REALISTIC ACCEPTANCE

Previously, we pointed out that a person does not change himself totally but remains fundamentally himself and learns finally to accept himself as he is. Others too must learn to know and accept him as he is rather than always trying to change him. So changes in the Church as a result of the Council will not change the historic Church essentially. Pope Paul said: "Neither a desire for return to old ways nor a continuous questioning of permanent truths and laws should mark today's Catholics."[14] As a person learns to do, the men in the Church must learn to work constructively within the framework of what the Church knows and has defined itself to be.

The transcendent, supernatural, and supereminent image of the Church as the sign and proof of God's engagement and concern for the world remains as the ultimate Christian ideal, inspiration, and goal. But considering the Church in its humanity, we must also consider the human limits of its potential in any given age and place. The Church is not only divine but existential. It exists in moments of time through "the men who belong to it." Its confusions and conflicts do not touch its transcendent and supernatural divinity. They consider rather its human agency. But, being human, the Church has all the strengths as well as the weaknesses of men. So perceiving itself and defining for itself human and realistic self-ideals, the Church should, like an individual person, be able with constant effort and insight to approach ever closer to this fully functioning personal state. The Church can, then, like a person, under the right psychological as well as religious conditions, grow more mature, responsible and committed to the age and circumstances in which it lives.

EXISTENTIAL RELEVANCE

Seen this way, "per carita" is no mask of benevolent kindness sparing us from disturbing truth; it is rather the searing therapy of truth without which all—Christians and non-Christians alike —will remain unchanged and bound to old self-defeating ways. One can never arrive at the truth that makes for freedom if one never even begins to question oneself. Vatican Council II has opened up this process of questioning and involvement in faith, hope and love between man—within and without the Church— and between man and God. In contrast to the image of the Church as static, monolithic and removed, we now have the image of the

Church in counsel—struggling to become existentially aware of and relevant to the meaning and needs of man today.

We might say then that the Church—and all peoples of the world sympathetically observing and sharing this counseling process—has concluded some measure of its self-evaluation. It is now engaged in striving for the integration of the means to carry out what it has arrived at in its research into itself and reality. In this sense its process of counsel continues and involves us all. The Church—like a person in counseling—has, indeed, arrived at its own self-concept. As in the later stages of counseling, too, we are all now engaged in the implementation of this new and exciting awareness.

PERSONAL COMMITMENT

The core insight, then, that the Council seemed finally to have focused on was the need for change in each Christian's self-regard, in order to implement this new self-concept. This was repeatedly emphasized in papal and Council statements defining both the importance of the person and the necessity of a restoration of genuine love between Christians themselves and with the world.

This is evident not only in the Council documents but even more in the remarks, interpreting the Council, made at various times by Pope Paul. Early Council statements stressed the need for a genuine effort to understand, respect and love one another; other Christians; other religions; and the world. This emphasis continued throughout the Council. The concluding schema on the relationship of bishops and priests underscores the biblical injunction that priests and the laity must be viewed as friends, not servants, and so must be included together in a genuinely positive dialogue.

So personal engagement and creative communication are here conceived as the heart of Christian witness. In his discourse to the Observers, Pope Paul emphasized the need for such genuine love in Christ, "so that the world will recognize we are truly his disciples because we have re-established among us a reciprocal love."[15] Addressing them as "Brothers, and friends in Christ," he said, . . . "We have begun again to love one another."[16] In his last speech to the Council, the Pope declared the restoration of Christian humanism and the person:

The Church of the Council has been concerned not just with herself and her relationship . . . with God, but with man—man as he really is today; loving man . . . man as the superman of yesterday and today, ever frail, unreal, selfish and savage; man unhappy with himself as he laughs and cries . . . man as he is, a creature who thinks and loves and toils and is always waiting for something. . . . We call upon those who term themselves modern humanists . . . to recognize our own new type of humanism; we, too, in fact more than any others, honor mankind.[17]

To the United Nations, the Pope said:

The hour has struck for our "conversion," for personal transformation, for interior renewal. We must get used to thinking of man in a new way; and in a new way also of man's life in common; with a new manner too of conceiving the paths of history and the destiny of the world, according to the words of Saint Paul: "You must be clothed in the new self, which is created in God's image, justified, and sanctified through the truth" (Eph. IV, 23). The hour has struck for a halt, a moment of recollection, of reflection, almost of prayer. A moment to think anew of our common origin, our history, our common destiny.[18]

What we see here seems to add up not simply to a series of plans and programs. Rather, what is demanded, as in personal counseling, is a deep and fundamental change in self-concept, a change necessary to establish the climate for a new and more mature religious experience and commitment.

If the contradiction between the Church's preaching love and the consistent failure of Christians to practice it—a contradiction which Pope Paul singled out—is ever to be remedied, it will be done by deep and painful self-awareness on the part of Christians themselves. What the Pope was calling for, therefore, and what he felt the Council had offered, was a new Christian relationship characterized by penetrating understanding, mutual respect and acceptance, and growing self-regard and regard for others. Such qualities in an individual relationship or in a group epitomize the best elements we know for furthering psychological and spiritual growth and development.

Reform or growth in the Church, then, would have as its goal this most complete kind of religious humanism. Only by striving to become a complete and integrated person can a Christian arrive at that truth about himself which will make him free. Since love is an action as well as a state, a religious man must struggle to love himself at the deepest level of his own person and reciprocally so to love others. The Christian community in turn must allow him the freedom, respect and regard which constantly furthers and enlarges his capacity to do this.

NOTES

[1] *Gli Italiani* (Rome: Arnoldo Mondodori Editore, 1965).

[2] *Ibid.*, pp. 431–432.

[3] *Chicago Sun Times,* Tuesday, May 20, 1962.

[4] *Ibid.*

[5] In report to Diocese of Columbus, Ohio, from Bishop Clarence G. Issenmann.

[6] *Time,* January 4, 1963.

[7] *Theological Digest,* 10, No. 4. (Autumn 1962), p. 177.

[8] *National Catholic Register* (Denver, Colorado), December 23, 1965.

[9] Barzini, *op. cit.,* p. 434.

[10] Robert E. McNally, S.J., "The Council of Trent and the German Protestants," *Theological Studies,* 25 (March 1964), p. 2.

[11] Associated Press release, *Rome Daily American,* Friday, October 22, 1965; complete Italian text, *Osservatore Romano,* Friday, October 22, 1965.

[12] "Creativity," *Carnegie Corporation of New York Quarterly, op. cit.,* p. 2.

[13] "It [the Church] is holy in its search for holiness. It is holy and penitent at the same time. It is holy in itself, sick in the men who belong to it." Pope Paul VI, *Osservatore Romano,* October 22 (Friday), 1965.

[14] *National Catholic Register, op. cit.*

[15] *National Catholic Register, op. cit.*

[16] *Osservatore Romano,* December 6, 7, 1965.

[17] *Newsweek,* December 20, 1965, p. 41.

[18] Address of His Holiness Paul VI to the General Assembly of the United Nations, October 4, 1965, *Tipografia Poliglotta Vaticana,* p. 21.

15

Religion as Community and Communication

WHAT WE ARE NOW WITNESSING, therefore, is a changing self-concept about religion itself, its relation to its own members, to other religious people and to the world. This change in self-concept is evident not only in many of the resolutions of Vatican II but in religious groups everywhere, large and small. There is ferment apparently as the leaven of religious values begins again to reassert itself and seeks new and fresh ways to permeate man's daily existence.

PERSONHOOD AND RELATEDNESS

We have considered various means by which counseling and psychotherapy might join with religion in this task of aiding man. The main thrust of their common effort could be said to center on the sense of depersonalization and alienation that seems to characterize our age. Counseling, psychotherapy and religion emphasize both the meaning and value of becoming a person and the fulfillment of the need to belong and to give oneself to others. So personhood and relatedness, then, are their common themes.

But personhood and relatedness are based on a person's capacity to communicate with himself and others. We are trying to find more adequate means of such creative communication. Only through that communication which truly brings communion does a man become a person and affiliate with others in a genuine community. Such a community is characterized by authentic involvement. The God-dimension or totally Other aspects of religion are included here because prayer must also be creative communica-

311

tion if it is a dialogue with the divine. The image of God as Persons in relation and belonging fits well, as we have said, as the model of what man himself now seeks and needs.

COMMUNION AND COMMUNICATION

The word "community," then, includes "communication" and "communion" and implies "union." "Communication" is what goes on in "communion," and "communion" is what happens in a "community." A genuine community is characterized by the richness, warmth and openness of the people who compose it. The model and ideal of a community, seen this way, would be the model of friendship.

The Saxon word "friendship," however, will not give us the same sense as its corresponding Norman adjective. If we were to say that it is an "amicable" relationship, this will lead us to "amor," the Latin equivalent of the Saxon word "love." But, it would be embarrassing to speak of a community of lovers; yet, rightly understood, that is what an amicable relationship obviously is. The idea of "community" then, in its full force and in its scriptural religious tradition, implies a place or relationship where people have freedom to love. A community would then be a place where love removes barriers and so creates both communication and communion.

But friendship demands communication and true revelation of self. Otherwise the relationship can be only a mask. Consequently a concept of "community" that implies simply living together in one house or on the same or adjacent streets can, in fact, be no real community at all but actual isolation. Enforced familiarity can further the necessity of masks. On the contrary, one often requires personal distance to engage oneself at those stress levels at which one's real individuality and uniqueness are made evident. Here one may need counsel with oneself or with another and time and distance for creative self-involvement in order to be able to relate in a genuine communication with others. Proximity may produce only group conformism and narcissistic manipulation and use of one another out of anxiety and defense. Such an enforced "living together" may only increase real isolation under the appearance of "getting along together." Such relationships inevitably appear "phony" to the sensitive observer, particularly the young.

Because the words "love" and "lover" are almost too intimate, the words "friendship" and "friend" are generally preferred in describing an authentic relationship. But "friendship" in its present usage can seem so cold and removed that it fails to imply necessary communion and communication. Nonetheless it is a safe word; there is no danger, no risk, no involvement, in its use. The word "love," by contrast, is threatening, in the sense that it implies a much more involved and intense relationship. But this is its special value too. For friendship really to have any significant personal meaning, it must be such a relationship of love.

MEANING OF LOVE

"Love," however, as we have seen, has a wide variety of meanings. We can consider again briefly three such implications. The first, that of eroticism, is the crowding into an aggrandized image of the sexual function a power and meaning which is fantasy and magic combined. This displaced eroticism shows itself, for example, in the constant use of feminine allure in advertising. In contrast to the Greek notion that a woman's body represented virtue, justice and the graces, it is now used to sell things.

The second image of love is both romantic and idolatrous in the sense that the possession of the other person is promised as the solution to all life's alienation and fulfillment. In songs, for example, the possession of the other, in a basically narcissistic way, makes him or her "mine alone." The only escape from alienation is this one relationship. One must search and find him or her —say, across a crowded room—or be forever alone. There is then only one man and one woman, and if a man does not find her, he is alienated. She in turn is lost. No gate could be as narrow or path to salvation as difficult as that.

Lovers are assured that their special love will outlast the mountains, and even though the wells dry up, such love will remain "true." The lover thus claims a kind of divinity for himself and his beloved. In this promise of love's eternal fulfillment in the lover alone, we have a kind of romantic idolatry.

The love of "friendship," by contrast, is, as we have stressed throughout, the gift of self. It is that moment in time when one person moves out of himself to the other. In such a moment of friendship, an act of genuine love has occurred. It is loving persons by wishing them the best fulfillment of their unique selves. We have seen that this resembles the counseling therapeutic relationship especially in those moments when the genuine outgoingness on the part of the counselor or therapist is totally for the other to be used for his most complete being and becoming. "Community" is then related to this kind of love—offering mature and respectful consensual validation of what is best for each person.

THE CITY

But the word "community" can also mean a city. While the word "city" is derived from French and Latin, its Greek form is "polis." The words "police" and "political" are obviously from this Greek form. But in modern usage "police" and "political" can appear to be almost contradictory terms to communion and communication. For a "city" now seems cold and impersonal, with little of the warmth and openness real communication and communion would imply. Rather the community idea of persons in a deep relationship of genuine union and belonging would be what alienated, anxious and faceless masses of people buried in the "inner" city genuinely seek.

We have already considered both St. Augustine's contribution to the richness of the modern concept of "person" and, briefly, his concept of the "City of God." He probed so thoughtfully into the nature of "person" that this concept gained a whole new religious and psychological depth and significance. He is far more widely known, however, for his conception of the "city"—applied to the Church as the "City of God." In the Introduction we suggested that this model of the Church as a city—albeit a city of God—now represents some values that are different from its original Augustinian conception. We will now pursue this further, especially as it relates to needs of community.

The Greek, and later Roman, idea conceived of a city as it conceived of a building—a rationalized orderly structure to be a safe and cultural place in which to live. It was protected and enclosed by a wall that kept some people in and others out. It was the wall that separated friend and enemy. Such a model supplied the foundation of normal living, some sense of "to each his own" in an orderly fashion.

INNER-CITY BELONGING

One reason why Christianity succeeded so well in large cities was that the Christian groups offered a sense of communion and communication to the faceless masses within. The word "pagani" did not originally mean "pagans" in our sense; it meant "farmers." Those were the people who lived outside the wall. Within the city, little groups of Christians came together in deep communication and communion and so fulfilled the human need for in-group sense of belonging. In other words, these groups had much the same needs as the inner-city masses of today, and religion gave them a sense of incarnate worth and significance as persons.

The nature of the Christian religion itself, its stress on community and the meaning of the person, all seemed to further its being at home with and suited to the people of large cities. McNeill points out:

None of the other mystery religions of the Roman empire had as much to offer. A noble ethic, sacred writings popularly written, yet backed by the sanction of ancient prophecy, a warm emotional brotherhood among the faithful, the promise of eternal and blissful life topped by a vivid expectation of an early overthrow of worldly injustices on earth; all these made a powerful appeal to the poor and dispossessed of the great cities of the Roman world and beyond Roman borders as well.[1]

THE CITY OF GOD

Bourke indicates how Augustine came, initially, by political circumstances to write the *City of God:*

In the midst of this active ecclesiastical career, a shocking political and military event occurred. The supposedly impregnable City of Rome was attacked and ravished by the Goths in the year 410. Suddenly the Empire which had ruled most of the civilized world for centuries was dying. Throughout the Roman world, astonishment was followed by recrimination: one persistent rumor was that Christianity had sapped the strength of Rome. The officials and citizenry of Rome were still divided into Christian and pagan groups. It takes no powers of imagination to picture the situation. A Roman official in North Africa, the Christian Marcellinus, wrote to Augustine, telling him about this charge against Christianity and asking him to refute it. This was the setting, then, which occasioned the writing of the *City of God*.[2]

We cannot, then, separate the extension of Augustine's model of the City and the political position in which the fall of Rome put the Church. As Gilson says:

. . . The great Bishop of Hippo probably would never have written it except for the fall of Rome and the ensuing controversies to which that event gave rise; nevertheless, when the challenge came he was prepared to meet it.[3]

Without the political situation as it was, there might have been no need for a model of the Church as a city. As a result, however, of the image of a holy city, St. Augustine, according to Gilson, apparently did not see any really valid continuing temporal order:

It was not through any failure to foresee the beneficent influence that the City of God, by the very fact of its existence, can and ought to exercise on temporal societies, that the possibility of a unified temporal order, valid and justifiable in itself from the point of view of its proper end, did not suggest itself to St. Augustine; rather, it was due to the close association between the two notions of *world* and of *evil,* so spontaneously linked together in his mind . . . as if the transcendent importance of the building of the City of God relegated the temporal order to a place so clearly secondary that it was no longer worth the trouble to consider it for itself or to organize it in view of its own ends.[4]

For Augustine, the earthly city is selfish and irreligious:

And so two loves made two cities. The love of self even unto the contempt of God made the earthly city, whereas the love of God even unto the contempt of self made the heavenly city.[5]

Describing the ancient Greek symbolization of the nobility of a great city in Homer, Steiner comments:

At the core of the Homeric poems lies the remembrance of one of the greatest disasters that can befall man: the destruction of a city. A city is the outward sum of man's nobility; in it, his condition is most thoroughly humanized. When a city is destroyed, man is compelled to wander the earth or dwell in the open fields in partial return to the manner of a beast. That is the central realization of the *Iliad*. Resounding through the epic, now in stifled allusion, now in strident lament, is the dread fact that an ancient and splendid city has perished by the edge of the sea. . . .

The remembrance of these ancient terrors, of city gates broken and towers burned, beats loud in the *Iliad*. The *Odyssey* speaks of the aftermath. It is the epic of the displaced person. The cities are down, and survivors wander the face of the earth as pirates or beggars.[6]

St. Augustine was caught up, no doubt, with something of this same tragic concern when news of the sacking of Rome came to him. We have already seen something of his own personal travail and anguish at the same time. It is understandable, then, that his sense of Rome's nobility as a great city should be transferred to his resplendent image of the Church as the magnificent and towering City of God. No matter, then, what happened to the "secular" city.

HOLY CITY

From the time of Augustine, this model of a city seems to have dominated the conceptualization of the Church in the World. It was the City of God—awesome and splendid in its high-walled and towered eminence, like a massive church towering above the roofs of a village. Protestants as a group, while changing many other things, never really changed this. Their alliances with governments, their early view of the United States, their position in the community, still held to the implication of a holy city above and beyond the secular.

As Bourke says:

. . . This was a mistake made by Charlemagne and his associates, who thought to realize the Heavenly City in the Holy Roman Empire. Still, out of the impetus of the civilization and political states which they established to fill the void left by the destruction of Rome have developed the social and political institutions of modern Europe and America.[7]

The influences of exceptional groups, such as the Quakers, were never reflected in the whole American Protestant attitude. As Marty comments:

The Reverend Jonathan Edwards towered over the religious landscape of pre-Revolutionary America. Today he is often thought of—and dismissed—as the last, most gloomy Calvinist. According to Alan Heimert, however, Edwards was actually a man of cosmic optimism, whose prophecy of the Lord's future kingdom was that "the latter-day glory, is probably to begin in America." The first religious revival in America, the Great Awakening of the 1730's, proved to Edwards and his colleagues that *here* was the place, *now* was the time: in the new land men could work confidently with God to advance the work of redemption. . . .

Did it turn out to be the Kingdom, the New Jerusalem? The followers of Edwards and the other Calvinists would not have comprehended its secularity, would have regretted the side-tracking of the churches in the nation's power alignments.[8]

To the barbarian, emerging out of the dark ages, the model of the city came to suggest the splendid ideal of civilization, culture, law and order. The very word "civilization" has, even now, these positive cultural overtones. One can see how a model of the "city" of God seemed apt for giving the exact dimensions of the civilizing and cultural mission of the Church as the Western world slowly began to re-form and re-educate itself through the Middle Ages.

But this model of the city contained also seeds of power and disorganization that slowly affected some of the positive values it implied. McNally points out how the early concept of the Church as a warm, loving person gave way to another picture:

The Church of Christ, once known in Antiquity simply and reverently as "the Mother of all the living" in parallel with the first Eve, took on in the high Middle Ages more and more the visage of a majestic, imperial queen. Law, more than life, seems to have become the significant element in the image of the Church. And this tendency, which was in accord with developments in contemporary society, manifested itself within the Church by the creation of a universal legal system which was served more and more by the faithful rather than itself serving them. The maternal aspect of the Church yielded to the regal, therefore. This was inevitable once ecclesiastical administration had become centralized under the papacy and had consolidated itself into a vast juridical bureaucracy which extended out over the whole Western world.[9]

The appearance and values of a bureaucratic organization are often seen by many as only those where cold, impersonal power structures dominate the "political" scene. These values are obviously not the values that religion best represents or that would appeal most to modern needs—however much this civilizing model attracted and appealed to an earlier period.

LIMITED MEANING

Images, then, and the values they implicitly represent have a way of shifting. Where before the "city" suggested the necessary legal and cultural values of a "civilizing" process, now this image may suggest a large indifferent mass, a bureaucratic structure. Both "politician" and "political," in addition to meaning positive civil service and dedication, can imply conniving, maneuvering and corruption. These are ambiguities.

But even in its most positive significance, the modern city no longer has the implication of intimate, secure and protective warm community structure that it had as Augustine conceived it. Rather it now carries threatening depersonalized aspects. "Polis" no longer suggests communion and communication. Even if the word community is used, it has only a limited application, usually to a small suburb. Consequently, the "city" model, suggesting values of law and power as it does now, has no longer the implications of the "civilizing" process it formerly had nor the closeness and sharing which the model of religious communion should have.

At the same time, in a way that Augustine never foresaw, the secular city has now its own new meaning and significance as a civilizing, educational and democratizing force. The great need now is, then, not more mass organizations of law and power, against or within other cities or power structures—secular or religious. The great need is for communion and communication in the restoration—as in the early Christian Church—of communities where genuinely religious and loving friendship give an experience of redemptive worth and meaning to each one.

One way, therefore, of describing what is now happening in religion is to say that the model of the Church as the "City of God," expounded by Augustine and enduring to our time, is receding into the background. Another model—also delineated by Augustine and also present in the Church—that of God as Persons-in-union, is now coming forward to occupy the foreground. In this model, such a union and community involves the communion and communication of knowing and loving persons.

Since the city model still has advantages and even features that may be considered essential to the Church, institutionally, this city model in some measure will no doubt be maintained. To what degree such a city model is still necessary, we are not yet in a position to see. What we do seem to be witnessing, however, is the emergence of other models of community to positions of great importance, emphasis and centrality. This, like some aspects of the early Church, highlights the necessity of authentic relationships that genuinely involve religious people not only in social issues but with one another and with others outside the group. This, rather than more organization, seems to be evolving as the main religious concern.

VALUE SYSTEMS

These changing models of the Church which time and history seem to be producing are important because, as we have seen, such models can contain implicit value systems which often determine our ways of viewing and acting toward ourselves and others. The

Church during a long period was forced, probably less by choice than by historical necessity, to take a direct and major role in the process of establishing and maintaining civilization. Christianity was seen as a city-thing, and its growth and civilization, whether by chance or necessity, went hand in hand. But the city model also contained the implicit values of removal, protection, exclusion, withdrawal and excommunication to the wilderness and danger outside. While this model still has value, since law and order and civilization are essential, we can now no longer exclude the outside world from it.

The change from the model of the city to that of the person involves, too, a change of values from an outer- to an inner-directed awareness. In the city, walks, streets, houses—exterior material structures—and laws, judges, police courts, all conspire to force order and reasonableness by external sanctions. In this sense, "police" and the Greek word for city—polis—go well together. But a person must achieve such inner order by subtle controls, reflections and persuasions within himself. Purely external forces are no real help here except by good example and fear. Aquinas remarks how a man controls his emotions and instincts in somewhat the same way free men are ruled—each one having a will and goal of his own. Both must be ruled by a kind of "gentle persuasion" if violence and rebellion are not to occur.

In this comparison between the manner of inner self-control and determination in a person and the best manner of ordering a city, Aquinas has touched a subtle and significant modern issue. For purely external law and order, or even adequate and just laws, are not enough. All the forces of each individual person must be constructively engaged as well if a city is finally to fulfill its democratic purpose for each citizen. And what is said here of a city applies as well to any organization—to the Church, the university and the school; to industry; to the whole scope of the community.

OPEN SHARING

Before the "City of God" was its dominating image, the Church as the Christian community is portrayed in pastoral scenes, images of fishermen, and similar models, drawn from the world of the people around Christ. These fill out the Gospel message with what is often now almost poetic imagery. While these concepts are still beautiful and appealing, they often lack the practical meaning that they had at the time Christ lived. To have present relevance they need to be made incarnate in present experiences in people's own lives.

In one of these, however, there is an interesting juxtaposing of city and person. The disciples are told to enter the city—take what it offers and leave only when they are clearly rejected. They are then to have no regrets in the sense that they are to wipe even the dust off their sandals. If we say this is not simply a city but more one's encounter with persons, one sees the need for open defenseless entering and giving oneself to someone—trusting them— which can at the same time involve the possibility of their hurting us. This is the risk in any open act of love. This idea, indeed, of disciples openly entering, sharing and so relating intimately with other persons in a small community of belonging and faith, is clearly different from the idea of a medieval walled and protected city—as a model of the Church.

To add to the model of a city—even if it is the City of God— the model of the earlier Christian and Jewish communities, that of persons-in-relation, is therefore to have something both new and old in the history of religion. To give a more secondary role to the concept of a city and its model of organization, planning, government, law, force and order is to alter in some measure the Church's outlook. With the model of the city as primary, the Church was engaged in a struggle either to be a civil government itself and control other governments by alliance and concordat or, at least, to influence the large design and mass movements of governments. So conceived, its arena was understandably the world of kings and princes and the political forum where the struggle for power raged.

EACH UNIQUE PERSON

When we turn, however, to the concept of a person—any human being in any part of the world of any color, race or religion—we are indeed face-to-face with a "new humanism." The models of government and statecraft, of law and the process of civilization, can be of little help in probing and striving to understand the anxiety and anguish, the hopes and joys, the ecstasies and despairs of each human being in his unique existence in a particular time and place. Tracts on government and law, abstract philosophy, and even rational ethics leave a vast gap between their models of excellency and performance and the actual existential state of each human being as we know him and encounter him in himself and in ourselves. The civilization process has perfected itself through long centuries of awareness and growth. Law has indeed become the rule of the land all over the world, granting that mass governmental powers are still in strained and, at times, violent disagreement over whose laws and whose civilization process applies where. The Church, while still concerned with these issues, is also equally concerned with the common man wherever he is. Its voice for peace and liberty, for economic justice, is speaking for him so that he may have an opportunity to both be and become his total potential as a human person.

ANCIENT AND MODERN

The most consuming religious interest, then, seems to center around those conditions of growth and development most favorable to the individual person. Present religious concern seems turned to and concentrated on individual man, existent and unique in himself, in all his complex psychosomatic commonality and singularity, his knowledgeableness and his mystery, his insights and his confusions, with his ever recurring measure of integration and conflict. Into this area, counseling and psychotherapy have already entered. They are a long way, of course, from any kind of comprehensive knowledge of man, but they have made a beginning of looking at him, not abstractly or ideally, or even as he ought to be, but as he is.

Person, then, and Personhood bring us by both ancient and modern congruence to a concept meaningfully applied to both God and man in one of the most consistent of cultural awarenesses, which extends from the time of the Hebrews, the Greeks, Christ and Augustine down to the latest modern study on personality growth and development. In seeing the Church after the model of a person then—and of persons in Union and Communion—we are at once seeing the Church in an ancient and yet relevant modern form.

When we say, therefore, that the model of the city applied to the Church is receding into the background, we do not mean it ceases to exist. We simply mean that the Church's organizing and legalizing function seems to be occupying a position that is decreasing in emphasis. The work of religion now seems to demand far more focus on the needs of the person—each person as "he laughs and cries." It still remains to be seen how many of the established city-model structures yet serve a significant purpose and how many will, in fact, slowly pass into obsolescence as new structures and relationships, formed after the model of "persons-in-relationship," take their place.

PERSONS IN RELATIONSHIP

So, in consciously shifting our model of the religious community, the people of God, from the "City of God" to "persons-in-relationship," we are not denying the past validity and even the present and future necessity of the city model. We are rather bringing forward, out of somewhat depersonalized abstraction, the richly human model of persons in relationship and the belonging, communion and community that this involves.

In implementing this idea of the religious personal relationship for our present age, counseling and psychotherapy can be especially helpful. They offer us a fresh starting place from which to develop and extend to greater depth the meaning of a person and his potentialities. They supply us models for new ways in which man can grow in the knowledge and love of himself, others and God.

As in earlier times the Church joined with the civilizing secular forces of the city, so now it would seem that in religious concern for the person, the Church should join with the forces which are striving to bring order and achievement to each man within himself, his own self-concept and his relations with others. These are the crucial pressing modern issues—issues that are fundamentally psychological and social. The order of the city, extending itself to the whole world, must still be achieved. This is now, however, the responsibility and the burden of the secular forces themselves. But even here this goal will best be achieved by fundamental changes in each man's attitude towards himself and others, so that he can achieve maximum communion and communication. Religion can further this as it focuses its strength to produce personal integrity and genuine relationships in a warm, creative community of personal fulfillment.

THE PROCESS OF INVOLVEMENT

In this sense, we can learn from the "civilizing" process which engaged both the Church and the city constructively together. For as the city grew under the support and aid of religion to acquire its own unique meaning and purpose, so counseling and psychotherapy and all phases of personality dynamics in psychology, psychiatry, sociology and similar fields can interrelate with, and receive support from, religion without endangering their own unique purpose. Rather, much as the process of civilization developed in the West, allied to and interrelated with religion but finally independent of it, an independent and mutually respectful cooperation may be anticipated between behavioral science and religion, and especially between counseling, psychotherapy and religion. Rather than the model of rival or competing cities, we need the sense of support and belonging seen in the simple model of salt savoring meat or yeast penetrating dough.

As religion formerly put itself so seriously to the process of civilizing, organizing and legalizing, so now, with equal or greater intensity, it might be said to be concerned with the process of involvement. But just involvement in social issues, while important and necessary, is not enough. It must, even more, enable each man to discover the conditions necessary to his becoming involved with himself and others at the deepest level of understanding and of self. Only in this way can a genuine relationship of persons, imitating the Augustinian model of Divine Persons, come about.

NOTES

[1] W. H. McNeill, *The Rise of the West: A History of the Human Community* (Chicago: University of Chicago Press, A Mentor Book, 1963), p. 373.

[2] St. Augustine, *City of God,* trans. Gerald G. Walsh, S.J., et al.; ed., with an Introduction, by Vernon J. Bourke; Foreword by Etienne Gilson (New York: Doubleday Image Books, 1958), Introduction, p. 8.

[3] *Ibid.,* Foreword, pp. 33–34.

[4] *Ibid.,* pp. 32–33.

[5] St. Augustine, *The City of God,* Book XIV, Ch. 28, quoted in Thomas P. Neill, ed., *The Building of the Human City* (New York: Doubleday & Co., Inc., a Dolphin Book, 1960), p. 81 and p. xx, Introduction.

[6] George Steiner, *Language and Silence* (New York: Atheneum, 1967), pp. 174–175.

[7] St. Augustine, *City of God,* ed. Bourke, p. 10.

[8] Martin E. Marty, reviewing Alan Heimert's *Religion and the American Mind: From the Great Awakening to the Revolution* (Cambridge: Harvard University Press, 1966) in *Book Week,* February 5, 1967.

[9] Robert E. McNally, S.J., *The Unreformed Church* (New York: Sheed and Ward, 1965), pp. 6–7.

16

Representation and Community

WE HAVE SAID that in religion we are focused on the operational values implied in the model of disciples entering cities and forming open and real relationships with all who receive them. This is the model of community, of persons in genuine relationship with one another. Such a model implies creative commitment if this kind of positive communion of persons and constructive communication is to result.

This seems to be needed everywhere: in marriage, in family life, among religious communities and groups, in churches, in schools and universities, in business and professional relationships, and in whatever other context one can mention—neighborhoods, peoples, nations. We seek a genuine and authentic environment and communication that is truly creative and constructive and so furthers the growth of what is best in each one. For it is not enough that civilization has the capacity of feeding and clothing and even educating each person. Ideal as this is, and necessary, these things alone still leave man at a loss with himself and others. Man indeed "does not live by bread alone," and "the lost must be found"— that is, some kind of really personal meaning, value and fulfillment must be added to these basic securities of food, clothing and knowledge if the promise of our time is to reach any measure of significant fruition. Given a choice, many might prefer to be cold and hungry, but with a sense of worth and love, rather than to be well-fed and clothed but alone and empty.

We have, throughout this book, attempted to present various conditions and skills that seem to further authentic involvement and creative communication in a variety of circumstances. In this chapter we will consider some additional elements that produce genuine relationships in groups and among individuals as well as factors that result in fraudulent or "phony" imitations of this. In addition to drawing understanding from counseling therapy excerpts, we can gain in this awareness from the perceptivity of the modern novelist. He too has been committed to studying the involved human condition. We will therefore also use some excerpts from modern novelists as a means of reaching and illustrating positive and negative factors in creative commitment.

INCARNATE REPRESENTATION

One of the issues—perhaps the most basic of all—is the nature of representation and how best to make it effective. In using *mimesis* for this, we mean something more than simple imitation, we mean "becoming like" of which imitation may be a first stage. (II Thessalonians 3:7–9.) We have seen how, in counseling and psychotherapy, the counselor or therapist might be said to represent a realistically ideal self toward which the person is striving. This seems to constitute the cylinder or dynamic continuum into which the forces of growth and change assemble themselves. We saw that this too appeared evident in the learning process, the representation of the godlike figure of the teacher—in one research project, the native language-expert—slowly became real and incarnate to the others when he was seen struggling to learn another language and when each experienced his warmth and acceptance as their language counselor. By such an incarnate process we saw that identification, belonging and learning were furthered. Representation became incarnate and so motivated others to "become like" what was represented.

The religious process too, we saw, must undergo this same transition of the representation of meaning into the incarnation of values. In the positive growth of constructive anxiety inherent in the religious faith-involvement, the religious person must move from a passive and infantile dependency on representative parent-figures—a "milk for babes" relationship—to a more mature and responsible self-identity.

IDEAL REPRESENTATION

In the model of the city and the tower, the purpose of the representation was to hold up, in all its splendor, an ideal image above and beyond the lowly human condition. Barzini, quoted earlier, describes how this could even go so far that the ideal and representation were thought to be this reality; when, in fact, the horrible ugly reality itself was ignored.

But in its original conception, the city towering above all the works of man, and its rulers decked in the magnificence of royal splendor, were seen as authentic models of excellence and genuine and real symbols of the mighty and awesome power and dignity of God. In this way, too, rulers in their removed isolation were seen as sharing the loneliness and alienation of the seer, the prophet and the artist.

Thomas Mann, in a novel aptly titled *Royal Highness,* addressed himself to this question. The novel, first published in 1905, was seen by Mann as symbolic of this very meaning of monarchy. In the Introduction to a new edition in 1939 Mann wrote:

. . . But the monarchy was not only the atmosphere of the book; it was also, quite precisely, its subject, treated, if only allegorically, as a form of existence. And this was at the moment when the monarchy was at its height.[1]

Here the isolated and lonely position of nobility was seen as representing all symbols of excellence and their need to accept a kind of artistic isolation—the loneliness of the seer who must represent what he sees long before others can share it. So in the Introduction Mann says:

. . . the personal and human experiences of those early years entirely condition its treatment of that favourite theme of my youth, the theme of the artist as isolated and "different." . . . Its subject-matter lends itself to allusiveness: it analyses the life led by royalty as a formal, unreal existence, lifted above actualities; in a word, the existence of the artist. The resolution of the royal complex is brought about by a fairytale, comedy love-affair; it leads to marriage and to the solution of certain problems in political economy as well. But even so, it exhibits a rejection of empty and melancholy formalism in favor of life and companionship, which is not without symbolic meaning and shows some sensitiveness to coming events.[2]

ISOLATED VISION

This sense of artistic isolation and excellence is similar to Van Gogh's insistence to his brother Theo that no matter how odd others thought his paintings were, he could not change, because this was how things really looked to him. Or the way in which Van Gogh goes to great pains to have Theo view a certain painting only with a golden frame and background because "It simply cannot be seen without such a setting" which "gives, at the same time, a brightness to spots where you would not expect it."[3] Here we witness the pained concern of the seer, pathetically anxious that others might share his vision and not miss it. In this loneliness of excellence and artistic vision, we have an approach to the alienation of Christ, crying over the city and judging its shortsightedness:

And as he drew near, and caught sight of the city, he wept over it, and said: Ah, if thou too couldst understand, above all in this day that is granted thee, the ways that can bring thee peace! (Luke 19: 41, 42).[4]

INDIVIDUAL VIEWPOINT

Moreover, in a manner perhaps difficult for us now to understand and appreciate fully, this view of monarchy's uniqueness and even eccentricity in some ways also heightened individual freedom. Our own period, with all its advantages in growing horizontal equality has, at the same time, become threatening for its "organization man" and its "lonely crowd." So Mann says:

. . . On its appearance thirty years ago *Royal Highness* was a portent, and the fact did not escape the knowing ones. It was a sign of that crisis of individualism which has since become a commonplace in the public consciousness; a sign of that surrender by the intellect of the individual point of view in favour of the communal, the social, the democratic, yes, the political, at the will of the times.[5]

REPRESENTATION OF EXCELLENCE

In the novel itself the views of the Prince's tutor catch an aspect of this ancient kind of representation which royalty and nobility shared with high churchmen, in representing excellence and godliness together. The Prince, Klaus Heinrich, at fifteen and lonely, has urges to confide in his tutor, Doctor Ueberbein. The tutor, however, wants no such experience of incarnation from the Prince. He wants from the Prince the pure, unadulterated representation of excellence:

His attitude of reserve relaxed, the experiences of his own fifteen years of life came crowding in upon him, he felt a longing himself to retail confidences, and he tried to tell Doctor Ueberbein all about himself.

But the funny thing was that Doctor Ueberbein himself checked him, opposed any such intention most decidedly. "No, no, Klaus Heinrich," he said; "full stop there! No confidences, if you please! Not but that I know that you have all sorts of things to tell me . . . I need only watch you for half a day to see that, but you quite misunderstand me if you think I'm likely to encourage you to weep round my neck. In the first place, sooner or later you'd repent it. But in the second, the pleasures of a confidential intimacy are not for the likes of you. You see, there's no harm in my chattering. What am I? An usher. Not a common or garden one, in my own opinion, but still no better than such. Just a categorical unit. But you? What are you? That's harder to say. . . . Let's say a conception, a kind of ideal. A frame. An emblematical existence, Klaus Heinrich, and at the same time a formal existence. But formality and intimacy—haven't you yet learnt that the two are mutually exclusive? Absolutely exclusive. You have no right to intimate confidences, and if you attempted them you yourself would discover that they did not suit you, would find them inadequate and insipid. I must remind you of your duty, Klaus Heinrich."

Klaus Heinrich laughed and saluted with his crop, and on they rode.[6]

On another occasion Doctor Ueberbein said casually: "Popularity is a not very profound, but a grand and comprehensive kind of familiarity."

Later, rising to his theme, the tutor goes on to say:

... I love the extraordinary in every form and in every sense. I love those who are conscious of the dignity of their exceptional station, the marked men, those one can see are not as other men, all those whom the people stare at open-mouthed—I hope they'll appreciate their dignity, and I do not wish them to make themselves comfortable with the slip-shod and luke-warm truth which we have just heard set to music for three voices. ... Nowadays the soul's thirst for veneration has to be satisfied with what it can get. Where will you find greatness? ... I only hope you may! But quite apart from all actual greatness and high-calling, there is always what I call Highness, select and sadly isolated forms of life, toward which an attitude of the tenderest sympathy should be adopted. For the rest, greatness is strong, it wears jack-boots, it has no need of the knight-services of the mind. But Highness is affecting—damme if it isn't the most affecting thing on earth.[7]

In representing a genuine and untouchable Highness, the Prince was seen as standing for man's highest dignity and excellence:

Once they heard the "Magic Flute," and on the way home to "Pheasantry" station, in the first-class carriage, Doctor Ueberbein made the whole collection of them laugh by imitating the way in which singers talk when their roles oblige them to talk in prose. "He is a prince!" he said with pathos, and answered himself in a drawly, sing-song parsonical voice. "He is more than that, he is a man!" Even Professor Kurtchen was so much amused that he bleated.

But the next day, in the course of a private lesson in Klaus Heinrich's study, with the round mahogany table, whitened ceiling, and Greek bust on the stove, Doctor Ueberbein repeated his parody, and said then: "Great heavens, that was something new in its time, it was a piece of news, a startling truth! There are paradoxes which have stood so long on their heads that one has to put them on their feet to make anything even moderately daring out of them. 'He is a man. He is more than that'—that is getting gradually bolder, prettier, even truer. The converse is mere humanity, but I have no hearty love for humanity, I'm quite content to leave it out of account.

"One must, in a certain sense, be one of those of whom the people say: 'They are, after all, mortal men too'—or one is as deadly dull as an usher. I cannot honestly wish for the general comfortable obliteration of conflicts and gulfs, that's the way I am made, for better or worse, and the idea of the *principe uomo* is to me, to speak plainly, an abomination. I am not anxious that it should particularly appeal to you. . . . Look you, there have always been princes and exceptional persons who live their life of exception with a light heart, simply unconscious of their dignity or denying it outright, and capable of playing skittles with the townsfolk in their shirt-sleeves, without the slightest attempt at an inward qualm. But they are not very important, just as nothing is important which lacks mind. For mind, Klaus Heinrich, mind is the tutor which insists inexorably on dignity, indeed actually creates dignity, it is the arch-enemy and chief antagonist of all human good nature. 'More than that?' No! to be a representative, to stand for a number when one appears to be the exalted and refined expression of a multitude. Representing is naturally something more and higher than simply Being, Klaus Heinrich—and that's why people call you Highness."[8]

WARMTH AND AFFILIATION

The difficulty now with this disincarnate view of the city model with its prince as an ideal representation of excellence, applied as it can be to any organization structure, is that it now can seem artificial, unreal and "phony." Present values seem to want to have excellence shared as a common incarnate ideal by people whose humanity and warmth radiate open communion and affiliation. The representative now must *be* as well as represent. This is itself most complicated and demanding of far greater personal integrity and genuine commitment. The older image may, in this way, be thought to be more kindly and easier to fulfill because it did not demand such an *integrity between representing and being*. Genuine leadership now is far more personally involving.

MANIPULATION AND CONTROL

This is not accomplished, therefore, simply by the process of becoming democratic and so voting for representatives in place of the older method of heredity or appointment from above. On the contrary, this may make representation appear even more fraudulent because it wears the trappings but does not really have the openness of a genuinely personal commitment.

In this light, the city model may simply be now seen as symboliz-ing "will to power," and its other necessary attributes neglected. Representation takes this fraudulent form when it appears in the figure of the powerful and maneuvering "politician." As such, he manipulates but never really relates to the people he represents, even though he gives an appearance of wanting to serve them. Representation for him is holding power by the skilled maneuver-ing of others. He thus represents and demonstrates a power-fulfill-ment which impedes any real community and genuine commitment.

Such an image—in its fraudulent "politician" model—often appears as symbolic of the value system of any power-centered and power-controlled organization structure. Such power focus impedes genuine communion and community. This can even be so in marriage or a family. Here relationships are for the purpose of appearance and masks. The real values behind these relation-ships are not those of open communion and communication but self-centered control and personal satisfaction.

In another novel, Edwin O'Connor has such a "politician," de-scribing how to "deal with" people:

"The thing to remember is that all pests are talkers," he had said to me one day. "The women are the worst, but the men are bad enough. There's no such thing as a pest who listens. A pest talks, and he talks all the time. Now, if one gets hold of you, there are a couple of ways of handling him. The first way is simply to stare at him while he talks to you. Just stare: don't answer back, don't say a word, don't make a sound: just keep looking right into his eyes. Sooner or later, this will get to him. Silence unnerves pests. They don't really want you to say anything, but they expect you to nod and make certain ritual sounds—'uh-huh' is highly acceptable—whenever they pause for breath. That proves you're there and listening. If you don't do that it throws them off; they start to stumble, pretty soon they stop talking, and then they go away. The only trouble is that they're apt to go away mad, and if you're in my profession it's necessary to remember that pests vote too. So I've settled for another way: matter of fact, I've become rather good at it. It's not necessary to listen to anything they say—you can keep right on going with your private thoughts—but every once in a while you have to cluck or shake your head and make little noises of commiseration. They won't pay any attention to *what* you say; it's the sound that counts. Once you get good enough at it you can say anything: you can spout Jabberwocky at them and they won't bat an eye. The secret is in using the proper tone. And then, when they're all done, you simply look at them, take them by the hand, and say, 'I thank you. You've done us all a great service.' Or words to that effect; I don't want to seem too rigid. You'll have to develop your own style. We've got a prize specimen coming in here in a few minutes; I may be able to give you a slight demonstration."[9]

There follows a description of how a constituent is let talk away about his troubles and concerns while the politician pretending sympathy, nods and then responds in non-sense language. The man, apparently satisfied, goes away, after being thanked for "being of service." The politician then continues:

". . . and if you want to say anything it's perfectly all right, as long as you say it in the right way. The manner is everything. Now go home and practice on a relative. Or the parish priest. First thing you know you'll be a virtuoso and you'll save yourself all kinds of trouble in later life."[10]

While such open fraudulency is not, in this case, without humor, it still demonstrates the maneuvering and manipulating of a person in place of seeking a genuine relationship with him. In a kind of self-fulfilling prophecy, if I consider a person a "pest" and give him no opportunity ever to be anything else, he, of course, will always prove me right. But he may, in fact, never have really had a chance to be different—no one ever respected him enough to allow him to function in any other way. In seeing people as "pests" in this way, one sees them as inimical, as "enemies," as we explained earlier, so they must be maneuvered and manipulated in order to protect oneself from them. In such an incapsulation they never have a chance to become "friends."

LOSS OF TRUST

One effect of such a manner of relating to others can be the gradual loss of genuine trust in others and even in oneself—the cause of final alienation. Later in the same novel, in a scene between two brothers, one (Charles), having now become such a consummate "politician," is addressed by the other:

"You see, I know you, Charles," he said. "That's why what looks like quitting or giving in on my part isn't that at all, because I know you won't accept the option. You should, but you won't, and you won't for only one reason: *it isn't quite as safe as the other way.* You know you can rely on the lockup, but you can't bring yourself to believe my word. Isn't that it, Charles? You don't dare to take the risk any more. That's another way of saying you don't dare to trust anyone any more. You can't believe anyone now—except Marie, and she's not a part of the politics. I told you the game would get you, and it has—isn't that clear to you yet? You haven't just sold us out: you've sold *you* out. At this point in your career your every move has to be insured in advance because it might damage your future. You have to have everything all wrapped up before you say a word. That's the way you operate now, Charles: you've become The Complete Pol. You can't do anything on trust any more because you've destroyed trust for yourself. And that's what I'm trying to show you now: just how much you've destroyed it, and how far you're willing to go without it."[11]

One of the corruptions of the power which "representing" can give, then, is that it takes away the trusting impulses and open regard for others that a genuine relationship seems to demand. Rather, the display of such power often demonstrates, in a highly sophisticated displaced form, many of the primitive self-preservation urges that animals and small children show openly. It cannot ever be loving because it is too anxiously wrapped up in itself—afraid really "to give up its life" of power. Here, certainly, Alfred Adler's basic conception of the "will to power" impeding the "will to community" is evident in one of its most destructive and self-alienating forms. One can also see here a special application of the text, "He that shall save his life, shall lose it."

PERSONAL ANXIETY

Paradoxical as it may seem, such power needs may be a mask of personal anxiety. This can result from the odd situation that an anxious person trusts others even less than he trusts himself, and so he seeks power to protect himself from having to trust others. Since, in his rise to power, he often masks this by self-effacement and seeking the approval of others, his anxiety works to his benefit here. Once having authority, however, he can often be close to panic in the way he exercises it, even though he does not outwardly show this anxiety. As a result, he may appear inconsiderate and at times even ruthless.

The following is a picture of this type of reaction:

The insecure and anxious individual gained a degree of assurance by evolving a life pattern of being self-sufficient, independent, or the "lone wolf," or on the other hand by gaining approval through extra effort, conscientiousness, "perfectionism," and meticulousness. Under the usual circumstances of his life, such a system seemed adequate, i.e., the individual was relatively comfortable and effective. Then, because of a change in his situation such as a new position, the assumption of new responsibilities in courtship or marriage, criticism from without was implied or expressed and this again challenged his adequacy. Feelings of insecurity and anxiety were then experienced. One reaction to this challenge was to increase efforts by more work, greater conscientiousness and "perfectionism." Another reaction was seen in the bolstering of self-esteem through additional assertions of independence and the shutting off of much needed affection. There developed frustration, resentment and hostility toward the person or situation which rearoused the feelings of insecurity and inadequacy, causing the fragile system to falter or break down.[12]

IMPERSONAL AND REMOTE

Such a person can come to represent "phoniness' because his apparent warmth, concern and service at some point are revealed as false. These kinds of people are then seen as cold and closed power-persons wearing masks—feared, perhaps, but not trusted. The implicit values contained in this model of an organization, power-centered man are impersonal and remote, with little or no communion and real communication. This works against the openness, warmth and trust of a genuine relationship.

FAMILY LIFE

Such a depersonalized model with its exaggerated will-to-power fulfillment has affected not only organizations but also methods of teaching and most human relations. It furthers caution, defense, mistrust and resentment on the part of many while it satisfies some —those who can maintain positions of manipulation and control.

Such a model has affected even the family community itself, where nonbelonging and remoteness, rather than commitment, often seem evident. We quoted and discussed in detail elsewhere the research indication of

an impasse in communication between married or otherwise related man and woman who would be presumed a priori, because intimate, to be in good rapport.[13]

RELIGIOUS FAMILY

But this can apparently be so even in formal religious communities. Here especially, as in the family, we expect ideally a living representation or mimesis of belonging and sharing together. Despite being dedicated to the model of a warm, close religious family, however, they too often can seem to some of their members to be more like an imitation of the depersonalized organization model. Even where a "democratic" process is in vogue, it may have failed to produce a constructive and creative relationship for many.

ILLUSTRATION

The following excerpts are taken from the latter stages of a counseling process in which the person is contrasting his experience in religious community life over many years with a more recent constructive work relationship:

Cl: It occurs to me that this is one of the real values of this kind of being able to talk about something and having somone listen. (INSIGHT) All my life I have been suffering from some kind of indigestion, cramming things in and cramming things in and never being able to get a proper hearing of it or a chance just to get it out and examine it or look at it. If I have bogged down in the past, and I have many times, and haven't been able to get going, I think maybe it was because I had gotten too much in me and didn't know what to do with it.

Co: You're struck by the value of a sharing or communication, the way it fulfills, stimulates and helps a person. What you see in the past is just too much taking in and not enough chance to get it out. There was no chance to get a feedback or communication about yourself. This was rather constipating, so to speak, that is to say, it blocked you rather than helped you.

Cl: Yes, and I think I've been experiencing the positive effects too in the last two years. (NEW RELATIONSHIP) In this new work, I now have a secretary and some others. I'm able to do a fair amount of this thinking out loud around what I'm trying to do and it's just tremendously valuable. You never know when there is going to be a breakthrough in one area or another but these things do happen. I think I've done more work in many ways in the last two years and yet I haven't felt the pressure in the old bogging down way. I have felt it at times to some extent but not nearly like in the past; my going out to this or that person was an attempt to get an audience for myself but in a kind of a compromise way.

Co: You're struck by the effects of having a secretary now, among others. This brings you a more integrated sense of yourself rather than the previous sort of chasing around which you now see was maybe your just looking for some hearing or chance to communicate. Having this channel to think something out in an organized, constructive way with someone, your plans are more adequate, they seem to come off better, and you yourself are more self-contained, so to speak.

Cl: I like that word, "self-contained." (*A deep sigh.*) (VALUE) With these persons with whom I've been working for the last two years there is a real sense now for personhood. It is an ongoing kind of a thing and a realization that there has to be a fairly free communication for a constructive relationship. . . . Something I think I've really suffered from—especially after I got into the Community and began to function in more responsible jobs, in discipline, with students or teaching, working on our publications—was the extreme isolation and alienation from others in this aspect of work I was doing eight hours or ten hours a day. I could almost not stand that. (INSIGHT) And I think this was part of the reason I was bogging down, not just because I was reading too much and getting too much in me that I couldn't properly digest and assimilate but also that I didn't have any kind of a relationship during these extremely lonely hours of work.

Co: All these have reinforced and produced a kind of isolationism through all these years. By contrast now these two years with a part-time secretary, and with persons with whom you can communicate and work, it's almost a totally different world, as I get it, and a world that makes the other astonishingly empty by comparison.

Cl: I wouldn't be able to go back to it. (ANXIETY) Right now I even have an anxious feeling, some sort of a tension in the diaphragm region, that this isn't going to last, and I'll soon flip back into the old way. (RELIEF) As I say this I relax a bit, but I think I have a kind of insecurity that I'm not too important and they could move me and the whole situation would be lost as far as future work goes. I don't know what I would do about that. . . .

In contrast to years of stagnation even though he was surrounded by a community, a really creative relationship, if only with a part-time secretary and others, frees and stimulates this person to achievement and purpose. In this sense, as he sees, it is similar to counseling therapy in that it is centered on a common productive activity where one person has the central and the other the auxiliary function.

GENUINE INVESTMENT

As this excerpt continues, the person comes to realize that the main aspect of his anxiety arises from having made a value investment for the first time in his life. He now has something he really cares about and his work has creative meaning and purpose. But built into this is his fear of loss. He sees how indifference and deadness were, in a way, safer and more secure, even though empty.

In response to the counselor's statement about this fear of loss, the person says:

Frightening is a good word. (INSIGHT) I guess that I realize that this could be taken away. In the past I've never worried about having anything taken away because I've never had anything anyway, so they could move me here or there—it really didn't matter much. (PAST OPERATIONAL SYSTEM) Presumably I'd have something to do when I got there, the same kind of a house set-up and so on, the same deadness, I suppose. But this would be different. Although I must say at the same time that I have found myself able to operate a lot easier and a lot better and to form relationships. I think I am much more adequate in this now. I think that probably along these lines of what I'm interested in, there are a lot more people interested in these things, so that if there were some kind of a loss or death or move or something, I think I would probably be able to find someone without it being too much of an issue. (POSITIVE CONFIDENCE) I think I would know so much better now how to enter into such a relationship and carry on what I see is a very necessary part of my life, some kind of real communication about my own work world, my own self, my own, well, about my whole life.

CONFIDENCE

Continuing to analyze his fear and himself, he later concludes that he need not be so anxious about change because these new values have been internalized and are now a part of his operational self. He can feel sure now that he will take them with him:

But I think a lot of this fear is gone now that I realize that I have changed and that I am different. I guess it is hard for me to realize that this is more than a very transient thing, this change; in other words, I have to admit that I have changed, but I'm always on the edge of the abyss kind of feeling that it'll all go back to the way it was.

Later, in the same vein, while he recognizes that the loss of this creative relationship and activity "would be awful," he reaffirms his confidence that he could now handle it:

Yes, that would be awful. But I guess it's one of those things that once you start to look at it, like any other kind of a skill, you've got this security and that's it. And it doesn't depend on your losing your arm or your leg or any of these things, it's not a muscular skill or anything in that physical order; its just a plain skill that will be there and I need to look at it in this way and realize that these fears are pretty groundless.

CREATIVE RELATIONSHIP

From a literary point of view, John Marquand, the novelist—in the character of Thomas Harrow, a playwright who we presume in some way resembles himself—reproduces the following scene between the writer and the same kind of creative relationship. Here it is compared with the playwright's relationship with his third wife (Emily):

The old coach house here, after it had been made over, was a pleasant office. . . . He was careful every year to have fresh layers of gravel copiously poured upon the drive as well as on the path beyond the turn-around leading to the coach house, and consequently it was almost impossible for Emily to reach the place. In an effort of hers to do so, the previous summer, she had twisted her ankle severely and, as he knew, Emily had not attempted the trip again. Thus the coach house was free of interruptions; and there was another room for Miss Mulford, so that, when he wanted, he could be entirely alone. . . .[14]

The following exchange occurs between himself and his secretary:

"Are you thinking of that boyfriend you had ten years ago?" he asked.
"Yes," she said. "But as you would say, you can't do it over again. I just wanted you to know I know exactly what you mean. . . ."
"You can't live it over and I'm glad he didn't take you away," he said. "I've said that to a good many women, but I've never meant it so completely as I do when I say it to you. And now let's change the subject, shall we?"
"Yes," she said, "let's."[15]

The following description—in this case contrasted with the marriage—suggests the open and defenseless quality of this kind of creative relationship. The rewards were not in power and competition but in understanding, acceptance and a sense of work fulfillment:

Her clear voice . . . made him believe that everything was pulled together. It was suggestion more than fact when he heard her voice, because she had always pulled things together and she had seen him in every mood. It had been years since he had thought it was necessary to hide his thoughts or feelings from her. . . . The great thing about the co-existence was that it was not conjugal. There simply was no competition and no need to put a face on things. She had seen him in every possible mood, drunk and sober, elated or discouraged, sad or angry. She could make a sound prediction of his reactions; she knew his weaknesses without using this knowledge as a weapon; she knew them much better than he knew hers, and the beauty of it was that he did not have to know about hers. The only effort necessary for him was to do his work, and there would be no disturbance, no extraneous detail. It was completely peaceful there as he heard her speaking.[16]

This relationship is obviously too contrived and artificial; a genuinely creative situation between two people would have to have much more stress than this. It is unfair, too, to imply that marriage must necessarily always be competitive and artificial. Despite this, however, the excerpt indicates something of the nature of an open and trusting regard and a mutually respectful and fulfilling engagement of two people working together. In this it is similar to the previous counseling excerpt.

CONSTRUCTIVE COLLABORATION

Describing his productive and creative relationship in the drama with George Kaufman, Moss Hart comments:

Actually the process of collaboration is exactly what the dictionary says it is: a union of two people working in agreement on a common project. . . . It pleased me to make a mystery of our playwriting partnership, for the sole reason that the mechanics of two people writing together are no less dull and flat than the mechanics of one person writing alone. . . .

There can be no mystery, however, about the fact that collaboration is an infinitely more pleasurable way of working than working alone. Most human beings fear loneliness, and writing is the loneliest of the professions. Writers agonize a great deal about the loneliness of their craft, and though the wailing is apt to be a little deafening at times, they are telling the truth. The hardest part of writing by far is the seeming exclusion from all human kind while work is underway, for the writer at work cannot be gregarious. If he is not alone, if he is with so much as one other person, he is not at work, and it is this feeling of being cut off from his fellows that drives most writers to invent the most elaborate and ingenious excuses to put work aside and escape back into the world again.

Collaboration cuts this loneliness in half. When one is at a low point of discouragement, the very presence in the room of another human being, even though he too may be sunk in the same state of gloom, very often gives that dash of valor to the spirit that allows confidence to return and work to resume. Except on the rarest of occasions, writing is a cheerless business . . . I am never unmoved by the suffering of a fellow writer when he cries out that he is "blocked." It is a protest, I think, against his unalterable fate of being alone, and it is a desperation I can understand and give full sympathy to. When later on I went back to writing plays by myself, I looked back to the warmth and companionship of collaboration with the nostalgia of the exile for his homeland, and I confess that I have moments of missing it still.[17]

CREATIVE IMPULSE

Speaking of the mystery of creative stimulation in itself and in what it represents and the manner in which one person's presence—in this case Beatrice Kaufman—could affect it, Hart observes:

The sparkling flood of light her presence seemed to create remained in the room like an afterglow long after she had gone. It took me a while to settle down to work after the door closed behind her, and then I was brighter for having caught even that fleeting glimpse of her than I had been in days. The creative impulse is a mysterious one. It ignites and flourishes under the strangest of stimuli. I do not know precisely why the sight of Beatrice Kaufman should have unlocked my creative mechanism and set it wildly in motion, except that she seemed to be so striking a symbol of the world which lay just behind success in the theatre that she made the goal itself seem tantalizingly nearer and the drudgery and the weariness worth while. Both drudgery and weariness seemed to have vanished now. I could have worked right through the night.[18]

We can say, then, that a creative relationship, both in itself or for what it represents, produces this kind of constructive, stimulating and fulfilling achievement. This would be the core effect of community. It would provide such creative consensual validation and encouragement, and so not only further each one's best realization of himself but also stimulate him and support him toward his most adequate productivity.

The art and skill of counseling and psychotherapy, while obviously not yet totally adequate, still offer us a beginning, at least, in ways of furthering these kinds of mature, constructive and creative experience. In addition to a positive set of procedures, such a process forces us to look at ourselves, to recognize the difficulties inherent in our own destructive and controlling needs. In looking at what we have called the "agency" of the self, a person can better see his own needs of mature self-containment.

DESTRUCTIVE RELATIONSHIP

If a person is simply fulfilling his own impulses and will-to-power satisfactions, however this is masked as regard for others, dedication or service, other people may not only be negatively affected; they may even be gravely impeded in their purpose and meaning.

In his autobiography of his early adult years in Paris, Ernest Hemingway writes of such a destructive relationship between a writer friend of his and the writer's wife. Commenting on the wife, Hemingway says:

She was jealous of his work and as we got to know them, this fell into a regular pattern. He would resolve not to go on all-night drinking parties and to get some exercise each day and work regularly. He would start to work and as soon as he was working well she would begin complaining about how bored she was and get him off on another drunken party. They would quarrel and then make up and he would sweat out the alcohol on long walks with me, and make up his mind that this time he would start off well. Then it would start all over again. He was very much in love with her and he was jealous of her. . . .[19]

And later:

But the way things were going, he was lucky to get any work done at all. She did not encourage the people who were chasing her and she had nothing to do with them, she said. But it amused her and it made him jealous and he had to go with her to the places. It destroyed his work, and she was more jealous of his work than anything.[20]

We see here how the will to power can affect two people in marriage or any other similar relationship, and by manipulation and maneuver turn the forces of love and need into destructiveness.

The very openness that love and trust demand can leave a person defenselessly "nailed" if the trusted person chooses to attack. This is the risk involved in an open and loving relationship. It is not difficult to see, then, how a will, or urge, to community has to sacrifice personal power and control.

In the case we have been discussing, the same forces which might have impelled and encouraged this writer to produce the works which were in fact never written turned instead into almost insurmountable barriers to fulfillment and communication. His earlier creativity and his significant promise were all but destroyed. This is the hidden tragedy of all uncreative and negative relationships. Since they are sterile and barren, no one ever knows what a positive and constructively reflective atmosphere might have accomplished. We are, apparently, in large measure what others help us to be by the way they see and reflect us in their own actions towards us.

AIDING OR DEFEATING

Consequently, whether we consider a broad organization structure of a city, business, religious group or school, or the simpler relationship of a family, husband and wife, or two people working together, the contrast of power and self-affirmation versus community seems always to be present. Harrow's secretary, in knowing "his weaknesess without using this knowledge as a weapon," represents the open trust and defenseless quality of a genuinely creative will to community. By comparison the author's wife who "destroyed his work, and she was more jealous of his work than anything," demonstrates the subtle but effective destructiveness that uncontrolled will to power takes.

RELIGIOUS CONVALIDATION

We have said earlier that maturity seeks the pursuit of each one's own excellence in an atmosphere of positive reflection and authentic involvement. One of religion's main purposes now would seem to be to further this process by restoring a genuine sense of representation, communion and communication to working relationships, marriage, the family; and to the community at large, education, industry, the city and the Church. This, as we have seen, was the great contribution of the early Christian community, and it was apparently one of the main reasons for its effectiveness. We are now in the same need of restored personal meaning and value at all levels of human relationship.

Previously, quoting McNeill, we pointed out how the warmth, closeness and security of the early Christian communities played an important part in Christianity's rapid spread, especially among the masses in great cities. On this same theme, McNeill comments:

Much of Christianity's early success rested upon the systematic charities through which members helped one another and upon the ritual weekly meetings. . . . The upshot was to create a cohesive community of believers. . . .[21]

While these early Christian communities were by no means ideal in their relations with one another or in their regard toward others, they did apparently have an intense sense of responsibility for one another that characterized them and made them a "cohesive community."

This cohesion was marked, too, by a disciplined and affectionate regard for one another which St. Peter calls "the discipline of charity," as he exhorts Christians to "give constant proof of your affection for each other, loving unaffectedly."

OPEN REGARD

It is, in fact, this kind of open, mutual regard—without guile or affectation—that is one of the ways in which, according to Peter, Christians share in the priesthood itself:

. . . Purify your souls with the discipline of charity, and give constant proof of your good-will for each other, loving unaffectedly as brethren should (I Peter 1:22, Knox).

You must put aside, then, every trace of ill will and deceitfulness, your affections, the grudges you bore, and all the slanderous talk; you are children new-born, and all your craving must be for the soul's pure milk, that will nurture you into salvation, once you have tasted, as you have surely tasted, the goodness of the Lord. Draw near to him; he is the living antitype of that stone which men rejected, which God has chosen and prized; you too must be built up on him, stones that live and breathe, into a spiritual fabric; you must be a *holy priesthood, to offer up* that spiritual sacrifice which God accepts through Jesus Christ. (I Peter 2:1–5, Knox; italics mine.)

St. Paul further adds to this picture when he stresses the open but gentle confrontation and the deep sense of a common sharing of the human condition that should characterize the Christian Galatian community:

Brethren, if a man is found guilty of some fault, you, who are spiritually minded, ought to show a spirit of gentleness in correcting him. Have an eye upon thyself; thou too wilt perhaps encounter temptation. Bear the burden of one another's failings; then you will be fulfilling the law of Christ. The man who thinks he is of some worth, when in truth he is worth nothing at all, is merely deluding himself. Everyone should examine his own conduct; then he will be able to take the measure of his own worth; no need to compare himself with others. Each of us, then, will have his own load to carry. (Gal. 6:1–5, Knox.)

These qualities of deep, open and committed caring followed from the strong emphasis which Christ Himself placed on shared love and its rich and joyful sense of belonging:

All this I have told you, so that my joy may be yours, and the measure of your joy may be filled up. This is my commandment, that you should love one another, as I have loved you. This is the greatest love a man can show, that he should lay down his life for his friends; and you, if you do all that I command you, are my friends. I do not speak of you any more as my servants; a servant is one who does not understand what his master is about, whereas I have made known to you all that my Father has told me; and so I have called you my friends. It was not you that chose me, it was I that chose you. The task I have appointed you is to go out and bear fruit, fruit which will endure; so that every request you make of the Father in my name may be granted you. These are the directions I give you, that you should love one another. (John 15:11–17, Knox.)

Quite within this spirit, then, is Aquinas's emphasis on friendship as the core idea and essential relationship of man to himself, to others and to God:

Charity is love. Now love, by reason of the nature of the power whose act it is, is capable of reflecting on itself; . . . wherefore from the moment a man loves, *he loves himself to love*.

Yet charity is not love simply, but has the nature of friendship. . . .[22]

SELF-REGARD BASIS

Aristotle and Aquinas anticipated the modern self-concept theory in their understanding that one's attitude toward oneself determines one's relationship to others. Borrowing from Aristotle's *Ethics* as well as the gospel text that we are to love others as we love ourselves, Aquinas comments:

. . . the love with which a man loves himself is the form and root of friendship. For if we have friendship with others it is because we do unto them as we do unto ourselves, hence we read in Ethic. ix, 4, 8, that the origin of friendly relations with others lies in our relations to ourselves.

It is written (Lev. xix, 18, Matth. xxii, 39): *Thou shalt love thy neighbor* (Lev. *loc. cit.,—friend*) *as thyself.* Whence it seems to follow *that man's love for himself is the model of his love for another.* But the model exceeds the copy.[23]

The way a person loves himself, therefore, is the model of which his love of others is the copy. Or in the reverse, if one has a distorted view of himself, he will make this self-attitude his model and copy from it all his relationships with other people.

Aquinas summarized Aristotle's exposition of friendship in five propositions:

The Philosopher proves this from five things that are proper to friendship. For in the first place, every friend wishes his friend to be and to live; secondly, he desires good things for him; thirdly, he does good things to him; fourthly, he takes pleasure in his company; fifthly, he is of one mind with him, rejoicing and sorrowing in almost the same things. In this way *the good love themselves,* as to the inward man.[24]

In this sense, a psychologically mature person should aim to be a genuine friend to himself as well as to others. Through his doing so, friendship permeates all his relationships.[25]

FOCUS THROUGH SELF-CONCEPT

This is also similar to the self-concept theory in which a person's idea of himself is said to determine how he tends to see his environment and his relations to other people. To put it another way, and negatively, if his attitudes toward himself are distorted and warped, his attitude toward others tends to be distorted and warped too. If he is negative, hostile, resistant and rejecting in an unloving way toward himself; if he is fearful and anxious about himself; then he will project these attitudes toward other people. He will, in Aquinas's terms, tend "to love himself to hate" in place of "to love himself to love."

Insofar, then, as a person has these unresolved conflicts and disturbances, he tends to see experiences and other people in a proportionately distorted way. Not unlike the person who needs glasses, he has difficulty seeing without distortion. Consequently, unless a man has a clear image of himself and a right regard for himself at a deep and subtle psychological level, he will have a somewhat difficult time knowing other people as they really are. In proportion as his own inner world of feeling, instincts and soma is disturbed, he tends to have a confused picture of everything he experiences.

If a husband and wife, family, group or organizational relationship is to be changed then, it will not be changed by purely external force or persuasion or mass activity—except in a conformist, extrinsic sense. For a relationship to really get changed from within, all the unique self-awareness of each person must be engaged.

NEW PERCEPTUAL FIELD

A change that is ultimately valid, then, is begun apparently only in the uniqueness of each one. As a person changes his attitude toward himself, his attitudes toward others change proportionately. When he sees new aspects of a right love of himself and begins to acquire them, he seems, at the same time, to begin to project this outward to others. His new self-attitudes will, like new glasses, then allow him to see others as they are, rather than in a distorting way. His model of his relationship to himself and others is, therefore, not that of a machine—"good" if it does what he wants or "bad" if it does not—but a right sense of love of himself and others. It is this kind of reasonable and respectful self-attitude that is basic to a personalist organizational structure and community relationship.

Unless this is so, relationships will tend to be depersonalized, defensive or controlling, not open and trusting. But such cold, impersonal, organizational attitudes and structures and the kind of mechanical and managerial interpersonal relationships they produce run the risk of becoming finally self-defeating. They can satisfy only the will-to-power fulfillment of some and arouse resistance and defensiveness in the rest.[26]

GOAL: BECOMING A PERSON

Here especially, counseling and psychotherapy can aid religion in its effort to establish again a "cohesive community" according to "the discipline of love," as St. Peter's Epistle described the model of the early Christian community. To fulfill this now, what is called for is a new sense of community, one that will be suffused by an atmosphere of acceptance and understanding, where each one will have the opportunity and the encouragement to become more truly a person—in the unique and rich sense of this term.

NOTES

[1] *Op. cit.,* p. ix.

[2] *Ibid.,* p. viii.

[3] *Letters of the Great Artists: from Blake to Pollock,* ed. Richard Friedenthal (New York: Random House, 1963), pp. 169–170.

[4] *The Holy Bible,* trans. Ronald Knox. Copyright Sheed & Ward, Inc.,

1944, 1948, 1952. Reprinted with the permission of the Cardinal Archbishop of Westminster.

[5] Mann, *op. cit.*, pp. ix–x.

[6] *Ibid.*, pp. 72–74.

[7] *Ibid.*, pp. 75–76.

[8] *Ibid.*, pp. 76–77.

[9] From *All in the Family* by Edwin O'Connor. Copyright (c) 1964, 1966 by Edwin O'Connor. By permission of Atlantic—Little, Brown and Co. Pages 153–155.

[10] *Ibid.*, p. 155.

[11] *Ibid.*, p. 413.

[12] Bela Mittelmann, H. G. Wolff and M. P. Scharf, "Experimental Studies on Patients with Gastritis, Duodenitis and Peptic Ulcer," *Psychosomatic Medicine*, 4, pp. 5–61; by permission of the authors and of Paul B. Hoeber, Inc., Medical Book Department of Harper and Brothers. Quoted in Rollo May, *The Meaning of Anxiety* (New York: Ronald Press, 1950), p. 74.

[13] John F. Cuber and P. B. Harroff, "The More Total View: Relationships Among Men and Women of the Upper Middle Class," *Marriage and Family Living*, 25, 2 (May 1963), p. 144.

See Charles A. Curran, *Counseling and Psychotherapy: The Pursuit of Values,* chapter entitled "Marriage Counseling."

[14] From *Women and Thomas Harrow* by John P. Marquand. Copyright (c) 1958 by Thomas P. Marquand. By permission of Little, Brown and Co. Pages 37–38.

[15] *Ibid.*, pp. 123–124.

[16] *Ibid.*, pp. 456–457.

[17] Moss Hart, *Act One* (New York: Random House, Inc., A Signet Book, 1959). From *Act One,* by Moss Hart, © Copyright 1959 by Catherine Carlisle Hart and Joseph M. Hyman, Trustees. Reprinted by permission of Random House, Inc. Pp. 263–264.

[18] *Ibid.*, pp. 252–253.

[19] Ernest Hemingway, *A Moveable Feast* (New York: Charles Scribner's Sons, A Bantam Book, 1964), pp. 178–179.

[20] *Ibid.*, p. 181.

[21] McNeill, *op. cit.*, p. 372.

[22] *Summa Theologica*, II–II, Q. 25, a. 2.

[23] *Ibid.*, II–II, Q. 25, a. 4. (Italics mine.)

[24] *Ibid.*, II–II, Q. 25, a. 7.

[25] See William Schofield, *Psychotherapy—the Purchase of Friendship* (New Jersey: Prentice-Hall, 1964).

[26] See Gordon W. Allport, "The Psychology of Participation," *Psychological Review*, 53 (May 1945), pp. 122–123.

Conclusion:
Characteristics of
Creative Communication

IF THE LOVE of self is the model of which the love of others is the copy and the copy will be as good or as bad as the original, then a climate which produces a respectful and insightful self-love is a basic prerequisite to the achievement of human belonging. It will also be basic to creative communication. Such love of self, valuing self as a precious gift at the disposal of others, is at the opposite pole to a narcissistic self-preoccupation. If we add a religious concept to this, we are called upon to ponder afresh, and with greater depth and intensity, the nature of religious love. If such a genuine climate is to be established, this calls for a profound reorganization within the inner self of each person as well as within the community itself.

In any creative communication, an assessment of the nature of representation and commitment seems also implied, as we have pointed out. This must be both personal and communal—with concern extending to every person. Each one must be loved with the same respect, regard and conviction with which he seeks to love himself. Only in such a climate can love really come to final fruition and maturity.

GENUINE LOVE

These are the demands of authentic psychological as well as religious love and the creative communication it would produce. Such a realization would seek to restore again, amidst all the weary

353

dronings of jukebox, movie, radio and television, something of the pristine and fresh meaning of love as an experience in genuine relationship. The direct opposite of the easy saccharine sentimentality of the popular image of love, even one act of genuine love involves a difficult, mature and demanding commitment. But only in this way can it avoid relationships that are "phony" and that finally repel by their sentimentality or disguised condescension and manipulation, rather than attract by their real integrity.

This too is the "noblesse oblige" of our time. It is no longer the parent-figure responsibility of the representative few, but a common horizontal dignity, meaning and responsibility shared equally. To achieve this, each one needs to grow and to be aided to grow in his mature and responsible sense of personal worth in himself and joined to others. By taking on the responsibilities of real choice, one ennobles and matures oneself and so moves toward internalizing a greater sense of self-excellence. At the same time, one can move to the other in respectful concern for each one's unique capacity for excellence in his own particular way.

EQUAL AND EXCELLENT

Involved in the common incarnate sharing of the human condition and in equality is the question of how to find adequate representation of, and means to, such excellence. It is not something commonly shared but must be an excellence appropriate to each one's uniqueness. Gardner has phrased the question, "Can we be equal and excellent too?"[1]

Religion can especially enter here in this matter of each one's own "excellence." One means to an ideal and incarnate representation of authentic excellence is to believe in something beyond man, and to believe that this became incarnate in such a way that each man could share it. This would then make possible a transcendent and transfigured human worth. The possibility of a relationship with the divine would then also represent the possibility of a relationship with total excellence. God so conceived is not only the Total Other but the Total Other which represents the highest kind of excellence—the goal of all human striving for dignity, worth and meaning.

ROYAL PRIESTHOOD

In the Epistle previously quoted, St. Peter addresses the whole community as a living "royal priesthood." Priestliness—in his juxtaposing of it with the adjective "royal"—could here be conceived as the projection onto the human condition of this representation of divine excellence. Priestliness, in this sense, in a person and shared by the whole religious community, in the way Peter's Epistle describes, would be a means of designating the human correspondence to highest Excellence. It would symbolize for each one the unique meaning of his own personal excellence and so motivate each person to strive for such fulfillment.

Of course, this would not take the place of the traditional concept of priesthood but extend it. Like our comparison with the language-learning process, the priest or other clergyman is himself especially religiously mimetic, as the French person is mimetic to the identification-absorption process of learning or, in our sense, "becoming" French. The priest, and of course the bishop, *personalizes* priestliness. He is, in a particular fashion, a pontifex, or bridge builder, between God and man as the French person in our comparison is a bridge to French. We do not imply, then, any change in the meaning or function of the personal priesthood. As we said in our discussion on "Pastoral Counseling," the ordained minister especially personalizes the faith of the believing community. His official sacramental, liturgical and teaching functions are basic to, and expressive of, this faith commitment of the whole "people of God."

The whole believing, cohesive community then would be seen as representing authentic excellence to one another. Through a faith commitment, this excellence would truly represent that which goes beyond, and corresponds to, man's highest yearnings. This might be thought of as a modern approach to majesty in an era when kings and princes no longer carry this meaning.

The realization of the symbolization of kingliness and royal priesthood would now be fulfilled and completed in this sense of excellence shared by clergy and people together. Their common "consensual validation" of one another's excellence and their trusting, open regard—their genuine "will to community"—

would constitute the unique and special "royal" quality of their relationship. This shared correspondent excellence would be reflected in the whole community. Each one's open and respectful gift of himself to another might be seen—in the light of the use of the word "sacrifice" in the Epistle text—as the final completion in one another of the sacramental Eucharistic and Communion liturgy.

COMMUNION ENGAGEMENT

To be sure, Protestant "fellowship," and especially Quaker "friend," conceptions have already been rich and effective in this. We propose deepening these concepts to give them a special purpose and meaning for modern man—with his marked tendencies toward alienation and worthlessness. Fellowship is, of course, a Pauline conception (Gal. 2:9). Friendship, used by Christ (John 15:11, 17), could be considered, at the same time, a Greek-Platonic-Aristotelian cultural inheritance.[2] By adding the further description that St. Peter's Epistle gives we mean to include not only a relationship of fellowship and regard but, in addition, one with a "royal" quality of the sharing and support in each one's pursuit of his own excellence.

St. Peter, in relating this community regard with "sacrifice" and "priesthood," seems also to suggest that the early Christian community saw such community engagement and commitment as a direct concomitant of their liturgical communion. The stress on "friendship" and "fellowship" would be a way of continuing and fulfilling this idea. But in using the designation "royal," St. Peter adds a special concept of excellence to this sense of community belonging and sharing.

CORRESPONDENT REFLECTION

This relationship, as we mean it, would become evident in the manner in which sacraments and liturgy result in correspondent reflection in the community's attitude toward each person. This would be a special religious relationship which shares in the royal sense of excellence between God and man. This representative relationship would include, as a result of its engagement and personal concern, all aspects of the community in the living embrace of redemptive excellence. So, in their genuineness and integrity and their respectful regard extending to each adult and child, such a "people of God" would seek to come alive together as "stones that live and breathe."

Kennedy comments:

If the Church and its teachers have had one truth to preserve through the ages, it is a realistic vision of the human family, an understanding of the person as the center of life and its meaning. If the law and the prophets are summed up in love, and if loving our neighbor is the only command Christ left us, then the Church is the guardian of the only truths that can make us free. God is indeed dead when men have forgotten the meaning of each other, when they have died themselves because the Spirit has been supplanted by the supposed symbols of his presence. But empty symbols will never do in a world that is weary and hungry and yearning in a thousand disfigured and disguised ways for real love.[3]

NEW PARISH DYNAMIC

New ways of relating and conceptualizing the parish dynamic are necessary if this vision is to begin to be realized. Society itself is changing, and we must get to persons immediately in open and trusting communication. We can no longer wait for long-time relationships to emerge. De Witt, in discussing "making a community out of a parish," observes:

In our mobile society, the tie to a physical place, the family seat, the neighborhood, no longer seems to serve as a strong basis for lasting personal relationships.

Today, in contractual, urban and mobile society, both in and out of the Church, we see the need for primary groups with strong bonds of intimacy, acceptance, loyalties and mutually shared responsibilities for the development and sustaining of the person.[4]

He points out, however, that this cannot be achieved by simply getting a large number of people together—even in a worship or liturgical sense:

Further, it seems that small groups have a great deal to do with being Christian. It is clear that group life, in smaller and larger groups, was the earliest form of Christian life. Jesus had the twelve and the seventy-two and "certain women who ministered to him with what means they had" (Luke 8:3). In Acts, we catch a glimpse of the first Christians meeting in each others' homes "occupied with the apostles' teaching and fellowship in the breaking of the bread" (Acts 2:42 ff.). They were so caught up in a common vision and spirit that "they shared all they had, selling possessions so as to distribute to all as each had need" (Acts 2:45). It would seem then that the New Testament provides us with the original Christian experience, which was profoundly communal, an experience against which we can compare our own to see how we measure up.[5]

REDEMPTIVE STRIVING

We have already suggested ways in which this small group closeness might be achieved by incorporating group and individual counseling skills. In addition, liturgical symbolism and actions and the form of religious worship could be viewed as a way of making affects both cognitive and symbolic, and so projecting and universalizing the basic life experiences and needs of each person.

Such a relationship would not only be "royal" in its representation of excellence but communal in somewhat the same sense that counseling and therapy are communal. As a married couple or a group is brought together and communion restored through communication with and through the counselor, so religious worship and liturgical sharing together would seek to symbolize and make cognitive the unique feelings, urges and communications of each person, and so extend and universalize them. Through the communities' shared sense of excellence, each one would reflect in himself and his actions and respond to the other according to the Pauline redemptive sense of being "purchased by a great price." Each would, in this way, convalidate the other's sense of the striving for his own unique fulfillment and purpose.

As Thomas Mann saw kingliness as the image and symbol both of excellence and of artistic striving, so this shared representation of the "beyond" in humanity would seek to be validated in the being of each person. In this it, too, could be said to represent artistic striving as well. In what might be called an artistic incarnate-redemptive correspondence, the artist, too, seeks a genuine being as well as representing.

POSITIVE BEING AND COMMUNICATION

This sense, then, of being oneself in one's own increasing sense of worth and excellence would result from an intense striving both to grow and to be. This being and becoming in pursuit of one's own excellence is evident in the psychological incarnate-redemptive process of counseling therapy, as we have seen. Rogers comments:

> . . . We have established the fact that in successful psychotherapy negative attitudes toward the self decrease and positive attitudes increase. We have measured the gradual increase in self-acceptance and have studied the correlated increase in acceptance of others. But as I examine these statements and compare them with our more recent cases, I feel they fall short of the truth. The client not only accepts himself—a phrase which may carry the connotation of a grudging and reluctant acceptance of the inevitable—he actually comes to *like* himself. This is not a bragging or self-assertive liking; it is rather a quiet pleasure in being one's self.[6]

Rogers reports an interview at length where a client is slowly and tortuously arriving at this kind of positive being and communication with herself. She has previously designated herself, on a self-rating scale, an "attractive personality." She is discussing the surprise and excitement of this new self-attitude:

> . . . I walked out of here one time, and impulsively I threw my first card, "I am an attractive personality"; I looked at it sort of aghast but I left it there, I mean, because honestly, I mean, that is exactly how I felt—a—well, that bothered me and I catch that now. Every once in a while a sort of pleased feeling, nothing superior, but just—I don't know, sort of pleased . . .

Later the therapist, putting himself in her place, responds:

T: I'm really a pretty rich and interesting person.
C: Something like that. And then I say to myself, "our society pushes us around and we've lost it." And I keep going back to my feelings

about children. Well, maybe they're richer than we are. Maybe we
—it's something we've lost in the process of growing up.

T: Could be that they have a wisdom about that that we've lost.

C: That's right. My time's up.

Rogers then comments:

Here she arrives, as do so many other clients, at the tentative,
slightly apologetic realization that she has come to like, enjoy, appreciate herself.[7]

COMMUNITY PARALLEL

As the relationship here has produced this sense of growing worth
and meaning for a person, so a constructive and committed community involvement would seek to radiate this same sense of
finding, appreciating and learning to be oneself. As Rogers suggests,
one repeatedly witnesses this struggle for a personal sense of
worth and meaning in people in the counseling therapy process. It
is apparently a widespread need evident everywhere. It would be
an extremely important contribution, therefore, if a community experience among people could convey, reflect and finally result in,
this growing sense of worth of each one.

FAITH-COMMITMENT

If we add a faith-commitment, this would give a religious dimension
to the convalidating community. In the community's giving evidence of this kind of intense joint striving for unconditional positive regard—"in the discipline of charity, giving constant proof
of our affection for one another," as St. Peter's Epistle prescribes—
a correspondent religious sense of excellence would see itself
radiated. This would be one way in which belief in the representation of the divine in humanity would become evident through a
commitment to the unique worth of each person. This would represent for each the consensual validation of the meaning and significance of the incarnate-redemptive process as it permeates the
whole community with sharing regard and belonging.

Cooke draws a distinction between the relationship one might have with another as a source of life—say, as a father is the means of life to a child—and a relationship that would be truly personal and free—a genuine and free love that could, and it is to be hoped does, emerge between father and child. It is this personal relationship that, in his view, constitutes the mystery of the Church as community. So he says:

There is our gift of ordinary life, and on that basis God is Father. If you say God is Father in this sense, then to some extent you are using the word "Father" metaphorically. That is not, however, what we refer to when we mention the mystery of the church. We mean a Fatherhood which is much more proper. We mean that in the gift of supernatural life God the Father is involved personally. God the Father, with the Son and the Holy Spirit, creates the world; they who are persons effect something. But that which they effect does not involve them personally: a personal relationship does not result.

When the communication of supernatural life happens, however, there is—this is a deep part of the mystery—an involvement of the three Divine Persons in a situation of friendship with mankind. It is in this context, the unique giving of new existence, that sonship in the church, the family of God, is to be understood.[8]

Explaining what constitutes this community in a religious commitment, Cooke says:

It follows that the bond that unites us in the church is communion in a common life . . . We are the *communio fidelium* because we accept and witness to this communally. The Word of God is presented to us *as a people*. As such we accept this and profess our faith in it.[9]

It is not enough, therefore, for people simply to live together in the same house or on the same street or neighborhood. This kind of enforced familiarity, as we noted earlier, may only reinforce masks and defensive but disguised distance. For this "communion in a common life" that Cooke describes to be really so, committed and sustained efforts at genuine relationship would be demanded on each one's part—the exact opposite of the alienation and state of noncommunication that seems so characteristic of many of our present relationships.

The involvement of God in friendship with man will be most

convincing when we see its reflection in a community and communion of persons together that genuinely reflect and communicate a validation of each one's worth in human friendship.

OTHER-CENTERED COMMUNICATION

Aquinas comments that the core of this friendship relationship is a deep and understanding kind of other-centered communication. He contrasts it with tendencies to use and manipulate others as one might an animal, or "eat them up" as one might food:

... It is written (Jo XV 15): "I will not now call you servants . . . but My friends," Now this was said to them by reason of nothing else than charity. Therefore charity is friendship.

According to the Philosopher [Aristotle] (Ethic viii, 3, 3) not every love has the character of friendship, but that love which is together with benevolence, when we love someone so as to wish good to him, If, however, we do not wish good to what we love, but wish its good for ourselves (thus we are said to love wine, or a horse, or the like), it is love not of friendship, but of a kind of concupiscence. For it would be absurd to speak of having friendship for wine or for a horse. Yet neither does well-wishing suffice for friendship, for a certain mutual love is requisite, since friendship is between friend and friend: and this well-wishing is founded on some kind of communication.

Accordingly, since there is a communication between man and God, inasmuch as He communicates His happiness to us, some kind of friendship must needs be based on this same communication, of which it is written (I Cor. i. 9): "God is faithful: by Whom you are called unto the fellowship of His Son." The love which is based on this communication, is charity: wherefore it is evident that charity is the friendship of man for God.[10]

To fulfill this, a man seeks to be a true friend to himself, a true friend to others and a true friend to God. In this sense, love and friendship are experiences in mutual regard. But we notice this is more than feelings of regard, according to Aristotle and Aquinas. There is added to this the difficult requirement of genuine communication.

COMMUNICATION: UNDERSTANDING CONCERN

Throughout this book we have observed how complicated and subtle all efforts at human communication really are. Real communication is difficult because we tend to crowd into any relationship many of our own overt and hidden needs. This is particularly true in any attempt to "help" others.

But such "will to power" self-seeking—"concupiscence," as Aquinas uses it—is ultimately self-defeating and alienating. The real pursuit of one's own excellence includes a moderating kind of maturing that insures an awareness of self-limits. Such an awareness gives place to the other, facilitates and takes joy in his growth in worth and excellence. The contrary of this is to use him, manipulate and control him—however subtly—for oneself. One must moderate this power affirmation; otherwise this deceptive urge, which acts as a surrogate for excellence, will go beyond what a person really is and so end in defeating and deluding him.

Communication would consist in this deep understanding concern for the meaning and value of each person and each relationship, and the constant effort of each one, by words and actions, to convey this. This would be a personalist concern for each one's best fulfillment of himself as well as the most adequate completion of any common task. Such a concept—describing a relationship of mutual regard toward personal excellence, worth and adequate achievement—would add a new dimension to the incarnate-redemptive meaning and purpose of community as well as give an additional extension to the representative significance of a community sense of shared excellence and orientation and dedication to common tasks and goals.

PERSONAL AND SOCIAL

In focusing only on social and political issues as means of showing concern for others, one may overlook these extremely difficult personal aspects of real communication. But it is this genuine and dignified reflection of themselves from others that people are seeking—in addition to the realization of basic rights and normal living conditions. Both phases of concern, social and personal, are necessary for a truly creative community climate.

STRESS NECESSARY

We are not proposing, obviously, that human conflict and confusion can ever be finally resolved. On the contrary, such conflicts are apparently necessary to us since they form the basic stresses through which our individual personalities unfold. In his analysis of the stress of life, Hans Selye makes the point that "it is only in the heat of stress that individuality can be perfectly molded."[11] If we know one another in proportion as we have arrived at uniqueness in ourselves and others, then this comes about, evidently, not by avoiding conflict and stress but by authentic engagement with our total self and with the totality of other persons. To escape stress and commitment and its ensuing anxiety by assuming a kind of impartial and uninvolved "empty organism" attitude is apparently to be afraid to live. As Kerr has said:

We have neglected knowledge by contact in our abstraction-centered lives, have in fact almost persuaded ourselves that it does not exist.[12]

GRATEFUL OR VENGEFUL

As a summation of his observation of many persons under stress from a wide variety of conditions, Selye concluded:

I think in the final analysis that gratitude and revenge are the most important factors governing our actions in everyday life; upon them also chiefly depend our peace of mind, our feelings of security or insecurity, of fulfillment or frustration, in short, the extent to which we can make a success of life. . . . Gratitude is the awakening in another person of the wish that I should prosper, because of what I have done for him. It is perhaps the most characteristically human way of assuring security (homeostasis). It takes away the motive for a clash between selfish and selfless tendencies, because, by inspiring the feeling of gratitude. I have induced another person to share with me my natural wish for my own well-being.[13]

Gratitude would seem to be, in this sense, a description of a relationship between people, a "benevolentia" that would be mutually beneficial and reinforcing. A grateful life-attitude, then, would be this secure response to life, in openness, hope and appreciation.

Religion would add a divine dimension to such gratitude. As Allport says:

> The main purpose of religion, I suggest, is not to make people healthy, but to help them fit themselves into the Creator's context for them . . . a personality, to be sound and fully human, requires a guiding philosophy of life.[14]

CORRESPONDENT GRATITUDE

Religious values would extend gratitude to its correspondent divine dimension. It would be that wish in another person for my benevolence out of his sense of grace in what he himself has been given by God—the Pauline "What have we that we have not received, and if we have received it, why do we act as if we had received it not?" It is from this that religious values would share with counseling therapy the awareness of the need, and the impulse, to love first—and thus, as we have seen, offer another an incarnate and redemptive consensual validation.

Selye contrasts gratitude with vengeful feelings which he considers a "malformation of our urge to teach":

> Now revenge is the awakening in another person of the wish that I should not prosper, because of what I have done to him. It is the most important threat to security (homeostasis). But it also has its roots in a natural defense reaction. It is a savage distortion of the natural wish to teach others not to hurt us. . . . Unfortunately, in practice, it is very difficult to draw the line between teaching by punishment for a constructive purpose and senseless, purely vindictive retaliation as an aim in itself, a morbid satisfaction of the urge for self-expression. Professional teachers must be especially careful to make this distinction in all their dealings with students. . . . We need not give much thought to revenge; it is nothing but a grotesque malformation of our urge to teach; a kind of "disease of the teaching instinct."[15]

Such vengeful attitudes seem to be marked by a resentment towards others, particularly those parents and parent-figures that a person somehow feels are responsible for his own condition.

ILLUSTRATION

Sometimes in the process of counseling therapy, people slowly come to see how this kind of revenge towards themselves and others is deceptive and self-defeating. One client expressed it this way:

Cl: It's very strong. I—that I know. It's terribly powerful.

T: Almost a dominating kind of force.

Cl: Of which I am rarely conscious. Almost never . . . Well the only way I can describe it, it's a kind of murderous thing, but without violence . . . It's more like a feeling of wanting to get even . . . and of course, I won't pay back, but I'd like to. I really would like to.[16]

In a later interview, speaking of the bitterness that resulted, she says:

Cl: And then of course, I've come to—to see and to feel that over this—see, I've covered it up (*weeps*). But I've covered it up with so much bitterness, which in turn I had to cover up. (*Weeping.*) *That's* what I want to get rid of! I almost don't *care* if I hurt.[17]

REWARD AND APPROVAL MASK

Unless this kind of vengeful feeling is seen and faced as this person faced it in counseling therapy, it can seriously impede any real communication with another person. In its self-deception, this resentment may be covered and masked in many ways, even by an apparent joviality and friendliness. But such an appearance of friendliness often turns out to be manipulatory. The basic resentment is uncovered when the other does not do what is expected of him.

This is not a genuine communication with the uniqueness of another person but a reward for and approval of a person's fulfillment of a predetermined plan. Such phrases as "in the end it came out all right" or "he did the right thing after all" can be genuine benevolent approval. But they also may mask a vengeful attitude which really sees others as friends only if they do what is set out for them, and as inimical and threatening if they choose to follow a path different from the one chosen for them. Personal relationships, then, turn out positively only when such relationships—like the analogy of a mathematical problem, a story or a voyage—have one answer, or an exact ending or a proper destination. In other words, a kind of scenario is written for a person and he is to act out his part according to the script.

THE GENUINE IS ENIGMATIC

But in the Bible, for example, or in any real relationship it is rather the risk of the uncalculated and unforeseen that seems to determine the authenticity of the commitment. It is in the midst of the unknown that faith, hope and love are most strained and tested. David in exile maintaining hope against despair; the wolf coming at the throat of the "good shepherd" who stays, in contrast to the one who escapes; the "going out into the wilderness" after the "lost" sheep; the leaving the "ninety-nine" safe and secure ones to search for the "lost" one; as well as the prodigal son theme; or even the reality of Mary Magdalene: all suggest some complex and subtle way by which love comes only after risk and even sometimes after tragic weakness. But somehow, strength and genuinely redemptive worth emerge out of such risk and sin. By contrast, in these episodes, the "safe" ones never open themselves to love. They are too enclosed and anxious, like the man who "buries his talent."

These episodes describe aspects of the human condition that we see not only in a religious setting but in other psychological relationships as well. Authenticity of relationship emerges in faith, hope and trust in face of the insecure and the unknown that can be both mysterious and threatening. To predetermine in what direction "everything should come out" before anything is permitted to begin can be to choke a relationship and snuff out all its spontaneity and freedom before it starts. It is doubtful that in a relationship so preconceived there could be any significant place for the mystery of love.

GRACILITY

Relating the word "gratitude" to its origin, it comes, of course, from "gratia," the Latin word for grace. We could therefore say that a life attitude of gratitude would involve both grace and two other words of the same origin—"graciousness," to describe the relationship itself, and "graceful," to describe the external consequences and effects of such a life attitude.

In an attempt to sum up what is basic in human relations, then, we might speak of a need for "graciousness." One might call the essence of this quality "gracility," to suggest its personal, mysterious illusiveness and its source in grace. By this we mean that a relationship between two people or within a group would be open, free, incarnate and redemptive, so that each would feel a deep and significant reflection of himself both as being in genuine communion with others and as having worth and meaning in his own unique condition.

"Gracious" as a description of this dynamic and creative communication would *correspond* to grace and gratitude. Grace belongs to the religious conviction that God first loved man, and so enhanced his meaning and value by making possible for each one a life of friendship and dialogue with the divine. Gratitude, as a life attitude, would follow from this. Such a gracious regard for others then would be seen, from religious values, as living the life of grace. For this to be effective, a static and fixed "state of grace" implication would not be enough. There would need to be a constant effort at the responsive expression of one's own sense of grace by the gracious way a person responded to others. This would continue the correspondence with God in grace.

Externally, one might see this reflected in the word "graceful," in that each person's manners and actions and the whole environment of the human city would aim to reflect and correspond to this gracious, civilized ambiance. Gratitude would be the life attitude which would follow from and motivate a person to strive to be both gracious and grateful.

PERMEATE ALL RELATIONSHIPS

Such a grateful life attitude, rather than a vengeful, hostile or manipulatory one, would affect all relationships. For people working together, it would bring a sense of each one's creativeness continually renewed and refreshed by the experience of community and communication. It would aim at people's feeling that they were not simply "working for a living" but genuinely experiencing a sense of living through and for their work—not as totally absorbing them but as releasing in them a flood of constructive forces. On a broad organizational scale, it would result in that sense of positive participation necessary to any constructive organization effort.

The need for this sense of graciousness, then, could be said to permeate all human relationships. Applied to marriage, for example, in place of implying "competition" and "the need to put a face on things" which Marquand describes, marriage would strive to be constantly gracious. Gratitude rather than revenge, communion rather than power, would signify that each is aware of grace and graciousness in regard to the other. Such a prototype would be the model for all creative human relationships, in the family, in larger groups, in industry, in the school, church and city.

FRESHNESS OF THE UNKNOWN

Grace and graciousness are tied up with mystery, with the continual renewal of the freshness of the unknown. They imply that God is sought not simply in the heavens but across the faces and hearts of each of us. This Mysterious Presence is to be found, however, not in those things that are familiar and reflect ourselves in a kind of Narcissus image but in those things in which each of us represents the unique. These are the ways in which we are most mysterious to one another, but at the same time most really ourselves. Faith, hope and love for one another is involved with the mystery, the undefined unknown, that each of us represents both to ourselves and to others. Without this sense of mystery neither faith, hope nor love can grow between men or beyond, with God. All freshness of life, and so all sense of the really creative, seems tied to the childlike wonderment at the mysterious. Without this enigmatic quality each one is "finalized" with the finality of ordered tombstones. Liberty itself is abandoned. As Selye comments:

The fairest thing we can experience (said Einstein) is the mysterious. It is the fundamental emotion which stands at the cradle of true art and true science. He who knows it not and can no longer wonder, no longer feels amazement, is as good as dead, a snuffed-out candle.[18]

THE UNCALCULATED

Considered this way, a relationship of people should never grow stale, as long as they never conclude that they have one another "figured out." All the answers are not in the back of their life book. One detects this terrible deadness between two people, particularly husband and wife, when they seem to have lost this sense of uniqueness and mystery. They relate to one another only in those fixed, cliché forms that endlessly repeat banalities from which the fineness and delicacy of respectful regard have gone.

This regard for mystery would bring out the uncalculated from each like the freshness of each new dawn and the sharp difference of each new day, as they relate together. In such an atmosphere each person would be free to express his uniqueness, and so convey those things about him that would have the most meaning and that others would treasure. Graciousness between people would require that they be always waiting for mystery and surprise and so be open to each one's expression of difference. Their grace would consist in this kind of openness together, and their readiness to put themselves at the disposal of the mystery of one another, never presuming that they have one another "solved."

This, of course, is no easy thing to do. Everyone seeks answers, and we have, in a way, mathematical minds. There is a satisfaction in a clear and precisely-figured-out solution. It is pleasant to feel that one has someone else "solved." More than that, it is safe and secure. A mystery is threatening, and even has an element of awesomeness about it; the uncalculated is risky and dangerous. And yet precisely this is the nature of love. By falling in love we let ourselves go into mystery and openness, trusting to the other person—like those dramatic trapeze acts where one falls and the other catches.

OPENNESS TO LIFE

So it is not only in the religious relationship of divine grace that faith and hope precede love—faith and hope precede love in human relationships too. The faith we talk about here is not simply believing people's words. It is also trust and commitment to them in the uniqueness of their own mystery. It implies an openness to life.

Religious values bring an additional confidence that people strengthened and supported by gracious love will be strengthened and supported by grace.

MYSTERY OF LIFE

Love, then, for all the banality of the phrase, is in fact "the sweet mystery of life." For the religious man, it is the mystery of divine grace itself. Psychologically it is the free gift of one person to another in openness and trust, confidence and faith. Such a relationship would be seen as radiating—like a rainbow reflected on the surface of a stream—the divine grace and mystery and love to which human grace corresponds.

In the vertical conceptualization of the relationship of God and man—as in the Psalms, for example—God's eyes are flashing and the hills are dancing with His power. The Psalms give an awesome sense of the heavens as the place of God, the ever changing clouds reflecting the beauty of God's face and His smile radiating forth in the warm rays of the sun. In the horizontal view, the heavens are just in front of us, but beyond. The heavens and the earth meet, as in a painting in which the blues so fuse in the distance that one cannot tell where the blue of the sea begins and the blue of the sky ends. Heaven and earth come together in that beyond. Across the face of the earth and other men is that beyond. In this symbolic sense, we can also find God in and through seeking genuine relationship with the other.

CREATIVE COMMUNICATION

The struggle of our age to find communion and communication therefore gives a special meaning, need and purpose to community. Man's central concern is not simply a law-and-order image of a city but how one fills the city or any other community with communion and communication.

Modern psychological concepts can give us the courage, confidence and at least beginning knowledge to start to establish authentic personal relationships with one another rather than remaining fearfully or indifferently in the shadows. Man seems to be yearning for and to need such creative affiliation. Counseling, psychotherapy and religion together, but each in its own way, can give us models from which to pattern such structures of affiliation as would seek to give each person the means of self-understanding, worth and fulfillment, so that he may seek to give himself genuinely to others and in a faith-commitment to the Total Other.

Such relationships would not be simply "permissive." On the contrary, as we have seen, maturity itself demands that one struggle through personal conflict and confusion. Life and religion challenge and confront us and so strain and push us, like an athlete or artist, to the best possible expression of ourselves. By such life stresses— strengthened and supported by others—and our own courage to be, we grow in the pursuit of our own excellence.

To achieve such authentic relationships of creative communication among people is a goal and common concern where counseling, psychotherapy and religion can join most richly in mutual support and reinforcement. This appears to be one of modern man's most pressing quests. With all its stresses and its sense of almost catastrophic expectation of destruction our age yet also seeks to explore and unfold each person's potentialities in a way never before thought possible. Through economic, political, scientific and educational means, it increasingly invites and encourages larger numbers of people to strive to be and become themselves—in the best sense. Religion joins and reinforces this humanistic effort.

Such a "new humanism" through the common effort of these forces together will, hopefully, uncover much-needed fresh ways of regarding man, enabling him to live by the wisdom of "To thine own self be true and . . . thou canst not then be false to any man." It may also help him—in addition to his goals of social, economic and political justice—to *understand* with greater effectiveness and so *experience* the strange paradox of love. This paradox is that one really saves one's life only when one has trustingly offered it to another—and so somehow was prepared to lose it.

NOTES

[1] John W. Gardner, *Excellence: Can We Be Equal and Excellent Too?* (New York: Harper and Row, 1962).

2 Thomas Gould, *Platonic Love* (New York: Free Press of Glencoe, Macmillan, 1963), pp. 1–17.

3 Eugene C. Kennedy, M. M., *Fashion Me a People: Man Woman, and the Church* (New York: Sheed and Ward, 1967), p. 63.

4 John J. DeWitt, "Making a Community Out of a Parish," Liturgical Conference, Washington, D.C. (2900 Newton St. N.E., 20018), pp. 8–9.

5 *Ibid.*, p. 8–9.

6 Carl Rogers, *On Becoming a Person* (Boston: Houghton Mifflin, 1961), p. 87.

7 *Ibid.*, p. 88

8 Bernard Cooke, "The Church as Community," *Religious Education,* 59, No. 2 (March-April 1964), p. 158.

9 *Ibid.*, pp. 158–159.

10 *Summa Theologica*, II–II, 2, 23, a. 1.

11 From *The Stress of Life* by Hans Selye. Copyright 1956 by Hans Selye. Used by permission of McGraw-Hill Book Company. Page 277.

12 Walter Kerr, *The Decline of Pleasure* (New York: Simon and Schuster, 1962), p. 214. © 1962 by Walter Kerr. Reprinted by permission of Simon & Schuster, Inc.

13 Selye, *op. cit.*, p. 285.

14 Gordon W. Allport, "Mental Health: A Generic Attitude," *Journal of Religion and Health*, 4, 1 (October 1964), p. 20.

15 Selye, *op. cit.*, p. 286.

16 Rogers, *On Becoming a Person,* p. 92.

17 *Ibid.*, pp. 93–94.

18 Selye, *op. cit.*, p. 292.

Bibliography

Allport, Gordon W., *The Individual and His Religion.* New York: Macmillan, 1950.

———— "Mental Health: A Generic Attitude." *Journal of Religion and Health,* 4, No. 1 (October 1964).

———— "The Psychology of Participation." *Psychological Review,* 53 (May 1945).

———— *The Person in Psychology: Selected Essays.* Boston: Beacon Press, 1968.

Altizer, Thomas J. J., ed., *Toward a New Christianity, Readings in Death of God Theology.* New York: Harcourt, Brace and World, 1967.

Anderson, George C., ed., *Religion in the Developing Personality.* Proceedings of the Second Academy Symposium of the Academy of Religion and Mental Health. New York: New York University Press, 1960.

Aquinas, St. Thomas, *Summa contra Gentiles,* Book III, Part I, trans. Vernon J. Bourke, Garden City, N.Y.: Doubleday, 1956.

———— *Summa Theologica,* trans. Fathers of the English Dominican Province. New York, Benziger, 1947.

Arnold, Magda B., Hispanicus, P., Weisgerber, C. A., and D'Arcy, P. F., *Screening Candidates for the Priesthood and Religious Life,* preface by Vincent Herr. Chicago: Loyola University Press, 1962.

———— *Emotion and Personality,* Vols. I and II. New York: Columbia University Press, 1960.

Augustine, St., "On the Trinity," *Basic Writings of Saint Augustine,* W. J. Oates, ed. New York: Random House, 1948.

———— *City of God,* trans. G. G. Walsh, S.J., D. B. Zema, S.J., G. Monahan, O.S.U., D. J. Honan; ed. V. J. Bourke. New York: Doubleday Image Books, 1958.

———— *The Confessions.* New York: Modern Library, 1949.

Bachmann, Dr. C. Charles, *Ministering to the Grief Sufferer*. Engle-wood Cliffs, N.J.: Prentice-Hall, 1966.

Bakan, David, *The Duality of Human Existence*. Chicago: Rand Mc-Nally, 1966.

———— "The Mystery-Mastery Complex in Contemporary Psychol-ogy." *The American Psychologist*, 20, 3 (March 1965).

Barth, Karl, *Church Dogmatics,* trans. G. T. Thomson. New York: Scribner's, 1936.

———— *The Word of God and the Word of Man,* trans. with new fore-word by Douglas Horton. New York: Harper and Row (Harper Torch Books–The Cloister Library), 1957.

Bassett, Rev. William T., *Counseling the Childless Couple*. Englewood Cliffs, N.J.: Prentice-Hall, 1967.

Becker, Dr. Russell, *Family Pastoral Care*. Englewood Cliffs, N.J.: Prentice-Hall, 1967.

Beerbohm, Max, *Seven Men and Two Others*. New York: Vintage Books, 1959.

Berthold, Fred J., *The Fear of God: The Role of Anxiety in Con-temporary Thought*. New York: Harper and Brothers, 1959.

Bigongiari, Dino, ed., *The Political Ideas of St. Thomas Aquinas: Representative Selections*. New York: Hafner Publishing Co., 1957.

Blees, Rev. Robert A., *Counseling with Teen-Agers*. Englewood Cliffs, N.J.: Prentice-Hall, 1967.

Bourke, Vernon J., *Augustine's Quest of Wisdom: Life and Philosophy of the Bishop of Hippo*. Milwaukee: Bruce, 1945.

———— *Ethics: A Textbook in Moral Philosophy*. New York, Mac-millan, 1951.

Bouyer, Louis, *The Meaning of the Monastic Life*. New York, Kenedy, 1950.

Bowers, Margaretta K., Jackson, E. N., Knight, J. A., and LeShan, Lawrence, *Counseling the Dying*. New York: Thomas Nelson and Sons, 1964.

Braceland, F. J., ed., *Faith, Reason and Modern Psychiatry,* New York: Kenedy, 1955.

Branan, J. M., "Client Reaction to Counselor's Use of Self-Experi-ence." *The Personnel and Guidance Journal*, 45, No. 6 (February 1967).

Brenner, Charles, *An Elementary Textbook of Psychoanalysis*. New York: Doubleday, 1955.

Broad, C. D., *Five Types of Ethical Theory*. Paterson, N.J.: Little-field Adams and Co., 1959.

Brown, Rev. J. Paul, *Counseling the Senior Citizens.* Englewood Cliffs, N.J.: Prentice-Hall, 1967.

Brown, Peter, *Augustine of Hippo: A Biography.* Berkeley: University of California Press, 1967.

Brown, Roger, *Words and Things.* Glencoe, Ill.: The Free Press, 1958.

Bruder, Dr. Ernest E., *Ministering to Deeply Troubled People.* Englewood Cliffs, N.J.: Prentice-Hall, 1967.

Buber, Martin, *I and Thou,* trans. R. G. Smith. Edinburgh: T. and T. Clark, 1937.

Carnap, Rudolf, *Philosophical Foundations of Physics,* ed. Martin Gardner, New York: Basic Books, 1966.

Chaning-Pearce, Melville, *Sören Kierkegaard: A Study.* London: James Clarke & Co., Ltd., 1945.

Charue, Msgr. A. M., *The Diocesan Clergy: History and Spirituality,* trans. Rev. Michael J. Wrenn. New York: Desclée Co., 1963.

Churchman, C. West, *Prediction and Optimal Decision: Philosophical Issues of the Science of Values.* Englewood Cliffs, N.J.: Prentice-Hall, 1961.

Clark, W. H., *The Psychology of Religion.* New York: Macmillan, 1958.

Clebsch, William A., and Jaekle, Charles R., *Pastoral Care in Historical Perspective.* Englewood Cliffs, N.J.: Prentice-Hall, 1964.

Congar, Yves M. J., O.P., *Lay People in the Church: A Study for the Theology of the Laity,* trans. D. Attwater. Westminster, Md.: Newman Press, 1959.

Cooke, Bernard, *Christian Involvement: Three Lectures Delivered at the International Catholic Auxiliaries.* Prepared in written form by John McCudden. Chicago: Argus Communications Co., 1966.

———— "The Church as Community." *Religious Education,* 59, No. 2 (March–April 1964).

Cox, Richard H., "The Pastoral Counselor—Who is He?" *Journal of Pastoral Care,* 19, No. 4 (Winter 1965).

"Creativity." *Carnegie Corporation of New York Quarterly,* 9 (1961).

Cuber, John F., and Harroff, Peggy B., "The More Total View: Relationships Among Men and Women of the Upper Middle Class." *Marriage and Family Living,* 25, No. 2 (May 1963).

Cullmann, Oscar, *Christ and Time: The Primitive Christian Conception of Time and History,* trans. Floyd V. Filson. Philadelphia, Westminster Press, 1950.

Curran, Charles A., *Counseling in Catholic Life and Education.* New York, Macmillan, 1952.

———— "Vatican II: A New Christian Self-Concept." *Journal of Religion and Health,* 5, No. 2 (April 1966), pp. 91–103.

———— "Personality Dynamics of Scrupulosity," in *Readings in Guidance and Counseling,* J. M. Lee and N. J. Pallone, eds. New York: Sheed and Ward, 1966.

———— "The Concept of Sin and Guilt in Psychotherapy," in *Guidelines for Guidance: Readings in the Philosophy of Guidance,* C. E. Beck, ed. Dubuque, Iowa: William C. Brown Co., 1966.

———— "Some Ethical and Scientific Values in the Counseling Psychotherapeutic Process," in *Guidelines for Guidance: Readings in the Philosophy of Guidance,* C. E. Beck, ed. Dubuque, Iowa: William C. Brown Co., 1966.

———— "Toward a Theology of Human Belonging." *Journal of Religion and Health,* 4, No. 3 (April 1965).

———— "The Physician's Understanding Heart." *Journal of the American Medical Association,* 188 (April 13, 1964).

———— "Counseling, Psychotherapy and the Unified Person." *Journal of Religion and Health,* 2, No. 2 (January 1963).

———— "Positive Anxiety in Judaeo-Christian Thought," in *Constructive Aspects of Anxiety,* S. Hiltner and K. Menninger, eds. Nashville, Tenn.: Abingdon Press, 1963.

———— *Personality Factors in Counseling.* New York: Grune and Stratton, 1945.

D'Arcy, Paul F., and Kennedy, Eugene C., *The Genius of the Apostolate—Personal Growth in the Candidate, the Seminarian and the Priest.* New York: Sheed and Ward, 1965.

DeBernardy, Françoise, *Albert and Victoria,* trans. Ralph Manheim. New York: Harcourt, Brace and Co., 1953.

Dicks, Dr. Russell L., *Premarital Guidance.* Englewood Cliffs, N.J.: Prentice-Hall, 1967.

———— *Principles and Practices of Pastoral Care.* Englewood Cliffs, N.J.: Prentice-Hall, 1967.

Donceel, J. F., *Philosophical Psychology.* New York: Sheed and Ward, 1955.

Douglas, William, *Ministers' Wives: A Study of 5,000 Wives of Clergymen in More than Thirty Protestant Denominations.* New York: Harper and Row, 1965.

Draper, Dr. Edgar, *Psychiatry and Pastoral Care.* Englewood Cliffs, N.J.: Prentice-Hall, 1967.

Duggan, C. H., *Hans Küng and Reunion*. Westminster, Md.: Newman Press, 1964.

Duncan, Chaplain Tommie L., *Understanding and Helping the Narcotic Addict*. Englewood Cliffs, N.J.: Prentice-Hall, 1967.

Dunphy, William, ed., *The New Morality: Continuity and Discontinuity*. New York: Herder and Herder, 1967.

Durkin, Helen E., *The Group in Depth*. New York: International Universities Press, 1964.

Edel, Abraham, *Ethical Judgment: The Use of Science in Ethics*. Glencoe, Ill.: The Free Press, 1955.

Edwards, Paul, *The Logic of Moral Discourse*. With Introduction by Sidney Hook. Glencoe, Ill.: The Free Press, 1955.

Eliade, Mercea, *Mephistopheles and the Androgyne: Studies in Religious Myth and Symbol*, trans. M. Cohen. New York: Sheed and Ward, 1965.

Evoy, John J., and Christoph, Van F., *Personality Development in the Religious Life*. New York: Sheed and Ward, 1963.

Fagothey, Austin, *Right and Reason: Ethics in Theory and Practice*, 3d ed. Saint Louis: C. V. Mosby Co., 1963.

Feifel, Herman, ed., *The Meaning of Death*. New York: McGraw-Hill, 1959.

Feuillet, André, S.S., "The Era of the Church in St. John." *Theology Digest*, 11 (1963).

Fletcher, Joseph, *Moral Responsibility*. Philadelphia: Westminster Press, 1952.

Ford, John, and Kelly, Gerard, *Contemporary Moral Theology*. Westminister, Md.: Newman Press, 1958.

Frankl, Viktor, "Self-Transcendence as a Human Problem." *Journal of Humanistic Psychology*, 6 (1966).

Frellick, Rev. Francis I., *Helping Youth in Conflict*. Englewood Cliffs, N.J.: Prentice-Hall, 1967.

Freud, Sigmund, *An Autobiographical Study: The Standard Edition of the Complete Psychological Works of Sigmund Freud*, trans. James Strachey. London: Hogarth Press, 1959.

—— *Collected Papers*, 2, *Clinical Papers, Papers on Techniques*. New York: Basic Books, 1959.

—— "The Interpretation of Dreams." *Standard Edition of the Complete Psychological Works of Sigmund Freud*, 4, 5. New York: Modern Library, 1950.

—— *The Problem of Anxiety,* trans. Henry A. Bonker. New York: The Psychoanalytic Quarterly Press and W. W. Norton, 1936.

Friedman, Maurice S., *Martin Buber: The Life of Dialogue.* New York: Harper and Brothers (Harper Torchbooks–The Cloister Library), 1960.

Fromm, Erich, *Escape from Freedom.* New York: Farrar and Rinehart, 1941.

—— *Psychoanalysis and Religion.* New York: Bantam Books, 1967.

Gardner, John W., *Excellence: Can We Be Equal and Excellent Too?* New York: Harper and Row, 1962.

Garrigou-Lagrange, Reginald, O.P., *Christian Perfection and Contemplation.* St. Louis: B. Herder Book Co., 1937.

Gassert, Robert G., S.J., and Hall, Bernard H., M.D., *Psychiatry and Religious Faith.* New York: Viking Press, 1964.

Gendlin, Eugene T., *Experiencing and the Creation of Meaning: A Philosophical and Psychological Approach to the Subjective.* New York: The Free Press of Glencoe, 1962.

Gilkey, Langdon, *Shantung Compound.* New York: Harper and Row, 1966.

Gilson, Etienne, *The Elements of Christian Philosophy.* New York: New American Library, 1960.

Gleason, R. W., S.J., *To Live Is Christ: Nature and Grace in Religious Life.* New York: Sheed and Ward, 1961.

Glenn, Paul J., *Ethics: A Class Manual in Moral Philosophy.* St. Louis: B. Herder Book Co., 1950.

—— *Psychology.* St. Louis: B. Herder Book Co., 1936.

—— *A Tour of the Summa.* St. Louis: B. Herder Book Co., 1961.

Godin, André, *The Pastor as Counselor.* New York: Holt, Rinehart and Winston, 1965.

Greeley, Andrew M., *And Young Men Shall See Visions.* New York: Doubleday Image Books, 1968.

Grisez, Germain G., *Contraception and the Natural Law.* With a Foreword by John Wright. Milwaukee: Bruce, 1964.

Guardini, Romano, *The World and the Person.* Chicago: Regnery, 1965.

Hagmaier, George, and Gleason, Robert W., *Counseling the Catholic: Modern Techniques and Emotional Conflicts.* New York: Sheed and Ward, 1959.

Haley, Joseph E., ed., *Proceedings of the 1960 Sisters' Institute of*

Spirituality: The Superior and the Common Good of the Religious Community. Notre Dame, Indiana: University of Notre Dame Press, 1961.

Haring, Bernard, C.SS.R., *Road to Renewal*. New York: Doubleday Image Books, 1968.

Harrington, Wilfrid, O.P., *The Promise to Love*. Staten Island, N.Y.; Alba House, 1968.

Harris, Chaplain Thomas A., *Counseling the Serviceman and His Family*. Englewood Cliffs, N.J.: Prentice-Hall, 1967.

Hartmann, Heinz, *Psychoanalysis and Moral Values*. New York: International Universities Press, 1960.

Harvey, John, *The Idea of the Holy*, trans. John W. Harvey. London: Oxford University Press, 1928.

Havens, Joseph, ed., *Psychology and Religion*. Princeton, N.J.: Van Nostrand, 1968.

Henry, Paul, S.J., *Saint Augustine on Personality: The Saint Augustine Lecture, 1959*. New York: Macmillan, 1960.

Herr, Vincent, S.J., *Religious Psychology*. Staten Island, N.Y.: Alba House, 1964.

Hiltner, Seward, *Preface to Pastoral Theology: The Ministry and Theory of Shepherding*. Nashville, Tenn.: Abingdon Press, 1958.

—— *Pastoral Counseling*. Nashville, Tenn.: Abingdon Press, 1959.

—— and Colston, Lowell, G., *The Context of Pastoral Counseling*. Park Ridge, Ill.: Cokesbury, 1968.

Hudson, Dr. R. Lofton, *Marital Counseling*. Englewood Cliffs, N.J.: Prentice-Hall, 1967.

Isherwood, M., *Faith Without Dogma*. New York: Harper and Row, 1964.

Jung, Carl Gustav, *Psychology and Religion*. New Haven: Yale University Press, 1938 (3d printing, 1961).

Kant, Immanuel, *Fundamental Principles of the Metaphysic of Morals*. Reprinted as "The Categorical Imperative" by Immanuel Kant in *A Modern Introduction to Ethics: Readings from Classical and Contemporary Sources*, ed. M. K. Muntz, trans. Thomas K. Abbot. Glencoe, Ill.: Glencoe Free Press, 1958. From *Kant's Critique of Practical Reason and Other Works on the Theory of Ethics*, 1898.

Kaufman, Fritz, *Thomas Mann: The World as Will and Representation*. Boston: Beacon Press, 1957.

Kelly, J. N. D., *Early Christian Creeds*. London: Longmans, 1950.

Kemp, Dr. Charles F., *Counseling With College Students*. Englewood Cliffs, N.J.: Prentice-Hall, 1967.

Kennedy, Eugene, *Fashion Me a People: Man, Woman and the Church*. New York: Sheed and Ward, 1967.

———— *Comfort My People: The Pastoral Presence of the Church*. New York: Sheed and Ward, 1968.

Kestel, Dorothy, ed., "Curriculum for Renewal." *Bulletin of the National Catholic Educational Association*, 63, No. 1 (August 1966). Report of the Proceedings and Addresses at the Sixty-Third Annual Convention of the N.C.E.A., Chicago, April 11–14, 1966.

Kierkegaard, Sören, *The Concept of Dread,* trans. with introduction and notes by Walter Lowrie. Princeton: Princeton University Press, 1946.

———— *Fear and Trembling and Sickness Unto Death,* trans. with introduction and notes by Walter Lowrie. Garden City, N.Y.: Doubleday, 1954.

Klein, Edward J., ed. *The Imitation of Christ*. (From the first edition of an English translation made 1530 by Richard Whitford.) New York: Harper and Brothers, 1941.

Klink, Thomas W., *Depth Perspectives in Pastoral Work*. Englewood Cliffs, N.J.: Prentice-Hall, 1967.

Klotsche, J. Martin, *The Urban University and the Future of Our Cities*. New York: Harper and Row, 1966.

Knowles, Dr. Joseph W., *Group Counseling*. Englewood Cliffs, N.J.: Prentice-Hall, 1967.

Kolesnik, Walter B., ed., *Catholic Education: A Book of Readings*. New York: McGraw-Hill, 1965.

Küng, Hans, *The Council, Reform and Reunion,* trans. Cecily Hastings. New York: Sheed and Ward, 1961.

Lackmann, Max, *The Augsburg Confession and Catholic Unity*. New York: Herder and Herder, 1963.

Lee, James M., and Putz, L., C.S.C., eds., *Seminary Education in the Time of Change*. Notre Dame, Indiana: Fides, 1965.

Legrand, Lucien, *The Biblical Doctrine of Virginity*. New York: Sheed and Ward, 1963.

Lepp, Ignace, *The Depths of the Soul: A Christian Approach to Psychoanalysis*. Staten Island, N.Y.: Alba House, 1966.

Littell, Franklin H., *From State Church to Pluralism: A Protestant Interpretation of Religion in American History*. Garden City, N.Y.: Doubleday Anchor Books, 1962.

Lonergan, B. J. F., *Insight: A Study of Human Understanding*. New York: Philosophical Library, 1957.

Luther, Martin, *Three Treatises*. Philadelphia: Muhlenberg Press, 1943.

McGuire, Frederick A., *The New Missionary Church*. Baltimore: Helicon, 1964.

McKenzie, John G., *Guilt: Its Meaning and Significance*. Park Ridge, Ill.: Cokesbury, 1966.

McNally, Robert E., S.J., "The Council of Trent and the German Protestants." *Theological Studies*, 25 (March 1964).

—————— *The Unreformed Church*. New York: Sheed and Ward, 1965.

McNeill, John T., *A History of the Cure of Souls*. New York: Harper and Brothers, 1951.

McNeill, W. H., *The Rise of the West: A History of the Human Community*. Chicago: University of Chicago Press, A Mentor Book, 1963.

Mairet, P., ed., *Christian Essays in Psychiatry*. New York: Philosophical Library, 1956.

Marian Studies. Proceedings of the Fourteenth National Convention of the Mariological Society of America held in Boston, Mass., on January 2 and 3, 1963. Paterson, N.J.: Mariological Society of America, 1963.

Maritain, Jacques, *De Bergson à Thomas D'Aquin: Essais de Metaphysique et de Morale*. Paris: Hartmann, 1942.

—————— *Saint Thomas and the Problem of Evil*. Milwaukee: Marquette University Press, 1942.

—————— *Reflections on America*. New York: Scribner's, 1958.

—————— *The Peasant of the Garonne*, trans. Michael Cuddihy and Elizabeth Hughes. New York: Holt, Rinehart and Winston, 1968.

Maurois, André, *De Gide à Sartre*. Paris: Librairie Academique Perrin, 1965.

May, Rollo, *The Meaning of Anxiety*. New York: Ronald, 1950.

Menninger, Karl A., *A Manual for Psychiatric Case Study*, 2d ed. New York: Grune and Stratton, 1962.

—————— and Martin Maymen and Paul Pruyser, *The Vital Balance*. New York: Viking Press, 1963.

Merton, Thomas, *No Man Is An Island*. New York: Harcourt, Brace and Co., 1955.

Mittleman, B., Wolff, H. G., and Scharf, M. P., "Experimental Studies on Patients with Gastritis, Duodenitis and Peptic Ulcer." *Psychosomatic Medicine*, 4 (May 1961).

Montini, Giovanni Battista Cardinal (Pope Paul VI), *The Christian in the Material World*. Baltimore: Helicon, 1963.

———— *The Church*. Baltimore: Helicon, 1964.

Moore, Thomas V., *The Life of Man with God*. New York: Harcourt, Brace and Co., 1955.

Moral Values in Psychoanalysis. Proceedings of the Sixth Academy Symposium, 1963. Academy of Religion and Mental Health with the aid of the Josiah Macy, Jr., Foundation. New York: Academy of Religion and Mental Health, 1965.

Moser, Leslie E., *Counseling: A Modern Emphasis in Religion*. Englewood Cliffs, N.J.: Prentice-Hall, 1962.

Mowrer, O. H., ed., *Morality and Mental Health*. Chicago: Rand McNally, 1967.

———— *The Crisis in Psychiatry and Religion*. Princeton: Van Nostrand, 1961.

———— "Sin, the Lesser of Two Evils." *American Psychologist*, 15 (1960), pp. 301–304.

———— "Religion as Thesis and Science as Antithesis." *The Hanover, Forum*, 1, 5 (1959), pp. 37–46.

———— *Psychotherapy: Theory and Research*. New York: Ronald, 1953.

———— *Learning Theory and Personality Dynamics*. New York: Ronald, 1950.

Munitz, Milton K., ed., *A Modern Introduction to Ethics*. Glencoe, Ill.: The Free Press, 1958.

Murray, John Courtney, *We Hold These Truths: Catholic Reflections on the American Proposition*. New York: Sheed and Ward, 1960.

"Myth and Modern Man." *McCormick Quarterly* (January 1965). Proceedings of a special colloquium at McCormick Theological Seminary, Chicago, October 22, 1964.

Neill, Thomas P., ed., *The Building of the Human City*. Garden City, N. Y.: Doubleday Dolphin Books, 1960.

Niebuhr, Reinhold, *Beyond Tragedy: Essays on the Christian Interpretation of History*. New York: Scribner's, 1937.

Nuttin, Joseph, *Psychoanalysis and Personality*, trans. George Lamb. New York: Sheed and Ward, 1953; also New American Library, A Mentor Book.

O'Doherty, E. F., *Religion and Personality Problems*. Staten Island, N. Y.: Alba House, 1966.

O'Doherty, E. F., and McGrath, S. Desmond, *The Priest and Mental Health*. Staten Island, N.Y.: Society of St. Paul, 1963.

Outler, Albert C., *Psychotherapy and the Christian Message*. New York: Harper and Brothers, 1964.

———— "Anxiety and Grace: An Augustinian Perspective," in *Constructive Aspects of Anxiety,* Hiltner and Menninger, eds. Nashville, Tenn.: Abingdon Press, 1963.

Pallone, Nathaniel, ed., "Readings for Catholic Counselors." *National Catholic Guidance Conference Journal,* 3d ed. Kenosha, Wisconsin: Romantini Printing Co., 1966.

Pope Paul VI in *Time,* June 28, 1963.

———— "Address of His Holiness Paul VI to the General Assembly of the United Nations." *Tipographia Poliglotta Vaticana,* October 4, 1965.

———— "Closing Address to Vatican II." *Newsweek,* December 20, 1965.

Péguy, Charles, *Le Mystere de la Charité de Jeanne D' Arc.* Paris: Gallimard, 1943.

Perrin, Joseph. *Secular Institutes: Consecration to God and Life in the World,* trans. Lancelot C. Sheppard. New York: Kenedy, 1961.

———— *Virginity,* trans. Katherine Gordon. Westminster, Md.: Newman Press, 1955.

Plé, Albert, ed., *Obedience*. Westminster, Md.: Newman Press, 1956.

Pope Pius XII, *Dear Newlyweds,* selected and trans. James F. Murray and Bianca Murray. New York: Farrar, Straus and Cudahy, 1961.

Pruyser, Paul W., "Anxiety, Guilt and Shame in the Atonement." *Theology Today,* 21 (1964).

———— "Phenomenology and Dynamics of Hoping." *Journal for the Scientific Study of Religion,* 3 (Fall, 1963).

———— *A Dynamic Psychology of Religion*. New York: Harper and Row, 1968.

Raimy, Victor C., "The Self-Concept as a Factor in Counseling and Personality Organization." Ph.D. Thesis, Ohio State University, Columbus, Ohio, 1943.

Rank, Otto, *The Trauma of Birth*. New York: Harcourt, Brace and Co., 1929.

———— *Truth and Reality*. New York: Knopf, 1936.

Reeves, Robert B., "The Total Response." *Journal of Religion and Health,* 4 (April 1965).

Ricoeur, Paul, *The Symbolism of Evil,* trans. Emerson Buchanan. New York: Harper and Row, 1967.

Rogers, Carl R., *Counseling and Psychotherapy.* Boston: Houghton Mifflin, 1942.

——— "APA Presidential Address." *The American Psychologist,* 2, 9 (September 1947).

——— "A Note on 'The Nature of Man.'" *Journal of Counseling Psychology,* 4, 3 (1957).

——— *Client-Centered Therapy.* Boston: Houghton Mifflin, 1951.

——— *On Becoming a Person.* Boston: Houghton Mifflin, 1961.

——— *The Therapeutic Relationship and Its Impact: A Study of Psychotherapy with Schizophrenics.* Madison, Wis.: University of Wisconsin Press, 1967.

Ryan, Louis A., *Design for Happiness Here and Hereafter.* Ohio: College of Mt. St. Joseph, 1964. (unpublished)

Rynne, Xavier, *Letters from Vatican City.* Vatican Council II (First Session) Background and Debates. New York: Farrar, Straus and Co., 1963.

Samson, Henri, S.J., *Spiritual Insights of a Practicing Psychiatrist.* Staten Island, N.Y.: Alba House, 1966.

Sartre, Jean-Paul, *Existentialism and Human Emotions.* New York: Philosophical Library, 1957.

Scherzer, Dr. Carl J., *Ministering to the Physically Sick.* Englewood Cliffs, N.J.: Prentice-Hall, 1967.

——— *Ministering to the Dying.* Englewood Cliffs, N.J.: Prentice-Hall, 1967.

Schleiermacher, F. E. D., *The Christian Faith,* trans. H. R. MacIntosh and J. S. Stewart. Edinburgh: T. and T. Clark & Co., 1928.

Schmaus, Michael, *Preaching as a Saving Encounter.* Staten Island, N.Y.: Alba House, 1966.

Schnackenburg, Rudolf, *The Truth Will Make You Free.* New York: Herder and Herder, 1966.

Schneiders, Alexander A., *The Anarchy of Feeling.* New York: Sheed and Ward, 1963.

——— "Mental Health in Religious Life." Sister Formation Conference, New England Region, Annhurst College, February 2–5, 1967.

——— "Mental Health in Teaching and Learning." *The Catholic Education Review,* 58, No. 3 (March 1965), pp. 173–182.

——— "The Nature and Origins of Guilt." New York Academy of Sciences, February 19, 1968.

———— "Clinical Manifestations of Guilt," in *Three Joint Symposia from the ACPA-APA Meetings of 1957, 1958, 1959,* W. C. Bier and R. J. McCall, eds., pp. 7–18. New York: Fordham University Press, 1960.

———— "The Dynamics of Religious Enhancement and Dissolution." Seminar in Mental Health and Religion. Assumption College, August 4, 1965.

———— "Endopsychic Causes of Guilt and Shame and Their Social Implications." Seventh International Congress on Mental Health. London, England, August 12–17, 1968.

———— "Failure of Communication," in *Marriage: A Psychological and Moral Approach,* W. C. Bier, ed., pp. 194–200. New York: Fordham University Press, 1965.

Schofield, William, *Psychotherapy—The Purchase of Friendship.* Englewood Cliffs, N.J.: Prentice-Hall, 1964.

Sellmair, Josef, *The Priest in the World.* Westminster, Md.: Newman Press, 1953.

Selye, Hans, *The Stress of Life.* New York: McGraw-Hill, 1956.

Shipp, Dr. Thomas J., *Helping the Alcoholic and His Family.* Englewood Cliffs, N.J.: Prentice-Hall, 1965.

Sloyan, Gerald S., *The Three Persons in One God.* Englewood Cliffs, N.J.: Prentice-Hall, 1964.

Smart, Niniah, *Philosophers and Religious Truth.* London: SCM Press, 1964.

Snyder, William U., *Casebook of Non-Directive Counseling.* Boston: Houghton Mifflin, 1947.

Steimel, Raymond J., and O'Brien, Michael J., eds., *Psychological Aspects of Spiritual Development.* Proceedings of the Institutes of Catholic Pastoral Counseling and the Conferences for Religious Superiors of Men under the auspices of the Director of Summer Session and Workshops. Washington: Catholic University of America Press, 1964.

Steiner, George, *Language and Silence.* New York: Atheneum, 1967.

Stewart, Charles W., *The Minister as Marriage Counselor.* Park Ridge, Ill.: Cokesbury, 1966.

Stoll, Rev. Raymond F., *The Gospel According to St. Luke: A Study of the Third Gospel with a Translation and Commentary.* New York: Frederick Pustet Co., Inc., 1931.

Sullivan, Harry Stack, *The Interpersonal Theory of Psychiatry.* New York: W. W. Norton, 1953.

Teikmanis, Dr. Arthur L., *Preaching and Pastoral Care,* Englewood Cliffs, N.J.: Prentice-Hall, 1966.

Terkelsen, Rev. Helen E., *Counseling the Unwed Mother.* Englewood Cliffs, N.J.: Prentice-Hall, 1966.

Thornton, Dr. Edward E., *Theology and Pastoral Counseling.* Englewood Cliffs, N.J.: Prentice-Hall, 1966.

Tillich, Paul, *The Protestant Era,* trans., and with concluding essay, by James Luther Adams. Chicago: University of Chicago Press, 1948.

———— *Systematic Theology.* Chicago: University of Chicago Press, 1951.

———— *The Courage To Be.* New Haven: Yale University Press, 1952.

———— "Psychoanalysis, Existentialism and Theology." *Pastoral Psychology,* October 1958.

———— "The Impact of Psychotherapy on Theological Thought." *Pastoral Psychology,* February 1960.

Tournier, Paul, *The Meaning of Persons.* New York: Harper and Brothers, 1957.

———— *Guilt and Grace: A Psychological Study,* trans. Arthur W. Heathcote assisted by J. J. Henry and P. J. Allcock. New York: Harper and Row, 1962.

Ungersma, A. J., *The Search for Meaning: A New Approach in Psychotherapy and Pastoral Psychology.* Philadelphia: Westminster Press, 1961.

VanderVeldt, James H., and Odenwald, Robert P., *Psychiatry and Catholicism,* 2d ed. New York: Blakiston Division, McGraw-Hill, 1957.

Van Deusen, Dayton G., *Redemptive Counseling.* Richmond, Virginia: John Knox Press, 1960.

Van Kaam, Adrian L., *Religion and Personality.* New York: Doubleday Image Books, 1968.

———— *Existential Foundations of Psychology,* Pittsburgh: Duquesne University Press, 1966.

———— *A Light to the Gentiles.* Milwaukee: Bruce, 1962.

Vergote, A., *Problems in Psychoanalysis—A Symposium.* Baltimore, Md.: Helicon, 1961.

Von Balthasar, Hans, *Thérèse of Lisieux: The Story of a Mission,* trans. Donald Nicholl. New York: Sheed and Ward, 1954.

Walker, Daniel D., *The Human Problems of the Minister.* New York: Harper and Row, 1960.

Weigel, Gustave, S.J., *Faith and Understanding in America.* New York: Macmillan, 1959.

Weil, Simone, *The Need for Roots.* Boston: Beacon Press, 1952.

Werner, H., and Kaplan, B., *Symbol Formation.* New York: Wiley, 1963.

White, V., *Soul and Psyche: An Inquiry into the Relationship of Psychiatry and Religion.* New York: Harper, 1960.

Wilmer, Harry A., "Transference to a Medical Center." *California Medicine,* 96 (1962).

Zuurdeog, W., *An Analytical Philosophy of Religion.* Nashville, Tenn.: Abingdon Press, 1958.

INDEX

393